CW00631251

PENGUIN BOOKS

CHILD HEALTH

CHILD
HEALTH

THE COMPLETE GUIDE

Consultant Editors

PROFESSOR DAVID BAUM

Dr SUSANNA GRAHAM-JONES

PENGUIN BOOKS

PENGUIN BOOKS
Published by the Penguin Group
Penguin Books Ltd, 27 Wrights Lane, London W8 5TZ, England
Viking Penguin, a division of Penguin Books USA Inc.
375 Hudson Street, New York, New York 10014, USA
Penguin Books Australia Ltd, Ringwood, Victoria, Australia
Penguin Books Canada Ltd, 2801 John Street, Markham, Ontario,
Canada L3R 1B4
Penguin Books (N.Z.) Ltd, 182-190 Wairau Road, Auckland 10, New
Zealand
Penguin Books Ltd, Registered Offices: Harmondsworth, Middlesex,
England

Penguin Books Ltd, Registered Offices: Hardmondsworth, Middlesex,
England

First published by Viking 1989

Published in Penguin Books 1991
1   3   5   7   9   10   8   6   4   2

Text copyright © 1989 by individual contributors as listed
Copyright © 1989 by Duncan Petersen Publishing Ltd

Except in the United States of America, this book is sold subject to the
condition that it shall not, by way of trade or otherwise, be lent, re-
sold, hired out, or otherwise circulated without the publisher's prior
consent in any form of binding or cover other than that in which it is
published and without a similar condition including this condition
being imposed on the subsequent purchaser

Filmset in Britain by SX Composing Ltd, Rayleigh, Essex
Made and printed in Spain by Graficas Estella, S.A., Spain

Conceived, edited and designed by
Duncan Petersen Publishing Ltd,
5 Botts Mews, Chepstow Road, London, W2 5AG

Editorial director: Andrew Duncan
Editors: Esther Caplan, Stella Maidment
Proofreading: Laura Harper
Editorial: Rosemary Dawe

Art director: Mel Petersen
Design assistance: Beverley Stewart, Chris Foley
Artwork: Sandra Pond and Will Giles

The ideas, procedures and suggestions in this book are not intended to
replace the services of doctors; they are intended to enable patients to
collaborate more effectively with health professionals in combating
illness and disease. All matters regarding health require some degree
of medical supervision, and any applications of treatments set forth in
this book are made at the reader's own risk.

INTRODUCTION

We are all the product of a wonderfully variable interplay of our genetic inheritance and the environmental forces which were active in our earliest formative years. There is no doubt that the nurture bed within which a child grows and develops exerts a powerful influence, made up of the atmosphere, relationships and physical forces that define the child's family home, neighbourhood and community.

In identifying and treating ill health in childhood, parents play the primary role: they are, in effect, 'health care professionals', supported by the family doctor, the community child health services and specialist paediatric services. In promoting the long-term health of the child and future adult, parents play the overridingly dominant role in setting the style of living, the sense of values, the daily menu of food, work, exercise and recreation, and proving models for personal health care. The single clearest example of this is the family pattern of cigarette smoking. Recognition of the central place of parents in providing health care for their children is the justification for this book.

Child Health is not intended to be an exposition on how to bring up your child – this is surely the prerogative of all parents whose individual practices will depend on their experiences of family life, personal traditions and mythology, some of which may reflect a religious or cultural heritage. The aim of this book is to provide, in an easily accessible form, insight into the vocabulary and practice of the medicine of childhood in contemporary terms and to enhance the value of the partnership between you the parent and the health care professionals in your community. I also hope the book will help you to react decisively to illness in your child, bearing in mind that no set of words should be allowed to interfere with your instincts and judgements, which are the greatest health care assets that your child has.

The vast majority of children's ailments are 'minor' and require parents to judge, as in the case of a feverish cold, when: to do nothing; to buy paracetamol from the local pharmacy (perhaps discussing the ailment with the pharmacist); to take the child to the family doctor or ask for an emergency home visit or, based on your perception of the child's illness, past experience and the particular time and circumstances of the crisis, to take the child to the emergency department at the local hospital.

If faced with serious illness, I hope this book assists you in understanding the problems both before and after you have been in consultation with specialists. It may indeed help you to formulate questions for the specialist that will oblige him or her to explain fully the risks and likely benefits of tests and treatments; and it should acquaint you with something of the vocabulary of the ordeal you face with your child. In long-term, chronic diseases of childhood, when parents play the hour-by-hour and day-by-day role as the primary provider of health care for the child, I hope the book will be a resource to supplement specialist information given by hospital doctors, the family doctor and health visitor.

In order for you to play your full role as the primary provider of health care for your child, little specialist equipment or provisions are required in the home. More important than any medical equipment is the establishment of your network of communication with your family doctor and health visitor, local child health services and your local hospital. Having a telephone at home or access to a telephone is then your most important piece of health care 'equipment'. Then, it is sensible to have paracetamol in syrup or tablet form, although even the use of this most fundamental of medications should be considered carefully in conjunction with your health visitor or general practitioner, perhaps assisted by reference to this book. Apart from a simple antiseptic and supply of sticky plastic for cuts and abrasions, I would not recommend any other medical or pharmaceutical supplies as being essential. Some parents like to have a thermometer in the home: my only reservation about this is that I would prefer that parents use their judgement as to whether the child is ill or not, rather than take a measurement, the interpretation of which can be difficult and sometimes misleading. A thermometer is not a priority: your judgement and interpretation of your child's well-being is essential.

In recent decades, the achievements of scientific medicine have been extraordinary. Twenty years ago, 70 per cent of babies born weighing less than 2¼lb (1,000 grams) died in the new-born period; today more than 70 per cent survive and grow up to be healthy children. Twenty years ago, 80 per cent of children with acute leukaemia died: today more than 80 per cent survive and remain healthy. Immunization has eliminated smallpox and virtually removed poliomyelitis, tetanus and diphtheria from the British scene, and indeed from developed countries. Tuberculosis and rheumatic fever are rarities, whereas 30 years ago the wards of children's hospitals were full of such afflicted children. While we rejoice in these achievements, they are, for the parents of today, the new baseline from which we work. They allow no complacency. We require that every possible effort is made to secure the safety and health of today's children in the face of today's diseases and health hazards. Thus while our children face the hazards of such diseases as diabetes, asthma and cystic fibrosis, we can nevertheless reasonably hope for advances, step by step, towards better treatment and prevention over the next decade.

Less clear is whether we can influence those maladies of adult life, such as coronary heart-disease and high blood pressure, that have their origins, at least in part, in childhood. And for certain dangers to our children's health, such as AIDS, road traffic accidents, those problems arising from a deranged society including child abuse and neglect, there seem to be no reasonable grounds for optimism this side of the next century.

Whatever the potency of modern medical science, the health team, from parent to paediatrician, still needs to marshal all the attributes of healing, sympathy, understanding, patience, and affection in the care of the sick child. At the same time, parents are entitled to assume that the trained professionals will base their practice on the foundations of scientific medicine in order to protect children from the uncharted hazards of fads and fashion. It is our job in the hospitals, universities and research centres such as the Institute of Child Health in Bristol, to pursue the advancement of treatment and prevention of disease, to safeguard the health of the environment and to champion the care, protection and human rights of children today in order that they may, as tomorrow's adults, build a better and healthier society.

But in all this the fabric of the home environment remains paramount in determining the health of your child. I hope therefore that this book proves to be a useful companion, should the health and well-being of your child be challenged.

David Baum
Institute of Child Health, Bristol
May, 1989

First and last, this is a book designed for easy reference. Just look up the topic that concerns you – all the entries are in alphabetical order and they feature not only illnesses but symptoms and general problems. There is no index.

Whenever, in the course of an entry, you see a word in *LARGE ITALIC CAPITALS*, this means that there is a full entry on the topic elsewhere in the book which it is advisable to look up in order to complete your understanding of the topic.

Cross-references in SMALL CAPITALS mean the entry is well worth looking up, but not essential.

Occasionally you will find a word in capitals that does not correspond exactly to the title of the entry itself. The reason for this discrepancy is simply convenience of expression.

Entries are generally of three types:

Main entries, usually divided into multiple sub-headings, cover the illnesses, diseases and other problems of childhood and adolescence.

Background entries, usually with few sub-headings, cover general topics such as major symptoms, typically COUGH, ABDOMINAL PAIN, CHEST PAIN: having read such an entry, you will almost certainly wish to look up further, specific entries to which you will have been referred. Background entries also cover important general topics such as ACCIDENTS IN THE HOME, ADDITIVES IN FOOD and first-aid .

'Signpost' entries direct to you the main entry where the topic is fully covered. They often feature coloquial terms for symptoms (for example NITS See *LICE*) but they may also cover technical terms or names for diseases which are covered under the other headings (for example HYPERVENTILATION see *OVERBREATHING, STRESS SYMPTOMS*).

Remember that the book features not only physical illness but mental problems too – indeed the coverage of psychological disorders is particularly full. Also covered are many peripheral, but essential topics such as FAMILY PROBLEMS, GIFTED CHILD, JEALOUSY, LIES AND FIBS, and SEAT BELTS.

Except for the extraordinarily rare disorders – those which most doctors see perhaps once in a lifetime – the book covers everything that could possibly have a bearing on your child's physical and mental well-being.

The illustrations on the following pages are designed as a complement to the textual entries in the body of the book. They identify the major organs and systems of the body, and explain some of the key terms associated with them.

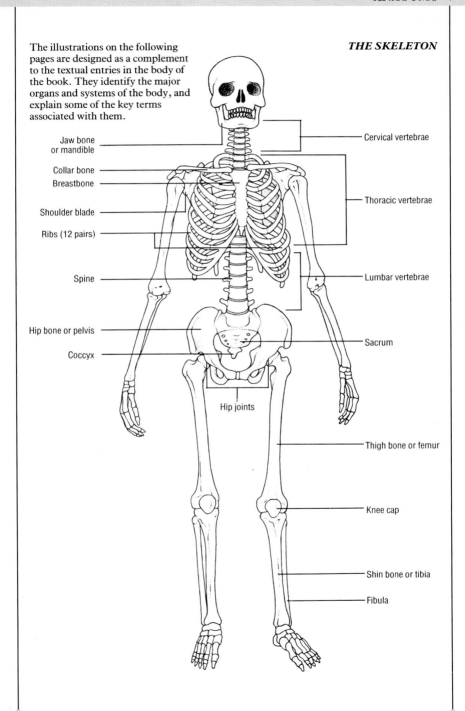

Jaw bone or mandible

Collar bone

Breastbone

Shoulder blade

Ribs (12 pairs)

Spine

Hip bone or pelvis

Coccyx

Hip joints

Cervical vertebrae

Thoracic vertebrae

Lumbar vertebrae

Sacrum

Thigh bone or femur

Knee cap

Shin bone or tibia

Fibula

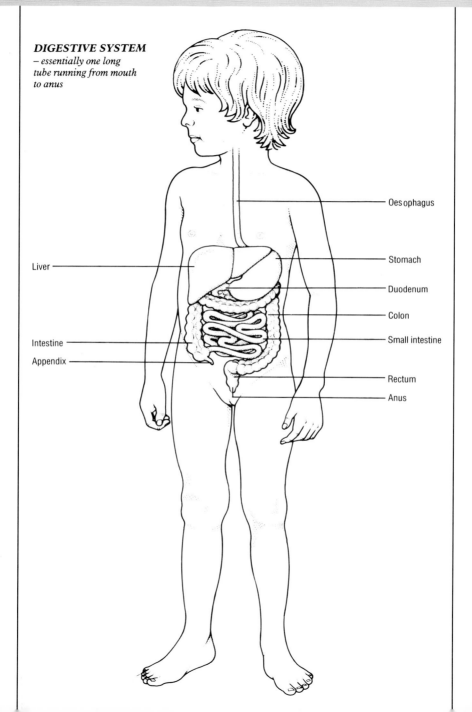

DIGESTIVE SYSTEM
*– essentially one long
tube running from mouth
to anus*

Oesophagus

Liver

Stomach

Duodenum

Colon

Intestine

Small intestine

Appendix

Rectum

Anus

THE HEART AND LUNGS

– work in harness: the heart is a muscular pump, driving blood to the lungs for re-oxygenization and to the rest of the body via the aorta; the lungs are a gas exchange system, enabling oxygen breathed in to pass to the bloodstream.

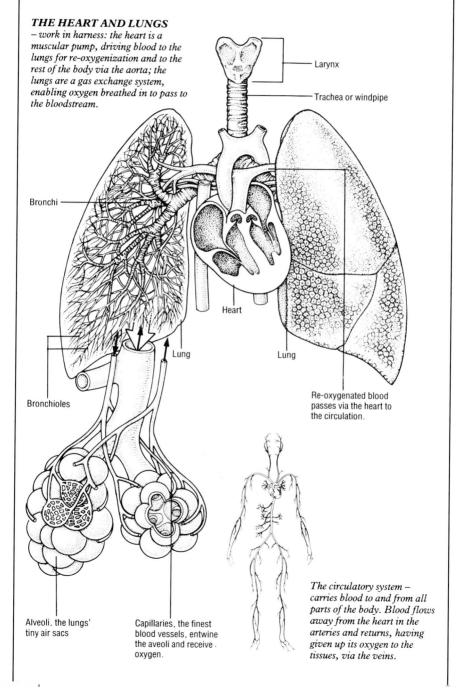

Larynx

Trachea or windpipe

Bronchi

Heart

Lung

Lung

Re-oxygenated blood passes via the heart to the circulation.

Bronchioles

Alveoli. the lungs' tiny air sacs

Capillaries, the finest blood vessels, entwine the aveoli and receive. oxygen.

The circulatory system – carries blood to and from all parts of the body. Blood flows away from the heart in the arteries and returns, having given up its oxygen to the tissues, via the veins.

THE HEAD AND NECK

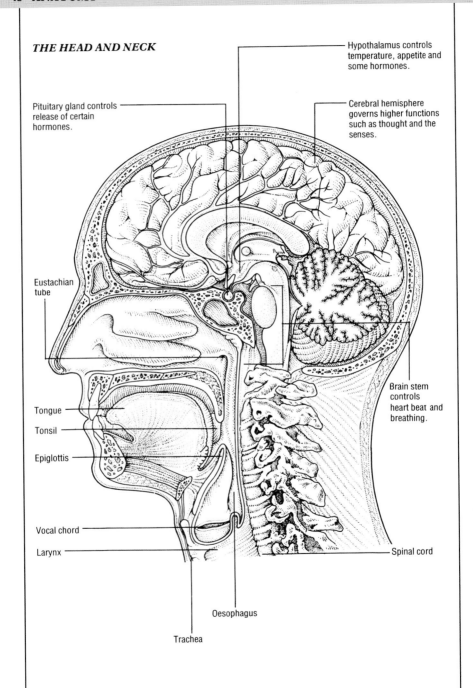

Hypothalamus controls temperature, appetite and some hormones.

Pituitary gland controls release of certain hormones.

Cerebral hemisphere governs higher functions such as thought and the senses.

Eustachian tube

Brain stem controls heart beat and breathing.

Tongue

Tonsil

Epiglottis

Vocal chord

Larynx

Spinal cord

Oesophagus

Trachea

THE EYE

Retina

Optic nerve

Bones of the skull

Eye muscles

Eyelid

Conjunctiva

Cornea

Iris

Pupil

Lens

Eyelid

THE EAR

Cochlea (turns sounds into nerve impulses)

Skull bone

Auditory nerve (carries sounds and balance sensations to brain)

Hammer

Anvil

Eardrum

Outer ear canal

Stirrup

Middle ear cavity

Eustachian tube

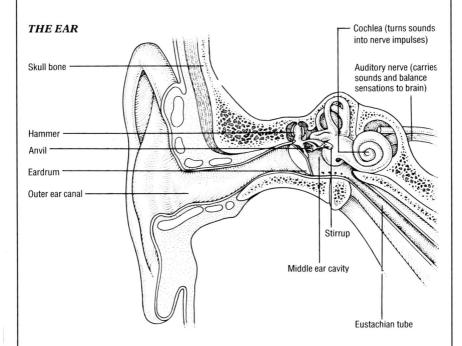

A

ABDOMINAL PAIN

Caused by different problems at different ages.

■ IN GENERAL If the child is otherwise well and can be distracted from the pain, the problem is probably a minor one, such as wind or indigestion. If the cause is serious, as with anything which may lead to PERITONITIS, the child looks unwell and cannot be distracted from the misery of the pain. There may also be other symptoms, such as loss of APPETITE, CONSTIPATION or DIARRHOEA, FEVER or VOMITING.

■ IN BABIES Crying babies are often thought to have wind or COLIC. The symptoms are thought to be due to swallowed air getting trapped in the intestine as an 'air bubble' causing distension and discomfort. However, the problem with a crying baby is rarely a matter of wind, and it is generally not helpful to wind babies obsessively after every feed.

■ ACTION Try to identify other reasons why your baby is crying. Does he look ill? Is he thriving? (See *FAILURE TO THRIVE*.) Is he in pain? The problem of an unsettled baby is common. A simple cause or explanation is rare. But if the problem persists or you think the baby is unwell or in acute pain – see *VOLVULUS* and *INTUSSUSCEPTION* – then get medical advice.

■ IN TODDLERS See *GASTROENTERITIS*, a common cause of episodes of diarrhoea, vomiting and abdominal pain. Many feverish illnesses such as sore throat, ear infections, may also cause a small child to complain of tummyache – see *MESENTERIC ADENITIS* for explanation. URINARY TRACT INFECTION is a cause of special importance, particularly in girls.

■ IN OLDER CHILDREN The child can describe the pain and separate it from other symptoms. Acute episodes of abdominal pain are usually clearly associated with general ill health and other symptoms, such as in gastroenteritis or urinary tract infection. However, recurrent or low-grade persistent abdominal pain in the absence of other symptoms is often less obviously explained – see also *RECURRENT ABDOMINAL PAIN*.

If you or your child are worried about the pain, get medical advice. In the child who is otherwise in good health, the origins may be psychological (such as pressure, teasing or stress at school; or tension or disharmony at home): the pains may nevertheless be real for the child. If the child is generally unwell, then many different and rare possible causes need to be considered, ranging from urine infections to inflammatory bowel disease. You should therefore get medical advice.

■ ACTION Try to get the child to tell you, calmly, as much as possible about the pain. What action you should take all depends on the severity, persistence and tempo of the complaint. Watch out for other symptoms: appetite, bowel habit? If the child does not seem ill and can move about normally, there is probably no need to go straight to your doctor; if in doubt, you might want to discuss the problem with your doctor on the telephone. If your child appears ill or develops any of the signs of peritonitis, get urgent medical help.

ABDOMINAL SWELLING

Toddlers often look pot-bellied at the age when they are learning to walk and run. Between the ages of two and five years, the belly becomes less prominent, flatter and more muscular. This is related to the natural straightening of the lower spine, together with strengthening of the muscular walls of the abdomen as the upright posture is established.

Other causes of generalized abdominal swelling are rare, but include a range of serious conditions including INTESTINAL OBSTRUCTION and enlargement of abdominal organs.

ABRASIONS

See *CUTS AND GRAZES.*

ACCIDENT-PRONE CHILD

See *CLUMSINESS.*

ACCIDENTS IN THE HOME, PREVENTION

A first-time parent quickly and automatically becomes aware of the need to make changes around the house to protect a child from accidents, above all when he is left unattended. Common-sense measures *do* save lives. As your child grows, yet more safety measures will be needed. See pages 17-19 for specific measures.

ACHONDROPLASIA

An INHERITED DISORDER diagnosed at birth: the baby is found to have short arms and legs – see *SHORT STATURE.* Adult height usually turns out to be less than 4½ ft (1.4 m). The back has a rather exaggerated curve and the head is large. Most such children enjoy otherwise good health and are of normal intelligence.

ACNE

The combination of blackheads and whiteheads on the face and upper trunk – a problem of puberty and adolescence.

■ CAUSE The underlying cause is the effect of the male sex hormones on the oil-producing glands in the skin. Both boys and girls produce these hormones as they approach puberty. They stimulate the activity of the sebaceous glands in the skin, which produce natural oils. The excess oil blocks the skin pores, forming blackheads and whiteheads. The oils in the resulting swellings are broken down by the normal BACTERIA on the skin, forming irritant acids which may result in painful inflamed spots that eventually burst.

■ ACTION Don't dismiss acne as an *Continued on page 19.*

ACNE

Acne commonly occurs on the face and upper trunk.

Development of spots

1 *Excess grease blocks the pores; blackheads or whiteheads form.*
2 *Normal bacteria breaks down the grease, producing irritant acids.*
3 *Painful red spots appear.*

■ SAFETY FOR THE SEMI-MOBILE CHILD A crawling baby should not be left alone. Many potential dangers, from glass ornaments to poisonous plants, are obvious but you cannot predict every eventuality.

Steps will be crawled down; corners bumped into; furniture pulled over. Rearrange the room, if necessary, so that he does not bump into sharp corners. Ensure that anything he might pull himself up on will not topple over.

– Keep a gate on the stairs, and across the doorway of any room which has not been baby-proofed.

– Guard all fires, and radiators if they get very hot.

– Take him to the door or telephone when you have to answer it. Or invest in a play-pen to pop him into at such moments.

– Pick up everything small enough to swallow, and put it out of reach.

– Cover electric points with safety plugs.

– Allow nothing breakable within 3 ft (one m) of the floor.

– Don't leave wires trailing, especially wires to electric kettles.

– Keep poisons in high cupboards.

– Move all the dangerous chemicals from the cupboard under the sink or fit a lock or child-proof catch.

– Check that none of the plants he can reach are dangerous.

ACCIDENT PREVENTION

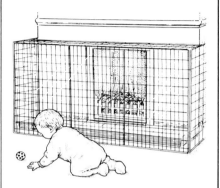

A fireguard must be stable and well-fitted in order to be effective.

– Check that he cannot crawl through the banisters on the landing.

– Keep cups of tea and coffee on a high shelf or table.

– Put away table-cloths for a year or so. He can easily pull everything on top of him if he tries to use the cloth to pull himself up.

– Keep drawers closed. If a child pulls up and leans forwards, the drawer can close on his fingers.

– Watch for children's fingers on the hinged side of the door.

– Swinging doors are lethal to babies.

– Wedge doors open.

– Wedge books into bookcases with folded newspapers.

Continued on next page.

■ SAFETY FOR THE MOBILE CHILD Once he starts moving about the house you will need to extend your child-proofing yet again.
– Once he can walk, he will also climb. Fit bars or locks to upstairs windows.

– Never leave him alone near water. A child can drown in a full bath someone has forgotten to empty.

– Keep all medicines in a locked cupboard.

– Keep all cleaning materials out of reach.

– Keep hiding places such as cupboards locked.

– Don't leave a toddler in the garden unsupervised.

– Make sure he cannot escape from the garden.

– Fill in garden pools until he is old enough to treat them sensibly.

– Make sure garden sheds and garages are locked.

– Make sure weed-killer and other garden poisons are out of reach, in case he does go into the shed.

– Don't leave fires unguarded.

– Make sure clothes are flame-resistant.

– Use the back burners on the cooker, and turn all pans so that the handles cannot be knocked.

– Be sure he cannot reach the kettle or the iron.

Hobguard, adjustable to fit any stove.

– Empty the kettle after use.

– Don't polish wooden floors so well that he will slip.

– Make sure rugs don't slip.

– Make sure he cannot lock himself in the lavatory, bathroom or any other room.

– Make sure he cannot open the front door.

– Never leave old fridges or freezers where he could climb inside.

■ ACTION Go round your house now and note all the hazards. Deal with them now, before the worst happens. Much can be achieved simply by moving all the most dangerous objects up and away from a child's normal reach. Do you need some extra high shelves?

SAFE TO PUT IN HIS MOUTH?

How safe it is for him to put objects into his mouth depends on the objects:

■ Too small and it could be swallowed.

■ Mouth-width objects may get stuck.

■ Loose and furry, and he may choke on little bits.

■ Long and thin, such as a wooden spoon, and it may get stuck down his throat.

■*Anything* sharp can cut.

■ Matchboxes and cigarettes are not good for babies to chew. The compound on the sides of matchboxes is poisonous; and a single swallowed cigarette delivers, for a baby, a dangerously large dose of nicotine.

■ If you are worried about germs, sterilize his toys.

■ Remember his neck is near his mouth: string, nylon, wool and ribbon could all get twisted accidentally around his neck. It is safest to use wool and elastic to tie toys to his cot; wool breaks and elastic gives if it ends up around his neck.

Beware of tying a dummy around a baby's neck; the ribbon could become twisted and strangle him.

untreatable hazard of growing up. It can be distressing for many teenagers, and mild acne can often be effectively treated by simple measures. These include squeezing blackheads carefully using a clean tissue and washing regularly with an antiseptic skin cleanser. Sunlight helps to clear acne, and *careful* use of a sunlamp may help.

■ GET MEDICAL ADVICE if the acne persists, and you are concerned about it.

■ TREATMENT Creams containing benzoyl peroxide may reduce the blockage of the pores by peeling off the top layer of skin. They can be bought from chemists without prescription. ANTIBIOTICS, taken for long periods (weeks or months on occasion), reduce the bacteria on the skin and prevent the breakdown of oils to irritant acids. The most commonly prescribed is tetracycline, or oxytetracycline. For girls, a pill may be prescribed similar to the contraceptive pill. This contains female hormones and neutralizes the effect of the male hormones.

If the acne is severe, and these treatments do not clear it, the doctor may refer your child to a specialist dermatologist.

■ LONG-TERM MANAGEMENT Antibiotics can be taken for several years if necessary. Not all teenagers grow out of acne, so long-term treatment may be required.

ADDICTION
See *ALCOHOL, SOLVENT ABUSE, SMOKING, DRUGS.*

ADDITIVES IN FOOD
Substances used in the processing of

food and drinks, typically as preservatives or colouring. They are identified by a number prefixed by the letter E, which means they are approved by the European Economic Community.

Pectin (E440), used to set jams, is a natural additive, as is lecithin (E322), made from soya beans, and used to stop foods separating. Some factory-produced additives are identical to natural substances; others are entirely artificial.

Additives are shown in the ingredients list on food packaging. The first ingredient, listed with its function and number, is present in the largest amount, the last one in the smallest.

Additives fall into four groups:

1 Those that enhance the flavour and appearance of food (E100-E180). There are more than 50 permitted colours, the commonest being caramel (E150), made by overcooking sugar. Another common one, beta-carotene (E160A), is a colouring extract of carrot converted to vitamin A in the body. There are no colourings used in the preparation of baby foods.

Flavour enhancers, which have no E numbers as yet, include monosodium glutamate and the best known sweetener, saccharin. Flavourings make up the largest group of additives, but are used in very much smaller quantities than the preservatives.

2 Those that act as preservatives (E200-E290): Potassium nitrate (E252) is a typical preservative: it kills micro-organisms, BACTERIA, yeasts and FUNGI, preventing food from rotting, allowing it to last longer and improving its safety.

3 Those that prevent food spoiling and maintain freshness (E300-E321): Antioxidant additives prevent or delay deterioration in fats by limiting the effect of oxygen, which causes fat to go rancid. VITAMINS are also preserved by antioxidant additives. They also prevent the discoloration of fruit and vegetables. Vitamin C (E300) is a commonly used antioxidant. The use of preservatives widens the range of available foods and can reduce their cost.

4 Those that aid food processing: These include acids which help release carbon dioxide gas necessary for raising bread; bleaching agents to whiten flour; bulking agents, emulsifiers, firming agents, freezing agents, glazing agents, humectants (to increase moisture), propellants, raising agents, anti-caking agents, releasing agents (to prevent food from sticking to packaging) and thickening agents.

▥ PROBLEMS WITH ADDITIVES

A tiny minority of people are affected by food additives. Those principally under suspicion are the yellow colour tartrazine (E102); the red colour erythrosin (E127); antioxidants E320 and E321; and some preservatives – E210-E213 and E220-E227.

Reactions include skin RASHES (URTICARIA), ASTHMA, HEADACHES and joint pains. Some asthmatics are sensitive to sulphites (E221-E227).

There may be a link between additives and HYPERACTIVITY in children. Conventional medicine regards the evidence for such a link as insubstantial; but some parents have found that their children have improved on additive-free diets. This means single-mindedly excluding additives (and aspirin), as well as some fruits and vegetables. Vitamin C supplements are necessary to compensate for the exclusion of fruit.

Such diets tend to work only if followed rigorously. Fashionable as the food additive issue may be, it is worth weighing up whether you cannot approach a problem such as hyperactivity in a less demanding way, keeping the additive-free diet as a last resort.

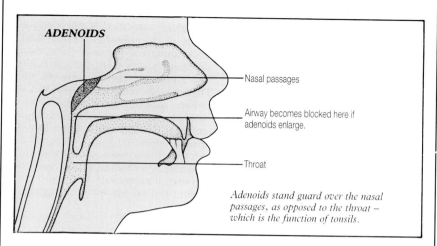

ADENOIDS

Nasal passages

Airway becomes blocked here if adenoids enlarge.

Throat

Adenoids stand guard over the nasal passages, as opposed to the throat – which is the function of tonsils.

ADENOIDS, ENLARGED

Adenoids consist of fleshy tissue lying at the back of the nose, having a structure and function similar to the tonsils, consisting of lymphoid tissue, and guarding against INFECTION. The adenoids are at their largest in the four- to seven-year age group; in individual children they may grow to be too big for the relatively small internal facial spaces, thus causing blockage of the space at the back of the nose.

▓ SYMPTOMS Persistent breathing through the mouth (the nose seems permanently blocked); nasal speech; repeated MIDDLE EAR INFECTIONS; partial DEAFNESS.

▓ ACTION If you suspect adenoid trouble, discuss the symptoms with your doctor.

▓ TREATMENT Symptoms may remit spontaneously or be relieved by nasal decongestants. Severe obstruction, recurrent middle ear infections, GLUE EAR and deafness may justify an operation to remove the adenoids. The decision to operate should take account of your views, together with those of your family doctor and an ear, nose and throat specialist. In the past, the operation was performed more often than is now thought necessary. It was also common to remove the tonsils at the same time, but this is no longer done unless there are specific additional indications.

▓ OUTLOOK As the child moves into adolescence, the facial bones enlarge, as do the cavities within; the child then literally grows out of the problem.

ADRENAL DISORDERS

The adrenal glands are situated on top of the kidneys, and their function is to produce various hormones. These secretions are vital for normal health. Over- or under-production causes a range of problems, which, for simplicity, are listed below under the names of the hormones involved.

The steroid hormones Too much cortisol causes Cushing's disease. This is a very rare disease in childhood. Over secretion by the adrenal glands often equates with an adrenal tumour. The effects of excess cortisol are much more commonly the result of high dosage treatment with cortisol-like agents. Clinically excess cortisol makes a child short, overweight and sometimes hairy.

Some children are born with a lack of both cortisol and aldosterone. This most commonly is the result of an abnormality in the synthetic pathways, which result in an overgrowth of the adrenal glands, termed congenital adrenal hyperplasia. The absence of the normal adrenal hormones causes serious problems in the first few days of life, which are life-threatening if not recognized. With treatment, however, the child can grow and develop normally.

Sex hormones In congenital adrenal hyperplasia the abnormal synthetic pathways result in masculinizing hormones instead of cortisol. These may result in an enlargement of the clitoris in a baby girl to the degree that sex identity may be difficult at birth.

In some children, over-production of sex hormones by an adrenal tumour can cause onset of early or precocious PUBERTY.

Adrenal disorders are rare; their clinical presentation is not usually obvious nor of sudden onset. However, once considered they are generally straightforward (for the specialist) to unravel, fully investigate, and treat. In most instances a complete cure can be effected, although this may be at the cost of life-long supportive medication.

AGGRESSION

See also *BEHAVIOURAL TREAT-MENTS, BULLYING AND TEAS-ING, SIBLING RIVALRY, TAN-TRUMS.*

All children are aggressive at times, both within and outside the family. Problems can arise in how aggression is expressed, such as in hitting, kicking, swearing, biting or spitting. The feeling of aggression is universal; its mode of expression is learned. Children punished physically are more likely to express aggression physically – imitation is a powerful form of learning, and children copy adults as well as other children. Aggression which succeeds in being rewarded is likely to be repeated. It can be an effective way of gaining adult attention. With age, children normally learn greater self-control and how to channel aggression in socially acceptable ways. Boys are naturally more aggressive than girls.

■ MANAGEMENT Don't retaliate aggressively. Don't allow aggression to achieve results. Ponder on situations in which your child has been aggressive, and ask yourself what may be causing it. When he fights, remove him from the 'arena' and leave him on his own for a few minutes to cool off. Explain briefly why it is wrong, and suggest an alternative method of dealing with the situation. In general, praise your child when he has shown self-control. When children are hit by others, parents have different philosophies on the virtues of hitting back. All children have to learn to stand up for themselves at some stage, but physical retaliation is not the only way.

Seek advice if your child is frequently aggressive, is difficult in a range of situations, and is constantly in trouble, all affecting his relationships inside and outside the home. Your family doctor may suggest discussing the problem with a child psychiatrist or psychologist.

AIDS (ACQUIRED IMMUNE DEFICIENCY SYNDROME)

A condition of depressed immunity caused by INFECTION with the Human Immunodeficiency VIRUS (HIV).

Children are most commonly infected during pregnancy because the mother has been infected (as a result of intravenous drug abuse or through intercourse with an infected partner). Another smaller group of haemophiliac children are infected through contaminated blood products given to them before the risk of AIDS was known.

■ SYMPTOMS Many children remain symptom free for the first year after infection. Most then develop non-specific symptoms which may include fever, diarrhoea, FAILURE TO THRIVE, enlargement of glands and a tendency to repeated ear, throat or chest infections. A smaller number develop progressive neurological problems, for example DEVELOPMENTAL DELAY, fits and symptoms of ENCEPHALITIS such as drowsiness, blurring of vision, neck stiffness and eventually COMA.

CONGENITAL ABNORMALITIES are a feature of children infected with the virus, and it seems likely that longer-term survivors will be prone to certain forms of CANCER. Some children suffer from BRUISING, ANAEMIA, HEPATITIS or unusual skin conditions.

■ ACTION A correct diagnosis is essential, and this is difficult because no group of symptoms is diagnostic. Some children born to infected mothers will not develop the disease even though blood tests may seem to suggest infection in the first few months of life. There are a variety of blood tests available but no single test is 100 per cent reliable, and expert advice should be sought in the interpretation of any test performed.

If a mother knows she is infected with HIV, she must consider whether breast feeding is advisable.

Recent studies suggest that there is a small but significant risk of mother to child transmission via breast milk.

If a child is proven to be infected, it seems likely, judging from current evidence, that he will eventually develop AIDS, although information is still limited because of the small numbers known to be infected. If the child is closely monitored and promptly treated for infections, it seems likely that survival can be prolonged. Get medical advice at the first sign of any symptoms which suggest infection.

■ TREATMENT There are no drug cures for AIDS. Clinical trials of anti-viral agents are under way, but at the present time their effectiveness is still not known.

There is no evidence that infected children are an infection risk to playmates, and they should not be segregated.

Counselling and social support for families is crucially important, especially as the condition progresses.

■ OUTLOOK is worst if symptoms develop early after infection.

ALBINISM
A group of rare inherited conditions in which there is absence of the pigment melanin.

■ SYMPTOMS Affected children have white hair, pale skin, blue-grey irises in the eyes, and abnormal vision, which is also due to lack of pigment.

■ CAUSE The inheritance of generalized albinism is recessive, which means that in a family, one in four children will be affected when both parents are carriers (see *IN-HERITED DISORDERS*). A separate form of albinism affecting only the eyes is inherited as an X-linked recessive, where some boys are affected, and girls are carriers.

■ ACTION Children with this relatively rare condition should be under the care of a specialist. There is no effective treatment, but sunbarrier creams will help to protect the skin from burning.

ALCOHOL ABUSE

Alcohol is the socially acceptable drug – indeed alcoholic drinks are regularly consumed by a third of all 14-year-old boys, and a quarter of all 14-year-old girls. While alcoholism is rare in the young, occasional and indeed regular drinking carries real health risks for children and adolescents.

■ SYMPTOMS of intoxication are the the same as for adults, only more pronounced and often quicker to take effect. The smaller the body size, the greater the impact. You will probably notice disinhibition, excitement and a loss of judgement; poor co-ordination, slurred speech, unsteadiness and a proneness to physical accident; and finally drowsiness, which can eventually lead to coma, with the danger of death by inhalation of vomit.

■ ACTION Obviously, make sure the intoxicated youngster is safe from risk of accident. If you think he has drunk a great deal – for instance, if a ten-year-old appears to have had several pints of beer or cider, or several glasses of sherry – get medical advice.

■ TREATMENT If the child (or teen-ager) is unconscious, place him in the RECOVERY POSITION. It is safe to let the youngster sleep off mild to moderate intoxication at home; hospitals occasionally admit children and adolescents recovering from exceptionally heavy bouts.

The adolescent who drinks regularly, and excessively, must be brought to realize the nature of the problem: that alcohol is a powerful drug with the potential to disrupt life and permanently damage health. The emphasis should be on *replacing* the stimulus with interests and activities which help the youngster to cope with life without the help of the drug. Is it friends he needs? More of your company? Professional help for young drinkers is available in many countries. Ask your family doctor's advice.

■ PREVENTION Effective education, from as early as primary school age, is the key to a responsible attitude to alcohol, but it is useless if parents set a poor example.

ALCOHOL IN PREGNANCY

Alcohol is best avoided, especially in early pregnancy. The occasional alcoholic drink, in the later stages of pregnancy, is probably harmless. Increasing amounts, for example two to three hard drinks each day, may cause LOW BIRTH WEIGHT, PREMATURITY and CONGENITAL ABNORMALITIES. A higher intake, that is, over five hard drinks each day, may lead to foetal alcohol syndrome: severely stunted growth, mental retardation and abnormal facial features.

ALLERGY

An abnormal reaction by the body to certain molecules, most commonly proteins, (ANTIGENS or allergens) which are foreign or extraneous to the body. The reaction results in the production of ANTIBODIES. Subsequent exposure to the same antigen results in antibody-antigen interaction which stimulates a cascade or chain of biochemical steps resulting in the allergic reaction.

■ INCIDENCE Allergy in one form or another affects 15-20 per cent of the population, and contributes to one third of chronic illness in childhood. It tends to run in families, but not every member of the family will have the same type of allergy, or be allergic to the same things. Many experts believe that prolonged breast feeding offers some protection against the development of some allergies.

■ CAUSES Common antigens include the house dust mite, certain pollen, animal hair, feathers, drugs, food and insect stings. A child may be allergic to one or many allergens.

■ SYMPTOMS depend on the type of allergy, and include ECZEMA, HAY FEVER, ASTHMA, CONJUNCTIVITIS, URTICARIA and FOOD ALLERGY. Anaphylaxis is a severe allergic reaction consisting of difficulty with breathing, a drop in BLOOD PRESSURE and a rapid heart rate. It is a rare, but life-threatening condition.

■ ACTION 1 Try to determine what causes the allergy through careful records and observation of the child:

– Notice the places where allergy is worst; indoors, out in the cold air, in a grassy meadow.
– Decide whether contact with animals has any effect.
– If allergy is seasonal, pollen could be the cause.
– Skin and blood tests may help

establish the likely causes of allergy (see below). 2 As far as possible avoid situations which you recognize may provoke an allergic reaction in your child:

– Exposure to house dust mite may be reduced by keeping the area where your child sleeps and plays as dust-free as possible. Chemicals are currently being developed to kill the mite, but these are not yet available for clinical use.
– Pollen is difficult to avoid completely in the spring and summer, but it is usually possible to take some avoiding action and thereby keep exposure to a minimum.
– Pets' hair can only be avoided by not keeping pets or avoiding homes of friends who do keep pets. Finding new homes for pets is, of course, easier said than done. You should seek your doctor's advice as to the likelihood of helping the allergic symptoms by removing the pet from the home.
– Foods can be excluded from the diet: reintroduction may clarify whether or not they cause symptoms. This should always be done with medical supervision: long-term dietary manipulation can in extreme situations lead to nutritional deficiencies.

■ TESTS can be performed which may help determine the causes of allergy. Blood tests may show whether allergy is likely to be present. It is also possible to test for some specific allergies. Skin tests may also be useful. Minute amounts of common allergens are introduced superficially into the skin. Redness and itching develop if the child is allergic. Otherwise these are without discomfort. Food allergies are not easily identified by any current laboratory or clinical test.

■ TREATMENT
– Antihistamines may relieve the symptoms but tend to cause drowsiness, (which in turn may affect school performance). Some recently developed antihistamines have a less sedative effect.
– Anti-allergic drugs such as sodium cromoglycate block the release of histamine. They are used to prevent allergic reactions, but are not useful in treating symptoms once they have developed.
– Steroids are often effective against allergy, and when used locally, for example as a nasal spray or inhaler), have very few side-effects. When taken by mouth, particularly at high dosage and for a prolonged course, the side-effects can be severe.

More details of treatment are given under specific allergies.

– Desensitization involves giving frequent repeated injections of small doses of the allergen. The dose is gradually increased until the child no longer reacts to the allergen.

Unfortunately desensitization is not, in practice, a particularly successful form of treatment because a child is often allergic to more than one substance; any protective effect wears off in time; desensitization can only be performed for certain specific allergies, such as house dust mite, pollen, animal hair and insect venom.

There is also a small risk of a severe allergic reaction to a desensitizing injection.

■ LONG-TERM MANAGEMENT
Allergies cannot be cured. Avoidance remains the best treatment, but when this is impossible, use the smallest dose of medication to relieve symptoms. If the allergy is seasonal, it may not be necessary to continue treatment all year round.

■ OUTLOOK Allergic reactions tend to become less frequent and less troublesome as a child grows up. About a third of allergic children lose their symptoms by the time they reach adulthood.

ALOPECIA
Hair loss or baldness from any cause.

■ CAUSES Many babies are of course born bald, or become bald soon after birth, before their proper hair grows. This is normal. Abnormal hair loss can be caused by: friction – babies who habitually lie on their backs often develop a bald patch; pulling – either as a habit (known in older children as trichotillomania), or as a result of over-vigorous use of curlers or plaiting; drugs – used for treating CANCERS; and INFECTION of the scalp by RINGWORM (a fungus). Additionally, hair loss may occur locally (*alopecia areata*) or more generally (*alopecia universalis*) for no identifiable reason.

■ SYMPTOMS Ringworm infection is likely to cause itching of the scalp; otherwise a bald patch is the only sign of alopecia.

■ ACTION Unless the cause is obvious, such as the baby's bald patch, or using curlers which are too tight, a doctor's opinion should be sought.

■ TREATMENT Infections of the scalp are treated by antifungal agents. *Alopecia areata* can be treated by steroid injections into the skin, though this is of doubtful effect and may have long-term effects on the scalp. Trichotillomania may be a sign of underlying emotional problems, for which psychological treatment may be necessary. It may, however, simply be a habit that will stop after suitable explanation and reassurance to both child and parents.

■ OUTLOOK Hair lost during anticancer drug treatment always grows again. *Alopecia areata* usually resolves in time; *alopecia universalis* is generally permanent.

AMNIOCENTESIS
See *ANTENATAL DIAGNOSIS*.

ANAEMIA
Deficiency of haemoglobin, the blood's oxygen carrier. This can occur because there are too few red blood cells; or because they don't contain enough haemoglobin, even though present in adequate numbers. There are several different types of anaemia, described below.

■ CAUSES Deficiency of the substances necessary to make haemoglobin gives rise to DEFICIENCY ANAEMIAS.
Excessive destruction of red blood cells produces the HAEMOLYTIC ANAEMIAS, which include THALASSAEMIA, SICKLE-CELL ANAEMIA and GLUCOSE 6-PHOSPHATE DEHYDROGENASE DEFICIENCY. A further form of the disease, APLASTIC ANAEMIA, is caused by underproduction of red blood cells in the bone marrow. Finally, chronic kidney disease, INFECTION, RHEUMATOID ARTHRITIS and LEUKAEMIA can all cause anaemia.

■ SYMPTOMS are similar, regardless of the cause. If the problem develops gradually, the symptoms may go unnoticed until the anaemia is severe.
– Tiredness, listlessness, loss of APPETITE and irritability are typical. The child may seem pale: his lips and the membranes of the lower eyelids are the best places to look. Don't suspect anaemia just because a child's cheeks are pale: this often happens, regardless of whether or not a child is anaemic.
– The child may be breathless when he runs about, and generally disinclined to exert himself.
– Other symptoms occur, specific to the different types of anaemia: see the separate entries.
– Severe anaemia can cause HEART FAILURE.

■ ACTION If you suspect anaemia, get medical advice. A BLOOD TEST is necessary to confirm the diagnosis, and the doctor may suggest immediate treatment with iron: iron deficiency is the most common cause of anaemia in childhood. See *DEFICIENCY ANAEMIA*.
Further action will depend on the type of anaemia.

■ TREATMENT depends on the cause. BLOOD TRANSFUSION may be necessary if the anaemia is severe. Heart failure should be treated in the usual way.

■ OUTLOOK depends on the cause of the anaemia; see the separate entries.

ANAESTHETICS
Drugs used to make surgical operations painless. General anaesthetics act on the brain to make the patient unconscious. Local anaesthetics block the action of the nerve supply to a specific part of the body with no effect on consciousness.
General anaesthetics may be given singly or in combination by inhalation, injection into a vein or, exceptionally,

as an enema. So if a child seriously dislikes injections, there are alternative ways of giving anaesthetics. Prior to a general anaesthetic for major surgery, it is common to give premedication with a tranquillizer. A drug is also given to dry secretions and protect the heart from excessive slowing of reflexes in response to procedures such as passing an airway (endotracheal tube) through the larynx. Today's general anaesthetic typically causes light unconsciousness but, combined with an analgesic, is also a powerful painkiller. The child wakes up quickly afterwards, and although some children feel 'hung over', most do not. This type of anaesthetic is also suitable for procedures such as CAESARIAN SECTION, in which case sedative effects on the baby are to be avoided.

Some general anaesthetics, however, cause deep unconsciousness and are used for major or prolonged operations.

It is common to give a paralysing drug as part of the anaesthetic in order to relax muscles. This allows, for example, a tube to be passed through the larynx, and it generally improves surgical access. Meanwhile breathing is controlled by artificial ventilation. One of the commonest reasons for general anaesthesia in childhood – dental procedures – is largely preventable by the use of fluoride and sound dental hygiene – see *TEETHING*.

Local anaesthetics are solutions given by injection. This may be given into the tissue under the skin where a local operation is to be carried out, or it may be given into the tissue round the nerve supply, for example at the base of a toe for ingrowing toe-nail surgery, to the nerve going to a tooth or in the neck for hand surgery.

Prepare your child for a general anaesthetic by explaining that it will simply put him to sleep for a while. See also *HOSPITAL, CHILD IN*.

ANAESTHETICS

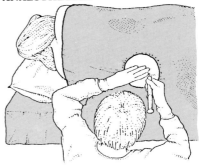

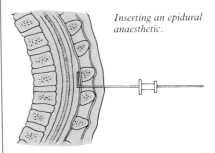

Inserting an epidural anaesthetic.

Parents should always be encouraged to stay with their child while an anaesthetic is taking effect and while it wears off. The child may not be allowed to drink straight after waking, but if he is, give him only a few sips. If he does not feel sick, let him drink more.

The range of modern anaesthetics means that there is a safe one for almost everybody, although there remains a remote but real risk of a child reacting adversely – and gravely. However, children are at no greater risk than adults. So *before* your child goes into hospital, make a note of everything you can about former illnesses, previous anaesthetics, any drugs the child is taking, especially steroids; any allergies, especially to sticking plaster; and any problems with anaesthetics experienced by a member of the family. Ensure that the doctor in charge of your child in hospital has all this information.

ANAL FISSURE

Straining to pass a hard stool can sometimes result in a small, superficial skin tear at the margin of the anus. If the child continues to be CONSTIPATED, the skin may stretch uncomfortably again and healing may be delayed. There may be slight bleeding at the site, and the child may become distressed before, during or after passing a stool.

■ ACTION Avoid constipation. Inspect the skin around the anus if your child cries when passing a stool, or if there is blood when his bottom is wiped. If there is a tear, make sure the area is kept clean and use a soothing antiseptic cream at night. It will probably heal within three or four days. If it does not heal rapidly, get medical advice.

ANAPHYLACTIC SHOCK

The most severe form of ALLERGY, which occurs within a few minutes of contact with a drug or other substance (see *BITES AND STINGS*) to which the child is allergic.

ANOREXIA NERVOSA

Self-induced weight loss by voluntary starvation, which usually occurs in teenage girls, sometimes associated with BULIMIA. Younger girls and some boys may also be affected. Once the child or adolescent is 15 per cent below the average weight for height, there is cause for concern. *Anorexia nervosa*, the psychological problem, is not to be confused with Anorexia, a term often used by doctors simply to describe loss of appetite.

■ CAUSES There is no single definite cause, but the illness often occurs in intelligent, hard-working and intense young people. An interest in health foods, diet and fitness may antedate the weight loss. A VIRAL illness with loss of appetite is sometimes seem at the start. Uncertainty about growing up and independence may also feature, though perhaps not recognized by the individual. How these diverse features come together to cause this potentially serious illness is not understood.

■ SYMPTOMS Dieting that does not stop when a reasonable weight is reached; dieting that is disguised; increased interest in food (sometimes with eating binges), sometimes with the preparation of elaborate meals for others; a sudden increase in exercise, even after dramatic weight loss. Menstrual periods usually stop, but the girl does not seen concerned. After serious weight loss, fingers and toes may become cold and blue, and downy hair grow on the trunk; the girl prefers to wear bulky clothing even in summer. Sometimes self-induced vomiting or the use of laxatives are added to promote or sustain weight loss (this last is characteristic of bulimia). An important symptom is the girl's denial that dieting or weight loss is a problem; often she is reluctant to seek help.

■ ACTION If your daughter is looking thinner than usual (especially if not overweight before) check her weight yourself. Take her to the doctor to be examined, and to establish what her weight should be. Discuss her diet with her; make sure it is a balanced one; and find out what is happening with her periods. The best chance of controlling or containing the disease probably lies in early recognition, with sympathetic attention to the girl's diet, weight and underlying worries.

If your daughter continues to diet, don't ignore it even if she makes excuses. Check her weight weekly and go back to the doctor; protest is part of the illness, which is harder to treat the longer it goes on.

If weight loss continues, you will probably be referred to a paediatrician, clinical psychologist or child and adolescent psychiatrist. You may be seen with your child (see *FAMILY THERAPY*) or separately, and hospital admission may be necessary.

▓ OUTLOOK Most recover, but some have lasting difficulties in maintaining normal weight. Extreme cases are rare, but include a risk to life.

ANTENATAL DIAGNOSIS

There continue to be rapid advances in the field of antenatal diagnosis, with the identification of more disorders of the foetus long before birth. The various antenatal tests can diagnose CONGENITAL or INHERITED DISORDERS, and assess the maturity of the foetus.

▓ ULTRASOUND SCAN is used:
– To assess the size and rate of growth and, towards the end of pregnancy, the maturity of the foetus at the time of expected delivery.
– To confirm MULTIPLE PREGNANCY.
– To assess the position of the foetus and placenta if AMNIOCENTESIS (see below) is under consideration.

▓ BLOOD TESTS The mother's blood can be tested to show whether the foetus has certain congenital abnormalities.

▓ AMNIOCENTESIS involves taking a sample of the amniotic fluid surrounding the foetus. The fluid can be tested to discover whether the foetus has certain congenital or in-

ANTENATAL DIAGNOSIS

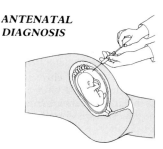

herited diseases. The fluid can also be tested late in pregnancy if there is a risk of premature birth to assess whether the foetal lungs are mature enough for the baby to breathe effectively outside the uterus.

An ultrasound scan (see above) is usually performed beforehand to confirm whether more than one foetus is present. An area on the lower abdomen is anaesthetized and a needle is inserted into the amniotic sac to withdraw a small amount of fluid. This contains cells from the foetus which can be examined for CHROMOSOMAL ABNORMALITIES (such as DOWN'S SYNDROME). This test is offered to older women in whom the risk of a Down's syndrome child is greater than average. Chemical tests can also be performed on the cells and the fluid to identify a variety of rare foetal abnormalities.

Amniocentesis is only offered if you would consider terminating your pregnancy should the test reveal a serious abnormality.

The procedure involves no risk to the mother and only slight discomfort. However, if an amniocentesis is carried out early in pregnancy, there is approaching a one per cent chance of it being followed by an abortion. When performed late in pregnancy to assess maturity of the foetus, the risks are small.

▓ CHORIONIC BIOPSY is a fairly

new procedure whereby a needle is inserted through the abdominal wall or via the vagina into the uterus. A few cells from the developing placenta are removed and tested for specific genetic and chromosomal abnormalities. The advantage of this test is that it can be done earlier than amniocentesis (see above); it may, however, carry a greater risk of causing an abortion. The risk to the mother is slight. Although uncomfortable, the procedure is not at all painful.

▨ FOETOSCOPY is a procedure used to examine the external appearance of the foetus, and also take blood samples to test for certain inherited abnormalities. A needle containing a device to inspect the foetus is inserted into the uterus. The risk of abortion following this procedure is about four per cent, so foetoscopy is only used when information cannot be obtained in any other way.

▨ PSYCHOLOGICAL CONSIDER-ATIONS are important. Before embarking on tests, make sure that you and your partner understand what they can predict, and what you will do if they reveal an abnormality. You may both be under a great deal of stress waiting for the results, and support from your general practitioner, or GENETIC COUNSELLING, may be helpful.

ANTIBIOTICS

These are drugs used to treat bacterial INFECTIONS. Most antibiotics work by killing the BACTERIA; others prevent the bacteria from multiplying and rely on the body's defences to eliminate them. Many infections suffered by children (COMMON COLD, EAR and THROAT INFECTIONS and DIARRHOEA) are caused by VIRUSES which are not destroyed by antibiotics. Occasionally, a bacterial infection may follow a viral infection, extending the illness; it may then be appropriate to treat the child with antibiotics.

It is sometimes difficult to be certain whether an illness is the result of a viral or bacterial infection. It is then reasonable for your doctor to prescribe antibiotics, particularly when an infection fails to improve over the course of several days. Certain illnesses are particularly likely to be caused by bacteria, as in the case of URINARY TRACT INFECTION.

▨ ADMINISTRATION Antibiotics may be given in liquid or tablet form. The daily dose depends on the age and weight of the child, and needs to be given at the intervals specified on the label. The duration of treatment will depend on the nature of the infection and pattern of the child's recovery. Antibiotics are most often prescribed for courses of between five and ten days. It is important to complete the prescribed course. If an antibiotic is not given regularly, or stopped too soon, the remaining bacteria, having built up resistance to the drug, may re-establish the infection.

The particular antibiotic prescribed will be determined by the type of bacteria likely or known to be causing the infection. If the child has received an antibiotic recently, the bacteria may have become resistant to its action; the doctor may then take account of this probability and choose to prescribe an alternative antibiotic. Other factors affecting the choice of antibiotic are the type and severity of the illness and the presence of other disorders, notably liver or kidney disease. Antibiotics may be changed during an illness if the child does not show signs of responding to therapy, or if laboratory tests show that the bacteria causing the illness are not destroyed by the antibiotic.

If a child is very ill, antibiotics may be given by injection, and more than one antibiotic may be given at the same time.

▓ SIDE-EFFECTS of antibiotics are usually mild and may include nausea, diarrhoea and loss of appetite. Uncommonly an ALLERGIC REACTION may occur, usually in the form of a skin rash. Your doctor should be notified at once and is likely to advise stopping the drug. Wheezing and difficulty with breathing may on very rare occasions follow the injection of an antibiotic; this is an emergency, and you should take your child at once to the nearest hospital accident and emergency department.

▓ OVER-USE OF ANTIBIOTICS Parents have reason to be anxious about the excessive use of antibiotics. Side-effects may occur, and bacteria become resistant to the commonly used antibiotics.

If it is not clear whether an infection is due to a virus or a bacterium, and if your child is not very ill, it is better to wait and see. If there is no improvement within a few days, it is more likely to be a bacterial infection and antibiotics may be necessary. If your doctor uses antibiotics frequently, discuss with him or her the possibility of reviewing the situation after a few days, rather than using antibiotics immediately.

ANTIBODY

A protein produced by white blood cells when they come into contact with an ANTIGEN. The antibody's function is to protect against INFECTION and other foreign agents. Antibodies react with the antigens and destroy them.

A BLOOD TEST can detect antibodies which often remain in the blood. This helps in the diagnosis of current or previous infection, and also helps in the diagnosis of ALLERGY.

Antibodies that remain in the blood continue to give IMMUNITY to that particular infection.

ANTIGEN

A chemical, usually a protein, which the body perceives as foreign. Proteins on VIRUSES, BACTERIA, FUNGI and PARASITES may constitute antigens, as may components of environmental particles such as pollen, animal hair and the house mite. An antigen stimulates the body's IMMUNE system to produce an ANTIBODY, specifically matched to the foreign body's chemical make-up. This is part of the body's response to eliminate foreign substances.

An organ which is transplanted into an individual also contains proteins which the body recognizes as foreign (see TRANSPLANTED ORGAN). Proteins that are eaten are digested into smaller particles called amino-acids before they are absorbed into the body. As the amino-acids are normally present in the circulation, they do not of themselves result in allergy.

ANTISOCIAL BEHAVIOUR

See *AGGRESSION, STEALING, SCHOOL ATTENDANCE PROBLEMS, TANTRUMS, LIES AND FIBS.*

ANUS, IMPERFORATE

This is a CONGENITAL ABNORMALITY which is detectable at birth – part of the routine examination of a new-born baby is to examine the anus carefully.

▓ TREATMENT If the anus is

obstructed, MECONIUM and subsequent bowel contents cannot be evacuated. Often the obstruction consists of no more than a relatively thin diaphragm of tissue. In such cases an operation to open up the passage can simply be performed.

ANXIETY

A normal experience of all children (and adults), both useful and necessary for keeping children safe and close to familiar adults (See *SEPARATION ANXIETY*) and making them think ahead, plan and prepare carefully, especially for new, strange or risky situations.

It is highly unusual for a child to be able to describe feelings of anxiety before adolescence. It is much more common to show behaviour which is a result of anxiety: being clinging or whining; having a tummy ache or headache which keeps the child at home and close to parents; finding reasons not to stay quietly in his own bed at night time; being nervous or tearful before a test at school. From an early age, some children are by nature more cautious and fearful than others and will show this type of behaviour more readily.

Anxiety is only a problem if it seems to be extreme and is preventing the child from developing new skills, from acquiring independence, or if the symptoms, or coping with them, are becoming a major part of your or your child's life.

▨ IN PRE-SCHOOL CHILDREN

Separation anxiety is an important way for a child to show anxiety at this age. He may also show excessive SHYNESS about speaking in front of strangers. Routines and rituals are often developed as a way of coping with anxiety: many bedtime routines are a way of coping with

anxiety about the dark and your child may insist on your following the routine precisely; see *SLEEP PROBLEMS*. Such routines are only a problem if there are too many of them, if the time they take is excessive or increasing (see *PHOBIAS*). Sometimes a timid or anxious child may have tremendous tempers or outbursts either unpredictably, or if the routines are not followed. These should be handled in exactly the same way as any other TANTRUM.

▨ IN SCHOOL-AGE CHILDREN

Many of the anxiety symptoms of younger children may persist into the school years, in particular routines, rituals and phobias. They may also reappear at times of stress or upheaval for the child, or for the family generally. At this age, anxiety is often shown by the child in physical symptoms such as headaches and stomach-aches. You will be able to observe how these symptoms arise in relation to stressful events, rather than as physical illnesses.

▨ ACTION Explain to the child that you know of his worries, talk about them and plan how he is going to prepare for the test/outing/new class/night away from home. Your confidence that he can cope after some preparation will help him more than avoiding the issue, which will raise his anxiety even more with the next challenging occasion.

Most children can quickly learn to cope with new or anxiety-provoking situations. If your child is not doing so, think about how you may be contributing to his anxiety. Is this an area where you had problems as a child and could this be making you uncertain about how he will cope? Do you feel worried because, for any reason, your child has special difficulties? If so, remember that your child will be less anxious if you have confidence in him, if you have talked to him about how he will handle each small step in the situation, and how he will behave, and who will help him if there are problems.

With this type of preparation, he will gradually master his anxiety. Praise him for his achievements and remind him of what he will gain from overcoming his anxiety. Always break preparatory talks down into small, manageable steps. If your child continues to be excessively anxious despite preparation, look for help in the setting where the problem arises.

APGAR SCORE

A rating to assess a baby's condition immediately after birth. It is named after the famous American paediatrician, Dr Virginia Apgar, who devised the system. The midwife or doctor present at delivery grades the baby according to heart rate, breathing, colour, response to stimulation and muscle tone. Up to a maximum of two points are given for each component of the score, amounting to a maximum of ten for the whole observation. The results indicate whether the baby at one minute and at five minutes has adapted to birth, or whether any active treatment is required.

APLASTIC ANAEMIA

A rare form of ANAEMIA, caused by faulty production of blood cells in the bone marrow.

▧ CAUSES It can be present at birth, or caused by certain drugs. Sometimes it occurs later in life for no apparent reason.

▧ SYMPTOMS are the same as for any anaemia. Sometimes only the production of red blood cells is affected, but if insufficient white cells and platelets are produced, both INFECTION and bleeding may also result.

▧ TESTS BLOOD TESTS will reveal an increased number of blood cells.

▧ TREATMENT BLOOD TRANSFUSIONS will tackle the acute problem. White blood cell and platelet transfusions may also be needed, and infection must be treated as soon as it occurs. Steroids may stimulate the bone marrow to function better. Bone marrow transplant may be a possibility for long-term treatment.

▧ OUTLOOK depends on the cause. Severe anaemia, bleeding and infections are the hazard.

APPENDICITIS

Inflammation of the appendix, a small finger-like part of the intestine situated at the junction of the small and large intestines. The cause(s) of appendicitis are unknown; there is no known way of preventing the condition.

▧ SYMPTOMS Appendicitis usually reveals itself as ABDOMINAL PAIN of fairly recent onset, often affecting the central area round the tummy button first, spreading to the right groin within a few hours. The child is usually unable to sit up comfortably or walk in an erect posture. Children of any age may be affected; it is rare, however, in infants and toddlers. There may also be vomiting, fever, diarrhoea or constipation. See *PERITONITIS* for details.

▧ TREATMENT is surgical: an operation is performed to find and remove the inflamed appendix.

■ OUTLOOK Expect the child to be in hospital for up to a week, after which recovery should be complete, with no complications.

■ COMMENT Chronic or 'grumbling' appendicitis probably does not exist as such – see *ABDOMINAL PAIN*.

APPENDICITIS

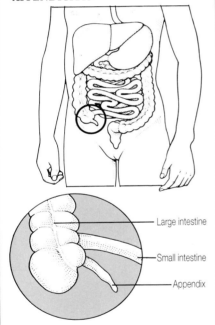

Large intestine

Small intestine

Appendix

APPETITE

Children vary enormously in their eating habits. Parents are often gratified by a child who eats vigorously, and worried by a child who 'picks at his food' (see *FEEDING PROBLEMS*). If the child is growing normally (see *GROWTH PATTERNS*), there is usually no cause for concern; but in a child who normally eats well, loss of appetite may be an early sign of illness.

■ CAUSES (Apart from normal variation between children): hot weather; any feverish illness; sore throat or mouth (see *TONSILLITIS*); unhappiness or emotional upset; excitement; as a concomitant of a variety of serious diseases.

Increased appetite may accompany or precede a growth spurt or recovery from illness.

■ ACTION and INVESTIGATIONS If you are worried by your child's sudden loss of appetite, especially if this is accompanied by such features as weight loss, you should contact your doctor. BLOOD, stool or URINE TESTS may be suggested, to check for a variety of possible causative conditions.

■ TREATMENT None is usually needed, unless investigations reveal a significant underlying cause.

■ SELF-MANAGEMENT Try to make sure your child drinks at least as much as usual, even if he refuses to eat. Dehydration causes more problems in the short term than lack of food.

■ OUTLOOK Changes in appetite usually accompany another disturbance. The eating pattern should settle as the underlying problem resolves.

ARRHYTHMIAS

Abnormalities in the heartbeat, which may be too fast, too slow, or irregular. Rare in childhood.

■ CAUSES Slow heart rates (bradycardia) can be present at birth as in congenital complete heart block. In older children, it is found occasionally in association with heart-disease.

Rapid heart rates (tachycardia) can occur in infancy and childhood as a result of abnormalities of the conduction network of the heart muscles. Sudden 'attacks' of very rapid beating of the heart (as in supra-ventricular tachycardia) can present as pallor, faints or panic episodes. Tachycardia can also occur in association with other HEART-DISEASE or systemic illnesses with fever or shock.

Some degree of irregularity of the heart rate is normal in childhood, as when the heart rate quickens and slows in phase with breathing (sinus arrhythmia). Greater irregularities occur in association with heart-disease.

▧ SYMPTOMS Slow heart rates may cause no symptoms, or there may be some tiredness or shortness of breath. Occasionally dizziness or fainting can occur.

Rapid heart rates can cause breathlessness, palpitations, dizziness and occasionally chest pain.

Irregular heart rate can give a sensation of a heart missing a beat, or palpitations.

▧ TESTS Principally, an ELECTRO-CARDIOGRAM (ECG). Sometimes a continuous tracing of the heart rhythm over 24 hours is recorded. Other tests may be done if heart disease is suspected.

▧ TREATMENT Slow heart rates don't usually need treatment in childhood. If fainting is due to a slow heart rate (but this is usually only as a manifestation of a complex irregularity of the heart rhythm), it may be necessary to have a pacemaker fitted to cure the lack of blood supply to the brain, but this is rarely used in children.

Rapid heart rates are usually treated with drugs such as digoxin. Irregular heart rates may not need treatment unless causing symptoms, in which case treatment is usually with drugs.

▧ OUTLOOK will depend on whether there is associated heart-disease. In isolation, the outlook is normally good.

ARTHRITIS

Pain and swelling of one or more joints. There are many causes including: INFECTION of the joint; injury to the joint (in children with HAEMOPHILIA, minor injury can cause severe bleeding into a joint); JUVENILE CHRONIC ARTHRITIS; VIRAL infections such as *RUBELLA*, particularly in older children.

There are also many other rare causes of arthritis such as LEUKAEMIA, LYMPHOMA, SICKLE-CELL ANAEMIA, HENOCH-SCHÖNLEIN PURPURA and RHEUMATIC FEVER.

▧ SYMPTOMS Pain in the affected joint or joints, made worse by movement; swelling of the joint, which also makes movement difficult; the joint often feels hot, and there may be redness of the skin over the joint.

These symptoms may develop slowly or rapidly, depending on the cause of the arthritis. Many children have vague pains in joints, particularly if they have a viral infection. This is not arthritis, despite the apparent similarity, and is usually not serious if it does not persist.

▧ ACTION Any painful, swollen joint should be examined by a doctor: infection in a joint can rapidly cause severe damage, so don't delay.

▧ TESTS are often necessary to make the diagnosis. These include BLOOD

TESTS and X-rays. Special types of SCAN are now also being used.

Occasionally, it is necessary to insert a needle into the joint to remove some fluid in order to test for infection. This is done under a local or general anaesthetic: not in itself painful, but the child will need distracting.

■ TREATMENT Analgesics are usually necessary for the pain, paracetamol being the usual first choice, especially in children under 12 years. If it is not strong enough, aspirin or other anti-inflammatory drugs will be prescribed. These may have dangerous side-effects (see *REYE'S SYNDROME*), especially in high doses. Never give more than the recommended dose without consulting your doctor.

Rest is usually necessary at the onset of a painful episode. Special splints can be used to rest joints in a position where they do not become stiff or difficult to use.

Bedclothes can press uncomfortably on painful knees and ankles: a 'cradle', used to raise the bedclothes, can help.

If there is infection in a joint, an operation may well be necessary in order to drain out the infected fluid. Antibiotics are also used to treat the infection; see also *OSTEO-MYELITIS*.

Joint injury usually improves with rest. If there has been bleeding, it may be necessary to remove some fluid with a needle.

Once the inflammation has been treated, the child should exercise to prevent joints from becoming stiff and muscles from becoming weak. First sessions are best done under the supervision of a doctor or physiotherapist. Exercises can be made into games so that they don't bore the child.

■ OUTLOOK depends on the cause.

ASPERGER'S SYNDROME
A rare condition in which children relate to others in an unusual way from early in life, thought to be similar to a mild form of AUTISM. The child's gestures and speech are odd, he has problems in making friends, behaves in an uninhibited way in social situations, is noticeably clumsy, and has peculiar and engrossing interests for a child of his age. Most grow up to lead normal, if eccentric, lives.

ASPHYXIA
See *EMERGENCY RESUSCITATION*.

ASPIRIN
See *REYE'S SYNDROME, POISONING*.

ASTHMA
The commonest cause of recurrent cough and wheezing in childhood. The disorder frequently runs in families. Its physiology is explained in detail below and in the illustration.

■ INCIDENCE One in ten children display features of asthma at some stage, but the majority grow out of it by adulthood.

■ CAUSES There is no one cause of asthma. Many factors predispose and interact, prominent among which are ALLERGIES to the house dust mite (found in all homes), animal fur and grass pollen. Allergy to specific foods may in rare instances initiate asthmatic symptoms. Attacks of asthma may be provoked in susceptible children by the COMMON COLD or other VIRAL IN-

FECTIONS, exercise, and by changes in atmosphere and air temperature.

■ SYMPTOMS are intermittent: children with asthma rarely have symptoms all the time. Wheezing (a continuous or 'musical' sound heard when the child breathes) is caused by three changes in the airways of the lungs: spasm of the muscular walls, swelling of the inner lining, and excess mucus (sticky fluid) production. These three reactions lead to a narrowing of the air passages, which prevents air getting through, and causes breathlessness and wheezing. Most asthma is mild to moderate, interfering little with the child's everyday life. In a small proportion of children, it can be severe, requiring emergency hospital attention.

Not all children have an audible wheeze: some only have a cough at night, or after exercise.

■ ACTION 1 If you suspect your child has asthma, get medical advice. It is not wise to use home remedies or other people's medicines for children who might have asthma. 2 If a child is known to have asthma, give the medicine or inhaler as prescribed by your doctor for use in an attack. See *INHALERS, NEBULIZERS*.

■ GET MEDICAL ADVICE if an attack of asthma gets progressively worse, or does not improve with the treatment.

■ RUSH THE CHILD TO HOSPITAL if he becomes cyanosed (blue) around the lips or unable to speak. Err on the side of caution: it is easy to underestimate the severity of an attack.

■ TESTS Lung function can be tested

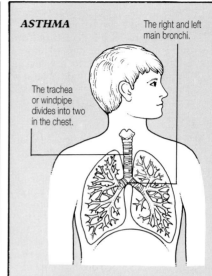

ASTHMA

The right and left main bronchi.

The trachea or windpipe divides into two in the chest.

Right and left bronchi divide into ever-smaller bronchi, and then into bronchioles.

simply with a PEAK FLOW METER. In this way the effectiveness of treatment can be objectively assessed. Skin tests may occasionally be used to identify specific allergies.

■ TREATMENT Drugs are used either to prevent bronchospasm or to treat attacks when they have started. Salbutamol, terbutaline and other bronchodilators, given as sugar-free syrup or in various forms of INHALER, are the most commonly used drugs for treating attacks. Aminophylline and theophylline given as tablets, capsules or syrups, may also be given as part of routine treatment. Sodium cromoglycate and inhaled steroids such as beclomethasone are used as preventive drugs, in various forms of inhaler. Steroids such as prednisolone are given for severe attacks, and very occasionally on a long-term basis to prevent attacks if a child has severe asthma.

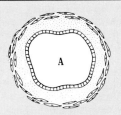

A *shows a (much magnified) normal bronchiole. The muscle is the thin band of surrounding cells. (Actual width may be as little as one mm.)*

In **B** *the muscle has contracted, narrowing the air passage. In a really bad attack, the bronchiole may be blocked completely.*

Rarely, desensitization may be attempted: see *ALLERGY*.

■ LONG-TERM MANAGEMENT Avoid those things that you know will bring on an attack, such as playing with a friend's dog, or rolling in a hay field in June. If your doctor has advised long-term treatment, such as inhaled sodium cromoglycate or steroid twice daily, encourage your child to use it consistently, as directed. Most children can master an inhaler by four years, with suitable training.

■ OUTLOOK Most children with asthma lead normal lives. For those who suffer from severe asthma, it should still be exceptional to miss time from school if a treatment plan is well devised and carried out. Occasionally severe attacks do occur which require expert and urgent hospital management.

ASTIGMATISM
A normal eyeball is more or less spherical, like a British football. If it is distorted – say into more the shape of a rugby ball – astigmatism may result. The shape of the eye is important because it plays a part in the eye's ability, as a lens, to bend rays of light, focusing them on the retina at the back of the eye. Imperfect curvature of the eyeball means distortion of the image formed on the retina. The strain incurred in attempting to focus may result in HEADACHES and/or PAIN IN THE EYE.

If your child complains of sight problems and headaches, an EYE TEST should be performed and SPECTACLES prescribed if necessary.

ATHLETE'S FOOT
The common name for a condition of the skin on the feet often, but not always, experienced when the feet are hot and sweaty for significant periods.

■ SYMPTOMS Common features include itching and soreness, uncomfortable red fissures, and the unpleasant 'cheesy' smell of the feet. Slight redness extending over the surface of the feet may be noticed. Perhaps the main feature is the dead, white shrivelled skin between the toes.

■ CAUSE FUNGAL INFECTION is commonly supposed to be the cause, but is demonstrably the cause in a minority of cases. Athlete's foot is neither caused nor transmitted simply by going barefoot at swimming-pools or in changing rooms.

■ TREATMENT If the rash spreads on to the surface of the foot your doctor may prescribe an antifungal cream. Treatment will probably need to be continued for some weeks in order to penetrate all the layers of the skin where the fungi are growing. Only when the affected tissue is entirely replaced can you consider the condition cured.

ATRIAL SEPTAL DEFECT
See *CONGENITAL HEART-DISEASE.*

AUDIOMETRY
A test of hearing, performed either to detect DEAFNESS (partial or profound), or to measure the type and degree of hearing loss. There are several types of audiometer, depending on the age of the child, and the purpose of the test. Some require the child to respond to a particular sound, made through headphones (pure-tone audiometry), while others measure the elasticity of the child's eardrum by applying slight pressure through a tiny tube inserted into the ear (impedance audiometry). Younger children are tested in a special room, where specific sounds are made under controlled circumstances and the child's behaviour is observed (free-field audiometry).

In every case, the results need to be interpreted by a specialist, and often to be repeated before the exact degree of deafness can be gauged. See also *DEAFNESS.*

AUTISTIC CHILD
A condition or group of conditions in which a child does not communicate normally in speech, gesture or eye contact.

▨ CAUSES The 'cause' of autism is unknown. There is no evidence that parents cause autism.

▨ INCIDENCE One child in 3,000.

▨ SYMPTOMS Some autistic children may appear normal for the first year of life. Others seem different from birth. Features of autism, which usually become evident before the child is five, are:
– He does not relate to others normally: he shows little interest in adults, in physical affection or eye contact; he is solitary and is unresponsive; he seems to be in a world of his own, although sometimes enjoying rough and tumble play.
– He plays in an absorbed, repetitive and non-creative way. He may, for example, repeatedly spin the wheels of a toy car, but never use it as a car.
– His speech development is delayed and speech abnormal when he does learn to speak. He may repeat what is said to him (echolalia). Sometimes the child never learns to speak at all.
– His development is delayed in many areas: most autistic children have serious LEARNING DISORDERS.

▨ ACTION Take your child to your doctor, child health clinic or health visitor. The diagnosis is never clear at first. It may require months or years of observation and consultation to reach a firm conclusion.

▨ TREATMENT There is no specific treatment for autism. Many children can be helped by attendance at a special nursery or school, often with speech therapy. A psychologist will usually be involved to assist with behaviour difficulties. Some authorities employ 'holding' as a technique, aiming to assist the autistic child with making relationships. Such an approach should only be used under careful supervision of an experienced person.

▨ OUTLOOK There is a range of disorders covered by the term autism. At its mildest, the outlook for an independent adult life is good; at its most severe, the prospect is currently one of substantial handicap.

B

BACTERIA

Micro-organisms which occur ubiquitously in our environment. Most bacteria do not cause disease and some are beneficial, such as those found in the digestive tract. Recognition of the type of bacteria causing an INFECTION is important, since specific ANTIBIOTICS are more effective against one type of bacterium than another. Bacterial identification is achieved by taking a swab or sample from the infected source (skin, urine, blood) and growing the bacteria in a culture medium.

▧ TREATMENT of bacterial infection is usually with antibiotics. The choice of treatment can be assisted by testing the bacterial culture against a range of antibiotics.

Certain types of bacteria are more likely than others to cause particular infections, such as TONSILLITIS or URINARY TRACT INFECTION. It is therefore sometimes possible to predict which antibiotic is most likely to be effective without tests being necessary.

BALANITIS

A BACTERIAL INFECTION of the foreskin and tip of the penis. Typical in babies, it causes redness and swelling, and may be accompanied by a slight discharge. A baby may cry when passing urine. You should keep the penis clean by bathing with warm water, change his nappies regularly and get medical advice. Your doctor may take a sample of the exudate for laboratory examination, and prescribe ANTIBIOTICS.

Once treated, your baby should have no further problems. Boys with recurrent balanitis may develop PHIMOSIS and require CIRCUMCISION.

BALDNESS

See ALOPECIA.

'BAT' EARS

See PROTRUDING EARS.

BCG

See TUBERCULOSIS.

BEDWETTING (ENURESIS)

Control of the bladder is acquired through physiological maturation – until this stage is complete a child cannot be dry at night. The age at which children become dry varies: some are dry at two years; by the age of five about 15 per cent still wet the bed; by the age of ten this drops to about 5 per cent of boys and 2 or 3 per cent of girls.

No consistent differences in depth of sleep, bladder capacity or other physical factors have been found between children of the same age who are wet or dry at night. Bedwetting tends to run in families. Some children suddenly stop bedwetting, while for others the process is more gradual. The first sign may be the occasional dry or drier bed. See also TOILET TRAINING.

If a child is worried about wetting the bed – and many are once they are in the early school years – or if wetting the bed elicits negative responses from parents, this can add a degree of anxiety to the problem. It is extremely rare for a child to wet his bed deliberately. Bedwetting can be a sign of emotional stress, particularly in children who have been completely dry in the past, and a small number of children wet the bed because of URINARY TRACT INFECTIONS or other medical conditions, such as DIABETES.

▧ ACTION Minimize the inconvenience as far as possible by using a plastic sheet. Don't keep your older child in nappies at night: he has learned that nappies are for wetting. Minimize the effect of bedwetting on your child by a matter-of-fact re-action to the problem: wash or bathe your child and change his bed linen each morning (if at all possible) to avoid unpleasant smells. Handle the subject tactfully so that the child is not teased or embarrassed.

▥ GET MEDICAL ADVICE if bed-wetting becomes a real problem for you or your child, or if your child starts again after a long period of dryness for no obvious reason.

▥ TREATMENT is rarely advised if a child is under six years of age. Your doctor will advise how best to deal with the problem. The most effec-tive preventive measure, if used cor-rectly, is the enuretic alarm – a safe wire mesh placed under the sheet connected to a buzzer which should wake the child when the sheet first becomes damp. Other preventive measures include reward stars for dry nights and exercises to improve bladder control. There is little evi-dence of the effectiveness of drugs such as imipramine.

BEHAVIOURAL DISORDERS

An unsatisfactorily general term for a range of psychiatric disorders includ-ing TICS, COMFORT HABITS and ANTI-SOCIAL BEHAVIOUR.

See *AGGRESSION, STEALING, SCHOOL ATTENDANCE PROB-LEMS, TANTRUMS, BEHAV-IOURAL TREATMENTS.*

BEHAVIOURAL TREATMENTS

Commonly used to help parents of children with behavioural problems, these fall broadly into two categories.

▥ BEHAVIOUR MODIFICATION aims to teach new skills, and to in-crease sociable behaviour. It is based on the theory that anyone is likely to repeat behaviour if it is re-warding. This applies to good and to bad behaviour: a child who has a temper tantrum in a supermarket and is given sweets to keep quiet is likely to do so again. The psychol-ogist would say that the child has learned that having a tantrum is a way of getting what he wants. Like-wise, most parents praise children who oblige on the potty during toilet training. Genuine praise is a potent reward and the toddler feels en-couraged to do the same again.

In behaviour modification, re-wards are used to build up desirable behaviour; bad behaviour is ignored and not rewarded in any way.

Rewards in this context are not the same as bribes. Bribing means telling the child that he will only get something if he does what is wanted. A true reward is given straight after the good behaviour and not dis-cussed beforehand.

Ignoring bad behaviour, though effective, can be difficult to achieve in practice. 'Time out' is perhaps the main technique: it usually involves simply putting the child alone some-where for a few minutes to diffuse the situation. Another approach is to encourage good behaviour which is incompatible with naughtiness. The child who helps his mother with the shopping will not need to lie scream-ing on the floor to get attention.

Consistency is essential to be-haviour modification. The parent has to reward and ignore the same behaviour every time so that it is clear what is expected.

Parents use these techniques in day-to-day dealings with their chil-dren without having to be guided by professionals. Only when problems get out of hand does the psychologist have a role – and it will probably be to devise a systematic, practical way of applying behaviour modification.

■ COGNITIVE BEHAVIOUR THERAPY is a treatment for ANXIETY, PHOBIAS and mood problems. The individual works with a therapist to define and understand the thoughts, feelings and behaviour involved in difficult situations. Once recognized, relaxation, gradual practice and confidence-building exercises are used to overcome the problem. Because children understand comparatively little about their difficulties, these methods are generally not useful before adolescence unless parents are actively involved.

BEREAVEMENT

Losing a close relative or friend may be just as upsetting for a child as for an adult, and sometimes more so. The situation is complicated by the child's level of understanding at different ages, how close the child felt to the person (which is not the same as how much time they spent together), and how the loss affects other people in the family. Many of the reactions children show are similar to those when facing DIVORCE, which is also a kind of bereavement for many children.

■ BELOW SEVEN YEARS, children don't understand the finality of death. Often, they may not appear particularly upset if told a relative or friend has died. This does not mean they did not care about the person. They may ask practical questions about where the person is, what they are doing or eating. It is best to answer these questions in as straightforward a way as you can. They will often be asked several times as the child tries to make sense of what has happened, and of your being upset. If a child had felt angry or in some way upset with the person who died, he may feel responsible for the death – although this is unusual. Some children may behave normally; others will show SEPARATION ANXIETY, or have problems with eating, sleeping or behaving properly, especially if the child's routine has had to be disturbed. In this younger age group, children may take anything you say literally: if, for instance, you say "Grandad died because he was sick" your child may think that if you (or he) is sick, that you (or he) will die too. So you will need to find an explanation for death which is obvious but does not apply to either you or your child: "Grandad was very old and tired; he had a special illness which old people have". The form of explanation will of course depend on your child's age and level of development, and on your personal and religious beliefs.

■ ABOVE SEVEN YEARS, children understand better that death is final and irreversible. Still, they may, like younger children, feel in some way responsible for what has happened if they had angry or negative feelings about the person. They are likely to show that they are upset in more obvious ways, but this may fluctuate frequently in the period after the bereavement: children's moods don't always last as long as adult's, but this does not mean that they do not care.

Older children may well show changes in their pattern of eating, sleeping, concentrating and behaviour at home or at school; and such changes may last for several months; the period will depend on how much the bereavement has affected everyone in the family, and its routines, as well, of course, as the child's feelings.

■ ACTION If your child is still showing a marked change in any aspect of his life a few weeks after the event, check how he is functioning outside the home at play group or school. If this confirms your worries, see your doctor and discuss the possibility of help from a clinical psychologist or child psychiatrist. Many reactions to bereavement can be quickly helped by a few sessions in which to talk about the feelings involved. This can prevent long-term DEPRESSION, or problems at school.

BILIARY ATRESIA

A CONGENITAL obstruction of the bowel duct system which leads from the liver to the intestine. It is a rare condition without an identified cause, although VIRAL INFECTION in pregnancy has been considered.

Obstruction may be partial or complete. Bile is prevented from draining from the liver, which becomes inflamed.

■ SYMPTOMS Persistent JAUNDICE with pale BOWEL MOTIONS lacking the usual brown pigment. The abdomen may be distended by an enlarged liver, and there may be associated CONGENITAL ABNORMALITIES.

■ ACTION Jaundice lasting longer than one week in a full-term baby, or two weeks in a pre-term baby (37 weeks or below), should be investigated, although jaundice caused by biliary atresia tends to occur later than other more conventional types.

■ INVESTIGATIONS BLOOD-TEST checks on liver enzyme levels, and other specific tests will help to make the diagnosis.

■ TREATMENT The diagnosis must be made early (within two months)

for surgery to be successful.

A diet of easily digestible fats will be necessary. The child will be given extra VITAMINS, particularly vitamins D and E and elements, for example iron and zinc.

■ COMPLICATIONS BACTERIAL INFECTION may affect the liver causing a high FEVER and a worsening of the jaundice. ANTIBIOTICS may be needed. Biliary CIRRHOSIS may develop (see CIRRHOSIS). Failure to take vitamin supplements may lead to RICKETS or neurological disorders such as unsteadiness and floppiness.

■ OUTLOOK The life span in untreated biliary atresia is less than two years. The results of surgery are variable and there are complications, but children with this problem can survive into adult life.

BIRTH ASPHYXIA

Lack of oxygen at birth. Before birth, the baby receives oxygen via the placenta. If this supply falls below a certain level there will be signs of FOETAL DISTRESS during labour and the baby may have to be delivered swiftly. After birth, he may have a low APGAR SCORE.

■ CAUSES are usually uncertain. Factors that increase the risk of birth asphyxia include prolonged pregnancy (more than 42 weeks), extreme PREMATURITY, MULTIPLE PREGNANCY, HYPERTENSION (as in toxaemia of pregnancy), and the separation of the placenta from the uterus.

■ PREVENTION Antenatal care identifies problems in pregnancy. Monitoring during labour reveals whether a baby is showing signs of FOETAL DISTRESS. If asphyxia is anti-

BIRTH ASPHYXIA

Oxygen provided by mechanical ventilator in hospital intensive care unit.

cipated, then qualified medical staff may expedite delivery and should be present at the birth.

■ TREATMENT is resuscitation. Most babies are given oxygen either via a face mask or breathing tube placed into the trachea. Babies with severe asphyxia may subsequently need INTENSIVE CARE.

■ OUTLOOK Three to four minutes after resuscitation, most babies are pink and active; such babies will not usually develop long-term problems. A very small minority are severely asphyxiated, and may develop some degree of handicap or CEREBRAL PALSY.

BIRTH INJURIES
Injuries to the baby during DELIVERY. They may result in damage to the bones, nerves or skin.

■ BONES Fractures are rare, affecting less than one per cent of babies. They are often associated with diffi-cult births, breech deliveries and big babies. The majority are fractures of the clavicle (collar bone), often only noticed when a hard lump or callus develops on the bone after a few days. No treatment is necessary. Fractures of the bones of the legs and arms are usually recognized immediately. The baby may not move the damaged limb. Treatment is simple splinting; the fracture normally heals quickly and without deformity. Fractures of the skull bones usually follow difficult deliveries associated with FORCEPS. Such fractures are usually small, give no symptoms and need no treatment.

■ NERVES Injuries to the nerves are rare. However, during DELIVERY the nerves in the neck known as the brachial plexus may be stretched and cause three types of injury. Erb's palsy is the most common and affects the nerves supplying the upper arm muscles. The arm hangs down at the baby's side and is turned inwards. Klumpke's paralysis is rare. It affects the nerves to the hand so that it looks like a claw. Rarely there is a combination of both types of injury in which the whole arm is affected. Sometimes the nerve to the eye is also damaged, resulting in a droopy eyelid and small pupil.

The nerve supplying the face may be damaged by FORCEPS, causing the side of the mouth to droop. Recovery is usually complete but takes a few days: until then, extra care may be needed with feeding.

■ SKIN After a forceps delivery, the baby's face may have minor abrasions or scratches. After a breech delivery the baby's bottom and genitalia may be bruised for 24 to 48 hours. Birth pressure on the head may result in CAPUT or CEPHALHAEMATOMA.

BIRTH, PROBLEMS OF
See *AGPAR SCORE, BIRTH ASPHYXIA, BIRTH INJURIES.*

BIRTHMARKS
A general term for various skin abnormalities apparent at or soon after birth.

■ SYMPTOMS Birthmarks are either red, due to abnormal blood vessels in the skin, or dark, due to skin pigment (melanin).

There are two main types of red birthmarks: the strawberry naevus, which is a raised swelling; and the port wine stain, which is flat. The strawberry naevus (capillary haemangioma) is not always visible at birth, but soon appears and enlarges for up to 18 months. From the age of about three years, it begins to shrink and disappear; and most have disappeared (leaving a fine papery nonpigmented area of skin) by six. They tend to develop on the face or upper trunk, and very occasionally become (transiently) large and disfiguring.

Port wine stains (cavernous haemangiomas) do not disappear. They may be present on any part of the body, most notably the face or neck, and can be extensive and disfiguring. There is a risk with port wine stains on the face and scalp of associated abnormality within the brain. Such children should at some stage be assessed by a paediatrician.

Pigmented birthmarks are less common than ordinary MOLES, which develop in later childhood. They are usually small and insignificant; rarely 'bathing trunk' naevi are present, which cover a large segment of the trunk.

Many babies born to parents of African, Asian and Mediterranean origin have blue areas of pigmentation in one or more areas over their backs and buttocks. These are known as 'Mongolian blue spots'. They become less evident with age. It is important not to confuse them with bruises resulting from trauma (see *CHILD ABUSE*).

■ ACTION Since by definition a birthmark will be noticed at or soon after birth, advice will usually be available from a doctor or midwife at that time. However, in the case of cosmetically worrisome marks, you may wish to discuss with your doctor whether a specialist opinion (paediatrician, dermatologist or plastic surgeon) would be helpful.

■ TREATMENT Strawberry naevus: no treatment is needed, indeed interference may lead to scarring. Port wine stains can be camouflaged by masking creams, or may be destroyed by laser treatment given by a plastic surgeon. Pigmented birthmarks need no treatment if small, but extensive ones may be removed surgically.

■ LONG-TERM MANAGEMENT Children with permanent unsightly birthmarks of the face may helpfully use cosmetic camouflage. Trained cosmetic counsellors are attached to most plastic surgery clinics. Occasionally additional psychological support is indicated.

■ SELF-HELP Treat the birthmark in a matter-of-fact way; don't discuss it casually with others within earshot of the child. A word to the school teaching staff may be helpful.

■ OUTLOOK Strawberry naevi disappear in four to six years. The port wine stains do not, but advances in plastic surgical techniques (including the use of lasers) offer improving cosmetic results.

BITES AND STINGS

Animal bites can be especially dangerous to children – see *RABIES*.

■ SYMPTOMS The bites of mosquitoes and other blood-sucking insects are trivial, but to children often excessively irritating. The reaction is caused by ALLERGY to the saliva of the insect, injected before it starts sucking blood. This results in an itchy lump, similar to URTICARIA.

Bee and wasp venoms contain poison which damages blood vessels, causing swelling and pain. Individuals who have been stung by wasps or bees can develop an allergy to the venom, leading to far worse reactions on subsequent stinging, the most severe form being ANAPHYLACTIC SHOCK. When a bee stings, it leaves behind a tiny barbed rod which should be gently removed with tweezers. A wasp sting is retractable, so can be used repeatedly; it is also likely to carry the germs of TETANUS.

The only poisonous snake in Britain is the adder, but its bite is hardly ever fatal. The immediate effects are slight, but over 48 hours there may be pain and swelling of the limb, or, in severe cases, more generalized illness.

■ ACTION *Mosquito and other bites:* common-sense precautions such as protective clothing at dusk, and insect-repellent creams, will help both in reality and as a placebo for the child who is especially irritable or fearful because of the possibility of being attacked. Don't allow the child to expect such measures to be 100 per cent effective.

Bites themselves can be relieved by an antihistamine taken orally. Bites can become infected through being scratched, and may then need an antiseptic cream.

Bee and wasp stings: paracetamol reduces pain; reassurance that the bite will not cause serious damage may be just as important. If an allergic reaction develops, or if the child is known to be allergic to bee or wasp stings, immediate treatment with adrenalin should be given. This is available as an aerosol or an injection, and should be carried by all allergic individuals on medical advice.

Desensitization by a series of graded injections is available for some allergic individuals through hospital specialists.

Snake bites: the only effective treatment is an appropriate anti-venom, available at the local hospital casualty department. There is no benefit from cutting the bite, or sucking out the venom, while a tourniquet can be dangerous. Gently splinting the bitten limb to prevent movement may reduce spread of the venom while getting the child to hospital as quickly as possible.

Much reassurance is needed that the treatment will be effective: snake bites cause intense fear, in both child and parents.

■ OUTLOOK Allergy to bee and wasp stings is potentially grave: children who have reacted badly to stings should be seen by a specialist for advice on further treatment. Some snake bites in specific parts of the world are very dangerous, or indeed fatal. Prevention is the simple cure: use everyday encounters with wasps or bees as opportunity to demonstrate how to evade such threats calmly – and how not to provoke insects or animals.

BLACK EYE

BRUISING of the tissues around the eyeball usually resulting from the direct impact of a blow. Rarely a black eye, if spontaneous in onset, may reflect an underlying disease such as a bleeding disorder. Normally, after trauma, despite the dramatic swelling and vivid colour of the BRUISE, the injury settles relatively quickly: the blue-black turns to yellow-green and the discoloration fades in a fortnight. No treatment is called for, unless there is pain, which may be relieved with paracetamol.

BLACK-OUT
See *FAINTING, EPILEPSY, CONVULSIONS, GRAND MAL SEIZURE.*

BLEPHARITIS
A generalized inflammation of the skin of the eyelids. The lid margins look red, swollen and feel sore and itchy. It may result from an infection of the eyelids (see also CONJUNCTIVITIS); it also occurs in children with greasy skin.

■ TREATMENT is to keep the eyelids from becoming crusted (in infants this may require bathing the lids with clean cotton wool and warm water) and dissuading the child from rubbing his eyes.

If the lids become unusually inflamed, an infection may have developed. You should then get medical advice. Your doctor may prescribe an ANTIBIOTIC ointment.

BLINDNESS
In developed countries, typically one in 2,500 children are registered as blind or partially sighted.

■ CAUSES These include: CONGENITAL ABNORMALITY of the eye; CONGENITAL INFECTION; CATARACTS; damage to the optic nerve which car-

ries the impulse for sight to the brain; damage to the area of the brain that deals with vision (see *HYDROCEPHALUS* and *CEREBRAL PALSY*); retinoblastoma (see *TUMOUR OF THE EYE*).

■ SYMPTOMS Suspect a problem if your baby takes no visual interest in objects when a few weeks old. He may have an obvious SQUINT, or his eyes might wobble from side to side (nystagmus) when trying to look at something.

■ ACTION If you suspect any problem with a child's sight, you must of course contact your family doctor. He or she may arrange a specialist referral for EYE TESTS. The eye doctor may well ask about any family history of blindness.

■ TREATMENT Cataracts can be treated by surgery. Unfortunately, most other causes cannot be treated.

■ SELF-HELP Babies with impaired vision need extra stimulation of the other senses to encourage learning. Plenty of holding and touching are also essential to convey love and reassurance. Speech, noise (but not so that it startles), textures and smells can all be used to enhance the baby's awareness of his environment.

When he begins to crawl, parents have to provide an extra-safe environment. See *ACCIDENTS IN THE HOME*. Don't despair about his co-ordination: it will improve with practice. Toys he can operate to produce a noisy response will help.

Mixing with other children and encouraging independence will improve his confidence in his own abilities. Some visually handicapped children can distinguish light and dark or see bright colours. Large, bright toys can encourage learning in these children.

Since visual cues are absent, talking to these children is especially important in building up communication skills.

▨ EDUCATION The decision about which school suits your child needs to be made with the help of professionals. Special schools may cater for the needs of visually handicapped children along with those who have other handicaps.

The classroom will need to be well illuminated. Tape recorders and typewriters can help overcome the inherent problems of reading and writing. Braille will probably be taught. Adolescence is a difficult time of change with exaggerated demands on the youngster for identity and independence. Skills acquired at school and the possibility of further education help the transition to independence.

BLISTERS

Thin-walled, dome-shaped 'bubbles' on the skin containing clear fluid.

▨ CAUSES There is usually a local cause: friction, BURNS or an insect bite; blisters are rarely due to a generalized skin disease. Particular types of blisters (called VESICLES) are characteristic of CHICKENPOX.

▨ ACTION Ordinary blisters, as from ill-fitting shoes, should be protected by a simple dressing. Avoid bursting them; this invites INFECTION. See *BURNS* for the treatment of these. Insect bites may result in irritating blisters. No treatment is needed, but an antihistamine cream can ease the itching.

▨ GET MEDICAL ADVICE if the blisters have no obvious cause, especially in a baby, where they may be due to a serious infection of the skin, IMPETIGO, or may very rarely be the first pointer to serious disease.

▨ OUTLOOK Depends on the cause. If in doubt, your doctor may refer your child to a paediatrician or dermatologist.

BLOCKED EARS
See *WAX IN EARS, EARS, FOREIGN BODIES IN, WATER IN EARS, EXTERNAL EAR INFECTION.*

BLOOD GROUP INCOMPATIBILITY
When mother and baby have different blood groups, the baby having inherited his from the father. Why the baby should inherit the father's rather than the mother's blood group is not fully understood.

The incompatibility (which is relatively uncommon) can cause problems because a baby's red blood cells often cross the placenta during pregnancy and join the mother's blood circulation. If these cells are of a different group to the mother's, she is likely to produce ANTIBODIES against them. If antibodies are produced in sufficient quantities, they can cross back through the placenta to the baby, and destroy the baby's red blood cells.

The result is usually mild ANAEMIA and JAUNDICE in the baby during his first few days of life; there will be no long-term problems.

Blood group incompatibility, also known as ABO incompatibility, may occur during a first pregnancy, or during a subsequent one. See also *RHESUS INCOMPATIBILITY.*

BLOOD IN STOOLS
See *ANAL FISSURE, CONSTIPATION, ULCERATIVE COLITIS.*

BLOOD IN URINE
See *HAEMATURIA*.

BLOOD PRESSURE
The pressure of the blood measured in the arteries. It is lower in a younger child and increases to adult levels at adolescence. Raised blood pressure is called HYPERTENSION.

To measure blood pressure, an inflatable cuff is placed around your child's upper arm and the pressure in the cuff increased until it is above the pressure in the artery. As the pressure is released, the blood begins to flow in the artery and this can be felt at the pulse or heard with a stethoscope. The procedure is not painful, but creates a sensation of pressure which a child may find alarming. Blood pressure can be raised if a child is crying. It is necessary for the child to be lying or sitting quietly to obtain an accurate reading.

BLOOD SUGAR
See *DIABETES, MELLITUS*.

BLOOD TESTS
There are many different types of blood tests: blood can be tested to:
– diagnose disease;
– determine the response to treatment;
– measure the function of organs such as the liver and kidneys;
– check the levels of certain drugs in the blood, to ensure that the correct doses are being given
– assess blood loss after injury;
– match blood when a transfusion is necessary.

Small amounts of blood can be taken by a finger prick, or heel prick in the case of young babies. When larger amounts are needed, this is taken from a vein with a needle. After the initial prick the procedure is not usually painful. You may prefer to hold your child

BLOOD PRESSURE

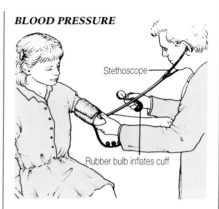

Stethoscope

Rubber bulb inflates cuff

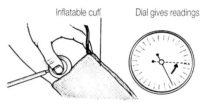

Inflatable cuff   Dial gives readings

yourself while this is done. Small children need to be held very still to complete the procedure as quickly as possible. Nurses are trained to do this, so either ask them to show you how best to hold your child, or let the nurse do it. If you become distressed this could further upset your child, so it is best if you can remain calm and reassuring. If you are anxious about it, discuss this with your doctor when the tests are suggested.

BLOOD TRANSFUSION
Giving blood taken from a healthy person to someone else who needs it. Likely reasons for blood transfusion include severe bleeding and ANAEMIA.

New-born babies may require an EXCHANGE TRANFUSION.

Before blood can be given, a sample of blood must be taken from the child to identify his blood group. There are four main blood groups (A, B, AB and

O). Only blood of a compatible group can be given. The child's blood must then be cross-matched with the blood which he will receive, to reduce the likelihood of an adverse reaction when the blood is given.

The amount of blood given depends on the weight of the child and the severity of the blood loss or anaemia.

A blood transfusion is never given unless it is absolutely necessary: transfusions can result in complications including a rash or a feverish reaction. The HEPATITIS and AIDS VIRUSES have, in the past, been transmitted by blood transfusion. This is now unlikely in developed countries because all donated blood is screened.

BLUE BABY

See *CONGENITAL HEART-DISEASE*.

BOILS

Superficial skin INFECTIONS caused by BACTERIA, commonly *Staphylococcus* or *Streptococcus* strains. Most children suffer the occasional boil, but if they recur frequently, the doctor may suggest a simple URINE TEST for sugar to check for DIABETES (recurrent boils may rarely be a first sign of diabetes). In older children and teenagers, boils tend to occur in sweaty places – armpits, groins, buttocks.

■ TREATMENT Most small boils will clear up within a week – keep the area clean and dry if possible. If the area is very painful, red and angry, take the child to the doctor, who will decide whether it needs a small incision to let out the infected pus, or whether a course of ANTI-BIOTICS is necessary.

In babies, boils should not be neglected, especially if accompanied by pointers to general illness.

BONDING

BONDING

Bonding describes the formation of the powerful emotional tie which develops between a parent and a new baby. The term refers generally to the mother-child relationship but a father also normally bonds with his baby.

Although parents are encouraged to hold their babies within moments of the birth to help develop feelings of attachment, those unable to do this (as, for example, following a CAESARIAN SECTION or if the baby is unwell at birth) can still bond successfully. Bonding is not necessarily an instant process and feelings of deep affection for and attachment to the baby develop over the first few weeks. How a parent reacts initially may depend on a number of factors such as the length of labour, previous experiences and personality.

Parents who are concerned about their feelings towards their new baby should consult their midwife, health visitor or family doctor. Mixed emotions are very common and discussing your concerns will be helpful. Occasionally mothers who feel detached from their babies are in fact suffering from postnatal depression.

BONE TUMOURS

Abnormal, undisciplined cell growth affecting the bone. Benign bone tumours grow slowly, do not spread and are not life-threatening. Malignant tumours – bone cancers – can spread around the body, destroying normal body tissue, and cause death.

▥ SYMPTOMS usually start as a bone swelling. There may be pain and redness of the skin over the swelling. Occasionally there is weight loss or fever. Sometimes a FRACTURE can occur at the site of the tumour, because it has weakened the bone.

▥ ACTION Early diagnosis makes treatment more effective, especially of malignant tumours.

If your child has any unexplained swelling or pain over a bone, see your doctor.

▥ TESTS are necessary to confirm the diagnosis. X-rays can show a tumour and also whether it has spread. An X-ray of the chest is performed to see whether the cancer has spread to the lungs. A bone scan and sometimes a scan of the whole body will help in the diagnosis.

Biopsy is often necessary to find out what type of tumour is present, and what treatment is best. This may be done through a needle, or at a minor operation. BLOOD TESTS may help the diagnosis.

▥ TREATMENT Surgical removal can cure most benign, and some malignant, tumours. If the tumour has spread, an operation may be necessary to remove further growth; indeed amputation of a limb may be considered to prevent the cancer from spreading, but this is much less common now that other kinds of treatment are becoming much more effective.

Radiotherapy and anticancer (cytotoxic) drugs can halt the growth of malignant tumours. Treatments are changing continually with the introduction of increasingly effective drugs.

The child will probably be looked after by both an orthopaedic surgeon and a paediatrician, so that the different forms of treatment can be co-ordinated.

▥ OUTLOOK with benign tumours is good; and long-term problems are unlikely.

Survival rates of children with malignant bone tumours are improving, and will probably continue to do so.

BOOSTER INJECTION

This is a further dose of a vaccine after the initial IMMUNIZATION. It stimulates the body to produce more ANTIBODIES so that the child remains immune to that particular INFECTION.

BORNHOLM DISEASE

See *CHEST PAINS*.

BOTTLE FEEDING

Formula milks are made up to have a nutritional content similar to breast milk. There are, however, important differences: formula milks do not contain the beneficial ANTIBODIES provided by breast milk. The protein used in formula milk is usually derived from cow's milk; soya bean protein is an alternative, soya-based formulae are sometimes used for babies thought to have COW'S MILK ALLERGY.

There are many brands of formula milk, and different types available for most brands. However, for most babies any normal formula is satisfactory. Your midwife or health visitor

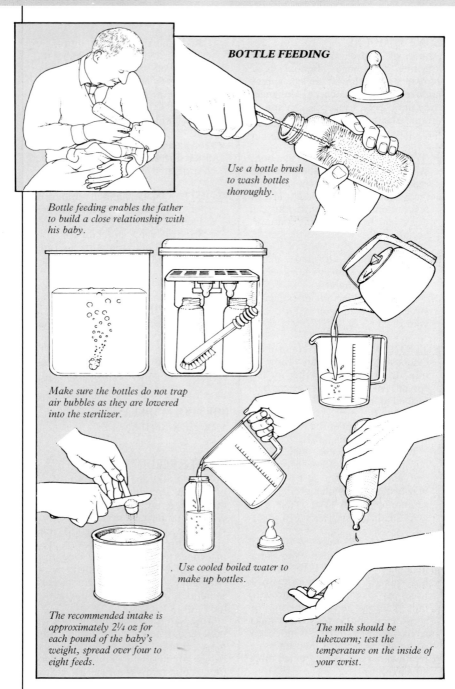

BOTTLE FEEDING

Use a bottle brush
to wash bottles
thoroughly.

Bottle feeding enables the father
to build a close relationship with
his baby.

Make sure the bottles do not trap
air bubbles as they are lowered
into the sterilizer.

Use cooled boiled water to
make up bottles.

The recommended intake is
approximately 2¼ oz for
each pound of the baby's
weight, spread over four to
eight feeds.

The milk should be
lukewarm; test the
temperature on the inside of
your wrist.

will advise you if you are in doubt as to which one to choose. There is normally no need to change the baby's formula until he progresses to weaning foods and domestic milk.

Bottle feeding offers a degree of convenience which may suit some families, allowing, for example, the father the opportunity to feed his baby. However, strict attention to hygiene in cleaning the bottle and teat, and preparing the formula feeds is essential. This is especially true in tropical countries: if bottles cannot be properly cleaned, and if made-up formula milk stands around and becomes a breeding ground for BACTERIA, there is a serious risk of GASTROENTERITIS, which in adverse conditions can be fatal.

Sterilizing and preparing bottles is time-consuming. You also have to decide how much milk to give the baby, and how often to feed. The recommended average intake for a 24-hour day is around 2¼ oz for each 1 lb (150 ml per kg) of the baby's weight, this amount being spread over four to eight feeds. (The volume taken and pattern of feeding is, of course, highly variable from baby to baby.) Babies should not be left with the bottle propped up in the cot: feeding should always be supervised because of the risk of vomiting and inhalation. Advice on all these matters should be readily available from your health visitor, G.P. or baby clinic, who will also be able to weigh the baby to check for steady weight gain.

BOW LEGS
Normal in infants and young children. In older children, bow-leggedness can be due to RICKETS, *OSTEOGENESIS IMPERFECTA* or other very rare bone abnormalities.

▪ SYMPTOMS are unlikely. You may notice that your child has bow

BOW LEGS

legs, or this may be pointed out by a relative or friend.

▪ ACTION If you are worried, get medical advice. It may be necessary for the child to wear a special shoe with an arch support and a wedge on the outer side.

▪ TREATMENT depends on the cause. Surgery is available, but rarely used.

BOWEL MOTIONS
The sticky dark green substance passed by a new-born baby is known as MECONIUM. It is replaced within a few days by semi-solid 'stool' – golden-yellow in the breast-fed baby, and greenish-brown in the bottle-fed one. As the child begins to take weaning foods, the stool changes again. The consistency and colour vary with the diet and with the individual make-up of the baby's digestive system. Most babies open the bowels (pass a stool or motion) daily or every other day with no evidence of discomfort. Occasionally, particularly at a time of change from breast feeding to formula milk, babies may become CONSTIPATED (strain and pass dry stools at irregular intervals). This can usually be man-

aged by simple expedients such as extra water or fruit juice in the diet. If this becomes a problem, get medical advice. See also *DIARRHOEA, CONSTIPATION, BLEEDING, MALABSORPTION.*

BRAIN DAMAGE

Permanent harm to the brain as a result of illness or injury. Once nerve cells in the brain are destroyed, they cannot grow again, or be replaced. Brain damage is a general term, and does not simply refer to problems at birth.

■ SYMPTOMS Effects of brain damage reflect the site involved. Damage to the front part of the brain (frontal damage) causes disinhibition, lack of initiative and concentration, and loss of ability to plan or control movements. Posterior damage can lead to blindness; damage in between may lead to loss of language, perception of shapes and distance or loss of sensation. EPILEPSY is a common consequence.

■ CAUSES Trauma; infective illness (including viral ENCEPHALITIS, MENINGITIS); biochemical disturbance (lack of oxygen or glucose; inborn chemical disorders); POISONING (typically from lead or carbon monoxide); lack of blood supply (cardiac arrest); bleeding (SHOCK) or raised pressure (for example in HYDROCEPHALUS). There may be widespread damage (say after violent shaking) or local damage.

■ INVESTIGATIONS depend on the circumstances, but emergency medical help is required if brain damage is suspected following an accident or in an acute illness. See *CEREBRAL PALSY, MENTAL HANDICAP.*

■ TREATMENT depends on the cause. If there is acute damage after injury, neurosurgery may limit damage. In acute illness, ANTIBIOTIC or biochemical treatment may help. In either case, life support in an INTENSIVE CARE unit may be required, including respiratory support, intravenous fluid and control of pressure in the head. If damage is long standing, treatment is by remedial therapy and teaching. See *CEREBRAL PALSY, MENTAL HANDICAP.*

■ OUTLOOK It does not necessarily follow that damage will lead to loss of function; although the damage is irreversible, related parts of the brain can sometimes compensate.

Most mentally handicapped children with symmetrical cerebral palsy have not suffered brain damage, but show the effects of abnormalities of brain development before birth.

BRAIN TUMOURS

These result from abnormal growths of brain cells; they may be benign (slow growing and confined to one site), or malignant (rapid growing and capable of spreading to more than one site). They may be primary (derived from brain cells) or secondary (from another part of the body). After LEUKAEMIA, brain tumours are the commonest of the childhood CANCERS.

Primary brain tumours may arise from the lining of the brain (meningioma), cranial nerves (neuromas), the choroid plexus (which secretes cerebro-spinal fluid), glial cells (glioma) or nerve cells. Commonest are gliomas.

■ SYMPTOMS include fits or convulsions, and symptoms of raised pressure inside the head, such as headache and vomiting (especially in the morning), deterioration in intellectual function, development of SQUINT or loss of vision, loss of balance or change in behaviour. Occasionally specific local effects of the tumour give rise to particular changes in body function, such as loss of ability to concentrate urine or the development of precocious puberty.

■ INVESTIGATION may include a brain scan, an electroencephalogram (EEG), and occasionally the injection of an X-ray opaque dye into the blood supply to the brain (angiogram).

■ TREATMENT depends on the site and nature of the tumour. Benign tumours can be removed surgically, either in part or totally. Malignant tumours may be removed in part, avoiding damage to the adjacent normal brain tissue. This is often combined with radiation (radiotherapy) and drugs (chemotherapy). If a tumour causes raised pressure inside the skull and cannot be removed, additional steps may be taken, such as the use of steroid drugs to reduce swelling of the surrounding brain, or the insertion of a shunt, a plastic tube which allows the high-pressure cerebro-spinal fluid to be relieved.

■ OUTLOOK A few malignant brain tumours are cured; for the rest, treatment is aimed to secure quality, rather than quantity of life. Survival rates are highly variable, from a few weeks to many years. A child with a brain tumour can usually lead a full and active life for a long time after appropriate treatment.

BREAST FEEDING

Breast feeding is the natural way by which the human mother (like other mammals) feeds her offspring. The food the baby receives is properly known as breast milk or human milk.

The alternative is BOTTLE FEEDING, in which case the baby receives a synthetic substitute called milk formula.

'Breast is best' is a slogan that symbolizes the return to fashion of breast feeding in developed countries. There is evidence to suggest that breast-fed babies suffer less from allergies and infections than babies who have been bottle fed from the start. Breast feeding is also encouraged because of the intimate contact and BONDING it promotes between mother and baby.

■ ACTION 1 Put the baby to the breast as soon as possible after birth, and allow him to feed for as long and as frequently as he wishes in the first few days. In this way your milk production and let-down will be stimulated. The first milk is a clear fluid, colostrum, which is rich in protein and ANTIBODIES and valuable for your baby; within three to four days milk flow will increase and the milk itself become more creamy. 2 Be patient. A healthy baby needs no other sustenance than colostrum and milk in the amounts naturally available, increasing over the first week after birth.

The majority of mothers comfortably establish breast feeding to their great satisfaction, and that of their baby.

Some mothers, especially with their first babies, need some expert assistance, particularly in ensuring that the baby is correctly positioned on the breast. This is especially so in the first week when the breasts become full.

Difficulties arise largely from confused and conflicting advice. Try to secure the support of one experienced midwife (with a special

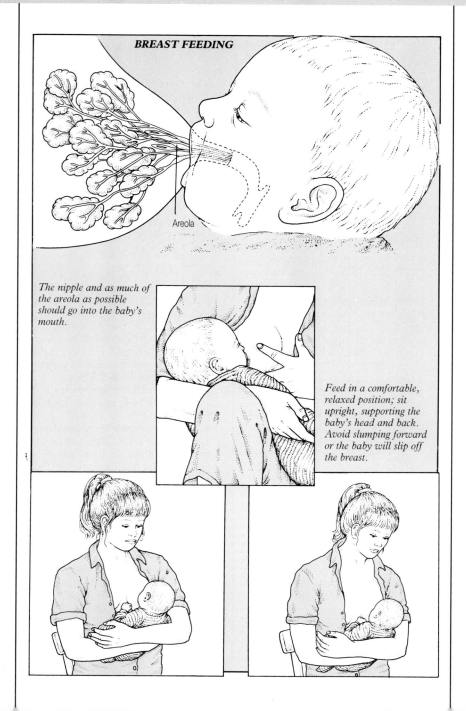

BREAST FEEDING

Areola

The nipple and as much of the areola as possible should go into the baby's mouth.

Feed in a comfortable, relaxed position; sit upright, supporting the baby's head and back. Avoid slumping forward or the baby will slip off the breast.

interest in breast feeding if possible). Avoid giving your baby bottled water or formula (unless specifically prescribed by a doctor): such supplements will reduce your baby's appetite, and hence the feeding stimulus to your milk production. **3** Breast care: A feeling of fullness of the breasts is normal in the first few days, as blood flow to the breast and milk production increase. If this becomes uncomfortable, or if your nipples feel sore when your baby is feeding, then ask for expert midwifery help. Most of the discomfort associated with breast feeding is avoidable if the baby is correctly positioned at the breast and feeding on demand. **4** Good positioning is essential. The nipple and most of the areola should go into the baby's mouth. This is best achieved by ensuring that your baby's mouth is wide open as he attaches to the breast. Allowing the baby to attach to the nipple alone will make you sore, and will not promote milk production and flow. **5** Don't let anyone worry you about the quantity of your milk supply. Your supply will naturally adjust to meet your baby's needs and demands. Let a 'hungry' baby feed often and well positioned at the breast.

■ OUTLOOK The great majority of mothers succeed in smoothly establishing and maintaining breast feeding. If you are having difficulties, get expert advice. This may be available from your midwife, health visitor, G.P., paediatrician or one of the voluntary groups that exist to support breast-feeding mothers.

BREATH-HOLDING ATTACKS
A child holds his breath or refuses to breathe: after a minute or so, he goes blue in the face and may lose consciousness. Breathing then resumes normally. Breath-holding attacks may occur during TANTRUMS and are a common expression of anger in toddlers. They are alarming for parents, but the child is not at risk: the body's natural response to shortage of oxygen is fainting which allows normal breathing to return automatically. If your child has an attack, stay calm; there is no need to intervene, but make sure he is in a safe position. Don't try to stop the attack by startling, slapping or splashing him with water. This is not effective, does not discourage future attacks and only increases tension.

BREATHLESSNESS
The combination of *difficulty* in breathing with *rapid* breathing.

■ CAUSES Breathlessness on exercise is of course normal; but if it occurs on minimal exertion, such as climbing a single flight of stairs, there could be something wrong.

ANXIETY can cause rapid or irregular breathing: see *OVER-BREATHING*.

ANAEMIA, with its associated lack of oxygen in the blood, tends to make the lungs work extra hard to compensate, and so cause breathlessness.

HEART-DISEASE, another cause, makes extra blood accumulate in the lungs. This in turn makes them stiff, and breathing becomes difficult.

Lung disease, and in particular ASTHMA and PNEUMONIA, result in rapid, laboured breathing, as can obstruction to the upper airways, as in CROUP or when an object is inhaled. Onset with these last is usually sudden.

SHOCK is a rare cause of breathlessness. It may be due to bleeding, anaphylaxis or any other cause of drop in BLOOD PRESSURE.

■ ACTION Try to determine whether your child is unusually breathless by comparing how he behaves on minimal exercise with a child of similar age. More than 50 breaths per minute is never normal, except just after heavy exercise.

If your baby becomes breathless when feeding, get medical advice.

Likewise, get medical advice immediately if a child has a sudden onset of rapid breathing, particularly if it is noisy.

■ TESTS will depend on the suspected cause. They could include chest X-ray, BLOOD TESTS to look for anaemia, and an ECG (ELECTROCARDIOGRAM). Sometimes lung-function tests are done by blowing into a special machine.

■ TREATMENT will depend on the cause. See appropriate entries.

■ LONG-TERM MANAGEMENT If your child has a CHRONIC ILLNESS causing breathlessness, find out from your doctor whether he needs to limit his activities. In almost all cases, a child can be allowed to determine his own limits. As long as he is allowed to rest if he is breathless, there is no danger.

BRONCHIECTASIS

A rare condition in which parts of the air passages (bronchi) become abnormally enlarged and infected.

■ CAUSES Bronchiectasis is occasionally inherited; more commonly, it is a complication of PNEUMONIA, severe attacks of MEASLES or WHOOPING COUGH, or a result of CYSTIC FIBROSIS.

■ SYMPTOMS The child has a persistent cough, producing coloured, offensive sputum. If a large part of the lungs is affected, he will be breathless after exertion. With infection, the child is tired and often febrile.

■ ACTION Children with this condition require specialist treatment, and prescribed routines should be clearly established.

■ INVESTIGATIONS A chest X-ray will usually be performed, but more specialized X-rays may also be needed to show exactly where and how widespread the trouble is.

■ TREATMENT Physiotherapy is the key: a physiotherapist teaches parents how to percuss the chest to clear lung secretions. It will usually be required twice daily. ANTIBIOTICS are usually prescribed, in higher doses and for longer periods than for simple infections.

Occasionally, if the disease is not controlled by the other methods, the damaged lobe of the lung is removed by surgery.

■ OUTLOOK One third of affected children recover completely, and more improve at puberty.

BRONCHIOLITIS

A serious chest INFECTION of young children occurring in epidemics, mainly in winter months.

■ CAUSE The respiratory syncytial VIRUS (RSV) is the major cause.

■ PREVENTION Attempts to produce a vaccine against RSV have so far been unsuccessful.

■ SYMPTOMS The baby, typically under six months, develops a cold, which rapidly progresses to involve the chest. Breathing becomes difficult and rapid, with a dry COUGH. Often, an older child in the family will recently have had a cold. There may be a FEVER, but it is not usually very high – say 100.5°F or 38°C.

■ ACTION Whenever a baby or young child develops rapid breathing and is in obvious distress, get urgent medical advice. Most children with bronchiolitis are treated in hospital, but mild attacks can be managed at home.

■ TREATMENT There is not yet a generally available drug to destroy the virus, so treatment comes down to assisting the breathing with oxygen, and providing adequate fluid and food, sometimes by tube feeding or intravenous fluids. Sometimes a drug is given to improve the breathing. New drugs are under development which can destroy the virus, but these are not as yet in general use.

■ OUTLOOK Most cases recover after about one week, but a significant number are left with a tendency to wheeze, which appears to be a form of ASTHMA.

■ LONG-TERM MANAGEMENT For those left with a persistent wheeze, treatment is the same as for ASTHMA. Most will recover completely as they reach adolescence.

BRONCHITIS

An INFECTION of the bronchi, or air passages (by various VIRUSES). In childhood, infection usually involves other parts of the respiratory tract as well.

■ CAUSES VIRUSES are normally responsible for bronchitis. Less com-

BRONCHITIS

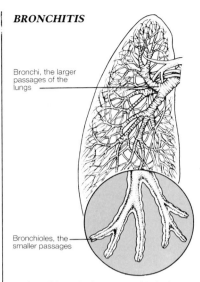

Bronchi, the larger passages of the lungs

Bronchioles, the smaller passages

Inflamed bronchioles: repeated infection damages their linings and makes them vulnerable to further infection.

monly, BACTERIA may infect the chest, but this is more likely if the child already has a disease such as CYSTIC FIBROSIS or BRONCHIECTASIS.

■ SYMPTOMS The child has a COUGH and wheezes, and may have a FEVER. In severe cases, wheezing (see also ASTHMA), breathlessness, and respiratory distress may occur, with difficulty in drinking or feeding.

■ ACTION If your child is known to have asthma and you recognize his symptoms as a mild attack, then treat him accordingly; otherwise he should see the doctor. You should give paracetamol to lower the child's temperature, and plenty of fluids to prevent dehydration.

■ TREATMENT ANTIBIOTICS may be prescribed, but are not required by most children. A bronchodilator drug such as salbutamol is often found to help the child who is wheezing.

Recurrent 'bronchitis' usually turns out to be asthma, which may flare up with a cold. He may need treatment over a prolonged period of time (see *ASTHMA*). If there is no other problem, an attack of bronchitis usually clears up quickly and completely.

BRUISING

Bruising is caused by blood oozing from broken blood vessels into the surrounding tissues under the skin. During the week following the injury, the blood is denatured and reabsorbed by the tissues. This causes the colour changes in the skin. Bruised areas are not necessarily painful; the pain arises from injured nerve endings and from the inflammatory process that causes swelling of an injured area, which often settles before the colour changes have completely resolved.

Toddlers and young children often get bruises on face, shins, forearms and back in the course of ordinary rough-and-tumble play. The patterns of bruising are characteristic, and the 'age' of the bruises corresponds with the timing of the injuries that have caused them.

Bruising that does not conform to these patterns may need investigation and tests.

■ TESTS There are two main categories of 'abnormal' bruising which call for special tests. 1 Disorders of bleeding and clotting. HAEMOPHILIA is an example: an hereditary bleeding disorder, causing bruising without injury, swelling of joints due to internal bleeding, and other unusual symptoms. Another example is Vitamin K deficiency, which disrupts the clotting mechanism in pre-

mature babies. There are many other disorders of bleeding and clotting, all of them rare. They can be distinguished only with blood tests. 2 Non-accidental injury – see *CHILD ABUSE*. If this is suspected from patterns of injury seen on the child, X-rays and BLOOD TESTS will be needed to rule out CONGENITAL ABNORMALITIES of bones and blood.

■ ACTION Bruising is not in itself painful; but pain arising from injury can be greatly relieved by paracetamol, or by a hot water-bottle or even an ice-pack.

BULIMIA

Secretive eating of large amounts of food, followed by self-induced vomiting or the use of laxatives. It is associated with *ANOREXIA NERVOSA*. It is a psychological disorder almost always affecting girls, from the teens onwards.

BULLYING AND TEASING

A sad – if toughening – fact of life both at school and at home for most children at some time or another. If the child is obviously different from others (being short, wearing glasses), the affliction may be long-term.

If your child is frequently upset by teasing, think up some techniques to help him stick up for himself. Try to discover from his teacher whether this is a widespread problem in school. Children who bully others are often insecure and unhappy themselves – in need of help. You could do worse than explain that to your child.

BURNS AND SCALDS

Burns are to blame for some 10 per cent of accidental deaths of children under five years.

■ IMMEDIATE ACTION *Minor burns and scalds:* Douse the affected area with cold running water – from the tap, shower, or by bowl or bucket. Continue immersion for ten minutes or so, or until the pain subsides. Remove any constricting clothing, including shoes and watches, from the burnt area before it starts to swell. At this stage get medical advice. If not readily

BURNS AND SCALDS

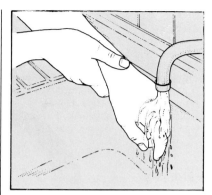

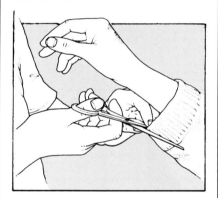

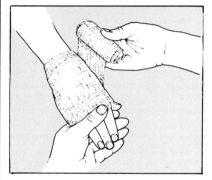

available, then dress the area with sterile material that does not produce fluff. Don't burst blisters, or put on lotions (nor butter, fat and so on) or use adhesive dressings.

Severe burns and scalds: Put out flames. Smother flaming hair or clothes with blanket, towel, coat or whatever is to hand. Remove child from source of heat. If child's clothing has been on fire, prevent him from running outside (breeze can fan the flames). Lie the child down, burnt side up, and douse the burnt area with water until the pain has stopped. Remove any constricting clothing or article before the area of the burn begins to swell. Don't remove clothing, or anything else, that is sticking to a burn. Call for medical help, or an ambulance, or take the child to your nearest hospital. You may judge it advisable to wrap the child in a blanket (not the cellular type) or similar heavy fabric for the journey. If you have called an ambulance, keep the child warm, flat on the ground, and stand by him until the first-aid team arrive.

Serious burns can bring on SHOCK. See that entry for treatment.

A child with any but the mildest burn should be checked at hospital.

■ OUTLOOK With modern skin-grafting techniques, horrifying damage can be patched up; but severe burns can still result in death, or permanent disfigurement and attendant psychological problems.

CAESARIAN SECTION

The DELIVERY of the baby through an incision in the abdominal wall and uterus. The use of Caesarian section varies from country to country. In the U.K., for example, it accounts for one in ten of births. It is generally done to facilitate the safe delivery of the baby.

Some Caesarian sections are anticipated, for example: if the mother has needed one at a previous delivery; if the baby's head is too large for the mother's pelvis; if the baby is in an unsuitable position – breech ('bottom-first') or transverse (crosswise); or if the placenta is lower than the baby's head (*Placenta praevia*).

Some Caesarians may become necessary for various reasons during labour: if, for instance, there is FOETAL DISTRESS or a prolapsed umbilical cord which might become trapped between the mother's cervix and the baby's head, hindering the flow of blood to the baby; or if there is failure of the labour to progress.

Caesarian section is performed either under an EPIDURAL or a general ANAESTHETIC. Both will usually be offered if the DELIVERY is not an emergency. In an emergency, a general anaesthetic is given. With an EPIDURAL, the mother remains awake during and after the delivery. The pubic hair may be shaved and a catheter (a small tube) inserted into the bladder to keep it empty (some maternity units avoid these procedures). An intravenous drip provides fluid and medication as necessary. When the anaesthetic has taken effect, a 'bikini line' incision is usually made through the abdominal wall and then into the uterus. The baby is eased out either by hand or, less often, using FORCEPS. The cord is cut and the baby is handed to his mother, or to his father if the mother is under general anaesthetic.

■ COMPLICATIONS After delivery the scar is sore and pain relief may be sought. The mother may not be able to move around easily, and will need help at first to care for her baby. She should be on her feet within 48 hours. Abdominal discomfort and constipation are more likely following a Caesarian section. It is helpful to be up and about as soon as possible after birth in order to minimize the risk of thromboses (blood clots) forming in the legs.

A mother who has had a Caesarian section will usually stay in hospital for about seven to ten days after the delivery. She can, however, still sit out of bed and play a full part in the care of her baby.

CANCER IN CHILDHOOD

Except for LEUKAEMIA, cancers are very uncommon in childhood. See *NEPHROBLASTOMA, TUMOUR OF THE EYE, BRAIN TUMOURS.* See also *CHRONIC ILLNESS, CHILD WITH, DYING CHILD.*

CANDIDA

See *THRUSH.*

CAPUT

The soft swelling that gives some new-

CAESARIAN SECTION

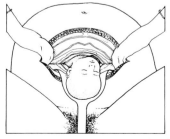

The baby is eased out, usually by hand, through a 'bikini line' incision.

born babies' heads a distorted shape. It is caused by normal pressure as the baby passes through the mother's pelvis. Caput disappears in a day or two. A swelling that remains may be a CEPHALHAEMATOMA.

CARBUNCLE
See *BOILS*.

CARDIAC MASSAGE
See *EMERGENCY RESUSCITATION*.

CARDIOMYOPATHY
Permanent damage to the heart muscle. The cause is usually unknown. See *HEART-DISEASE*.

CAST IN EYE
See *SQUINT*.

CAT SCAN
Computerized axial tomography is a convenient, but expensive, way of producing a series of cross-sectional images of an object, shaded to reflect changes in density. Often used to examine head or abdomen for suspect swellings. Painless, but can be lengthy; may eliminate need for investigations which may be painful or cause side effects.

CATARACTS
The lens of the eye becomes clouded. This can affect the whole lens, or only a small area in an otherwise clear lens. Rare in children.

▓ CAUSES Can be inherited: the child may be born with a cataract, or the problem may develop within the first few years. Cataracts can occur in children whose mothers contracted RUBELLA during the pregnancy. But in many cases the cause is unclear.

▓ SIGNS AND SYMPTOMS Parents may notice a white, clouded area within the pupil. If your child is old enough, he may complain of difficulty with vision.

▓ TREATMENT There is no way to reverse the clouding which is like a scar. However, the cataract can be removed by a simple operation performed at any age.

▓ OUTLOOK After the removal of the cataract, SPECTACLES and/or contact lenses are needed to replace the affected lens. This is essential to bring a focused picture on to the retina at the back of the eye.

It is important to treat cataracts early, so sometimes the operation is performed on babies only a few weeks or months old. In these cases, soft contact lenses are given.

Regular follow-up eye checks are necessary to change the strength of the lenses.

How successful the treatment will be depends on a number of factors, including how old the child was when the cataract developed, and the presence of other eye disease.

CATARRH
See *POST-NASAL DRIP, COMMON COLD*.

CELLULITIS
A spreading BACTERIAL INFECTION of the skin and soft tissues.

▓ SYMPTOMS The site of infection is angry and red, often with a raised edge. The skin feels hard, hot and tender. The child is generally un-well, and has a FEVER.

■ ACTION This condition needs urgent medical treatment: the child should see a doctor immediately.

■ TREATMENT An ANTIBIOTIC, chosen for its action on the bacteria that usually cause cellulitis, given by mouth or, if necessary, by injection.

■ OUTLOOK If not treated, cellulitis may progress to an abscess, and from this the infection can spread to involve the lymph glands or blood stream (leading to septicaemia). Correct antibiotic treatment is normally rapidly effective, and the condition heals with no long-term effects.

CEPHALHAEMATOMA
A collection of blood under the skin covering the skull bones of a new-born baby. It is caused by bruising during the DELIVERY (see also BIRTH INJURIES). It can be felt as a softish bump, usually on one or other side of the scalp. It is harmless and generally subsides over four to six weeks.

CEREBRAL PALSY
Cerebral palsy as a term covers an enormous range of problems. The most minor may present as no more than an infant who is a late walker who grows up to be a somewhat clumsy child. The most severe represents a major lifelong challenge for the child and his family.

Disorders of posture, movement and co-ordination usually become apparent in late infancy or toddlerhood. Although the effects of cerebral palsy change as the child grows, the disease does not get worse.

Cerebral palsy (CP) may be classi-fied into several types, according to how the different parts of the body are affected. Spastic cerebral palsy is the commonest (two-thirds of the cases). The child's muscles show increased re-sistance to passive movement and tightness on exertion.

Athetoid cerebral palsy involves writhing movements of the arms, legs and mouth muscles, which are outside the control of the child. Ataxic cerebral palsy is characterized by a lack of balance of the trunk and general un-steadiness of co-ordination. Cerebral palsy severely affecting all four limbs may be accompanied by severe intel-lectual deficiency (or MENTAL HANDI-CAP), and accounts for about 5 per cent of types of CP.

If all four limbs are affected, this is called quadriplegia; diplegia means the legs are most affected. When one half of the body is affected, it is described as hemiplegia. Ataxic diple-gia means a lack of trunk balance, plus spasticity in the legs.

Associated conditions include EPI-LEPSY; mental handicap or retardation; visual or hearing defects (up to a tenth of cases); language and communica-tion problems; and in the more severely affected, drooling of saliva and FEEDING PROBLEMS.

About two in every 1,000 children suffer from cerebral palsy.

■ CAUSES Damage to the developing brain during pregnancy, birth or the early postnatal period. Causes in-clude: CONGENITAL ABNORMALI-TIES, INFECTION in pregnancy (in-cluding *RUBELLA*, cytomegalovirus), BIRTH ASPHYXIATION, complications of PREMATURITY (despite INTENSIVE CARE), MENINGITIS or ENCEPHALI-TIS, or physical injury in early in-fancy.

■ TREATMENT Since CP is a com-plex manifestation of structural

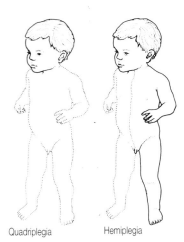

Quadriplegia   Hemiplegia

BRAIN DAMAGE, there is no cure or simple treatment. Management includes a wide-ranging and long-lasting programme of special education with particular attention to physiotherapy, speech therapy and occupational therapy. Aids, appliances, adapted footwear or orthopaedic surgery may be required. Psychological and social support for the child and whole family may be indicated.

Drugs may have a place for such associated problems as epilepsy or CONSTIPATION.

With a well-planned, co-ordinated and concerted effort, the child may achieve more than may seem possible as judged in infancy. Occasionally, athetoid children, thought to be mentally retarded in infancy, turn out to be of average or above average intelligence, but require special communication systems before they can express their abilities effectively.

■ OUTLOOK Facilities for children with cerebral palsy tend to be based in child development centres or in special schools; adolescent and young adult rehabilitation services are also available. Many countries, including the U.K., have organizations and societies established that are very effective in supporting individuals and families with CP.

Most children with CP can be expected to live a normal length of life.

CHEST PAIN
An unusual symptom in childhood.

■ SYMPTOMS The nature of the pain, and other symptoms present may well indicate the cause.

If the child has a sharp pain in his chest which is made worse on breathing, suspect an injury such as a bruised or torn muscle or a FRACTURED rib. The commonest cause of chest pain is in fact a minor muscle injury.

A similar type of pain can be due to inflammation of the lungs (as in PNEUMONIA and PLEURISY) or a VIRAL INFECTION. There is usually a cough (which can make the pain worse), fever and sometimes general muscle pain.

Pain caused by HEART-DISEASE is always related to exercise, lasts for a few minutes, and is relieved by rest. It is best described as a tight feeling in the centre of the chest and, in childhood, is very rare. An older child may be concerned that a pain could be due to a heart problem, and unless you have reason to suspect that this is true, you can do no harm in explaining these facts to the child.

Young children may complain of pain in the chest when the cause is in another part of the body.

■ ACTION Look for signs of injury, typically of BRUISING. Determine whether the pain is associated with coughing or breathing, or is related to exercise. Take your child's temperature to establish whether an infection is implicated.

An older child may need reassurance that chest pain is not due to a heart condition, especially if someone in the family has CORONARY ARTERY DISEASE.

Get medical advice if the pain occurs with breathing or on exercise, or if it persists for more than a few days.

■ TREATMENT Muscular pain needs no specific treatment, but a painkiller such as paracetamol may help. Chest-wall injury is normally also treated with a simple painkiller.

Pain from pneumonia, pleurisy or a viral infection is likewise treated with a painkiller, but the child must see a doctor in the case of the first two infections; an ANTIBIOTIC will probably be necessary.

Chest pain that could be due to heart-disease must be followed up with the family doctor and/or a specialist.

■ TESTS A chest X-ray helps to diagnose a fractured rib, pleurisy, pneumonia or heart-disease.

An ECG (ELECTROCARDIOGRAM) will be necessary if heart-disease is suspected.

Bornholm's disease, a viral infection of muscle, can cause chest pain. There is stabbing pain and the disease can mimic more serious illnesses. Recovery is in about seven days.

CHICKENPOX

A highly INFECTIOUS disease, mainly but not exclusively confined to childhood, caused by one of the herpes group of VIRUSES. It is transmitted by direct contact or airborne spread from an infected person. It is most infectious before the RASH appears, so it is very difficult to prevent your child from coming into contact with it. It tends to be mild in childhood (and very unpleasant in adulthood), so it makes sense to let your child catch it. The IN-CUBATION PERIOD is 14 to 21 days from the contact.

■ SYMPTOMS 1 There is often a mild FEVER, HEADACHE and a feeling of being generally unwell, particularly in older children. This may or may not give warning of the onset. 2 The rash occurs mainly on the trunk, but in severe cases it develops on the face, scalp and limbs. It consists of raised red spots which rapidly turn into itchy blisters. These gradually dry to form crusts, which can last for a few weeks. They do not leave a scar unless they are scratched, or get infected. New spots occur in batches, so while some are forming crusts, others may be appearing for the first time. Several spots may crop up in the mouth.

There are few serious complications of chickenpox, but PNEUMO-NIA or ENCEPHALITIS do occasionally occur. In children with reduced IM-MUNITY, including those on steroids, chickenpox can be severe.

■ ACTION The fever can be treated with an analgesic such as paracetamol; give cool baths if necessary.

Keep your child's nails short and clean to prevent him from scratching, and infecting the spots. Calamine lotion will help to reduce the itchiness.

Bed rest is unnecessary, unless your child is more comfortable in bed.

If you suspect PNEUMONIA or EN-CEPHALITIS (see the separate entries), get urgent medical advice.

Your child is infectious until new blisters have stopped appearing – usually about a week. The crusts are not infectious.

■ TREATMENT If the itchiness is really causing problems, your doctor may prescribe an antihistamine, usually as a syrup. Creams containing antihistamines can sometimes cause ALLERGIC reactions and are not generally used.

Minor skin infection can be treated with an antiseptic soap or cream, but more severe infection may require ANTIBIOTICS. Don't ignore spots that are much more red or painful than the rest of the rash: infection can spread rapidly.

As a viral infection chickenpox is, however, essentially untreatable.

■ OUTLOOK There are few long-term problems, but a child who has had chickenpox may develop shingles many years later. The virus lies dormant in the nerves of the spine. The shingles rash contains the virus, and this can cause chickenpox in someone who has not had the disease. However, a child with chickenpox will not pass on shingles to an adult; but he may, of course, pass on chickenpox to anyone who has not developed immunity by having the disease.

CHILD ABUSE

The main forms of child abuse are non-accidental injury, neglect and emotional abuse, but see also *SEXUAL ABUSE*.

■ INCIDENCE Accurate information is impossible to obtain because there is no single standard of parental care. However, a typical (U.K.) statistic is one child per 300 or 400 at risk of abuse at any one time.

■ SIGNS include bruises, weals or burns for which no satisfactory explanation can be given. Neglect and emotional abuse result in avoidable

DEVELOPMENTAL DELAY, FAILURE TO THRIVE, apathy or BEHAVIOURAL PROBLEMS, including DEPRESSION, furtiveness or AGGRESSION.

■ ACTION If you suspect that a child is being abused, contact your local social service department. A specialist medical opinion will almost certainly be needed. If there are reasonable grounds for suspicion, and the child is thought to be in immediate danger of further serious abuse, it may be justifiable to remove the child from the family home to a safe place. This is not a step that is taken lightly, and modern social workers are trained to balance the need to protect a child with intrusion on privacy, individual liberty, and indeed the possible ill-effects of removing a child from the family home.

■ INVESTIGATIONS The child is screened for bleeding tendencies and X-rayed for evidence of former fractures. The family and other carers will be interviewed – usually by a paediatrician and a social worker. Within days, a case conference of all professionals known to the family and other relevant agencies (including the police) will be called. It may be that further information will dispel suspicion.

■ TREATMENT The aim is a long-term plan of action for protecting the child. This typically includes everyday support for the family from an experienced social worker. Ways of reducing pressure on the child, and on the abuser, will be sought: the problem will be looked at in the light of everything that affects the family. Prosecution of the abuser will be considered. If there is no alternative, the child may be placed in care away from the family home. The aim, not always the reality, is that this should be a temporary measure. Only if continued abuse is considered inevitable or extremely likely is long-term care, away from the family, contemplated.

In most cases, child abuse is a short-term, remediable difficulty within the family.

Where tragedies have occurred, whether deaths of children or unjust accusation against parents, failure of co-operation between professional agencies has been a consistent feature. In Britain now, health authorities have multi-disciplinary child protection committees to review local practice.

▓ PREVENTION Better education in school about standards of behaviour could make a difference. Housing, employment, recreation, child care, benefits and support services – indeed anything that affects quality of life – has a bearing on this appalling problem.

▓ SELF-HELP Parents or other carers who have abused children and learned to cope, with support, can sometimes help families experiencing this kind of trouble for the first time.

▓ OUTLOOK Abuse of any type has grave long-term consequences for physical, mental and emotional development of a child. The sad fact remains that today's abused child can all too easily turn into tomorrow's child abuser.

CHILD PSYCHOTHERAPY

A psychological treatment for children with emotional problems based on the theories of psychoanalysts such as Anna Freud or Melanie Klein. It involves the child in regular sessions with a therapist, usually over a matter of months or years. PLAY THERAPY may be used to help the child in hospital deal with anxieties or fears; it may also serve to distract the child between ward routines.

CHOANAL ATRESIA

A rare congenital obstruction of one or both nostrils. If both sides are blocked, a baby cannot survive without emergency surgery.

CHOKING

Whole or partial blockage of the airway, interfering with the child's breathing. It occurs typically when a child inhales an object such as a peanut or button; rarely a baby may choke if left unattended with a propped up bottle.

▓ IMMEDIATE ACTION If possible, ask someone to call a doctor or an ambulance. Then remove anything tight from around the child's neck. Resuscitation is not to be undertaken lightly: however, if your child is at risk of dying from airway obstruction, then there is no alternative but to start EMERGENCY RESUSCITATION. If the chest fails to rise, take the steps below:

In babies and children under two years: Hold the child upside down or over your knee, tummy down, head lower than feet. Bang four times on his back between the shoulder-blades with the flat of your hand. This should dislodge the object. Turn the child over and give four squeezes to the chest as in cardiac massage (EMERGENCY RESUSCITATION, step C). Repeat if not successful first time.

In children above two years: If blows to the back (as for younger

CHOKING

Action for children under two years.

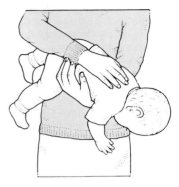

Action for babies.

Then wrap both your arms tightly round the child just below the rib cage. Pull sharply and quickly inwards. This is meant to force the object upwards and out of the airway. Repeat if not at first successful.

If the object is obviously within reach at the back of the mouth, hook it out with your finger(s).

If all these fail, start artificial ventilation (EMERGENCY RESUSCITATION, steps A and B) in the hope of forcing air past the obstruction.

If the child is unconscious: Turn him on his back and immediately start artificial ventilation (EMERGENCY RESUSCITATION, step B). If this is unsuccessful, try to dislodge the obstruction as described above. Check whether the obstruction has been moved by looking in the mouth. If the choking continues, repeat artificial ventilation and once more check whether the obstruction has been dislodged. Again, make sure that a doctor or ambulance has been summoned. Keep repeating until the obstruction is dislodged, and the child is breathing. Put him in the RECOVERY POSITION and arrange transport to hospital.

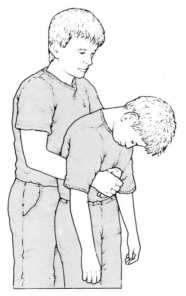

The Heimlich manoeuvre, for children over two years.

children, above) fail to work, try the Heimlich manoeuvre. (This is a potentially dangerous thing to do; but if there is no alternative, you will have to proceed.) Firstly make sure, if at all possible, that someone has called for a doctor or an ambulance.

CHOLERA

An acute, sometimes lethal infection, associated with severe DIARRHOEA and VOMITING. It develops after a short incubation period and is caused by a BACTERIUM, *Vibrio Cholera*, transmitted in contaminated food and water. The disease occurs typically in epidemics after a breakdown of sanitation. It is essentially a problem of developing countries and IMMUNIZATION, which lasts up to six months, is recommended before a visit to a cholera risk area.

▨ SYMPTOMS Profuse, painless watery diarrhoea and vomiting. There may be muscle cramps. DEHYDRATION develops rapidly.

▨ INVESTIGATIONS Culture of the BOWEL MOTIONS for the bacteria.

▨ TREATMENT Fluids, either by mouth or by intravenous drip. Antibiotics may be necessary.

CHOREA

Sudden, jerky, non-repetitive involuntary movements. These may be associated with athetoid CEREBRAL PALSY or may occur after streptococcal throat infection (Sydenham's chorea – now rare in the U.K.). Chorea due to Huntington's disease is a disease of adulthood. The childhood concern with Huntington's chorea relates to matters of genetics and counselling.

CHROMOSOMES

Parts of a cell which contain the GENES. They transmit the inherited characteristics from parent to child. Each gene has a particular place on a chromosome. Every nucleated cell in the body contains 23 matching pairs of chromosomes. An ovum and a sperm each have one of every pair, so the new cell produced at fertilization contains 23 pairs. The two chromosomes from each pair are identical in size and shape, except for those in the 23rd pair. These determine sex. Females have two identical sex chromosomes – the X chromosomes – while males have one X chromosome and a smaller Y chromosome. The sex of a child depends on whether an X or a Y chromosome is inherited from the father. An X chromosome from the father together with one of the X chromosomes from the mother will result in a female. A Y chromosome from the father together with one of the X chromosomes from the mother will result in a male.

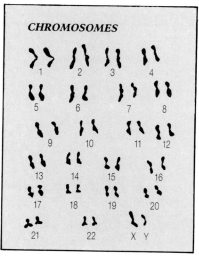

CHROMOSOMES

A set of human chromosomes, with the matching pairs numbered; number 23, the one that determines sex, is here shown as an X with a Y: the genetic code for a boy.

CHRONIC HEPATITIS

Inflammation of the liver continuing without improvement for longer than six months. It is uncommon. The problem is caused by an abnormal IMMUNE response in the liver. See also *HEPATITIS*.

CHRONIC ILLNESS, CHILD WITH

The principles of care of children with chronic medical conditions and those with mental or physical handicaps are similar in many respects. Whether your child has, for example, ASTHMA or DIABETES, a physical or mental handicap, certain restrictions on activity may make him different from others. Parents, too, have their own problems in coping. A child with a chronic disease has specific needs, but these are in addition to, and not instead of, those of other children. He requires a loving, stable, stimulating environment. Contact with other children is also important.

ADJUSTMENT IN THE FAMILY
It takes time to accept that a child has a problem. Discuss your worries with your doctor. Your whole family is involved. An ill child takes up time that would otherwise be shared with the rest of the family. If your partner and the other children take part in the decision-making and the day-to-day activities of your ill or handicapped child, they are likely to feel more involved and understanding. Frank discussion with your other children will help them to accept the situation better. Marital discord and child abuse tend to be more common in families where there is a handicapped child.

GENERAL ADVICE
– Make sure that any specialists or educationalists who see your child write to your G.P. He or she is often the person you see in an emergency, and can only advise if fully informed.
– Don't be ashamed to ask for help if you need it. Stress can affect your judgement and ability to handle difficult situations.
– Look carefully at all educational possibilities and obtain the best advice about school placements.
– Get an accurate idea of what your child's potential is and don't expect too much or too little.
– Don't over-protect your child.

PRE-SCHOOL
Your child will be largely in your care. Support from friends is invaluable and local self-help groups can offer practical advice. Such support is important: if you are having difficulty coping, the family will suffer. It is especially important to help the child build his self-confidence by praising his achievements.

SCHOOL
Once your child is approaching school age, you should seek advice regarding the future. Your G.P. or community child specialist will usually co-ordinate special services, and facilities for the child with particular needs. A paediatrician or educational psychologist may be asked to help define the capabilities of your child and help you to make decisions on the aims of his education.

If your child is at a normal school, inform teachers and the school doctor about his illness or disability. They should know what treatment he is receiving, what symptoms to look out for, and what to do in an emergency; if there are any restrictions on his physical activity; and what learning problems he may have. If your child is not doing well (or is unlikely to do well) at the local school, discuss the problem with all the health and educational professionals involved, before deciding to send him to a special school.

Special schools have advantages and disadvantages. They have better facilities for specific handicaps, such as ramps for wheel chairs and special educational equipment; also fewer children per teacher so that each child receives more individual attention. In a special school, a child with learning problems will not be struggling to do well against more able children, and he is less likely to feel different. The disadvantages of special schools are that the child is in a protected environment and may later find it difficult to adjust to the real world; the degree of competition and incentive will depend very much on the individual teaching staff; and your child may have to live away from home.

▓ ADOLESCENCE presents specific problems. The striving for independence can result in the rejection of authority, and long-term treatment is less likely to be adhered to regularly (as in DIABETES and ASTHMA). A young person with a severe handicap will have to rely on others for help with washing and dressing. The lack of independence and privacy may make him very resentful. He may also have problems meeting other young people and may experience problems with SEXUALITY. Sex education is essential and specific sexual problems should be discussed with a doctor.

CIRCUMCISION
The surgical removal of the foreskin, which covers the glans of the penis. The new-born baby's foreskin is attached to the glans and cannot be pulled back. It becomes progressively retractable from one year of age onwards.

Circumcision is performed worldwide for religious and cultural reasons. Occasionally, circumcision is necessary on medical grounds; for example, following recurrent BALANITIS, for PHIMOSIS and paraphimosis (when the foreskin has been forcibly pulled back

and is trapped in the retracted position. The operation is normally performed under general ANAESTHETIC.

CIRRHOSIS OF THE LIVER
Chronic (long-term) damage to the liver. It is an uncommon complication of HEPATITIS, or may be associated with other rare diseases; or the cause may be unknown.

▓ SYMPTOMS Early signs of liver disease include skin changes and JAUNDICE. The child will be unwell and poorly nourished. There may be generalized itching; also swelling – due to excess fluid – of the abdomen and limbs (OEDEMA) caused by low protein levels in the blood. The spleen may be enlarged. There may be internal bleeding. Eventually there may be liver failure, with an effect on brain function. There will be personality changes, tremor (fine shaking of the limbs), speech disorder and lethargy leading to deep COMA and death.

▓ INVESTIGATIONS Liver-function tests; ultrasound, X-ray, CAT SCAN or radio-isotope scan of the liver; liver biopsy.

▓ TREATMENT In early cirrhosis, an adjusted protein diet and fat-soluble VITAMINS will be necessary. Control of oesophageal bleeding, BLOOD TRANSFUSION and correction of clotting disorders may be required. Surgery may be needed to control bleeding.

▓ OUTLOOK There is no cure once cirrhosis is fully developed, but a liver transplant may be possible.

CLEFT PALATE
An abnormality of development in

which the two sides of the roof of the mouth fail to join together, either totally or partially. It is often accompanied by a cleft of the upper lip.

■ INCIDENCE Cleft palate, cleft lip, or both together, occur about once in 700 births.

■ CAUSES Unknown, but once it has occurred in a family, there is a slight risk of recurrence.

■ TREATMENT Feeding: is usually possible in the normal fashion by breast or bottle. Extra care and some expert advice may be needed. However, with the most extensive bilateral clefts, feeding by cup and spoon may be necessary.
Surgery: one operation to correct the cleft lip, another to repair the cleft palate. Usually a series of planned operations is required to improve the function and appearance of palate and lips. Opinion varies as to the best timing of the operations. Frequently correction is performed at about three months, while repair of the palate is initiated between three and six months.

■ LONG-TERM MANAGEMENT Cleft lip alone seldom leads to problems with speech, and the cosmetic result from modern surgery is excellent. Cleft palate can result in 'nasal' speech, which may be improved by further surgery, and by speech therapy.

■ OUTLOOK With a cleft palate there is an increased risk of MIDDLE EAR INFECTIONS and DEAFNESS. Regular hearing tests are advised. Teeth may not grow straight; so planned orthodontic care is necessary. However, children with a cleft lip or palate can expect to lead full and normal lives.

CLUB FOOT

The commonest CONGENITAL ABNORMALITY of the foot. One or both feet may be affected. The cause is not fully understood: an imbalance of the muscles of the foot may be implicated, with the muscles of the inner side of the foot pulling it inwards.

■ SYMPTOMS All new-born babies are examined routinely for evidence of club foot. Most have feet that turn in, but this can usually be corrected by gently moving the foot into the normal position.
In babies with a true club foot, this turned-in position is quite marked and the foot cannot be straightened. The range of movement of the ankle joint is restricted and calf muscles under-developed.

■ TREATMENT should be started soon after birth. The foot is manipulated into the correct position and then fixed by a plaster cast, a splint or adhesive strapping.
If the foot is not back to normal, both on examination and on X-ray, after about three months, an operation is recommended. The tight ligaments and tendons on the inside of the foot are lengthened. After the operation, a plaster cast is worn for a few months to allow healing in the correct position.
Children who have not had early treatment usually need surgery. The same applies when the problem recurs after early treatment.

■ OUTLOOK depends on the age at which treatment is started, and its effectiveness. Early treatment is usually successful; but even with prompt treatment, some children can have a relapse when treatment is discontinued. This is most likely in children who have especially under-developed calf muscles.

CLUMSINESS

The term covers a range of severity, from the normal child lacking in dexterity, to the child who has a clear specific MOTOR DEVELOPMENT difficulty. Clumsiness may affect balance, co-ordination, hand function or speech. Overall, about 2 per cent of children might be termed 'clumsy', in association with which can be found the whole range of intelligence. In its more severe forms, however, it is commonly associated with learning difficulties and other problems.

■ MANAGEMENT Accept the problem, and find activities in which the child can experience success, particularly those which can be shared with you, or hobbies which can be shared with other children. Occasionally, speech therapy, physiotherapy or occupational therapy may be useful, as well as special help with handwriting.

■ OUTLOOK The majority of clumsy children grow into normal adults, who perhaps lack co-ordination skills in such matters as handwriting, ball games and dancing.

COARCTATION OF THE AORTA

A narrowing of the artery which carries blood from the heart (aorta). It is a CONGENITAL HEART-DISEASE and if severe will cause HEART FAILURE in infancy. If it is not severe, it may be noticed because the pulses in the legs are weak, a HEART MURMUR is heard, or HYPERTENSION is discovered. Tests will be necessary to show the severity of the narrowing. Surgery is usually necessary.

COELIAC DISEASE

A chronic illness caused by intolerance of wheat and rye protein (GLUTEN). It is characterized by MALABSORPTION; abnormal small bowel lining; and improvement when wheat and rye cereals are excluded from the diet.

Coeliac disease may be detected at any age in childhood, or in adult life.

■ FEATURES Poor APPETITE and FAILURE TO THRIVE in infancy soon after the introduction of cereals in the diet, usually at three to four months. Abnormal BOWEL MOTIONS (pale, large, and difficult to flush down the lavatory), ABDOMINAL SWELLING, thin muscles (usually buttocks and thighs) and floppiness may be noticed. The child is usually miserable. RICKETS or thickening of fingernail beds (clubbing) may be associated, but these are rare.

A coeliac crisis is unusual, but consists of ANOREXIA, VOMITING, DIARRHOEA and generally feeling unwell with accompanying, acute abdominal swelling.

Some patients are diagnosed in adult life, with ANAEMIA, recurrent diarrhoea, unsteadiness and even infertility.

Unusual associations are a blistering skin rash or *diabetes mellitus*.

Prolonged GASTROENTERITIS, diarrhoea, bowel INFECTIONS, SUGAR INTOLERANCE, COW'S MILK ALLERGY, CYSTIC FIBROSIS and toddler diarrhoea can all suggest the condition.

■ TESTS Confirmation of anaemia; oral sugar (xylose) absorption test; BLOOD TEST for raised gliadin (gluten ANTIBODIES); X-ray of hand to show delayed bone age due to inadequate NUTRITION.

A jejunal biopsy is necessary before and after treatment: this is safe and involves passing a fine tube via the stomach into the small bowel (the jejunum), under sedation. A cutting device painlessly collects a tiny piece of tissue, which is examined under a microscope. In coeliac disease, the fine projections of the normal lining of the bowel are flattened by inflammation. When the biopsy is repeated after treatment, the lining should have returned to normal.

■ TREATMENT All foods containing flour or cereal from wheat or rye grain should be removed from the diet. A dietician will advise. Gluten-free food, most of which is available on prescription, has special symbols on the packaging. Eliminating gluten results in a bland but manageable diet, which should be continued indefinitely.

● Corticosteroid drugs may be necessary in a coeliac crisis.

■ OUTLOOK This is usually a permanent problem. However, a repeat biopsy after reintroducing gluten into the diet may confirm in later childhood that the initial illness was due to a temporary intolerance.

A child with true coeliac disease on the appropriate diet will feel well and gain weight satisfactorily, although it may take some time to catch up on lost growth.

COLD SORES

Caused by the herpes VIRUS, which lies dormant in the body after initial INFECTION, which may or may not cause symptoms. The sores tend to occur in older children and adults, and can be activated by an infectious illness, overexposure to sunlight or emotional upsets; but often no cause is found.

■ SYMPTOMS Initial infection can cause mouth and lip ulcers which are extremely painful and associated with a high FEVER. The lymph glands in the neck may be swollen and the illness can last for a week or so. There may be loss of APPETITE.

Recurrent cold sores develop on the lips and around the nose and mouth when the dormant virus is reactivated. They begin as a tiny but painful crop of blisters. There is usually no fever, but the pain may be severe enough to make the child miserable. It lasts a few days and the sore then dries to a scab.

■ ACTION 1 Initial infection: painkillers such as paracetamol can be used against the fever and pain, particularly if a baby is not feeding well. A dose given about half an hour before a feed may be useful. Occasionally, the pain and fever are so severe as to prevent feeding and cause DEHYDRATION, so keep a note of how much your baby is taking and if you are in any doubt, get medical advice. 2 Recurrent cold sores: Analgesics may be necessary if the pain is severe. Avoid excessive exposure to sunlight if this seems to be a cause. Prevent secondary BACTERIAL infection by discouraging scratching of the sore. Cold sores are infectious and can be spread by kissing. They are especially tiresome in children who already have ECZEMA.

■ TREATMENT Viral infections are generally difficult to treat because the virus is within the body's cells. However, there are several antiviral drugs, such as acyclovir, that can be given for herpes infections as a tablet or as a suspension, or for local application on the skin. If used early, they can clear the sore up quickly. They do not, however, prevent recurrences of cold sores.

■ COMPLICATIONS are rare, but herpes infection of the eye can be serious if not recognized and treated. In children with reduced IMMUNITY, such as those on high doses of steroids or those with LEUKAEMIA, the herpes virus may spread through the body and cause severe illness.

▨ OUTLOOK Herpes mouth ulcers do not usually recur. Cold sores tend to become less frequent with time.

COLIC
Spasms of ABDOMINAL PAIN. They can occur in babies or in older children in relation to bowel obstructions such as INTUSSUSCEPTION.

Many babies have bouts of crying associated with colic during their first three months ('three-month colic'). There are episodes of abdominal pain, persistent crying, and occasional mild ABDOMINAL SWELLING from gas which may be secondary to air swallowing. Alleged causes are excessive wind, a poor winding technique, or over- or underfeeding. There may be an unsatisfactory relationship between the baby and the mother, but this can be secondary to the disturbance due to the colic. COW'S MILK, and possibly soya milk protein ALLERGY, may be associated. Colic can occur in breast-fed babies, some of whom improve when their mothers stop taking cow's milk.

▨ SYMPTOMS Bouts of crying are most common at night. The baby stops crying briefly when offered a feed, but then starts to cry again during the feed. The legs are often drawn up over the abdomen.

▨ INVESTIGATIONS Diagnosis is usually made from the history and, where possible, observation of the child. INFECTION needs to be excluded by the doctor.

▨ TREATMENT Antispasmodic

drugs may help. Soya milk may be tried if cow's milk allergy is suspected. Severe cases may need to be admitted to hospital for a few days for advice on feeding and handling. Most infants, however, lose their colic by three months and don't need such specific therapy. Colic in the older child may indicate an INTESTINAL OBSTRUCTION which will need investigation and treatment.

COLOUR BLINDNESS
Inability to distinguish between certain colours, typically red and green. It usually causes few problems.

It is much more common in boys than in girls: about 5 per cent of males have some degree of colour blindness. Some children may have difficulties at school if things are colour coded. If parents and teachers are aware of the problem, appropriate allowances can be made.

COMA
A state of UNCONSCIOUSNESS that may last for hours, days, or longer. It is not a disease as such, but a manifestation of disease in which brain function is deranged.

Degrees of coma range from light unconsciousness with reactive pupils, restlessness and response to being touched, to deep unconsciousness with fixed dilated pupils, no response to stimuli and the need for artificial ventilation.

The outcome really depends on the underlying cause of the coma. In general, however, the lighter the degree of coma and the shorter it lasts, the better the outcome. Full recovery from deep coma can occur, for example after barbiturate poisoning. Slow and progressive recovery from deep coma of other origins can continue over weeks or months.

■ CAUSES include HEAD INJURY, EN-CEPHALITIS, very low or persistently high blood sugar in DIABETES, drug poisoning, post-convulsive states, and brain swelling in a wide range of medical conditions, most notably liver failure.

■ OUTLOOK If coma proves irreversible, it is taken to represent very severe brain damage. A point may then arise when a difficult decision has to be made on whether or not to continue life support treatment. The doctors will be looking for an agreed set of physical signs that indicate with a fair degree of certainty that the brain is damaged beyond any chance of recovery, so-called 'brain death'. The signs include no spontaneous breathing, no response to stimulation and no pupil reaction to light or eye movements when the ears are syringed with ice-cold water. The tests are usually repeated after 12 to 24 hours; it is usual to involve at least two experienced doctors. Occasionally an EEG RECORDING (ELECTROENCEPHALOGRAM) may be performed to confirm the absence of electrical activity of the brain. At this stage, it may be appropriate to discuss the prospects of the child being a donor of an organ for TRANSPLANTATION surgery. In that case, life support will continue until the transplant has been carried out.

COMFORT HABITS

Automatic repetitive actions such as rocking, THUMB SUCKING and HEAD BANGING, which appear to be reassuring because of their familiarity. They may be irritating to the parents, but are not directly harmful to the child. Punishment is both ineffective and inappropriate; distracting the child's attention or encouraging alternative actions may help. The habits frequently reflect anxieties and worries which the child may be too young or be otherwise unable to express.

COMMON COLD

A viral INFECTION of the nose and throat, which can be caused by many different VIRUSES. Infection is spread by droplets containing the virus sneezed or breathed out by an infected person. Overcrowding thus favours the spread of colds. Cold weather does not cause colds, but rapid changes in body temperature may make the body more susceptible to infection. Infection by one of the cold viruses does not give IMMUNITY to others. The average child has about four colds a year.

■ SYMPTOMS The INCUBATION PERIOD is two to three days. The illness begins with sneezing, a sore throat, followed by a watery discharge from the nose; in younger children particularly the nose may be blocked; there may also be FEVER and general malaise. The symptoms usually last for a week. Secondary BACTERIAL infection is rare: in such cases, swelling and inflammation caused by the virus block normal anatomical pathways and allow bacteria to multiply, giving rise to such problems as SINUSITIS and OTITIS.

■ ACTION 1 An older child (say three years upwards) often has mild symptoms, and it is not usually necessary to get medical advice. Rest in bed or at home is not necessary. If the child does not feel ill and has no fever, he can go to school. 2 If a child under six has a fever and has previously suffered from a febrile convulsion, be on your guard against a repetition. 3 Colds in small babies can be distressing for the infant and the parents. A blocked nose may interfere with feeding. In extreme cases you may need to feed your baby with a spoon. However, if you are BREAST FEEDING you should certainly continue if at all possible. **4** Encourage your child to drink plenty of clear fluids: both fever and breathing through the mouth can lead to DEHYDRATION.

■ GET MEDICAL ADVICE if the child:
 - is under six and has a high fever;
 - is not feeding properly;
 - has failed to improve within a few days;
 - has other symptoms such as EARACHE, VOMITING or a persistent COUGH.

■ TREATMENT There is no specific treatment. You can give medicines that you find helpful to relieve significant symptoms. ASPIRIN should *not* be given to children under the age of 12 because of the risk of REYE'S SYNDROME.
 - Paracetamol is an analgesic that may help the sore throat and malaise, in addition to reducing fever.
 - Decongestants act by drying up the nasal secretions and reducing the swelling of the nasal passages; however they are not often very effective. Many decongestants contain antihistamines, which may cause drowsiness. They should not be given to children under one year.
 - Decongestant nose drops act in the same way as those taken by mouth. However, they can irritate the nasal membranes, causing further congestion; don't use them for more than a week at a time.
 - When buying cold remedies, choose single-ingredient medicines rather than those with an analgesic and decongestant combined, which reduce control over dose.
 - ANTIBIOTICS are not indicated for

the common cold, except (arguably) for certain patients with heart-disease or lowered immunity to infection, since they have no effect on viruses.

■ ALTERNATIVE TREATMENT There is a view that VITAMIN C reduces the severity and frequency of colds. Medical trials do not support this theory. It is inadvisable to give large doses of vitamin C to babies.

■ LONG-TERM MANAGEMENT Colds usually get better without treatment. Secondary bacterial infection usually responds to an antibiotic. A child who has cold symptoms lasting for months probably has a nasal ALLERGY.

■ OUTLOOK The illness rarely causes serious complications.

CONCUSSION
A state of altered awareness following HEAD INJURY. The child is disoriented, confused, drowsy and may be sick. It is usually brief, with full recovery.

In younger children, if you judge that the blow to the head was other than trivial, or that the concussion lasts longer or is more severe than you think reasonable, get medical advice.

If the doctor is in doubt, he or she may advise an X-ray of the skull (to look for a skull fracture), and perhaps overnight observation in hospital to ensure complete recovery.

CONGENITAL ABNORMALITIES
Any abnormality present at birth. Approximately one baby in a hundred is born with a significant congenital abnormality.

During the nine months of pregnancy, vast changes take place, from the fertilized egg to the embryo, to the foetus to the new-born baby. Any deviation from the normal process of development can result in a congenital abnormality.

Congenital abnormalities may arise as a result of inherited factors or environmental factors, or the interplay of the two. In most instances, no simple or single cause or explanation for the occurrence of congenital abnormality can be found. The frequency of such abnormalities may also be affected by the age of the mother: for example, a mother over the age of 35 is more likely to have a child with DOWN'S SYNDROME.

Most organs are formed in the first 12 weeks after conception, so any noxious influence acting during this time may result in a congenital abnormality. Such environmental factors include:
– certain specific infections such as RUBELLA;
– disorders of the mother's biochemistry, particularly around the time of conception, as may occur, for example, in poorly controlled *Diabetes mellitus* and phenylketonuria;
– rarely drugs or medicines taken by the mother (note that any drug known to affect the developing baby will be either banned completely or carry a clear warning not to be taken in pregnancy). See *DRUGS IN PREGNANCY*.
– Alcohol has been shown to cause congenital abnormalities (FOETAL ALCOHOL SYNDROME). The precise quantity that will have an effect is unknown, but it is likely to be a combination of the frequency and amount taken during pregnancy.
– X-rays of the mother's abdomen or directly of the developing embryo may slightly but significantly enhance the chances of the child developing cancer in later life. Thus while the result is not a visible malformation, it is a congenitally abnormal predisposition. This justifies the general advice to avoid exposure to X-rays throughout pregnancy.

Damage can be done in the first few weeks of pregnancy, even before you can be sure that you are pregnant. You should avoid all risks such as alcohol, smoking, drugs and exposure to X-rays if there is any possibility of your being pregnant.

If there is a history of inherited disease or congenital abnormality in your family, it is advisable to seek GENETIC COUNSELLING before you become pregnant.

Some congenital abnormalities can be diagnosed during pregnancy (ANTENATAL DIAGNOSIS).

The management of a baby born with a congenital abnormality will, of course, depend on its type and severity. In some cases no treatment is needed, or a simple operation can correct the problem: as, for example, with an extra little finger. If the condition is more severe, it may be necessary to embark upon a long-term plan of stage-by-stage reconstructive surgery, as in a severe cleft lip and palate (see *CHRONIC ILLNESS, CHILD WITH*).

CONGENITAL DISLOCATION OF THE HIP

The hip is a ball and socket joint, the socket formed by the pelvis, the ball by the top end of the thigh bone (the femur). If the socket is not properly formed, the femur tends to slip out – in other words to dislocate. The problem is often inherited. Girls are more commonly affected than boys, and if one girl in a family suffers from the abnormality, there is a high risk that her sisters will too.

▓ SYMPTOMS All babies are checked at birth for the abnormality. In many there is a slight click as the hip is moved, but if the hip

CONGENITAL DISLOCATION OF THE HIP

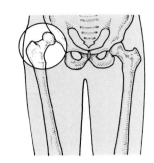

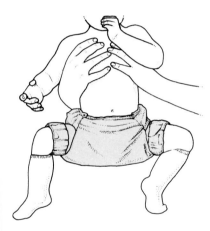

otherwise moves normally, it is unlikely to be dislocated.

If a child has a dislocation which was not discovered after birth, this will show up when he begins to walk. He will probably walk late and may have a LIMP or an unsteady, waddling walk.

■ ACTION If there is a family history, tell your doctor so that particular care can be taken with the examination at birth.

Examination becomes increasingly difficult as the baby grows bigger and stronger, but he should be examined for the problem again at six weeks and at six months, so it is important not to miss these routine checks.

If there is a click in the hip, your doctor may suggest that the baby wears a double terry-towelling nappy. This holds the legs further apart than usual, keeping the bone in the socket.

■ TESTS If examination suggests that there is dislocation, an X-ray of the hip is usually done to confirm suspicions. An ULTRASOUND SCAN of the hip joint may in the future be used for early detection.

■ TREATMENT If there is definite evidence of a dislocated hip, the child may have to put up with a splint. How long this lasts tends to be governed by natural growth of the hip joint. Eventually, the joint tends to develop of its own accord so that it functions properly.

If dislocation is not discovered until the child is walking, traction is necessary to set the ball back into the socket, followed by a plaster cast to stop it coming out again. Sometimes an operation is the only option.

■ OUTLOOK If diagnosed before the child starts to walk, the problem is usually easy to manage. If made late, ARTHRITIS may develop prematurely in the hip.

CONGENITAL HEART BLOCK
See *ARRHYTHMIAS*.

CONGENITAL HEART-DISEASE
Heart-disease with which a child is born. The heart is formed in the first 12 weeks of embryonic development. Any abnormality in this process can result in a heart that is not perfect in its structure.

(Read this entry in conjunction with the general entry, HEART-DISEASE; also see the diagram of the heart and lungs under ANATOMY. Much of the information that follows cannot be understood without a visual aid.)

■ CAUSES Usually no cause can be identified. Certain babies have a higher than average chance of having a congenital heart defect. These include: the infant of a mother with DIABETES (though the risk is higher than normal, it is still less than one case in 20); infants with the CONGENITAL *RUBELLA* SYNDROME and with DOWN'S SYNDROME. Up to half of these will have a heart defect.

If you have had one child with congenital heart-disease, the chance of having another child so affected is about one in 50. If more than one child in a family has congenital heart-disease, it is advisable to seek GENETIC COUNSELLING to determine the risks to future children.

■ TYPES OF CONGENITAL HEART-DISEASE *Holes in the heart* The common types are: ventricular septal defect, in which the hole is between the two ventricles; atrial septal defect, where the defect is between the two atria; patent ductus arteriosus, where the vessel which communicates between the aorta and pulmonary artery (which is open before birth) fails to close after birth.

Any communication between the right and left sides of the heart will result in blood passing from the high-pressure left side to the low-pressure right. If the hole is small, the amount of blood passing across will cause no problem, although a HEART MURMUR will almost always be present.

But if the hole is large, excess

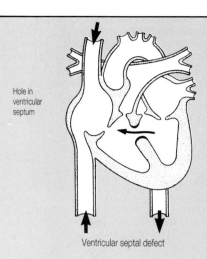

Hole in
ventricular
septum

Ventricular septal defect

CONGENITAL HEART-DISEASE

Types of congenital heart-disease: The three most common holes in the heart and (bottom) two most basic valve abnormalities.

Valve opening
is normal

Valve opening is
inadequate – stenosis

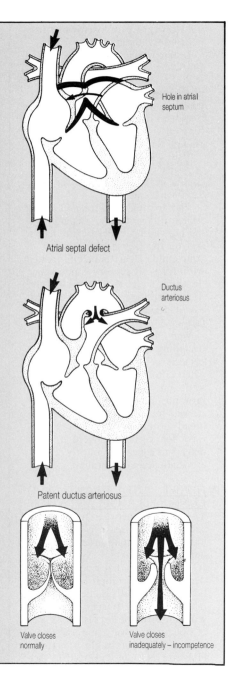

Hole in atrial septum

Atrial septal defect

Ductus arteriosus

Patent ductus arteriosus

Valve closes normally

Valve closes inadequately – incompetence

blood passes from the right side of the heart to the lungs, resulting in increased flow and pressure of blood on the vessels of the lungs. In time this causes damage which in turn puts back pressure on the heart.

Valve abnormalities There are two basic varieties: narrowed or stenotic valves (most commonly, affecting the pulmonary and aortic valves), and leaking or incompetent valves (in this case any of the four valves in the heart may be affected – mitral, tricuspid, pulmonary or aortic).

If the valve abnormality is slight, there will be little effect on the heart, although a murmur may be heard. If the valve is severely affected, whether stenotic or incompetent, the heart has to pump harder to sustain the circulation. The extra work leads to enlargement of the heart and eventually to HEART FAILURE.

Coarctation of the aorta This is a special variant of stenosis in which the main great artery that leaves the left ventricle, the aorta, is itself narrowed beyond the site of the aortic valve. Clinical features include a heart murmur, absence or weakness of pulses to the lower half of the body coupled with high blood pressure in the upper half of the body. If severe, coarcation can lead to heart failure and needs surgical treatment.

Combinations of abnormalities, such as a hole and an abnormal valve, can occur. The effect is variable depending on the particular combination and severity. In some cases, de-oxygenized blood passes directly from the right to the left side of the heart, and is pumped into the general circulation of the body without first going through the lungs to take up oxygen. This can result in the child appearing blue or cyanosed. Among the most common causes of this variety of cyanotic congenital heart-disease are Fallot's tetralogy and transposition of the great arteries.

■ SYMPTOMS depend on the type and severity of the abnormality. Symptoms are not always present at birth, and if the abnormality is mild, symptoms may never develop and the only evidence of the defect may be a heart murmur (and in many instances the defect and murmur will disappear with age, especially in the case of small ventricular septal defects).

■ ACTION If you suspect any of the symptoms above, get medical advice.

■ TESTS See *HEART-DISEASE.*

■ TREATMENT *Hole in the heart* If it is small, no treatment may be necessary, although your child will usually be seen by a paediatrician or cardiologist every few years to ensure that there is no heart strain and to determine whether the hole is closing. If your child has a patent ductus arteriosus, he may need surgery, sometimes even in the newborn period (especially if very small or premature).

If a hole is large, medical treatment for heart failure may be needed. Large holes seldom close on their own, and surgery is often necessary. A patch is usually sewn over the hole. The operation may be done during infancy, particularly if the child has symptoms of heart failure or signs that the pressure in the blood vessels of the lungs is high.

Valve abnormality Narrowing of the valve can be treated by stretching the valve with a flexible tube passed via a vein into the heart (cardiac catheterization); or by opening the valve surgically. This is only necessary if the narrowing is severe;

milder degrees of narrowing may need no treatment.

Leaking valves can only be treated surgically. Repair, or replacement with an artificial valve, is a complicated procedure, only undertaken if the leak is severe. Drug treatment can help to improve heart function if the leak is not severe enough for surgery.

Your child will need to see a cardiologist at intervals so that any change in the condition of the valve can be assessed.

The treatment of *combined and complex abnormalities* depends on the type and severity of the defect, and on the health and progress of your child. Heart failure is treated with drugs. If surgery is necessary, the age at which the operation – and it may require a series of operations – will depend on many individual factors.

Many heart defects carry a risk of becoming infected: for example, if bacteria is released into the blood when a tooth is extracted, it may settle on the damaged valve and grow into a bacterial colony. For this reason most cardiologists recommend prophylactic antibiotic therapy for certain congenital heart defects to cover certain procedures, especially dental treatment.

■ HEART AND HEART AND LUNG TRANSPLANTATION There was a time when treatment of severe kidney disease in children by kidney transplantation seemed cavalier and experimental. Not so today. It seems likely that over the next decade serious complex congenital heart-disease may also be treated by transplantation. If successful, this will transform the anguish of a series of operations over years and years into a 'curative' single operation. However, society will need to face the ethical aspects of this development and the question of heart donation may be more difficult than that of kidney donation.

▓ LONG-TERM MANAGEMENT and OUTLOOK See *HEART-DISEASE.*

CONGENITAL INFECTION
See *RUBELLA, TOXOPLASMO-SIS, CYTOMEGALOVIRUS.*

CONGENITAL *RUBELLA* SYNDROME
See *RUBELLA.*

CONJUNCTIVITIS
An inflammation of the conjunctiva, thin coverings of the inside of the eyelid and over the front of the eyeball.

▓ CAUSES Usually an INFECTION either by BACTERIA or VIRUSES, but it can also result from irritation of the eye by a foreign body, chemicals, trauma or an ALLERGY.

▓ SYMPTOMS The eye is red and watery, and feels sore and itchy. There may be a discharge. Sometimes the eyelids are stuck together with yellow pus. The eyelids may look puffy.

▓ TREATMENT Bathe the eye frequently with water to remove the pus and keep the eye clean. Search for any irritant particle. If found, it should be removed carefully – see *EYE, FOREIGN BODY IN.* In mild cases this may be the cure. If the symptoms continue, or the eye is swollen, get medical advice. If your doctor thinks the conjunctivitis is due to a bacterial infection, ANTI-BIOTIC eye drops or ointment may be prescribed. The most commonly used is chloramphenicol. Putting

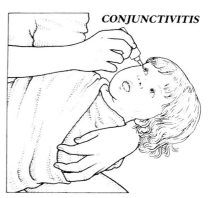

CONJUNCTIVITIS

Wrapping child tightly in towel helps keep him still when applying eye ointment or drops.

drops or ointment into a child's eye can be difficult – see the illustration. There is no specific treatment for a viral infection of the eye.

The redness and itching may be caused by an allergy. This is likely to be a recurrent problem; in which case the allergen may be recognizable and should be avoided.

▓ OUTLOOK A seven-day course of antibiotics usually clears a bacterial infection. Viral conjunctivitis usually clears spontaneously in several days.

CONSTIPATION
True constipation is defined as infrequent opening of the bowels leading to pain on opening the bowels, distress or SOILING. Control of bowel opening is achieved by 50 per cent of children before two years, and in most by three.

Bowel movements may be influenced by a number of factors. Inadequate fibre in the diet may be associated with hard BOWEL MOTIONS. A previous ANAL FISSURE may have resulted in pain on passing stools and subsequent constipation. Uncommonly, a simple external congenital narrowing (anal stenosis) may prevent the passage of stools.

The constipated child may suffer rectal bleeding and pass exceptionally large stools. Severe degrees of constipation may indicate HIRSCHPRUNG'S DISEASE. Inappropriate TOILET TRAINING (undertaken too early or with undue emphasis) and negative behaviour can be factors in a pattern in which constipation also plays a part. A further factor may be unpleasant school lavatories.

▒ SYMPTOMS Withholding of stools and continuous distension of the rectum leading to a reduction in the normal urge to open the bowels: stools may be retained for several days. Liquid faeces may escape past the hard motions to stain the underclothes and there may be ABDOMINAL SWELLING.

▒ ACTION If a child has hard, infrequent stools and difficulty opening the bowels, get medical advice without delay.

If the child has long-standing constipation, referral to a paediatrician will be necessary.

▒ INVESTIGATIONS General examination may show poor growth and abdominal swelling, with hard stools palpable in the bowel. Often, however, these signs are not so obvious. The anus may be either abnormal or satisfactory, but examination of the rectum by the doctor may identify firm motions or, very occasionally, a tightness suggesting HIRSCHPRUNG'S DISEASE.

Abdominal X-ray will determine the extent of the constipation. A barium ENEMA may show a distended bowel above a narrowed segment in Hirschprung's disease.

▒ TREATMENT Helping the parents, and child, understand the process of digestion and bowel action can give results. Laxative agents to soften and clear the hard stools may be necessary, although often added dietary fibre is enough. A drug that helps the intestine to pass the motion by stimulating bowel movement (peristalsis) may be offered.

A regular pattern of toilet training, particularly after meals, is important. Rewarding success by means of a star chart can be positive – and amusing.

A child with marked problems may require an ENEMA given at home by the local nurse, or in hospital, in association with bowel training. An anal fissure will need regular anaesthetic creams to stop the pain and allow the bowels to open.

Laxative agents may have to be continued for some weeks, and the distended bowel will need to settle before adequate bowel movements occur. Even after stopping laxatives, they may need to be used intermittently for some time until regular bowel movements are established. Surgery is necessary for anal stenosis and Hirschprung's disease.

A psychiatrist's opinion or family therapy may be considered when the child is using constipation and soiling to upset the family.

▒ OUTLOOK depends on the cause. Surgical problems are usually easy to correct. Dietary changes, laxatives and toilet training will help many children. When constipation is part of a BEHAVIOURAL problem, improvement may take a long time.

CONVULSIONS

Also described as fits, seizures or EPILEPTIC attacks, these are states of altered consciousness or behaviour associated with involuntary stiffening/ jerking (tonic/clonic) movements. They can affect the whole body (generalized) or only part of the body (partial) and are caused by transient, disorderly electrical activity in the brain. They are relatively common: one child in 20 suffers at least one fit during childhood.

The essence of a convulsion is involuntary movement; but not all epileptic attacks are convulsive.

▓ SYMPTOMS Twitching or jerking with associated states of mental confusion, automatism, pins and needles, stomach pains; dizziness or visual disturbances such as flashing lights. In some children, aura or focal seizures may precede a generalized convulsion.

Convulsions need to be distinguished from FAINTING, when the heart slows or stops; also from OVER-BREATHING associated with ANXIETY; and from BREATH HOLDING; from vertigo, a spinning sensation; from NIGHT TERRORS, rigors, TANTRUMS and psychological attacks.

▓ ACTION A child having a generalized convulsion should be placed in the RECOVERY POSITION until he comes round. With a focal convulsion, he should be kept safe and quiet until it passes. Rush the child to hospital if the convulsion continues for more than ten minutes. The child should be transported in the recovery position. In any case, call a doctor once the child has recovered, unless he happens to be a known epileptic.

▓ CAUSES Between the ages of five and 15 years, convulsions can be provoked by flashing lights, looking at patterns, or light on the surface of water. They can also be started by sudden high fever in infants aged six

months to five years – FEBRILE CONVULSIONS. Night-time convulsions may also occur, with a sense of fullness or choking in the mouth. All of these cease of their own accord in later years. See also *EPILEPSY*. Convulsions can also be caused by genetic or biochemical disorders, brain malformation or BRAIN DAMAGE.

▓ TREATMENT If convulsions are recurrent, prolonged or severe, they can be treated with anti-epileptic drugs. See *EPILEPSY*.

▓ OUTLOOK Despite their disturbing aspects, convulsions are usually not harmful unless prolonged or frequent. Your national epilepsy association may have a branch in your area; give them a try – these organizations often have a valuable contribution to make in problems such as this.

CORONARY ARTERY DISEASE
Damage to heart muscle caused by blockage of the coronary arteries. Rare during childhood.

▓ CAUSES are not always clear, but there are a number of risk factors which are thought to be important.

A diet consistently high in animal fats may (probably only in those with a genetic predisposition) raise the fat level of the blood (HYPERLIPIDAEMIA). This is associated with an increased risk of coronary artery disease.

Cigarette smoking is known to be associated with damage to the coronary arteries.

OBESITY is an additional risk factor for coronary artery disease.

Coronary artery disease can be inherited. Certain types of hyperlipidaemia are passed on as a dominant

GENE, and appear in half the children of an affected parent. In these cases, coronary artery disease may appear early in adult life.

DIABETES and HYPERTENSION predispose to coronary artery disease.

▨ ACTION Prevention is better than cure. Although much remains to be learned about the precise risks and mechanisms involved, it would seem prudent to advise parents and children to avoid too much animal fat in their diet, not to smoke cigarettes, to avoid obesity and to develop a habit for regular exercise.

▨ TESTS If there is a history of coronary artery disease occurring in young adults in the family, discuss with your doctor the possibility of BLOOD TESTS to check for the presence of familial hyperlipidaemia.

▨ TREATMENT If fat levels in the blood are high, a low fat diet plus certain medications are recommended which may succeed in lowering the level of fat in the blood.

▨ OUTLOOK This is one of the most common causes of premature death in the developed world. International statistics suggest that lifestyle can influence the disease; and that little improvement in the U.K. can be reported to date.

COT DEATH

An apparently healthy infant dies suddenly at home and the most careful enquiries fail to answer the parents' anguished question 'Why did this happen to my baby?'

In most countries of the world, two in every 1,000 babies die in the first 12 months in this way, the peak incidence being around three months.

The problem of cot deaths (sudden infant death syndrome or SIDS) is sufficiently well known that many parents, particularly with their first baby, spend agonising hours watching patterns of breathing. No one could reasonably persuade them otherwise; one can only say that there is little evidence that one or other intervention would have prevented the catastrophe.

Some babies do have prolonged breathing pauses or periods when they turn a poor colour and look desperately ill. Such children are usually rushed to hospital or given mouth-to-mouth resuscitation while awaiting medical attention. Sometimes such events are explicable in terms of serious, recognizable illness; at other times they are not and then, occasionally, the term 'near-miss cot death' is used. Since we do not know the cause of these episodes, nor do we know the cause of SIDS, it is supposition that one is a near-miss version of the other. Nevertheless, some parents become so worried that they wish to have a breathing monitor attached to the baby before they can face taking him home. While this is understandable, most authorities on the subject think that monitors do not actually help prevent sudden death and may cause more false alarm signals than they are worth. However, there are occasions when a home monitor may be helpful.

There are many theories, of course, as to why babies die suddenly and unexpectedly. The very range shows that no single cause has been identified and indeed makes it likely that the condition may arise from a number of causes and factors acting in rare and unhappy constellation. Theories include: unidentified, virulent VIRAL infections; the regurgitation and inhalation of food; a massive ALLERGIC reaction to environmental allergens; overheating; miscellaneous rare errors of biochemistry; and, inevitably, the occasional question is raised relating to non-accidental injury. Balance of opinion currently favours no single explanation. Much research into the subject is currently funded by the Foundation for the Study of Infant Deaths in London, which also offers a network of lay counsellors and doctors to support families in their time of crisis.

COUGH

The mechanism by which mucus or other foreign material is expelled from the passages of the lungs.

▦ CAUSES Mucus may be produced in the nose and throat, as in COMMON COLD or HAY FEVER; or in the chest, as in ASTHMA, PNEUMONIA, CYSTIC FIBROSIS, or in TUBERCULOSIS.

▦ SYMPTOMS depend on whether the mucus is produced in the nose or in the chest. If in the nose, it drains down the throat into the airways and will be associated with a runny or blocked nose or sneezing, and is often worse at night. If produced in the chest, the cough is associated with wheezing, rapid breathing, or other sounds in the chest.

▦ ACTION A cough, in itself, can be treated by two entirely different types of medication:
– If the cough is caused by excess mucus production in the nose, it can be reduced by a decongestant, or, in the case of HAY FEVER, a specific anti-allergic preparation. It is important for the child to blow his nose regularly to minimize the amount of mucus draining away from the nose into the chest.
– If the cough is caused by excess mucus production in the chest, medication can loosen the mucus and make it easier to cough up. Drugs that do this include mucolytics, expectorants, and bronchodila-

tors. A combination of mucolytic and bronchodilator may be used.
    A dry, unproductive cough tends to be caused by thick mucus in the chest. DEHYDRATION can make the secretions thicker, so encourage your child to drink plenty of clear fluids.
– If a dry cough is being caused by irritation in the throat, it can be suppressed, but cough suppressants are rarely necessary in children, and should only be used when there is no mucus in the chest or if the cough is exhausting the child and preventing him from sleeping.

▦ GET MEDICAL ADVICE if:
– a cough is accompanied by FEVER that lasts for more than a few days.
– the cough is associated with rapid breathing or shortness of breath.
– the mucus coughed up is green, yellow or contains blood.
– there is pain in the chest on coughing. See *CHEST PAIN*.
– the cough continues for more than ten days.
– your child has recently choked on something which could have been inhaled into the chest.

▦ TREATMENT **1** Decongestants and anti-allergic medications usually contain antihistamines, and may cause drowsiness or irritability as side-effects. They should not be used for more than one week at a time. See *HAY FEVER* and *ASTHMA*. **2** Expectorants and mucolytics are supposed to 'loosen' mucus, but there is little evidence to support their use in children (or adults). **3** Bronchodilators dilate the airways, so making it easier to cough up mucus. They are used for asthma. **4** Cough suppressants such as codeine act on the cough centre in the brain and suppress the cough. They should not be given to young children, or those with asthma. 5 ANTIBIOTICS are seldom necessary as the most common causes of cough are VIRAL infection or allergy.

■ TESTS If a cough persists, or if there are signs of chest infection, lung function tests (see *ASTHMA*) or an X-ray of the chest may be necessary. It is difficult to obtain a sputum specimen in a child, but if this is possible it can be tested for BACTERIA.

■ LONG-TERM MANAGEMENT Chronic cough caused by hay fever or asthma are discussed under the separate entries.

■ OUTLOOK Most coughs get better without treatment.

COW'S MILK ALLERGY

Intolerance of cow's milk protein affects primarily the gastro-intestinal tract, but is also associated with other complications. It is not uncommon, but usually resolves by two years of age. Easily confused with LACTOSE IN-TOLERANCE.

■ SYMPTOMS There is a wide range, related to different systems in the body. Acute symptoms can be severe enough to cause SHOCK, general swelling as a result of excess fluid (angioneurotic OEDEMA), URTI-CARIA, or VOMITING and acute DIAR-RHOEA associated with DEHYDRA-TION – although these symptoms are more likely to be due to infective GASTROENTERITIS.

Babies who have early acute symptoms are likely to be atopic – having a background of ALLERGY – as may other members of their family, and will often later develop ASTHMA and ECZEMA.

Usually the effects of cow's milk

allergy are gradual and consist of MALABSORPTION, persistent diar-rhoea, COLIC, ABDOMINAL SWELL-ING, FAILURE TO THRIVE, gastro-intestinal bleeding and low protein levels in the blood. Diarrhoea is of variable severity and is due to an immune reaction in the lining (the mucosa) of the small intestine, which may be a primary effect, or may occur after gastroenteritis leading to secondary damage with cow's milk intolerance.

The diarrhoea faeces contain blood, either obvious or in microscopic form. In the primary type, a milk-induced COLITIS can develop, with frequent stools containing mucus and fresh blood. Sometimes the baby vomits blood (haematemesis), or has iron deficiency ANAEMIA. Excessive gastrointestinal protein loss can occur with subsequent oedema and MALNUTRI-TION, but this is rare. Symptoms can occur in breast-fed babies because of the presence of cow's milk protein in the mother's diet passing into her breast milk.

■ ACTION If symptoms suggest cow's milk allergy, discuss the baby's diet with your family doctor; a change of milk should be considered.

■ INVESTIGATIONS The doctor who investigates the problem will want to know about any links between symptoms and feeding changes; gastroenteritis; and any family history of allergy. The baby will need a thorough examination to exclude INFECTION and to look for allergic manifestations such as asthma or eczema.

A BLOOD TEST for milk ANTIBO-DIES, may help, but is unlikely to be conclusive.

Internal examination of the colon

is sometimes necessary and may reveal inflammation and ulceration. The main investigation, however, is a trial period with no cow's milk in the diet, giving instead alternative types of milk. Subsequent careful challenge with a small amount of cow's milk, usually under supervision in hospital, will be necessary.

▓ TREATMENT   Avoiding cow's milk in any form is, of course, the mainstay of the treatment. A hospital dietician will help devise a workable new regime, often incorporating soya milk; but it is bound to mean extra work for parents.

▓ OUTLOOK   Cautious reintroduction of cow's milk protein, starting with small amounts, and building up over a few days, can be considered, usually after the first birthday. A few children remain intolerant well after their first year. In some unlucky children, sensitivity to soya protein may also occur, in which case other milk formulae will have to be found. Babies whose families have a strong history of allergy and who are breast-fed may benefit from the mother excluding cow's milk and other dairy products from her own diet.

CRADLE CAP
A common scalp problem in early infancy, consisting of a thick scaly mat covering all or part of the head.

▓ SYMPTOMS   None – the appearance is the only problem.

▓ ACTION   Careful but firm washing of the whole head, using a baby shampoo, will prevent cradle cap forming, and can clear a mild cradle cap. When the build-up of scales is thicker, olive oil, or a cream which softens hard skin, such as 1 per cent

sulphur and 1 per cent salicylic acid in aqueous cream (obtained from a chemist) used overnight will gradually clear the scales. There is no need to be afraid of washing over the soft part of a baby's scalp.

▓ GET MEDICAL ADVICE   if the cradle cap does not clear with these simple measures. Occasionally it can be a sign of another skin disease, such as ECZEMA or PSORIASIS.

▓ TREATMENT   Apart from the simple cream to soften to scales, no treatment is necessary.

▓ OUTLOOK   Provided the baby's head is washed properly, cradle cap should not recur. It is not a sign of a developing skin disease.

CRAMP
Involuntary muscle spasm. It can be caused by exercise (particularly in the cold), if muscles are tensed to an exceptional degree, or if there is a deficiency of salt or other minerals in the blood. Often enough, there is no apparent cause. Cramp frequently occurs at night.

Gentle massage of the muscle will gradually ease the spasm, as with the manoeuvre illustrated below. Children don't usually have severe cramp, but if it persists, get medical advice.

CRETINISM
See *HYPOTHYROIDISM*.

CROHN'S DISEASE
An uncommon chronic inflammatory disease of the bowel which may affect any area of the gut, from the mouth to the anus, but most commonly concentrated in the small bowel. The cause is unknown.

▓ SYMPTOMS   depend on how much bowel is involved and how active the inflammation is. They include:

ABDOMINAL PAIN, which may be acute and similar to APPENDICITIS; or intermittent and chronic. The pain is mainly in the lower abdomen and can be worse on defecation. COLIC may occur from incipient small INTESTINAL OBSTRUCTION.

DIARRHOEA: mild and intermittent. Occasionally there is blood and mucus in the stools.

FEVER: frequent in the early (childhood) stages; sometimes associated with ARTHRITIS or joint pain.

ANOREXIA and poor APPETITE. WEIGHT LOSS can occur, and over a long time this can be associated with growth retardation.

There may also be an abdominal lump, which a doctor can detect by feeling. There may be ulcers, abscesses, fissures, or skin tags around the anus. Communicating channels (fistulae) may develop between the bowel and the skin near the anus. MOUTH ULCERS may develop. A skin rash may be present – thickened, purple-coloured swellings of the shins – and associated eye inflammation (uveitis).

■ INVESTIGATIONS BLOOD TEST; checks on VITAMIN levels and on blood viscosity; stool culture; barium meal and X-ray.

Examination of the bowel under sedation may be necessary, as may biopsy of the bowel lining and the peri-anal skin.

■ TREATMENT A high-calorie diet. Milk exclusion may help. A diet of simple, easily digested liquid food, or intravenous feeding may be required. Anti-inflammatory drugs such as sulphasalazine can help. There are some uncommon side-effects with this treatment. Steroids can be given as an ointment to the anus, by suppository, or as an ENEMA. Treatment of the anal problems will probably be essential for children persistently ill with Crohn's disease.

Immunosuppressive drugs may be needed if the response to steroids is poor.

Surgery may be necessary to deal with a peri-anal abscess or fistula, intestinal obstruction and other associated problems.

■ OUTLOOK Crohn's disease is an upsetting, chronic problem with a risk of death, but the long-term outlook for most is good these days.

CROUP
The noisy cough younger children have with an INFECTION of, or around, the larynx.

■ CAUSES are VIRUSES, such as parainfluenza viruses. Rarely, a BACTERIUM, *Haemophilus influenzae*, causes a very serious form of croup called EPIGLOTTITIS.

■ INCIDENCE Viral croup is usually a noisy manifestation of widerspread infection called LARYNGOTRACHEO-BRONCHITIS. This is common, occurring in winter months. Once a child has had an attack, he is a little more likely to have further bouts of croup. Epiglottitis, while relatively rare, is very serious and if neglected can become life threatening over a period of hours.

■ SYMPTOMS The cough sounds like the bark of a sea lion. In simple (viral) croup, there may be no other symptoms, but the child will often have a runny nose and hoarse voice or cry. Some children also have a FEVER, and seem generally unwell. The cough is often worse at night. If the croup is more severe, there will be noisy breathing, or STRIDOR.

■ ACTION For simple croup, warm drinks and paracetamol will generally comfort the child and reduce the temperature. Some children may benefit from inhaling steam. You may be able to provide this in the bathroom by running the hot taps, but the result is rarely so good as to justify the inconvenience.

■ GET MEDICAL ADVICE if your child has difficulty in breathing or swallowing, or if he becomes lethargic or distressed.

■ TREATMENT Although viral infections are not affected by ANTIBIOTICS, these may be prescribed as a precaution against further infection, or if there is doubt over the possibility of early epiglottitis.

Children with severe laryngo-tracheo-bronchitis normally require admission to hospital for observation and treatment. Any child suspected of having epiglottitis must be admitted to hospital fast.

■ OUTLOOK Even after a severe attack of croup, children recover fully and quickly. Although the croupy cough tends to recur, this becomes less common as their throats grow larger, and is rare after about five years. In the case of epiglottitis, if treatment is commenced early, recovery is normally complete with no long-term effects.

CRYING

The universal dilemma of parenthood: is the baby (or toddler) crying because of some definite problem which ought to be corrected, or just because babies will cry?

The possible causes are perhaps best divided into three categories: **1** When there is no illness or injury: If the child has no obvious signs of illness or injury, crying can be due to discomfort, hunger, boredom, fatigue, fear, sadness, loneliness or frustration. **2** With minor illness, crying can be due to COLIC, TEETHING, FEVER or a COMMON COLD. **3** With definite disease, crying can be due to EARACHE, HEADACHE, SORE THROAT, MENINGITIS, other INFECTION or severe pain, typically ABDOMINAL PAIN.

■ ACTION If the child has no obvious signs of illness or injury, and can be pacified by food or other attention, it is reasonable to assume that the problem is not major disease.

Anxiety on your part can be sensed by your baby and this can make him more fretful: so try to remain calm. Young babies need human contact, so don't hesitate to pick him up.

If you suspect colic, teething or that the baby feels generally unwell because of a common cold, a painkiller such as paracetamol can usually relieve the discomfort. In babies under three months of age this should only be given on a doctor's prescription. See also *FEVER*.

If your child continues to cry, some undetected illness or injury should be suspected. A young child cannot localize pain well, and earache and tummy-ache can give the same apparent symptoms. If you remain uncertain.

Your child cannot injure himself by crying, although he can make himself vomit.

CURVATURE OF THE SPINE
See *SCOLIOSIS*.

CUSHING'S DISEASE
See *ADRENAL DISORDERS*.

CUTS AND GRAZES
■ ACTION Clean cuts and grazes as soon as they happen, simply by dousing them with water. This is the

key to treatment because it painlessly and efficiently removes dirt, and with it the likelihood of INFECTION. Clean the surrounding skin with water applied with a clean flannel, handkerchief or cotton wool. Wipe away from the wound. If you have a suitable antiseptic solution (for example, iodine or TCP), this may be applied to the wound. Such agents sting and may cause your child to cry out. Comfort the child afterwards. Don't dislodge any blood clots that form. To dry, dab gently. If bleeding does not stop, apply firm pressure over the wound. This stops bleeding by flattening the blood vessels in the area of the wound. Blood flows more slowly, which can encourage clots to form. Be prepared to keep up the pressure for five to 15 minutes. If something is buried in the wound, apply pressure beside and around it. If the wound is in a limb, raising it may reduce bleeding by reducing local blood pressure. Cover the wound with a sterile dressing.

▓ GO TO HOSPITAL if there is glass debris or a foreign body in the wound: removing such material is best performed by a trained person. Large, jagged or gaping wounds will also need the attention of a doctor, preferably at your local hospital casualty department.

▓ OUTLOOK Is the child IMMUNE to TETANUS? If not, get medical advice, even if the wound appears 'clean'.

CYSTIC FIBROSIS

An uncommon, chronic INHERITED DISORDER consisting of repeated chest INFECTIONS and MALABSORPTION with FAILURE TO THRIVE. There is excess salt in the sweat and thick mucus in the lungs and pancreas.

Incidence: one in 2,500 births.

▓ CAUSE An unidentified abnormality of the cells, possibly also a deficiency of certain proteins and abnormal cellular salt transfer. This leads to production of thick secretions which block the ducts of the pancreas and lungs. The problems occur from birth and eventually lead to degeneration of these organs, known medically as fibrosis.

▓ SYMPTOMS Bowel problems: Sticky stools in infancy may obstruct the bowel. The baby may vomit bile and have ABDOMINAL SWELLING. Similar symptoms can occur in an older child. There may be RECTAL PROLAPSE in an older child, although cystic fibrosis is not frequently associated with this.

FAILURE TO THRIVE: Blockage of the pancreatic ducts prevents release of enzymes which are necessary for food digestion. Malabsorption of nutrients will result in poor growth despite a good appetite. Smelly, pale stools containing excess fat and protein will be present from birth.

Repeated chest infections: The child has a frequent, productive cough with thick yellow (infected) sputum. There may be associated VOMITING. PNEUMONIA and chest infections with certain BACTERIA may require management in hospital. The child may also develop wheezing due to allergic ASTHMA.

Abdominal problems: The obstruction of the pancreas will lead to fibrosis which, if severe, may also stop insulin production. The child may then develop *diabetes mellitus*, usually from adolescence onwards. Fibrosis (CIRRHOSIS) of the liver will cause back pressure on the blood in the veins to the liver. This in turn may cause distension of the veins around the oesophagus (the varices) and this can make the child vomit blood. As a result, the spleen may become enlarged.

Cardiac complications: Fibrosis of the lungs will restrict the blood supply from the heart. Increased pressure in the lung circulation may lead to heart strain with swelling of the legs, and eventually to HEART FAILURE.

■ INVESTIGATIONS A sweat test can reveal abnormal salt content, giving a firm diagnosis. An X-ray of the chest showing scattered areas of acute and chronic infection may suggest the diagnosis. Low levels of pancreatic enzyme, raised levels of fat in the stool and excess trypsin in the blood, may be helpful indicators when screening infants.

■ MANAGEMENT Clearing away sticky bowel contents, preferably using special ENEMAS or surgery.

Use of pancreatic enzyme preparations regularly with meals to aid digestion. High calorie diet with VITAMIN supplements.

Appropriate ANTIBIOTIC treatment, possibly long-term.

Chest physiotherapy to help the child cough up the secretions.

INHALERS and treatment for asthma if the child is wheezy.

Treatment for diabetes; appropriate management for cirrhosis and vomiting blood.

Diuretic drugs to help remove extra fluid in right-heart strain.

■ OUTLOOK Although children with cystic fibrosis are now surviving with normal intellect into adult life, their life span is considerably reduced. Treatment will help to keep them as well as possible. Heart/lung transplantation is now being tried, with some success.

Most males will be sterile, but girls can produce normal babies.

The risk of a further child having cystic fibrosis is one in four. The condition can be diagnosed by sampling tissue from the foetus in early pregnancy. The parents will need GENETIC COUNSELLING.

CYSTITIS
See *URINARY TRACT INFECTION*.

CYTOMEGALOVIRUS INFECTION
A common VIRAL INFECTION. Older children and adults usually have a mild form but if it occurs during pregnancy, it can be transmitted from mother to baby, causing serious illness.

■ SYMPTOMS IN BABIES The birth weight is often low; JAUNDICE and ANAEMIA may develop; the liver and spleen may be enlarged.

MENTAL HANDICAP can occur, but if the signs are not marked, this may only be noticed later in childhood. Inflammation of the eye can lead to BLINDNESS. Some babies can carry the virus without it causing significant problems.

■ SYMPTOMS IN OLDER CHILDREN FEVER, COUGH, HEADACHES and muscle pains; but the infection may well have no symptoms at all and be discovered by accident.

■ TESTS URINE and BLOOD TESTS confirm the diagnosis.

■ TREATMENT There is no effective treatment.

■ OUTLOOK In babies, this depends on the severity of the infection. A mother who has an infected baby is unlikely to have problems in another pregnancy, but it would be advisable to get medical advice before becoming pregnant again. Older children usually have no long-term problems.

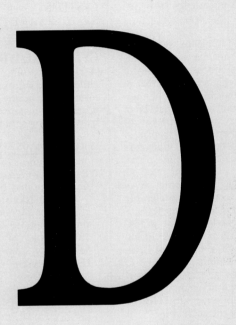

DARK URINE

The colour of the urine varies with its concentration. Urine formed during the night is more concentrated, and therefore looks darker than daytime urine. Urine that has been standing for a while may go cloudy, and this may look similar to the 'smoky' colour caused by NEPHRITIS. Eating red sweets and sometimes beetroot makes the urine red.

If you are worried or suspect there is blood in your child's urine, take a sample to your doctor to be tested.

DEADLY NIGHTSHADE

See *POISONING*.

DEAFNESS

The medical description for any loss of hearing, mild or severe. There are two main types of deafness: conductive, when there is disease or damage obstructing the passage of sound from the outside to the sensitive inner ear; and perceptive, when the problem lies in the inner ear itself, or with the nerve connecting the inner ear to the brain.

▓ CAUSES Perceptive, or nerve deafness, is commonly present from birth, and may be due to a variety of causes, especially birth injury or congenital *rubella*. Babies are routinely checked for hearing, at various ages, at well baby clinics, or by their health visitor or doctor. It may also be caused by VIRAL INFECTIONS in childhood, or by certain drugs. Conductive deafness is usually due to an obstruction in the sound pathway, such as MIDDLE EAR INFECTION or GLUE EAR; and, most commonly, by WAX IN EARS.

▓ SYMPTOMS vary according to the child's age. Youngest babies will normally 'startle' at a loud noise. As they get older, normal babies respond in many ways to even the softest sounds, such as a carer moving quietly round the room, or soft talking; deaf babies, on the other hand, may be startled by suddenly *seeing* someone beside the cot. Once a child is beginning to understand speech – say at two to two-and-a-half years old – you can test hearing by whispering in the child's vicinity, but remaining out of sight.

Hearing is necessary for the development of speech: deaf children do not learn to speak, while partially deaf children show delayed speech. Older children who develop deafness may lose interest in school, and may be wrongly labelled 'backward'.

▓ ACTION If at the age of 2½ years you suspect that your child's speech is not developing like other children's, you should consult your health visitor or G.P. – they can refer you to a hearing specialist. Early detection and treatment are essential to minimize developmental delays. Children who have had middle ear infections should be checked for hearing loss and they should be monitored until they recover. Before school entry any children with speech difficulties should see a hearing specialist for thorough assessment.

▓ TESTS If severe congenital deafness is suspected in a baby, audiometric and electrical tests are done to measure how much hearing and at what frequencies (pitch) it is present. These tests are also used to assess what sort of hearing aid will be best for the child. In older children, hearing can be assessed either by pure tone AUDIOMETRY, or by impedance audiometry, or by using spoken words in a special room.

■ TREATMENT The sooner you help a severely or totally deaf child to face the communication problem, the better. It is essential to try to understand his difficulties. You may have to help him adapt to a hearing aid, or go through special training in sign language and lip reading. Conductive deafness due to glue ear is often temporary, but if it persists, GROMMETS may be inserted. If the conductive deafness is due to a perforated eardrum, usually following middle ear infection, repair of the drum may be carried out after the infection has completely cleared.

■ LONG-TERM MANAGEMENT Hearing aid technology continues to improve, and deaf children have a better chance than ever before of receiving their education in normal schools.

Although hearing aids may take some getting used to, it is worth persevering. It is important that profoundly deaf children receive as 'normal' an education as possible, and mix with hearing children to help their integration into society as adults. In some cases, special educational help may also be on offer.

DEFICIENCY ANAEMIA

ANAEMIA caused by a deficiency of one of the substances necessary to make haemoglobin, which acts as the blood's oxygen carrier.

■ CAUSES 1 Iron deficiency is the commonest in childhood. It is usually due to an inadequate diet, but poor absorption (as in COELIAC DISEASE), or blood loss, can sometimes be to blame. Premature babies, twins and triplets, who have not built up stores of iron in their bodies before birth, are particularly at risk. Babies born at full-term have iron stores to last until about six months. Thereafter, they need adequate iron in their diet. Weaning diets during the first year of life, especially if the range of food is limited and unmodified cow's milk is introduced early, often have insufficient iron. For these reasons, iron deficiency anaemia is most likely to occur between six months and two years.

Foods which contain iron include red meat, wholewheat flour, brown rice, apricots, guavas, green leafy vegetables (typically spinach), and iron-enriched cereals. 2 Folic acid and vitamin B12 are also needed to make haemoglobin. Lack of folic acid is uncommon in children, but premature babies or those with MALABSORPTION can be at risk. Folic acid is found in meat and green leafy vegetables. Vitamin B12 deficiency is very rare in children.

Adults and children who are vegans (eat no animal products) may be at risk of anaemia due to these deficiencies.

■ SYMPTOMS Similar to other causes of anaemia. They usually begin gradually, and are difficult to recognize.

Anaemia can be caused by blood loss (for example during surgery). This may not be severe enough to require a BLOOD TRANSFUSION, but extra iron may be needed to replace that lost.

■ ACTION If your baby was premature, or one of twins or triplets, discuss with your doctor whether iron and folic acid supplements are necessary.

Ensure that your child has a balanced diet. See NUTRITION. If he does not have a good appetite, make sure that what he does eat is healthy. Don't be tempted to fill him up with 'just anything'. This will further decrease his appetite and make healthy eating even less likely. Discuss with your doctor the possibility of iron and folic acid supplements.

If you suspect anaemia, always get medical advice.

▓ TESTS A BLOOD TEST will show whether there is anaemia, and what has caused it. Occasionally, it is necessary to test for unnoticed bleeding of the bowel as a cause of anaemia.

▓ TREATMENT Iron and folic acid can be given as a syrup. Folic acid causes no side-effects, but iron can cause constipation, diarrhoea and nausea in children. If the anaemia is not severe, it may be possible to increase the amount of iron and folic acid naturally in the diet. Iron syrup and tablets can cause serious poisoning if taken in overdose, so keep the bottle away from children.

Treatment takes about a week to start working. The body's iron store can be replenished in a few months; folic acid is not stored for long, so a constant intake is required.

▓ OUTLOOK This is an easily treated form of anaemia, usually causing no long-term problems.

DEHYDRATION

Caused by loss of body fluids, as in severe DIARRHOEA and VOMITING. The danger is that the circulating blood volume may be reduced, with a fall in BLOOD PRESSURE. This can, if not corrected quickly, result in life-threatening SHOCK.

▓ SYMPTOMS to watch for in a child with severe diarrhoea or vomiting: thirst – a typical response to early dehydration, but one that is not always obvious in infants, especially if the baby is generally ill and vomiting; passing less urine than usual – a sign that the body is having to conserve fluid; eyes looking sunken; dry mouth and tongue; shallow breathing and general weakness; rapid pulse rate.

▓ ACTION Dehydration requires prompt action to replace body water. See *GASTROENTERITIS*.

If severe, and the child is unable to drink clear fluids, contact your doctor who will arrange immediate admission to hospital, where fluids will be administered if necessary by intravenous 'drip'.

In common gastroenteritis of childhood, dehydration can usually be avoided by giving water mixed with special salts (which your G.P. can prescribe). This so-called oral rehydration therapy will often succeed, even in the presence of continuing diarrhoea and some degree of vomiting.

▓ OUTLOOK Given prompt treatment, the child will have no long-term ill effects.

DELIRIUM, DELIRIOUS CHILD

An old-fashioned term for the confusion a child may experience in association with a high FEVER, as in TONSILLITIS and lobal PNEUMONIA. The child may cry out or scream while half-awake and appear highly disturbed. Nowadays, fevers are usually treated quickly and effectively with sponging and antipyretic drugs such as paracetamol. As a result, delirium is uncommon and short lasting.

For action and treatment, see *FEVER*. See also *HALLUCINATIONS*.

DEPRESSION

You are no stranger to your child's sad and tearful moods in response to frustration, disappointment or failure. A child may be suffering from depression only if such episodes occur without external provocation, are frequent and long lasting, and are accompanied by other symptoms (see below). Before adolescence, it is unusual for children to complain explicitly that they are depressed.

■ CAUSES Any big change, especially if this involves losing a valued close relationship (be it a relative, a friend, even a pet), can initiate a period of sadness. Parental unhappiness, worries or discord can also cause unhappiness in a child. However, the term depression implies something deeper and longer-lasting, usually against a background of previous episodes of being low.

■ SYMPTOMS Tearful, unhappy moods which seem to arise spontaneously or for trivial reasons; irritability; problems with concentration; a falling off in performance of school work (this can be an effect as well as a cause). Awkward, contrary, naughty behaviour may also be a part of the picture, as may poor sleeping patterns and a change in appetite.

■ ACTION Obviously you will try to identify what may be upsetting your child, and talk to him about it. This is an obvious and important step, which may be quite difficult with a teenage child. Young children often feel responsible for things which are not their fault: for example, if a parent has been ill, the child may think his naughtiness has caused it – see also BEREAVEMENT and DIVORCE. However, it is not always clear to the parents or child himself what may have initiated the depressive state. Talk to your family doctor if the change lasts longer than a few weeks, or if the symptoms are worsening.

■ TREATMENT Your doctor may feel that the help of a child psychiatrist or psychotherapist is needed. Such problems are best dealt with by therapists as a whole family concern even if only one member appears to be affected. Antidepressant drugs are rarely used, but they can be useful, even in young children. Your doctor may also want to consider whether depression could be a symptom of some underlying physical illness.

DERMATITIS

Literally, this means 'inflamed skin', but the term is now commonly used interchangeably with ECZEMA, when it refers to various forms of ALLERGIC skin disease.

■ CAUSES There are two main types: irritant dermatitis, and contact dermatitis. Irritant dermatitis is caused by the direct action of chemicals on the skin – a common example is NAPPY RASH, where the irritant is ammonia, formed by the breakdown of urine. Contact dermatitis is an allergic reaction to a substance which has been in contact with the skin. One of the commonest is nickel, the metal found in bracelets, necklaces, and watch straps, but there are many possible causes of this allergy.

■ SYMPTOMS The skin becomes red, and feels sore or itchy. In more severe forms, blisters and cracks are seen. The rash is limited to the area in contact with the irritant or allergy-producing substance, often leaving tell-tale shapes under straps, or rings, or babies' nappies, or on the hands.

▨ ACTION If the cause can be identified, simply removing it and avoiding further contact may solve the problem. Simple soothing creams, or mild hydrocortisone cream (now obtainable from chemists) will relieve the itching.

▨ GET MEDICAL ADVICE if the rash persists, or if you cannot identify a cause.

▨ TESTS If a child with contact dermatitis is referred to a hospital clinic, tests can be done to find out what substances might be causing it. Patches containing various chemicals are applied to the child's skin. Allergy is shown by a red reaction to the patch.

▨ TREATMENT Once a cause is found, care must be taken to avoid it. Sometimes the allergy is one of the common constituents of skin creams, such as lanolin.

▨ OUTLOOK Children who show allergic rashes on contact with certain substances are likely to have other forms of allergy, and may have some allergic symptoms throughout life. Many, however, will grow out of them.

DEVELOPMENTAL DELAY
See 'NORMAL' DEVELOPMENT.

DIABETES MELLITUS
A disorder resulting from insulin deficiency. Insulin is a hormone produced by the pancreas gland. Its main function is to help glucose enter the body's cells where it can be used for energy and growth. If there is surplus glucose, insulin directs it into the liver for storage.

▨ CAUSES The cause(s) of childhood onset diabetes is uncertain. The current view is that it probably results from an 'insult' to the insulin-secreting cells of the pancreas. The 'insult' may take the form of a VIRAL infection that activates the body's immune system to attack the insulin-producing cells of its own pancreas. These then fail to produce insulin, and, as a result, the child's blood glucose level rises.

▨ SYMPTOMS The excess glucose in the blood spills over into the urine carrying with it an excess of water, Thus the untreated diabetic child passes ever increasing volumes of urine; he may have to get up during the night perhaps many times to pass urine, or he may wet the bed. He will be excessively thirsty to compensate for the loss of water, and he will lose weight as energy which should be built into tissues is wasted as glucose in the urine.

He may become tired, irritable; his breath may smell of pear drops or acetone; and if the condition remains undiagnosed and untreated, it may progress to a dangerous state in which the child becomes unconscious, dehydrated and begins to breathe heavily and deeply.

▨ ACTION If your child develops these symptoms, you must of course get medical advice. Your doctor will do a URINE TEST for glucose (there is normally none present) and a BLOOD TEST for a raised glucose concentration. If the result is positive, the doctor will either refer the child to a specialist or arrange his urgent admission to hospital, depending on his clinical state.

■ TREATMENT The basis of treatment of childhood diabetes is replacement of the missing insulin. It must be given for life as the body is unable to make its own insulin. Insulin is usually given by injection once or twice a day; it cannot be given by mouth as it is destroyed by the intestinal digestive secretions. Most children readily adjust to the daily discipline of their injections. On average they begin to show an interest and ability in managing their own injections from the age of eight to 12 years. Once the family have adjusted to the shock of the diagnosis, the clinical routine is not in itself difficult to adopt: the difficulty is in the permanency of the routine and the necessity for an abnormally organized lifestyle for the child and family.

Regular blood and/or urine tests are necessary to monitor the blood glucose level. The levels during a particular day can then be charted. This becomes the currency of attendance at the diabetic clinic at which control is assessed and discussed, and supplies (for finger pricking, blood or urine glucose testing and insulin) are provided.

A child with diabetes is advised to eat essentially normal foods as part of a normal, well-balanced diet. The restriction is sugary foods (sweets, chocolates and many energy-dense 'junk' foods), because they cause sudden rises in blood glucose. To balance the effects of the injected insulin, and to keep blood glucose levels steady, the carbohydrate intake is calculated and spread over the snacks and main meals of the day. The carbohydrate should preferably come from whole foods, for example fruit, and foods rich in natural fibre, for example cereals, wholemeal bread and beans. Meals need to be eaten at regular times; it is prudent to keep animal fats to a minimum. Most children usually adjust well to the dietary discipline, at least initially. Great ingenuity, stamina and support are needed to help the child sustain the diet for years and years.

■ PROBLEMS IN DIABETIC CONTROL HYPOGLYCAEMIA – a low blood glucose level, which may result from extra exercise, a missed snack, too much insulin, or sometimes for no obvious reason. The individual child may display pallor, irritability, hunger, dizziness or sudden loss of consciousness. Treatment includes immediate extra glucose from a drink, sugar or tablet; or may require the emergency use of glucagon, an injectable hormone that works as an antidote to insulin. Medical help may be required. After recovery, thought needs to be given as to why the episode occurred. It may be preventable next time.

HYPERGLYCAEMIA occurs if the blood glucose rises too high. The initial symptoms of diabetes return, with frequent passage of urine, thirst and weight loss. Vague lassitude and headaches may have gone before. The condition may arise from too little insulin (or the child outgrowing his previous dose); from eating more than usual; from a change in lifestyle or exercise; from worry over school work; or as a result of infection. In diabetic children, blood glucose tends to rise during infections, even though they are eating less.

The key to coping with hyperglycaemia is frequent thoughtful measurements of the child's blood glucose, judiciously injecting extra quick-acting insulin, maintaining fluid intake and keeping in touch with the doctor.

■ SELF-HELP Always carry an emergency supply of glucose (most conveniently in the form of glucose tablets) to counter an unexpected fall in blood glucose.

Change the site of the injection from day to day. This will help maintain the injection sites in a smooth and supple state, and will help the regular pattern of insulin absorption.

Don't let diabetes restrict your child's lifestyle. Encourage him to participate in his friends' activities, and particularly in exercise. Unaccustomed, vigorous and lengthy exercise may need forethought, in providing extra carbohydrate before and often after the bout, to offset a fall in blood glucose concentration.

■ OUTLOOK With adequate control of his diabetes, and his blood glucose levels, your child will grow up to lead a near-normal adult life with very few restrictions. The discipline of diabetes will still be required; and certain jobs may not be open to him such as army service or piloting aeroplanes.

Childhood diabetes may, in a minority of cases, result in problems and complications in adulthood. These may include: changes in the small blood vessels of the eyes, kidneys and feet, with additional problems affecting the nerves and heart in some instances. Such problems are worrisome to parents and children alike, but they are a long way off and should not cloud the life of the diabetic child. It is true that there is some relationship between control of blood glucose in childhood and future health. But, in coming decades we can expect improvements in the care and prospects of diabetics; and so it is fair to take an optimistic, but careful view of a diabetic child's future health. You may wish to discuss these matters with your doctor or paediatrician, and with your child, especially, perhaps, when he becomes a teenager.

DIABETIC PREGNANCY

A pregnancy in which the mother has DIABETES. A woman may have diabetes before she becomes pregnant or develop it during pregnancy. All women are screened for diabetes during pregnancy by testing their urine for sugar. A BLOOD TEST is usually necessary to confirm the diabetic state.

Whatever the type of the mother's diabetes, the health of the foetus may be affected. If the mother's BLOOD SUGAR level is not well controlled, the extra sugar crosses the placenta and may make the foetus large and fat. As a rebound effect, after birth the blood sugar may drop severely (see *HYPO-GLYCAEMIA*).

Diabetic mothers run a slightly increased risk of STILL BIRTH in late pregnancy, so many obstetricians advise induction of labour at 38 weeks of gestation.

DIALYSIS
See *RENAL FAILURE*.

DIARRHOEA
The passage of frequent, loose or watery bowel motions. Often caused by a VIRUS (if accompanied by vomiting, this is GASTROENTERITIS). However, diarrhoea may accompany a variety of conditions, such as INFECTIONS of the ears or throat.

Rarely it may be a pointer to a more serious abdominal problem such as APPENDICITIS. Many toddlers are, however, prone to short episodes of non-specific diarrhoea which need not cause concern if they last no longer than a day or two. *GIARDIA* should be considered as a possible cause if the diarrhoea is long lasting.

■ ACTION A child with diarrhoea may have a poor APPETITE for a few days. This does not matter, but it is important to ensure sufficient fluid intake in order to prevent DEHYDRATION. Avoid formula milk, which may make the diarrhoea worse. Give frequent drinks of clear fluids and water. If you are breast feeding, you should continue supplementing your milk if necessary with watery drinks. Change nappies frequently to avoid soreness due to the acid content of the faeces – also use a barrier cream.

Get medical advice if there are any signs of dehydration, if the child is generally unwell, or has abdominal pain or vomiting, or if the diarrhoea lasts more than three to four days.

■ TESTS A specimen of the child's faeces may be sent for laboratory microscopic study for VIRUSES, BACTERIA or parasites.

■ TREATMENT The only treatment needed in most cases of diarrhoea is fluid replacement to avoid dehydration. Powders to make up into 're-hydration fluid' can be bought over the counter from your chemist, and should be used when diarrhoea is severe and frequent, to replace fluid and salt loss. Medicines that 'stop' the diarrhoea by reducing bowel mobility should be avoided, especially in children. If a faeces specimen shows a parasite such as *Giardia*, your doctor may prescribe a specific medicine.

DIPHTHERIA

Now rare in most developed countries because of IMMUNIZATION. It is caused by BACTERIA spread by exhaled droplets. The bacteria produce a toxin which can damage the heart, nerves and other organs in the body. The INCUBATION PERIOD is between two and seven days.

■ PREVENTION Diptheria immunization is safe and efficient.

■ SYMPTOMS FEVER, HEADACHE and feeling generally unwell are early signs. The glands of the neck become very large. A membrane forms in the back of the throat and in the nose, causing difficulty with breathing. Complications include muscle PARALYSIS, PNEUMONIA and HEART FAILURE.

■ ACTION Get medical advice. Your doctor will arrange admission to hospital.

■ TREATMENT In hospital, an antitoxin injection is given, plus ANTIBIOTICS.

If the membrane is obstructing breathing, a tube may have to be passed down the windpipe in hospital. If the muscles of breathing are paralysed, the child may need a ventilator (life-support machine). See the separate entries for treatment of heart failure and pneumonia.

■ OUTLOOK This illness, now rare, is most severe in younger children. Convalescence is usually long, and the complications can occur late in the course of the disease.

DISLOCATION OF A JOINT

A joint becomes dislocated when the 'ball' (see diagram) loses proper contact with its 'socket'. As might be expected, this is almost always caused by injury. Joints commonly dislocated are those of the shoulder, elbow and fingers. One type of dislocation is present at birth: CONGENITAL DISLOCATION OF THE HIP.

■ SYMPTOMS The injury is usually obvious, and there may be exceedingly painful swelling and deformity of the joint.

DISLOCATION OF JOINT

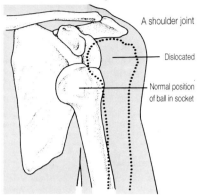

A shoulder joint

Dislocated

Normal position of ball in socket

▓ ACTION Get medical advice or take the child straight to a hospital casualty department. An anaesthetic may be necessary, so don't give him anything to eat or drink, otherwise the anaesthetic may well have to be postponed.

▓ TESTS An X-ray may be necessary to make the diagnosis. It is usually repeated once the dislocation has been treated, to make sure that everything is back to normal.

▓ TREATMENT The joint is manipulated into its normal position, a procedure usually done under an anaesthetic. A sling may be used to rest the joint for a few weeks.

It is important to exercise other joints and muscles in the body as usual, otherwise they will become stiff and weak.

▓ OUTLOOK is usually good, but if ligaments, tendons and muscles around the joint are badly torn, the joint can be weakened, giving rise to repeated dislocation.

DIVORCE

The sad truth is that in many Western countries, marriage break-up affects one child in six, and that this rate is still increasing. There is no disguising the fact that divorce causes children tremendous distress. And it is hard for parents to cope with this because at the time they themselves are tense and upset.

Recent research shows that, however bad the marriage, children like their parents to stay together. You may know this is impossible, but remember your child may secretly wish and hope it for years.

Unless the parent who leaves has been violent, most children want and need to keep in contact with the parent who has left. It is important to try to maintain this relationship, and to allow that the person who has left can be a good *parent* though not a good *spouse*.

Access will often be regulated by the court which grants the divorce, but it is in your child's best interest for this to be predictable, planned and (depending on the age of the child) for long enough to maintain a relationship.

▓ REACTIONS TO DIVORCE
Pre-school children: Babies and toddlers are unlikely to show specific reactions, but may be upset if the parent is absent. A slightly older child may be concerned about the absent parent's welfare in a practical sense: 'Will Daddy have a bed to sleep in?' 'Will Daddy have food to eat?' Children at this age may also feel that their naughtiness has caused problems between the parents and need reassurance that this is not the case.

Five to eight/nine years: Children are still likely to feel responsible for what has happened and they may also worry that the absent parent has died. It is important to reassure them and to encourage communication by cards or brief telephone calls if access is a problem. The child may be tearful and upset and wakeful at night and there may be difficult behaviour at home or at school. Warn your child's teacher of what is happening.

Nine to 12 years: The child will probably not feel responsible for the break-up, but may take sides. He may show considerable emotional distress; and his behaviour may become very difficult indeed: a challenge, perhaps, for the remaining parent to demonstrate whether he or she can really manage alone.

Teenagers are likely to argue quite vehemently for or against one of the parents. They may well feel strong loyalty to the absent parent and should be given some say in access and where they will be living. They need to be kept informed about what is happening. They may be upset for several months, with difficult behaviour and worse marks than usual at school. There may be SCHOOL ATTENDANCE PROBLEMS.

▨ ACTION Remember you are bound to be upset and this will make matters even more difficult for your children. Apart from trying to keep up contact with the absent parent, maintain the children's routines as far as possible and allow them to miss the absent parent without feeling they are disloyal to you.

Don't let them take sides, and encourage them to keep their own photos of the family group. Try to preserve 'space' for the child or children, even though you need to give everything you have to keeping yourself together.

If a child's reaction to separation and divorce is severe and lasts longer than a few months, ask your doctor to refer him to a child psychologist or psychiatrist for help before the problem becomes entrenched.

DIZZINESS

A sensation which children may describe in a variety of ways, including 'muzziness', light-headedness, a sense of spinning (also called vertigo). It is a rather vague symptom with many possible underlying causes ranging from MIDDLE EAR problems, side-effects of medication, drug abuse or OVER-BREATHING. It rarely justifies major investigation or treatment.

DOWN'S SYNDROME

A relatively, and distressingly common CHROMOSOMAL abnormality in which children are born with an extra chromosome number in their cells. It affects approximately one in 700 children, and the likelihood increases with a mother's age: the chance of a woman who is over 44 having a Down's child is one in 40.

▨ ANTENATAL DIAGNOSIS Down's syndrome may now be diagnosed during pregnancy by amniocentesis, which allows analysis of foetal chromosomes. Recent research has suggested that a BLOOD TEST done before the 16th week of pregnancy can also be useful in making a diagnosis.

▨ FEATURES OF DOWN'S SYNDROME The child's facial features have a characteristic 'Mongoloid' appearance: the eyes slant upwards and outwards, and may be widely separated. The bridge of the nose tends to be flat and the ears small. The tongue may protrude between the lips. Other identifying features include a single crease line across the palm of the hand. The baby may be especially quiet and placid. He has a tendency to CONGENITAL HEART-DISEASE, and may be born with a blockage of the bowel (DUODENAL ATRESIA).

■ PROBLEMS AFTER BIRTH As with any other baby, you can breast or bottle feed. However, he takes longer to feed because he finds sucking difficult. He may also be slow to put on weight at first.

An operation for either the bowel or heart problem may be necessary. The hospital doctors should discuss with you in detail the risks and different possibilities for surgery.

■ PROBLEMS IN CHILDHOOD During their first few years, children with Down's syndrome tend to have minor infections of the eyes and ears. They are more prone than other children to colds and chest infections.

The main point, however, is that they can, and do, achieve all the usual childhood skills: the Down's child will walk, and talk, albeit more slowly than others. Techniques for assisting development have improved enormously and with professional help, parents can ensure that the Down's child reaches his full potential.

Down's children are typically affectionate, lovable and good mixers. They need to be included, stimulated and treated as normally as possible.

They will, it must be faced, have a low I.Q.: educational needs must be realistically assessed and usually a special school is chosen.

■ ADOLESCENCE AND ADULTHOOD When a child is nearing school-leaving age, further careful assessment is needed of his future. Some Down's children are fully self-supporting in unskilled or semi-skilled jobs. However, most need help from an adult training centre to develop daily living skills or to gain employment.

The critical time for Down's syndrome adults tends to be middle age. With their own parents in old age, and the possibility of serious health problems resulting from congenital heart-disease, the outlook can be uncertain. But provision for this type of handicap is improving, and today's Down's child may well fare better in middle age than parents dared hope in the 1960s and 1970s. Your national association for Down's syndrome may well offer real support.

DROWNING

Most drownings occur in swimming-pools, in ornamental ponds, in canals and lakes, or in the bath. A young child can drown in a few inches of water. With hindsight most accidents appear easily preventable by adequate supervision at swimming-pools or during domestic bathtime, provision of life jackets in boats and fencing off ornamental ponds in gardens, public places and private swimming-pools. Additionally, children should all be taught to swim.

■ IMMEDIATE ACTION Summon an ambulance. Even if the child appears to be dead, start EMERGENCY RESUSCITATION. Try to give the child a few breaths even as you pull him from the water. Be prepared to continue artificial ventilation until professional help arrives, even if this is for several hours. If possible, wrap the child in a blanket (or suitable substitute such as a jacket), since chilling can lead to HYPOTHERMIA.

● When the child starts breathing, put him in the RECOVERY POSITION.

■ OUTLOOK Best in those who recover consciousness soonest, but it is always worth attempting emergency resuscitation and persisting until medical help arrives. Even after prolonged periods of UNCON-SCIOUSNESS and artificial ventilation, some children make complete recoveries.

DRUG ABUSE
A rare but potentially grave problem, which includes 'street' drug abuse and occasional GLUE SNIFFING. Taking medication prescribed for a parent is a separate, also dangerous problem which should never be ignored.

Illegal 'street' drugs such as heroin, cocaine, hallucinogenics, amphetamines or their derivatives may be sniffed, smoked, injected or taken as tablets. For some social groups, drug abuse, particularly of heroin, is an increasingly serious threat in adolescence. The expense of purchasing the drug may lead the youngster into crime. Risks to health include AIDS from shared needles, quite apart from the spectre of addiction and the general undermining of a youngster's self-respect and direction.

■ SYMPTOMS Sudden changes of mood after being out with friends – being suddenly elated, laughing inappropriately, then quickly becoming depressed and withdrawn; hiding parts of the body where drugs have been injected; a sudden need for money; intoxication although there is no smell of alcohol; all are grounds for suspicion. If a teenager has needle puncture marks, typically on the forearms, or if you find needles or syringes amongst his possessions, take immediate action.

It is unusual for drug abuse to be a teenager's first problem: it usually occurs when there is already trouble with family relationships, school work, SCHOOL ATTENDANCE or with the law.

■ ACTION Confront the youngster and produce the evidence. Go to the family doctor together or seek help from local counselling services or the drug dependence team; be prepared to undergo counselling.

DRUGS IN PREGNANCY
No drugs are allowed on the market which are known to cause malformations of an unborn baby. However, rare, minor or subtle effects may be associated with many 'drugs' (including aspirin, herbal remedies, alcohol, tobacco and drugs of addiction). So it is prudent to avoid, as far as possible, all drugs in pregnancy. If in doubt, get medical advice.

DRUGS, ALLERGIC REACTIONS TO
Not all unwanted effects of drugs or medicines are allergic in nature; some are the direct effect of the drug itself, often mistaken for an ALLERGY. However, many drugs can produce genuine allergic reactions when given more than once, and occasionally these reactions can be serious.

■ TYPES OF ALLERGIC RE-ACTION Rashes are the best known, and are most likely when the drug – typically an ANTIBIOTIC or an antihistamine – has been used directly on the skin. Any form of skin rash can be caused by allergy, including: URTICARIA, ECZEMA, DERMATITIS, BLISTERS, and rashes that resemble MEASLES.

Drug allergies can also cause ASTHMA and ALLERGIC RHINITIS, various blood disorders such as APLASTIC ANAEMIA or, most serious of all, ANAPHYLACTIC SHOCK. However, this last is most unlikely, except when the drug is given by injection. Emergency remedies are always on hand whenever injections are given.

▨ CAUSES The drugs most likely to cause allergic reactions include: penicillin and other antibiotics; sulphonamides, like antibiotics; aspirin (not now used in children under 12); dyes used in colouring medicines; vaccines.

▨ ACTION If you suspect a child is suffering from an allergic reaction to any drug or medicine, you should report it as soon as possible to your doctor. If the symptoms are severe, immediate treatment should be obtained, but if less severe, such as an itchy rash, there is less urgency.

▨ TREATMENT Removal of the drug, and stopping any further exposure to it, are obvious steps. If anaphylactic shock has occurred, emergency treatment with injections of adrenalin, antihistamine and hydrocortisone will be given. Less severe reactions may be treated with an oral antihistamine or sometimes by a corticosteroid. Blood disorders will require special investigations and treatment in hospital.

▨ TESTS It is not always possible to prove that a reaction is due to a drug allergy, but BLOOD TESTS are available which may help to determine the cause. Skin tests for drug allergy can themselves be dangerous, and are only used under certain circumstances. Patch tests for skin allergies are widely used in dermatology clinics, and are helpful if allergy to a contact substance is suspected.

▨ OUTLOOK Once an allergy has been demonstrated, it is important for the child to avoid further contact. However, many so-called allergies, for example to penicillin, are not genuine, and doctors may

reasonably test a small dose of the drug by mouth, in order to discover whether in fact a reaction occurs.

DUODENAL ATRESIA
An uncommon CONGENITAL ABNORMALITY of the duodenum (the small bowel connected to the stomach, and forming the first part of the small intestine). A short section does not develop properly in the foetus and fails to function properly at birth, leading to obstruction of the bowel.

▨ SYMPTOMS Vomiting bile, inability to feed properly.

▨ TREATMENT Surgery to remove the narrowed section and rejoin (reanastomose) the bowel.

▨ OUTLOOK is excellent: no further problems need be expected.

DWARFISM
See *SHORT STATURE.*

DYING CHILD
No amount of rationalization can relieve a parent's sense of shock and injustice when faced with the prospect of a dying child. But although each family is unique and the ability of family members to cope is often unpredictable, it is possible for even this tragic experience to enhance rather than destroy their integrity and emotional well-being.

There can be no absolute rules to guide anyone through the ordeal; the following suggestions are based simply on the observations and experiences of others who have suffered similarly.

▨ COMMUNICATION After parents have been told that their child's illness will have a fatal outcome they will have to deal not only with their own shock and disbelief but also, in the ensuing days and weeks, with meeting many different people: relatives, friends, health professionals, religious pastors, in addition to the child. Expressions of anger or a retreat into silent grief may be natural but will help nobody, and may disturb the child's precious final days.

Parents should ask health professionals to explain all the facts clearly. It is often useful to write down questions before meeting senior doctors and nurses as it is easy to forget what to ask in the heat of the moment. Don't be afraid to ask the same thing time and again.

It may be helpful to meet with parents who have been through a similar ordeal or whose child had the same condition. Ask the ward sister or your family doctor for details. Treat the child in a routine way: children are concerned with living normally, and if artificial celebrations are created – an early Christmas or birthday celebration – they may feel subtly pressurized.

Many religious pastors will be a source of great comfort at this time and parents should not be reluctant to involve them, even if their previous contact has been slight.

Friends of the family may be uncertain how to cope and parents may need to encourage them to visit the child, or sometimes to discourage them if their interest and concern becomes too intrusive.

▓ THE PROCESS OF DYING Although death frightens most people, the physical process of dying should be, and can be, dignified and pain-free. Don't be afraid:
– to arrange for the child to die in a particular place – at home or in a favoured room or bed in the hospi-

tal. Talk to the nurses about making the surroundings as warm and homely as possible;
– to include (or occasionally to exclude) relatives and friends in the visiting schedule;
– to discuss arrangements for pain relief repeatedly with the doctors or nurses;
– to talk to the child and to comfort him physically. The decision about what to tell the child will vary with the illness and circumstances. If in doubt, discuss this with the child's doctor;
– to be with the child after death.

▓ BEREAVEMENT Although the pain of grief is intense, have no doubt that time is a great healer and that the mourning process will bring a sense of perspective and emotional stability, usually after a period of about nine months.

Depression may well disturb patterns of eating and sleeping. Social contacts may be avoided. These are usually harmless unless they last indefinitely. But problems in a marriage, or at work, may follow if one parent finds it exceptionally difficult to cope with grief when the other does not. Be aware that this is a potentially destructive situation.

DYSLEXIA

A controversial term describing severe difficulty in reading or spelling inconsistent with the child's level of intelligence. It is the result of one or more specific aberrations in the complex process of learning to read. A child with dyslexia is now usually described as having a specific learning disorder. Very mild forms of dyslexia are actually quite common. The child will usually profit by specialized help with learning to read, usually in a normal school. See *LEARNING DIS-ORDERS*.

E

EAR INFECTION
See *MIDDLE* and *EXTERNAL EAR INFECTIONS*.

EARACHE
Any pain in or around the ear.

▓ CAUSES are MIDDLE EAR INFECTION (especially in association with VIRAL INFECTIONS of the nose and throat), EXTERNAL EAR INFECTION and EAR, FOREIGN BODY IN. It is commonest in young children, whose Eustachian tubes are short, enabling infections to travel easily from the throat to the middle ear.

▓ SYMPTOMS Infants have non-specific symptoms such as FEVER, crying and VOMITING. Toddlers and older children will hold their ears or complain of earache – which can be *very* painful. See *MIDDLE EAR INFECTION (OTITIS MEDIA)*.

▓ ACTION If you think your child has earache, get medical advice. While awaiting medical attention, you could give your child a simple painkiller such as paracetamol. The urgency depends on the severity of the pain and the degree of general illness, especially in infants. If untreated, middle ear infection may resolve spontaneously, but may on occasion lead to EARDRUM PERFORATION. When this happens, the pain may remit: there may then be a need for specialist attention to the perforated drum.

EARDRUM PERFORATION
The eardrum may be perforated by direct injury, by extreme changes of pressure, and most commonly by MIDDLE EAR INFECTIONS, in which case a discharge may appear in the external ear canal.

▓ SYMPTOMS Discharge (see above); pain and/or bleeding.

▓ TREATMENT If the cause is a middle ear infection, it is likely that your doctor will prescribe an ANTIBIOTIC. Perforations usually heal without treatment. Occasionally specialist attention may be needed, particularly if there is any suggestion that hearing has been impaired.

EARS, FOREIGN BODY IN
Any object, animal, vegetable or mineral, lodged in the ear canal, where it can cause irritation, swelling and lead to infection.

▓ SYMPTOMS Pain, itching, or simply a complaint of a blocked ear. If it has been there for some time, a smelly discharge may be noted.

▓ ACTION Many foreign bodies, including insects, can be removed by lying the child on his side and gently pouring warm water into his ear. Make sure the water is not too hot. Some objects will have to be removed by a doctor, who will syringe the ear to wash out the unwanted matter, or use a special probe or tweezers to pluck out the offending object.

▓ TREATMENT If the ear canal is inflamed or infected, ANTIBIOTIC drops may be prescribed.

▓ OUTLOOK There should be no long-term problems, but young children who have put things in their ears tend to do so again.

ECG (ELECTROCARDIOGRAM)
A test to measure the function of the heart. The patient is connected to a machine by little metal plates or suck-

ers attached to the arms, legs and chest. A paste or jelly is used to aid contact. A tracing is then recorded of the electrical activity of the heart. This is completely painless – there is nothing to feel while the tracing is taken. But the child must stay fairly still for a few minutes. The ECG can show whether the heart is beating irregularly, and whether there are signs of strain on the heart caused by HEART-DISEASE.

ECG

A typical ECG print-out.

ECZEMA

In childhood, an itchy, scaling or weeping rash, often associated with other allergic conditions such as HAY FEVER and ASTHMA. It tends to run in families.

■ SYMPTOMS Childhood eczema usually starts in infancy. Initially it is prominent in the nappy area; later in childhood it presents as a symmetrical rash affecting the hands and wrists, the creases of the arms, ankles and behind the knees, and in more extreme cases the face, neck or trunk. The rash is pink or red, and may be dry and scaly or develop cracks and become wet and weepy. It is usually itchy.

■ ACTION Because of the family pattern, many parents recognize eczema when it starts. While treatment is not necessarily urgent, it is wise to get medical advice early on as with the diagnosis and treatment of any skin rash.

■ TREATMENT It is important for parents to realize that however unsightly, eczema is not contagious, and usually lessens in severity in later childhood, often completely clearing by the teens. It does not lead to scarring, although a dryness of the skin may remain even in adulthood.

There are four main groups of therapeutic agents employed in the treatment of eczema: **1** Emollients – creams or ointments to keep the skin soft, supple and moist – should be used freely. Emulsifying agents in place of soap for bathing, play a most important role in the everyday skin care of children with eczema. **2** Steroid creams. These can completely clear the skin, but excessive use leads to side-effects: thinning of the skin, and an increased risk of infection. If too strong a cream is used for too long, there is even a risk of the steroid being absorbed into the body, causing serious side-effects. Thus the weakest cream or ointment that proves effective for your child should be used. One per cent hydrocortisone is the weakest, and is often effective in mild eczema. It is available over-the-counter in many countries. Nothing stronger should be used on the face, except under medical supervision.

Stronger steroids (for example betamethasone) may be prescribed for limited use, for localized angry patches and for periods when the skin becomes particularly troublesome. **3** Antihistamines, given as syrup or tablets, relieve itching and, taken before bed, will help the child sleep. This may be of particular importance for the child and parents alike in early infancy. **4** ANTIBIOTICS, usually by mouth, will be prescribed if there is evidence of infection of the skin. Sometimes steroid creams are combined with an antibiotic. See *IMPETIGO*.

■ SELF-HELP Persist with moisturizers – childhood eczema tends to cause a very dry skin, and drying out of the skin tends to make eczema worse. Soaps and detergents can irritate eczema, so avoid them. For affected infants and young children, mittens or gloves may help reduce scratching, especially at night. Dress the child in cotton. Wool and synthetic fibres tend to irritate if worn next to the skin. Clothes, and bedclothes, should be cool and loose: itching is worse when the body is hot. If a child with eczema is shown to have a specific allergy (this is not commonly the case), then allergen avoidance is naturally advisable, as for example in COW'S MILK ALLERGY.

■ DIET For some children, the removal of certain items from the diet may improve the eczema: your doctor will advise you, as it can be harmful to alter a child's diet too drastically. The principal culprit foods include cow's milk, eggs, cheese and chocolate.

■ OUTLOOK Eczema persists through childhood in many children, waxing and waning in severity, so a long-term approach may be needed. Children are naturally sensitive about their appearance, and may need moral support, sometimes including professional psychological help. If in real difficulties, ask to be referred to a skin specialist. Occasionally, it is necessary to admit a child to hospital for a period of intensive treatment. Remember that children with eczema are healthy and normal in other respects, although they do sometimes have the related problems of asthma or hay fever.

EEG RECORDING (ELECTROENCEPHALOGRAM)

A test of brain function, obtained by placing special electrodes on the scalp. The brain's surface electrical discharges are detected, and through a system of amplification are transcribed on to paper as a wave pattern. The equipment is expensive, and the technique requires specialized training for performance and interpretation.

Miniaturization of electronics has allowed ambulatory monitoring: the leads from the scalp electrodes are connected to a tape recorder worn on a belt. The child's EEG can thereby be monitored over periods of hours as he walks about freely. The EEG tape can then be played back for detailed study.

EEG is commonly used in childhood to confirm the diagnosis of EPILEPSY, and characterize its type and source. The diagnostic value of EEG may be enhanced by asking the child to breathe deeply and to look at a flashing chequer board or lamp. Sleep recordings may also be helpful. The test is safe and painless, and can be used at any age from birth onwards. With reassurance, most children co-operate happily.

ELECTRIC SHOCK

Electric shock can cause a variety of injuries from superficial BURNS to FRACTURES and widespread internal damage. The most immediately serious threat may be that the heart will stop beating. See *EMERGENCY RESUSCITATION*.

■ ACTION 1 Disconnect or switch off the source of electricity. If this is impossible, don't touch either the child or any conductive surfaces – such as metal – that are in contact with him, or you may also receive a shock. If necessary, use a broom handle or some other non-conductive object (for example, anything made of wood), to dislodge him from the source of electricity. 2 Assess the situation – see *EMERGENCY RE-SUSCITATION*. If breathing and pulse are absent follow steps A, B and C. **3** Look for burns at the entry and exit sites of the electric shock. For emergency treatment, see BURNS. All burns caused as a result of a shock should be assessed by a doctor, since internal damage may well exceed the extent of the superficial burn.

▓ ACTION AT HOSPITAL If necessary, the child will be resuscitated. Burns and internal injuries will then be assessed and treated.

▓ OUTLOOK depends on the severity of the shock and the extent of the injuries.

EMERGENCY RESUSCITATION
▓ IMMEDIATE ACTION IN A LIFE-THREATENING EMERGENCY **1** Make sure there is no further danger to you or to the child. **2** Call for assistance to help with resuscitation. **3** Call an ambulance.

▓ OUTLOOK Best if resuscitation starts immediately and the child responds fairly quickly. But never be in doubt that it is worth trying to resuscitate, even if it seems to you to be too late.

▓ ASSESS THE SITUATION What has happened to the child? See *DROWNING, CHOKING, BURNS AND SCALDS, SUFFOCATION, POISONING* for appropriate first-aid measures. If there could be damage to the neck, only move the child if absolutely necessary. If you *must* move the child, and no trained person is present, summon help and support the child's neck, head and shoulders at all times. Unless the neck is kept im-

mobile, there is a risk of causing damage to the spinal cord, which might result in paralysis. See the illustrations of blanket lift and manual lift.

Next, look at the whole child and try to observe problems:
– Is the child breathing? Listen for sounds of breathing, look and feel for the rise and fall of the chest. If breathing is noisy and difficult, see *CHOKING*. If there is no breathing, follow steps A, B and C below.
– Is there a pulse? Try feeling for the radial pulse, at the wrist near the base of the thumb; or the brachial pulse, on the inner surface of the straightened arm at the level of the elbow; or the carotid pulse, felt in the neck, below and inwards from the angle of the jaw. Alternatively listen to the heart over the central and left side of the front of the chest. If there is no pulse, follow steps A, B and C below.
– Is the child unconscious? If so, turn him on to his side in the RECOVERY POSITION, with his head and mouth tilted towards the floor. If the child is sick, vomit will be more likely to spill out of his mouth and not be inhaled. Contine to check that breathing and pulse remain satisfactory.
– Is the child bleeding? Use firm pressure to control bleeding. See *CUTS AND GRAZES*. Preferably apply a pad of clean material, but if unavailable, use firm hand pressure over the wound. Steps A, B and C can best be learnt by attending a first-aid course.

Step A: Clear the airway. Lie the child flat on his back, choosing a firm surface. Clear the mouth of vomit and/or any other obstructing matter. Tilt the head back and support the chin.

EMERGENCY RESUSCITATION

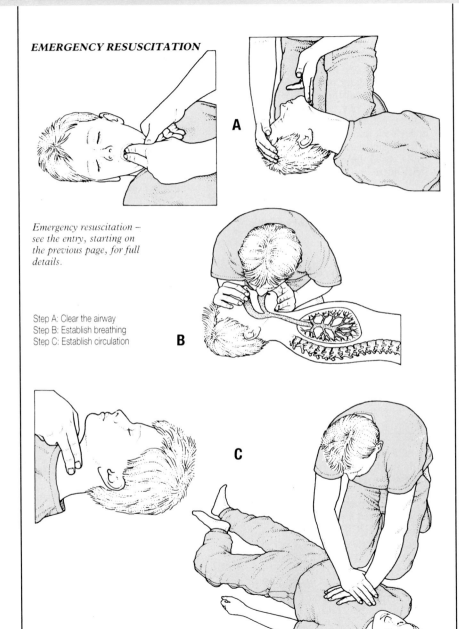

*Emergency resuscitation –
see the entry, starting on
the previous page, for full
details.*

Step A: Clear the airway
Step B: Establish breathing
Step C: Establish circulation

Step B: Establish breathing. If step A does not start the child breathing, begin artificial ventilation. 1 Squeeze nose shut. 2 Cover mouth of child with your mouth. 3 Breathe into child's mouth. Take care not to blow; 'breathe' really does mean what it says: gently exhale from the base of your lungs. If the casualty is a baby, cover both nose and mouth with your mouth. Breathe four times, then check for pulse. Check that the chest moves as you breathe into the child. If chest wall is not moving, repeat step A and consider whether an object has been inhaled. See *CHOKING*.

Step C: Establish circulation. If no pulse is felt, start cardiac massage immediately. Make sure the child is on a firm surface. If the casualty is a baby, use your hands quite forcibly to depress the sternum (breastbone). Give 100 compressions a minute. Allow a pause between compressions (think to yourself 'press and press and press'). Give a mouth to mouth breath (step B) every five compressions.

For older children, you will need to press more forcibly. Avoid fracturing a rib, but remember you are trying to squeeze the heart and make it pump the circulation.

What to expect at hospital: The child's vital supply of oxygen to the blood (and hence brain) will be enhanced by delivering oxygen through a mask. The hospital staff may also try intubation: a tube passed through the mouth (or nose) into the lungs to deliver a supply of oxygen directly to the airways. An intravenous drip will be set up to supply essential fluid and/or drugs. An ECG will monitor heart function. Defibrillation – an electric shock to the heart – may be needed

to restore proper function. When these essential life-support systems are running, attention will then be directed to the cause of the collapse.

ENCEPHALITIS
An acute dysfunctional illness of the brain. Causes include viral infections, biochemical abnormalities (for example in liver failure), REYE'S SYNDROME (probably related to treating viral infections with ASPIRIN). An encephalitic illness may also rarely follow two or three weeks after a viral infection or, *extremely* rarely, IMMUNIZATION against WHOOPING COUGH.

ENCOPRESIS
See *SOILING*.

ENEMA
An enema is a liquid inserted into the lower bowel through the anus from a container with a nozzle. It usually consists of a softening agent to relieve CONSTIPATION, but may contain medication for other conditions, for example, corticosteroids for ULCERATIVE COLITIS. A barium enema is used in a radiological procedure to outline the lower bowel to show, for instance, the extent of inflammatory bowel disease (ulcerative colitis), or to identify and reduce an INTUSSUSCEPTION.

ENURESIS
See *BEDWETTING, WETTING, URINARY TRACT INFECTION*.

EPIDURAL ANAESTHETIC
The injection of anaesthetic drugs into the epidural space - the space surrounding the nerves of the spinal cord. An epidural anaesthetic may be used (in some hospitals more than others)

during labour to relieve painful uterine contractions and to anaesthetize the pelvis if forceps are to be applied. An epidural may also be used in place of a general anaesthetic for a CAESARIAN SECTION.

The woman lies either on her side or leans over forwards. A small area of skin on her lower back is numbed with local anaesthetic and a needle containing a fine plastic tube is inserted into the epidural space. Small amounts of anaesthetic drug are continually infused through the tube.

Epidural anaesthesia gives excellent pain relief but it may prevent the woman pushing effectively, and increase the chance of a FORCEPS delivery. Occasionally an epidural results in a drop in blood pressure; this will require treatment with intravenous fluids and drugs.

EPIGLOTTITIS

A rare, but serious, bacterial INFECTION of the epiglottis causing obstruction to breathing.

■ CAUSE *Haemophillus influenzae*, a BACTERIUM causing various respiratory symptoms.

■ SYMPTOMS The child rapidly becomes unwell and lethargic, with a fever and distressed noisy breathing, with drawing in of the space under the ribs. The throat will be sore, so that he refuses food and drink, and dribbles saliva. Although the condition is similar to CROUP, the dribbling (due to difficulty swallowing saliva) is distinctive. The symptoms differ from those of croup in several other important ways: the noise is more of a rattle, occurring with every breath, not just with the cough; the child is much more feverish and toxic.

■ ACTION 1 Keep the child sitting up, leaning forwards. 2 Summon urgent medical help. *This is an emergency.* If a doctor is not available, send for an ambulance.

■ TREATMENT If the condition is advancing towards obstruction of the airway, then an experienced anaesthetist will be called upon to insert a tube into the child's windpipe, through his mouth or nose. This will be left in place for a few days, allowing him to breathe freely. ANTIBIOTICS (ampicillin or chloramphenicol) will be given, initially by injection or intravenous drip.

EPILEPSY

The experience of recurrent seizures over a period of months or years. There are many types and most start in childhood. Some only occur in children or adolescents. About eight in 1,000 children compared with five in 1,000 adults are epileptic.

■ SYMPTOMS depend on the part of the brain where the seizure discharge begins. In generalized seizures, the onset is sudden with loss of awareness or consciousness (see *GRAND MAL* and *PETIT MAL SEIZURES*). In focal or partial seizures there may be awareness of twitching, pins and needles, flashing lights, odd smells, tummy-ache, a sense of choking, hallucinations, dizziness, inability to talk or confusion, even fear. Such seizures may become generalized or remain focal. (But note that these symptoms have many other causes.)

■ ACTION Place the child having a seizure in the RECOVERY POSITION (see *EMERGENCY RESUSCITATION*) and protect him from danger, especially fire and sharp edges. If you suspect epilepsy, you should of course take your child to the family doctor, who will arrange specialist investigation and advice about treatment. Make a precise note of the circumstances and what happened.

■ INVESTIGATIONS The most helpful information comes from an accurate description of the events by the child and a witness. Provoking factors, for example lack of food or sleep, feeling ill, standing up, watching TV or even just a fright, may help to distinguish between a FAINTING attack and an epileptic seizure. An EEG RECORDING helps to decide between generalized and partial epilepsies. BLOOD and URINE TESTS may be made to look for chemical causes (rare). A scan is only helpful if symptoms, seizure type and an EEG suggest a focal cause, or if other physical findings are present. Skull X-ray rarely shows the cause of epilepsy, but may show signs of uneven growth of the brain in older children.

■ CAUSES Everyone has a seizure threshold. Children with epilepsy have a lower threshold than average, but why one suffers from epilepsy and another does not is often impossible to answer. Two-thirds of children with epilepsy are otherwise normal. Seizure threshold is lowered by structural brain disease associated with mental retardation (see MENTAL HANDICAP), CEREBRAL PALSY or HYDROCEPHALUS, and a third of children affected by those problems will have epilepsy (compared with one in 200 children with no neurological disability). Epilepsy does not cause these disabilities to appear – it is a symptom of them. It is not infectious. There are some specific genetic causes of epilepsy, but the genetic risk is low – about 3 to 5 per cent of children with epilepsy have an affected parent. Genetic risk is higher for generalized than for partial seizures. If no obvious cause is found, the epilepsy is described as idiopathic.

■ TREATMENT Ensure that the child, relatives and teachers understand the problem. Promote a regular and healthy lifestyle and deal with worries. Consider medication if seizures are frequent or prolonged (usually anticonvulsant tablets twice daily for two to five years). Drugs control generalized seizures in 80 per cent of children and partial seizures in 50 per cent but the greater the associated disability, the harder it is to find effective drugs.

■ SELF-HELP Regular and sufficient sleep, meals and recreation will probably help. Encourage the child to develop his talents. He can learn to swim under supervision, and cycle off busy roads. He should wear a necklace or bracelet if seizures are likely outside the home. Check if drugs for other conditions interact. Avoid alcohol. Consider anti-smother pillows. Consider showers rather than unsupervised baths. Join a self-help group or the national association.

■ OUTLOOK depends on type and frequency of seizures and associated disabilities. Best chances of recovery are with idiopathic generalized and benign partial seizures, when few seizures have occurred and the child is otherwise well. Altogether, a third of children with epilepsy recover, a third continue with seizures but are treated successfully with drugs, and a third have incompletely controlled seizures in adult life. Social attitudes to epilepsy are improving slowly.

Future employment prospects depend on seizure type, frequency and associated disabilities. Advice should be sought in childhood to avoid unrealistic expectations at school-leaving age. *The Epilepsy Reference Book* by Peter M. Jeavons and Alec Aspinall (Harper and Row, 1985) is useful reading.

EPISTAXIS (BLEEDING FROM THE NOSE)
See *NOSEBLEED*.

EXCHANGE TRANSFUSION
The replacement of much of the blood in the body. This is usually performed if a new-born baby has a rising concentration in his blood of bilirubin (see JAUNDICE). A small amount of the baby's blood will be slowly drawn out from a large blood vessel - usually the UMBILICAL vein. The same amount is then replaced by donor blood. This procedure is repeated many times until the washout or exchange transfusion is judged to be complete.

EXTERNAL EAR INFECTION
Uncommon in children, this is an IN-FECTION of the skin lining the outer part of the ear, up to the eardrum. It can be confused with a MIDDLE EAR IN-FECTION.

■ SYMPTOMS The ear may be blocked by a mixture of WAX and discharge, leading to DEAFNESS. Itching is often a feature, especially if the child also has ECZEMA.

■ ACTION Any child with these symptoms should be seen by a doctor, both to find out exactly what is causing it, and for treatment.

■ TREATMENT The discharge or wax may be gently removed by syringing, although some children find this too frightening. ANTIBIOTIC ear-drops or ointment are commonly prescribed.

■ OUTLOOK If the problem recurs, there might be an underlying skin disorder such as eczema. Usually the infection settles quickly, with treatment.

EYE, FOREIGN BODY IN
See the illustration showing how to examine a child's eye.

If a foreign body, or indeed an eyelash, is stuck on the white part of the eye, it is worth giving the child's tears (a normal response to the irritation) a chance to wash it out naturally: blinking and blowing the nose may assist the process. Try to dissuade your child from rubbing his eye.

If this does not work, and the particle is not stuck fast, lift it off using a damp corner of a clean handkerchief.

If the foreign body overlies the coloured part of the eye (the iris), don't try to remove it. Cover the child's eye with a clean pad or persuade him to keep his eyes closed, and take him to a hospital casualty department. If an object is embedded anywhere on the eyeball (see *EYE INJURY*), don't try to remove it; take the child straight to hospital.

If a foreign body is caught under the upper lid, ask the child to look down. Grip the eyelashes of the upper lid and pull the lid out and down. The lower lid lashes may brush the particle off. If this fails, you may be able to persuade your child to blink under water, when the irritant may float off.

If this fails, cover the eye with a pad and get medical advice.

If in doubt, always get professional advice. Untreated, a minor eye injury may progress to become serious.

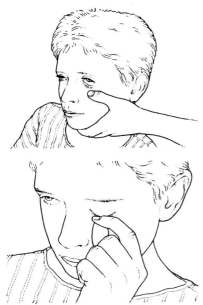

Top, *pulling down lower lid to examine eye and* **above,** *action for object under lower lid.*

EYE INJURY

See the illustration showing how to examine a child's eye at EYE, FOREIGN BODY IN.

Obvious damage or penetration of the eye by an object requires urgent medical treatment. Internal damage may lead to infection and blindness. Cover the eye with a clean pad: this helps to prevent the child moving the eyeball and worsening the damage. If the child will allow it, cover the good eye too: this makes movement even less likely. Alternatively, ask your child to keep his eyes closed.

It may be difficult to know whether an object has actually penetrated the eye. If in any doubt, get urgent medical advice.

Chemicals in eye: Act quickly to prevent damage to the eye's surface. Don't let the child rub his eye.

Hold the eye open under running water (from a tap or jug). If the eyelid is shut as a reaction to the pain, you should nevertheless try firmly to hold the lids open to allow irrigation. Dress the eye lightly with a clean pad. Alternatively, ask your child to keep his eyes closed. Take the child to hospital without delay.

EYELID, SWOLLEN
See *BLEPHARITIS, ALLERGY.*

EYE TESTS
These are important because visual disorders in childhood are relatively common; untreated, they may result in learning difficulties.

Children are more likely to have eyesight problems if there is a family history of SQUINT or LAZY EYE, or if they were born very PREMATURELY.

To measure the vision of a child requires patience and skill. A baby's eyesight may be assessed by his ability to follow a moving light or object. A toddler may be asked to match shapes or toys with others at a distance. After three years, single letters or shapes on cards can be used.

■ TESTS FOR SPECTACLES On the basis of the above tests, an eye specialist may decide that your child is either LONG- or SHORT-SIGHTED, or that he has a more complex focusing problem, or a squint. Further examinations are required to fit the correct SPECTACLES.

Tests for older children are the same as for adults. Different lenses are fitted into a frame, and the child is asked to look at a chart and say which lens gives the clearest picture.

As eyesight changes with age, eye tests need to be performed regularly, and the lens prescription of the spectacles must be adjusted accordingly.

FAILURE TO THRIVE

A usefully vague medical term for infants who are lacking in vitality and failing to gain weight normally. See *GROWTH PATTERNS*. In well-baby clinics, it is usual good practice for babies to be weighed regularly to check whether they are growing at a normal rate. If a baby fails to gain weight normally, or loses weight, this calls for close attention: is this a pointer to ill-health or undernutrition? If the baby is otherwise well, you may simply be encouraged to feed your baby more often (breast or bottle), and increase the energy (calorie) content of solid (weaning) foods in his diet. If weight gain is still poor, or the child is otherwise unwell – that is failing to thrive – then your doctor will refer you to a paediatrician for a specialist opinion and possible investigations.

▓ TESTS It is unusual for a single or simple test to resolve the child's problem. The specialist will want to take a broad view of all aspects of your child's development. You will be asked questions about his birth weight, diet, behaviour and development; and about family relationships and the dynamics of your household. Special tests may be performed to rule out particular conditions. Examples might include a URINE TEST to look for urinary INFECTION; a stool sample to search for PARASITES such as *Giardia* in the bowel; BLOOD TESTS for hormonal problems such as an underactive thyroid gland; a 'sweat test' for cystic fibrosis; an examination of the upper bowel for evidence of COELIAC DISEASE.

▓ OUTLOOK Many specific causes of failure to thrive respond well to treatment. It is often the case, however, that the child turns out to be essentially healthy but displaying a pattern of transient slow growth; in which case, apart from your natural concern, the outlook is excellent.

FAINTING

A transient form of unconsciousness equally common in boys and girls, caused by transient inadequate blood circulation to the brain.

▓ CAUSES Fainting occurs typically when standing in a warm room, or when experiencing something unpleasant or after a fright.

▓ ACTION Allow the child to lie flat on the floor. Recovery will follow naturally and speedily.

▓ SELF-HELP If a child is prone to recurrent fainting when standing, teach him how to contract his leg muscles: this may prevent fainting.

▓ OUTLOOK Fainting is rarely significant. It may require investigation if it occurs during vigorous exercise, or in association with palpitations. It can be confused with EPILEPSY.

FALLOT'S TETRALOGY

See *CONGENITAL HEART-DISEASE*.

FALLS

See *CLUMSINESS, CONVULSIONS*.

FAMILY PROBLEMS

Almost any family problem will affect children, even if they are not the cause. Children are sensitive to, and react to, changes or upset feelings in their parents, whether or not they know or can understand the cause.

■ PROBLEMS OUTSIDE THE
FAMILY Unemployment, or the
threat of it, moving house, illness in
a grandparent or family friend,
BEREAVEMENT, money worries,
changes or upheavals in the community or school, racial harassment:
all these may affect your child indirectly through their effect on you,
or directly from what the child
reads, hears or sees. Don't pretend
these things are not happening. Try
to explain in a reassuring way what
is causing the worry and what you
are feeling and doing as a result.
Give what reassurance you can
about what will *not* change: various
routines, your love, affection and
protection for the child.

Try to consider *his* level of understanding. You may need to spell out
several times everything which remains normal, and how the child
should cope with any change.

■ PROBLEMS WITHIN THE
FAMILY Marital unhappiness,
separation, DIVORCE or remarriage,
illness or the need for medical investigation, problems with the law:
all will produce stress in parents and
this will affect a child. Give a simple
and straightforward explanation,
tailored to his age and understanding. Your child may show ANXIETY
or STRESS SYMPTOMS, SLEEP or FEED-
ING PROBLEMS or BEHAVIOURAL DIS-
ORDERS, or SCHOOL ATTENDANCE
PROBLEMS. These can all be kept to a
minimum if you explain what is happening and as far as possible avoid
disrupting routines.

Sometimes a problem with one
child can affect the others. Illness or
school difficulties, step families,
problems of adolescence are all
typical culprits. Sometimes you may
need to reassure the other children
that this problem will not necessarily beset them, or, conversely, that

you still love them even though you
are preoccupied with the child in
difficulty. Make special efforts not
to forget children who are *not* causing anxiety. The symptoms a child
may show in these circumstances
will vary with age.

■ ACTION Air problems if at all possible. Talk about it together, read
the relevant section in this book, or,
or if it persists, see your doctor who
will suggest other sources of help.

FAMILY THERAPY
A form of treatment which enables
families to sort out problems, usually
identified with, or brought to light by,
one of the children. It is based on the
premise that difficulties in family relationships are associated with psychological problems, and that they can
best be helped by involving all members of the family concerned. Family
therapy may also help when one family
member has a problem, but the family
as a whole can be of general help and
support. This can be a powerful way of
effecting change. It is practised by a
range of professionals including psychologists, social workers and child
psychiatrists. Often more than one therapist will be involved. In a broader
sense, however, most professionals
working with children admit the importance of the family. See also
*FAMILY PROBLEMS, BEHAV-
IOURAL TREATMENTS.*

FEARS
Fear is a natural and self-protective in-
stinct, which all children develop
naturally as part of their own self-
defence. During the first few years all
children have frights and develop
fears; normally they acquire the confidence to deal with them unaided. See
also *ANXIETY* and *PHOBIAS.*

FEBRILE CONVULSIONS

Usually generalized (rather than focal) CONVULSIONS of sudden onset in association with a FEVER in susceptible infants and young children from six months to five years, but mostly under three years. They need to be distinguished from FAINTING attacks and rigors during febrile illnesses.

They can run in families, and boys appear to be more susceptible than girls.

■ ACTION Place the child in the RECOVERY POSITION. When he recovers, give frequent drinks (typically, half cup of milk or juice per hour during the waking day) and paracetamol (two 5 ml doses three times per day) to reduce fever. Don't give aspirin – see *REYE'S SYNDROME*. Future febrile illnesses should be treated in the same way to reduce risk of febrile convulsions. See *FEVER*. There is some risk of BRAIN DAMAGE if the convulsion lasts for more than 30 minutes. Get medical help immediately if a convulsion continues for ten minutes or longer. Always get medical advice when an infant under 18 months has a febrile convulsion, in case it is a first sign of MENINGITIS.

■ TREATMENT Anticonvulsant drugs will not prevent recurrences, and they have side effects.

■ OUTLOOK Most febrile convulsions are brief and harmless, though alarming to parents who may even think the child has died. If a child has had one febrile convulsion, there is a one in three risk of it happening again. A third of children who have had two will go on to experience another. About 5 per cent of all children experience at least one febrile convulsion, but only one in 50 of those go on to experience EPILEPSY in later childhood.

FEEDING PROBLEMS

These tend to occur at times of change – see WEANING. The baby (or toddler) simply finds the next stage of development tiresome or difficult. VOMITING or regurgitating is often associated with the introduction of solids. In three-year-olds and above, the problems are usually faddiness, poor appetite or overeating.

■ CAUSES Almost all day-to-day feeding problems are to do with difficult behaviour rather than poor health. They usually arise for a combination of reasons:

The child may be eating enough, despite what parents think. Particularly for toddlers, food can provide an ideal opportunity to assert independence.

Suspecting a child may not be getting adequate nourishment causes anxiety; anxiety leads to pressure on the child to eat: a battle of wills with the child in an ideal position to win. Deliberate vomiting is often associated with this conflict.

Children, like adults, can be conservative in their tastes and may dislike trying new food. They do become more willing to try out new foods as they grow older.

Meal times in many families provide an opportunity for demonstrating individuality in public through food choice. Having something prepared especially for you is not only a treat; it is a useful and comforting demonstration of parental attention.

■ AVOIDING PROBLEMS Have a routine; take meals in a relaxed atmosphere – let the child eat at his own pace; encourage independence, and allow likes and dislikes, without over-indulging.

– Make a game of persuading the child to eat, rather than fussing, cajoling, threatening or bribing.

– Avoid battles: remove food if it is not eaten after two or three attempts at gentle encouragement. But don't reward the child's refusal with sweets or ice-cream to follow.

– Put too little, rather than too much, on the child's dish or plate. He can always be offered more if it is finished.

■ ACTION If you are really worried that the child is not eating properly, ask yourself or check with the family doctor, whether he is gaining weight at the normal rate for his age and height. Try recording everything that your child eats and drinks, not just at meal times. It may be more than you think.

If weaning a child, don't allow him to make up for uneaten food with milk. Reduce his milk intake and give other drinks instead. Give him a baby beaker or cup instead of the bottle. Gradually increase the consistency of food, offer finger foods, and allow him to do as much for himself as he wants.

Don't feel that you always have to cook alternatives for poor or faddy eaters. Discourage eating between meals and encourage your child always to try a little of anything new.

Get medical advice if vomiting seems related to illness or occurs at most meals.

The advice of a clinical psychologist may be suggested if severe feeding problems persist. It may be necessary for him or her to come and observe the problem during meal-times at home.

See also *WEANING, OBES-ITY, ANOREXIA NERVOSA, FAILURE TO THRIVE, BREAST FEEDING, BOTTLE FEEDING.*

FEVER

A temperature of more than 98.4°F or 37°C. The most common causes of fever are VIRAL and BACTERIAL INFEC-TIONS. However, a fever may also be a sign of a less common underlying general disease, such as inflammation of the joints (ARTHRITIS) or bowels (CROHN'S DISEASE). The child feels generally unwell and may appear miserable and irritable. If the temperature is rising steeply, he may shiver and feel cold; if the temperature is steady or falling, he may look red, sweat and feel hot. Other symptoms may be associated depending on the cause of the fever.

■ ACTION 1 The term fever is rather dramatic. If it is mild (say up to 101°F or 38.5°C), then probably no action is called for other than loosening the child's clothing.

The higher the temperature, the more important it is for the child to be seen by a doctor. After all, the fever is a symptom or sign to an underlying disease, and treatment may confuse the picture for the doctor.

Nevertheless, the child will feel more miserable the higher the temperature, and on these grounds there is a case for trying to reduce the fever (preferably after consultation with the doctor). The exception to this general approach is the child who has had a fit or convulsion with a fever. In such children, up to the age of six years or so, there is a case for bringing the temperature down as quickly and effectively as possible. Certainly undress the child, at least. For infants under two years of age, who may be at risk of a first FEBRILE CONVULSION, there is a case for unclothing, sponging and anti-pyretics.

But remember: fever is not a disease; it is a pointer to a disease.

Paracetamol is the safest and most effective fever treatment (antipyretic). Aspirin should *not* be given to a child under 12 years old, because of the risk of REYE'S SYNDROME. The dose of paracetamol will vary with the age of the child, and is shown on the bottle. It may be given up to every four hours. **2** A cool bath is an effective way of treating fever. It is best to put your child into a warm bath and gradually lower the temperature by adding cold water. The child remains in the bath for 15 minutes or so. It may be necessary to repeat the cool bath during the night as he is likely to sleep more easily if his temperature is brought down. **3** Dress your child in light clothing to make heat loss from his body easier. **4** Encourage your child to drink clear fluids. This is generally comforting and avoids dehydration.

■ GET MEDICAL ADVICE if the fever continues or recurs, or is very high (say over 102°F or 39°C), or if your child is irritable or has other symptoms.

The doctor will advise additional treatment or tests depending on the pattern and duration of the fever, and the constellation of associated features. Tests may range from urine culture (for suspect URINARY TRACT INFECTION), chest X-ray (for suspect PNEUMONIA) to a lumbar puncture (for suspect MENINGITIS).

FINGER INJURIES

Hands and fingers are precious, so injuries need prompt treatment. Don't delay in seeking treatment for anything beyond a small cut – in children as well as adults. The 'pulp spaces' in the fingertips and palms are especially prone to infection, and may need a full course of ANTIBIOTICS. Tendon injuries are another common problem,

so get medical advice if the hand doesn't seem to work properly after an injury, or if there is any numbness which may indicate damage to nerves. Whether you attend your family doctor or a casualty department at your local hospital, you may be referred on to a special hand clinic where the injury can receive specialist treatment.

FIRE, SETTING ON

Some children find fire fascinating and, if they have the means, will seek to light one. They may do this by copying what they have seen adults do, for instance poking paper into gas fires for a light. Keep matches and cigarette lighters away from children. Teach respect for fire by showing and telling them what they should do, and by doing the same yourself. *Never* leave a young child alone with an unguarded domestic fire. See also *ACCIDENTS IN THE HOME, BEHAVIOURAL TREATMENTS.*

FITS
See *CONVULSIONS.*

FLAT FEET
Common, particularly in children who are overweight. All babies and young children have flat feet until bone growth gives the necessary modelling.

■ SYMPTOMS Loss of the normal arch of the foot, so that the sole is in contact with the ground over its whole length. The heel tilts inwards and the front of the foot turns outwards. Shoes bulge inwards and the heels wear down quickly on the inner side. Sometimes the child also has KNOCK KNEES.

Flat feet are not usually painful, but the child may complain of sore legs or want to avoid rough games.

■ <u>ACTION</u> Usually there is no action necessary. There is a wide range of normal postures and shapes of feet; only the most severe (and therefore the most extreme and obvious) forms of flat foot require treatment. If in doubt, ask your doctor, who may refer your child to an orthopaedic surgeon.

As he grows older, get him to practise picking up things with his toes to develop natural curvature.

■ <u>TREATMENT</u> is not necessary under three years of age. Sometimes it helps to build up the inner side of the shoes. Surgery is rarely recommended and only after the child has stopped growing.

■ <u>OUTLOOK</u> Not a serious problem, unless the child (or later the adult) has to stand a great deal, in which case uneven strain on the muscles may cause pain in the feet.

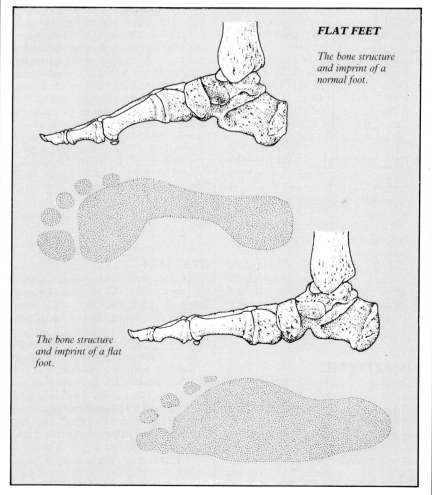

FLAT FEET

The bone structure and imprint of a normal foot.

The bone structure and imprint of a flat foot.

FLU
See *INFLUENZA*.

FLUORIDE
See *TEETHING*.

FOETAL DISTRESS
The foetus is in a state of distress. This may arise from problems of circulation or oxygenization, usually due to problems of placenta function. If the distress is unrelieved, the health and life of the foetus may be in danger.

▓ SIGNS Green-brown staining of the waters (due to the foetus emptying MECONIUM from his bowels as a response to distress): if the waters break at home and are seen to be green-stained, go to hospital immediately. The baby's heart rate changes in response to distress, sometimes rising (to rates greater than 160/min) or, more seriously, falling (to rates below 120/min). Changes in foetal movements may also point to distress, especially if foetal movements become less frequent or stop altogether. If you think your baby has stopped moving, contact your doctor or go to hospital without delay.

▓ TESTS The baby's heart rate can be monitored either by listening in with a trumpet stethoscope or by electronic monitoring (see *DE-LIVERY*). If foetal distress is suspected, a sample of blood may be taken from the foetal scalp. In skilled hands, this is harmless to the baby, and a minimally discomforting procedure for the mother. The blood is then analysed for acidity: the more acidic, the greater the severity of the foetal distress.

▓ ACTION Your obstetrician, often in consultation with a paediatrician, will decide whether any immediate action is called for. Often careful observation as pregnancy or delivery progresses is all that is indicated. At other times, particularly if the pointers are to severe distress, the decision may be made to deliver your baby urgently, by forceps or Caesarian section.

▓ OUTLOOK In the majority of cases, the baby comes to no harm, and is well at birth and thereafter. Occasionally distress proceeds to asphyxia: if delivered, the baby will then need vigorous skilled resuscitation; if undelivered, the foetus is in danger of dying.

FONTANELLES
The gaps or soft areas between the bones of the baby's skull. There are two: one at the front, of about ½-one in (15-30 mm) in diameter in the newborn period, which closes when the baby is around 18 months old; and a second, smaller fontanelle at the back of the skull, which closes in the early weeks after birth.

The size of the fontanelles varies greatly. They allow the brain to continue to grow rapidly, as it does in the first year or so after birth.

FONTANELLES

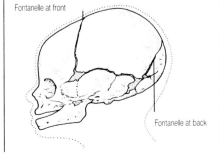

Fontanelle at front

Fontanelle at back

FOOD ALLERGY

A form of food intolerance, which is an unpleasant, adverse reaction to a specific food or ingredient. It can occur repeatedly. Examples include LACTOSE and SUGAR INTOLERANCE and reactions to FOOD ADDITIVES. Such reactions are typically unexpected when they first occur and entirely different to a child's psychological attitude to a food he may, for reasons of his own, dislike.

In true food allergy there is definite evidence of an abnormal immunological reaction to food (see *ALLERGY* and *IMMUNITY*). But this is, as yet, a poorly understood and in some respects controversial subject.

■ CAUSE See *ALLERGY*. The body tends to develop sensitivity between the first and second exposure to the substance; so the reaction occurs the second time the food is eaten. The commonest food allergens affecting children are cow's milk, egg, dairy products, cereals, fish, nuts, chicken meat, vegetables, fruit and drugs, but see also *ADDITIVES IN FOOD*.

There are two types of reactions:

Immediate reaction is within one hour of eating. People with a family history of allergy are prone to such reactions.

Delayed reactions take hours or days to develop. A common example is ECZEMA.

■ SYMPTOMS of immediate reaction include wheezing, sneezing, coughing, runny nose, itching and OEDEMA. The gravest of all is anaphylactic shock – see *ALLERGY*.

Symptoms of delayed reaction can affect different parts of the body:

Respiratory symptoms include rhinitis (see *HAY FEVER*), recurrent mild chestiness, swelling of the lips or occasionally the mouth.

Gastro-intestinal symptoms include heartburn, flatulence, indigestion, repeated abdominal pain and diarrhoea.

Neurological symptoms include headaches, tiredness, convulsions, hyperactivity and depression.

Musculo-skeletal symptoms tend to be vague aches and pains. Together with these there may also be vomiting, diarrhoea, croup, bronchitis, asthma, eczema, colic and FAILURE TO THRIVE. URTICARIA occurs occasionally. Sore throats and earache may be due to allergy, but this is disputed.

■ ACTION If symptoms suggest food allergy, see the family doctor.

■ INVESTIGATIONS include skin tests, blood tests, jejunal biopsy and challenge tests.

■ TREATMENT As might be expected, the mainstay of treatment is avoiding the allergen. With immediate allergy this is often readily identifiable, and avoiding the culprit food is easy. But children can have allergies to several foods, some of them constituents of commercially prepared foods. In such cases parents need a knowledge of diet to ensure exclusion.

FOOD POISONING

Acute DIARRHOEA and VOMITING caused by food-borne toxins produced by BACTERIA in contaminated food. Meat that has been inadequately cooked or stored without refrigeration, and had limited reheating, or cream and pastry are typical culprits. Several members of the family are likely to be afflicted at once.

■ SYMPTOMS Rapidity of onset depends on the bacteria involved. Vomiting, ABDOMINAL PAIN and profuse diarrhoea occur two to seven hours after staphylococcal food poisoning, and last one day. Symptoms due to *Bacillus cereus* or *Clostridium perfringens* (botulism) occur seven to 24 hours after eating the contaminated food.

■ ACTION Get medical advice if your child develops acute and severe symptoms (see *GASTROENTERITIS*). Admission to hospital may well be required. ANTIBIOTICS and other drugs are not usually given.

■ TREATMENT Oral or intravenous fluids to correct DEHYDRATION. Antitoxin injections and ventilation may be necessary for the rare peripheral nerve complications of botulism, which affect the control mechanisms of respiration.

■ OUTLOOK Most cases of food poisoning are mild. Even in severe cases, early treatment limits the risk of death. See the entry on *GASTROENTERITIS*.

FOOT INJURIES
Apart from SPRAINS AND STRAINS, the most common injuries to the feet are caused by dropping heavy objects on to them. Symptoms may well include BLEEDING, BRUISING, or possibly FRACTURES. The worst of the swelling and pain of the injury will start to subside after two days unless there is a fracture, in which case the child may still be unable to walk on the affected foot. Fractures of the bones of the foot are uncommon in childhood, but you may wish to take your child to a casualty department for an X-ray, just in case. Fractures of the small bones of the toes can occur, but are usually treated with strapping or left to heal by themselves. Fractures of the ankle may occur in older children. These need prompt treatment and immobilization

in plaster to ensure full recovery.

■ ACTION Use hot and cold compresses for pain at the site of injury. A painkiller such as paracetamol will also help. If the child is unable to put any weight on the foot after 24 hours, or if there is marked swelling or bleeding, then it makes sense to get medical advice in order to be sure there is no fracture.

FORCEPS
Spoon-shaped instruments placed either side of a baby's head to aid DELIVERY. Forceps delivery may be used to facilitate the delivery of the baby when there is FOETAL DISTRESS, or if the baby has difficulty in descending through the birth canal, or if the mother is judged to need help in the second stage of labour, when she is pushing with the contractions of the uterus. The mother's legs are put in stirrups and she is given a local anaesthetic if she has not already had an EPIDURAL ANAESTHETIC. An EPISIOTOMY is usually performed, the forceps slipped round the baby's head, and then pulled gently but firmly as the mother pushes with each contraction. Forceps delivery rarely results in BIRTH INJURY. Sometimes marks are visible on the baby's face which disappear in 24 hours.

FORCEPS DELIVERY

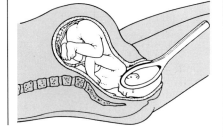

FRACTURES

This is the medical term for broken bones. The pliability of young bones, however, means that they may often bend rather than break, hence the term greenstick fracture.

You may also hear the term undisplaced fracture: one in which the normal line of the bone is not changed by the fracture, and the two ends remain in contact.

▦ SYMPTOMS There has usually been an obvious injury, but this is not always so.

There is pain and swelling or other deformity over the place where the bone is fractured. The pain may be severe, and aggravated by the slightest movement.

The child is usually extremely relucant to move the limb.

Sometimes the pain is not particularly bad because the fracture is stable: there is not much movement at the site of the fracture when the bone is not being used, or indeed on slight movement. Occasionally, the fracture can be so stable that the child continues to use the limb. However, in these cases, there is usually some swelling that does not settle, or slight but persistent pain.

Occasionally, a fracture may be so severe that one end of the bone comes through the skin (an open fracture). This kind of fracture can cause OSTEOMYELITIS.

▦ ACTION The pain can be relieved by keeping the fracture area still. If it is a limb, a sling or splint is helpful.

The swelling can be eased by an application of ice or elevating the limb.

If you suspect a fracture, you should get medical advice or go directly to a hospital where an X-ray can be taken.

FRACTURES

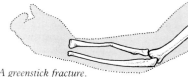

A greenstick fracture.

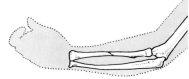

An undisplaced fracture.

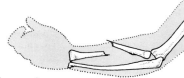

An open fracture.

If there is a chance that your child may need an anaesthetic for an operation to get the bones back into normal position (reduction of the fracture), don't give him anything to eat or drink since this will postpone the anaesthetic. If in doubt, get medical advice.

▦ TESTS X-ray is the common, reliable means of making the diagnosis. It is also useful for checking that the bone is healing normally.

▦ TREATMENT A painkiller such as paracetamol (do not give aspirin – see *REYE'S SYNDROME*) will ease the pain.

Fractures usually require a plaster cast to keep the bone from moving as it heals.

It is important to keep exercising those parts of the injured limb which are not in the plaster cast. This prevents the joints from becoming stiff and the muscles weak.

A child will usually exercise

naturally if it does not cause pain: there is no need to discourage him from doing so.

If his fingers or toes are swollen, encourage him to use them.

Occasionally, a plaster cast becomes too tight because of swelling of the tissue around the fracture a few hours after the plaster cast has been put on. This can affect important arteries and nerves, and is the reason why your child may be kept in hospital overnight after receiving a plaster cast. If you notice that his fingers or toes have become pale or blue, or if he complains of numbness, tingling or severe pain, let the nurse or doctor know immediately and make sure that it is carefully checked.

Some fractures do not need a plaster cast, usually because the fracture is stable. These include fractures of the collar-bone (clavicle) and the bone of the upper arm (humerus).

Fractures of the skull need special treatment because of the risk of damage to the brain.

Fractures heal more quickly in children than in adults, particularly the greenstick type. Healing occurs by the natural production of a bridge of bone between the two broken ends. Extra bridging is needed in bones that take weight, such as the leg, and these take longer to heal.

The bone will only regain its normal strength after several months, but this will happen fastest if the bone is used. Physiotherapy may help.

▨ OUTLOOK Most fractures in children heal completely without any long-term complications.

FRAGILE BONE DISEASE
See *OSTEOGENESIS IMPERFECTA*.

FRIENDS – REAL OR IMAGINARY
Making friends may start as early as the third year, but what the relationship means at this age may of course be different from later on. At this age, or later, when your child's imagination is very rich, he may acquire an imaginary friend, whether or not he has real friends. This friend often seems to have rights and possessions your child would like. Sometimes he, or she, vanishes as a younger brother or sister starts to talk and makes increasingly good company. It is a phase which usually passes naturally and can be regarded as perfectly normal.

FUNGI AND FUNGAL INFECTIONS
In medical terminology, fungi are organisms such as moulds and yeasts. Most fungi are harmless but a few can cause INFECTION, particularly of the skin, hair, nails and the membrane linings of the mouth and vagina. Common fungal infections include THRUSH, ATHLETE'S FOOT and RINGWORM.

Serious or recurrent fungal infections may represent a complication of extensive antibiotic therapy or, rarely, point to an IMMUNE deficiency.

THRUSH, however, expecially in infancy, is common (as a form of NAPPY RASH, for example)

▨ TREATMENT Common thrush is usually cured by a cream or medication. Other fungal infections of skin and nails are more difficult to cure and may need to be treated for several weeks until all the infected tissue, often several layers, has been replaced by healthy tissue.

FUNNEL CHEST
A deep hollow in the centre of the chest.
See *PECTUS EXCAVATUM*.

GALACTOSAEMIA

A condition in which digesting galactose, a form of sugar, results in toxicity symptoms because of an inherited deficiency of an enzyme essential for its metabolism.

▓ SYMPTOMS appear usually soon after birth and within a few days of starting to feed on milk. VOMITING and DIARRHOEA, FAILURE TO THRIVE, prolonged JAUNDICE and enlargement of the liver are all common in the first month of life. In severe cases, the abdomen may become swollen with fluid and the child may develop septicaemia. Some children have CATARACTS (opacities of the lens in the eye) and if the condition is not recognized promptly, brain development will be impaired – see below.

▓ TREATMENT depends on the elimination of galactose from the diet. Completely avoiding it is the goal, but this may be difficult. There are several milk preparations available which are virtually galactose free, including soya milk.

Dietary advice must be followed closely as the child grows. There are lists of permitted foods available, and it is essential that parents become well-versed in dietary do's and don'ts if treatment is to be successful. If an affected child does drink cow's milk or eat foods containing galactose, vomiting and diarrhoea will quickly develop. In the long term, inadequate control of the diet may result in poor growth and MENTAL HANDICAP.

▓ OUTLOOK Those children identified in the first month of life (and correctly treated) will have normal INTELLIGENCE, although minor LEARNING and BEHAVIOURAL DISORDERS may develop later. Close psychological follow-up is advisable: minor problems can be dealt with early, and the child motivated to keep up dietary control.

Children diagnosed late, or whose dietary control is poor, may be below average intelligence and have problems with perception. Girls may be infertile.

GASTROENTERITIS

A common condition of infants and toddlers: it usually consists of DIARRHOEA accompanied by VOMITING coming on quite suddenly, and lasting a few days. Usually caused by VIRUSES of various types, and passed from one person to another through physical contact, or as droplets in the air. In the U.K., epidemics are usually limited to nurseries, hospital wards and schools.

▓ ACTION Keep the child away from others (especially from other small infants) until the worst is over. Don't worry if the child has no appetite – a few days without solid food will do him no harm. But it is important to maintain an adequate fluid intake to compensate for the fluid losses in the faeces and vomit – see DEHYDRATION. This is the most significant danger of gastroenteritis. Concentrate on encouraging the child to have frequent drinks of clear fluids, despite the vomiting. The necessary fluids and salts are rapidly absorbed, so even if the child vomits soon after a drink, some will have been retained in the body.

Traditionally, milk is considered to be poorly tolerated by the bowel in gastroenteritis; however, for the breast-fed baby, it is often preferable to continue breast feeding.

If the symptoms continue for more than a day or so, or if your baby shows other signs of illness or dehydration, then get medical advice. The smaller or younger your baby, the sooner you should see your doctor.

▓ TREATMENT Most doctors do not give medicines to sedate or slow down the bowel; the emphasis is on maintaining your baby's fluid intake while allowing the body's natural defences to eliminate the virus.

▓ OUTLOOK This is a common illness, and recovery is normally complete within ten days. Appetite then improves and the child eats normally and puts on weight. Occasionally, following a severe bout of gastroenteritis, there is a period of LACTOSE INTOLERANCE, in which case milk and milk-containing foods continue to be poorly absorbed and to cause diarrhoea. If these are avoided for a few weeks, complete recovery follows.

GENES

Biological codes containing the inherited characteristics are passed on from parent to child. Every body cell, except the spermatozoa and ova, has 23 pairs of CHROMOSOMES, and each chromosome carries hundreds of genes. Each gene has a matching gene on the other chromosome of a pair. For every inherited characteristic, a child inherits one gene from one parent and another gene from the other parent. Genes responsible for a particular characteristic can be dominant or recessive. If the child inherits one gene for blue eyes and one for brown, then he will, generally, have brown eyes: the gene for brown eyes is dominant over the gene for blue eyes. Deficiencies or abnormalities in the chemical structure of genes can result in disease, which can be passed on in this way from parent to child. These are called INHERITED DISORDERS.

GENETIC COUNSELLING

Genetic counselling is of value if you have a family history of a particular disease, or if you have a child with an INHERITED DISORDER or CONGENITAL ABNORMALITY. Genetic counselling aims to explain the nature of an inherited disorder – its severity, treatment, complications and likely outcome – as well as the genetic mechanisms which cause the disease; most important, it also aims to define and advise upon the risk of the disease recurring in future pregnancies. The calculation of the risk is based on a variety of factors, including the recognized disease frequency in relatives of the child. Whether or not you decide to embark upon future pregnancies will depend on the severity of the disease and your attitude to the disease; additionally, in the case of a disease that can be identified in pregnancy, you would be helped to decide your own attitude towards termination of a pregnancy. Specific tests may be used to determine the risk of a particular disease in a family. Physical examination and BLOOD TESTS may indicate whether relatives are carriers of the disease. Research in this field is expanding rapidly, but we are a long way from being able to test for all genetically inherited diseases in this way.

If the risk of a recurrence of the disease is unacceptably high to you, you will need to discuss such matters as contraception, and the possibilities of adoption or artificial insemination by donor. If you are already pregnant, ANTENATAL DIAGNOSTIC tests may ascertain whether or not the foetus is affected, and termination of the pregnancy can then be considered.

GERMAN MEASLES

The common name for the viral infection *RUBELLA*. See that entry.

GIARDIA

Giardia lamblia is a PARASITE which inhabits the small bowel (see diagram of intestine, page 12), and interferes with absorption of food (see *MALABSORPTION*). The INFECTION can be contracted in this country from infected water or food; the risk is higher in, but not restricted to, tropical, developing countries.

■ SYMPTOMS may come on gradually, with the child eating poorly, being tired and irritable and losing weight. The faeces may be loose, pale and float in the lavatory pan because of non-absorbed fats. However, the symptoms may be more severe, with nausea, vomiting or stomach-ache, as in GASTROENTERITIS. Others in the family may be similarly affected.

■ TESTS *Giardia* may be detected in stool samples examined by a microbiologist. However, many samples may need to be studied to find the parasite.

■ ACTION Make sure everyone washes their hands thoroughly after going to the lavatory. (This is, of course, normal good health practice, but especially important if a member of the household has diarrhoea.) Get medical advice if your child is acutely unwell or the symptoms are seen to continue for more than a few days.

■ TREATMENT In proven or suspect cases, your doctor may prescribe metronidazole, an ANTIBIOTIC which is specifically effective against *Giardia*.

■ OUTLOOK A marked improvement in symptoms should follow in a few days after starting treatment with metronidazole. There is a risk of reinfection; this is best prevented by hand washing and culinary hygiene.

GIFTED CHILD

Children are defined as gifted if they have an I.Q. in excess of 140. Less than 0.5 per cent of all children fall into this category. (An average I.Q. is 100.) Many experts consider that gifted children have special educational needs: their abilities may make them stand out from their peer group, which can lead to social isolation. However, there is little clear evidence that exceptionally bright children as a whole have special difficulties, or that they do not achieve as well as expected in normal schools. It is important, as far as possible, that they are not made to feel special at home: this can lead them to behave as if they are superior to other children. It will require careful consideration to direct their scholastic performance at school in relation to non-academic interests. If you feel that your child is very bright and is not performing as well as expected, or if he seems unhappy at school, discuss the matter with his teacher. If the problem cannot be easily resolved, the teacher may refer your child to an educational psychologist for assessment.

GILLES DE LA TOURETTE SYNDROME

A severe form of TIC which typically takes the form of repeated words or phrases, sometimes rude or even obscene. The child cannot stop these utterances, but may be able to control them for a few minutes.

GINGIVITIS ('GUM DISEASE')

Gingivitis, or inflammation of the gums, is the first stage of 'gum disease' (periodontal disease): the start of a process which, if neglected, results in tooth loss. In children, it is usually just the gums that are affected.

- ■ CAUSES Plaque (a film containing bacteria) collects on the teeth and in the crevices between the teeth and gums, as a result of poor cleaning.

- ■ SYMPTOMS Soreness and bleeding from the gums, often during toothbrushing.

- ■ TREATMENT The process is easily reversed by regular and effective removal of the plaque by brushing, often initially with a soft brush. If bleeding persists, consult your dentist or doctor.

GLANDULAR FEVER

A VIRAL illness also known as infectious mononucleosis; it occurs most commonly in older children and adolescents. It is only mildly INFECTIOUS. The INCUBATION PERIOD is between four and 14 days.

- ■ SYMPTOMS Onset is gradual. There is a mild FEVER and loss of APPETITE, and the child feels generally unwell; some of the lymph glands enlarge and become tender. These may be in the neck, under the arms, or in the abdomen. ABDOMINAL PAIN arises from enlargement of the lymph glands or spleen. A sore throat is common and the tonsils are usually enlarged.

  Occasionally, a RASH occurs, either as little red spots, a blotchy red rash, or tiny bleeds into the skin, the last being due to minor problems with blood clotting.

  The fever and enlargement of the glands can last for several weeks.

- ■ ACTION There is no specific treatment. Symptoms can be relieved with analgesics such as paracetamol. ANTIBIOTICS can do more harm than good: ampicillin may cause a severe skin rash.

  The malaise and tiredness may persist for many months, particularly in adolescents. Occasionally, this is severe enough to interfere with school work and other activities. Understanding and support from the family, together with plenty of rest and a balanced diet are a sensible approach.

- ■ TESTS The diagnosis can be made on a BLOOD TEST if there is any doubt.

- ■ COMPLICATIONS Serious problems are rare, but if the spleen is enlarged, sports involving physical contact should be avoided because of the risk of rupture of the spleen and internal bleeding.

  In rare cases, inflammation of various organs can cause MYOCARDITIS, HEPATITIS, PNEUMONIA and MENINGITIS.

- ■ OUTLOOK The long-term outlook is usually good, but the feeling of vague ill-health, lasting for months, can be troublesome.

GLOMERULONEPHRITIS
See *NEPHRITIS*.

GLUCOSE 6-PHOSPHATE DEHYDROGENASE DEFICIENCY

An INHERITED DISORDER which can cause a HAEMOLYTIC ANAEMIA. There are slightly different symptoms in different ethnic groups around the world.

- ■ SYMPTOMS JAUNDICE can occur in new-born babies and may be severe enough to require EXCHANGE TRANSFUSION. If a baby or child has the condition, acute INFECTIONS, and certain drugs, can trigger a marked breakdown of red blood cells resulting in severe ANAEMIA and jaundice. The drugs include some ANTIBIOTICS and anti-malarial drugs, and a few other preparations seldom given to children.

Between episodes, the child is usually well. But in some children the breakdown of red blood cells continues all the time. This results in increased red blood cell production in the liver, spleen and bone marrow; if this does not compensate fully, a mild anaemia can result.

■ ACTION The child should wear a bracelet stating he has G6-PD deficiency, to ensure that he is not given inappropriate medication.

A BLOOD TEST can reveal the diagnosis, and if there is a family history this precaution should not be neglected.

■ TREATMENT Infections require immediate action: get medical advice. A BLOOD TRANSFUSION can be given to treat severe episodes.

■ OUTLOOK Usually good, once the disease has been diagnosed and culprit drugs identified.

GLUE EAR
The accumulation of sticky fluid in the middle ear behind the eardrum.

■ SYMPTOMS Partial deafness is the main symptom. The child may say his ear feels 'full'. The symptom may first arise following a MIDDLE EAR INFECTION.

■ ACTION Any suspicion that a child has hearing problems should be raised without delay with your doctor – see *DEAFNESS*.

GLUE EAR

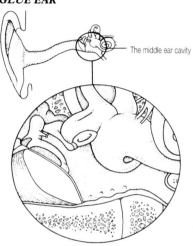

The middle ear cavity

Sticky fluid accumulates here.

■ INVESTIGATIONS If examination by a doctor confirms any degree of deafness, you will be referred to a specialist for full-scale hearing tests – see *AUDIOGRAM*.

■ TREATMENT Glue ear often clears up in two to three months without treatment, or with simple decongestant medicines. It is usual to wait three months, then re-check the child's hearing, before considering the insertion of GROMMETS (small tubes) through the eardrum to help drain remaining fluid.

■ OUTLOOK Hearing may vary in infancy and may affect early LANGUAGE DEVELOPMENT. In the long term, however, the outlook for health, hearing and speech is normally good.

GLUE SNIFFING
See *SOLVENT ABUSE, ADDICTION*.

GOITRE

A swelling in the neck caused by an enlarged thyroid gland. This can signify HYPERTHYROIDISM, HYPOTHYROIDISM, or result from a deficiency of iodine in the diet (now rare in the U.K., since all packet salt contains added iodine). The goitre itself usually requires no treatment (other than occasionally for cosmetic reasons) unless it is so large that it causes obstruction to the airway. In such cases, surgical removal or thyroidectomy is indicated. Treatment is directed towards the underlying cause of the goitre.

GONORRHOEA

A sexually transmitted BACTERIAL INFECTION. If a mother is infected when giving birth, it can give her baby severe CONJUNCTIVITIS. If this is not treated with ANTIBIOTIC eye drops, damage to the eyes can result.

Older children can catch the infection from an adult carrier through SEXUAL ABUSE.

Symptoms include ARTHRITIS, RASH and conjunctivitis. Vaginal infection in young girls may cause no symptoms, or a slight VAGINAL DISCHARGE. A swab of the infected area, or a BLOOD TEST, will confirm the diagnosis.

Treatment with antibiotics is rapidly effective.

GRAND MAL SEIZURE

The most florid form of EPILEPSY in which the child loses consciousness and may be variously rigid, or jerk some or all parts of the body. It may also be described (loosely) as a fit, seizure or CONVULSION.

■ SYMPTOMS There is stiffening of the whole body ('tonic phase'), followed by generalized shaking ('clonic phase'), followed by deep sleep when the breathing may be stertorous or snoring. The child may bite his tongue, lip or cheek during the attack, and produce frothy saliva around the mouth; he may also pass urine. On recovery, the child may rarely have a temporary loss of speech or limb paralysis ('Todd's paralysis'), he commonly feels groggy and may have a headache.

■ ACTION See *EPILEPSY*. Place the child in the recovery position. *Rush the child to hospital* if the convulsion lasts more than ten minutes, or if the child has not had previous convulsions.

■ TREATMENT A prolonged convulsion can be brought to an end by an intravenous injection of an anticonvulsant drug. In infants and for all children, emergency treatment may alternatively be given by suppository.

■ OUTLOOK See *EPILEPSY*.

GRITTY EYE

See *CONJUNCTIVITIS*.

GROMMETS

Small plastic tubes inserted by an ear surgeon through a child's eardrum. They allow free passage of air in and out of the middle ear. By assisting in the pressure regulation of the middle ear, the accumulation of fluid (and 'glue') is reduced. If a child is experiencing partial DEAFNESS as a result of GLUE EAR, insertion of grommets by minor surgical operation (no painful after-effects) can be very effective, both in improving hearing and the frequently associated BEHAVIOURAL DISORDERS. Grommets often work free after six to 12 months. Follow-up visits to a specialist will establish whether they need to be removed or replaced.

GROWTH PATTERNS

The weight of a baby together with his maturity (or gestational age) at birth represent the first measurements against which early postnatal growth and development are judged. Most babies lose weight in the first few days after birth, and regain their birth weight within ten days. They should then increase in weight month by month throughout childhood. The steepest increases are in the first year, with the additional major or steepest growth spurt in the years leading up to and around the time of PUBERTY.

Growth charts display the normal range of children's weight and length according to age. An individual baby or child's growth will depend on many factors: maturity and weight at birth, the mother and father's height, illnesses, family relationships, and diet or nutritional intake.

WELL-BABY CLINICS will check your baby's growth and development through the first years of life. Your family doctor can also help if you are worried about your child's growth, and will refer you to a paediatrician

GROWTH PATTERNS

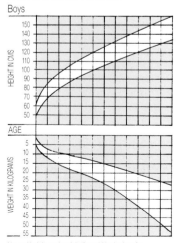

Normal height and weight lies within the bands

if you think his growth is abnormally delayed (see *FAILURE TO THRIVE*), or indeed excessive.

GUILLAIN-BARRE SYNDROME

Also known as infectious polyneuritis.

■ SYMPTOMS Progressive weakness and numbness often following two weeks or so after a VIRAL illness.

■ CAUSE Inflammation of the nerve roots where they emerge from the spinal cord.

■ TREATMENT There is no specific treatment and management is supportive in the acute phase, with attention to rehabilitation and physiotherapy in the recovery phase.

The most serious complications, which are rare in childhood, are breathing difficulties and disturbances of heart rhythm or BLOOD PRESSURE, which may require intensive care including artificial ventilation.

■ OUTLOOK The majority of cases are transient and recovery is complete.

GUTHRIE TEST

The test invented by Guthrie was, in fact, a laboratory test for PHENYLKETO-NURIA. However, the term is now generally used for collecting the blood samples for a variety of neonatal screening tests, including tests for neonatal HYPOTHYROIDISM and phenylketonuria. In many countries, it is performed on every baby around the sixth day after birth, collecting a sample of blood by pricking the heel and allowing the blood to drip on to a specially prepared card made of a heavy filter paper.

H

HAEMATURIA (BLOOD IN THE URINE)

This is rare in babies but commoner (though still rare) in older children. It can be a symptom of a URINARY TRACT INFECTION, NEPHRITIS, injury to the kidneys or bladder, WILM'S TUMOUR or HENOCH-SCHÖNLEIN PURPURA. If the number of red cells in the urine is enough to give it colour, it will appear pink or brown. Other substances can cause red or DARK URINE, and these may be confused with blood. Get medical advice if you suspect blood in your child's urine. Treatment will depend on the cause.

HAEMOLYTIC ANAEMIA

ANAEMIA caused by increased breakdown of red blood cells.

▥ CAUSES There are many, but the most common include THALASSAEMIA, SICKLE-CELL ANAEMIA and GLUCOSE 6-PHOSPHATE DEHYDROGENASE DEFICIENCY (G6-PD deficiency).

▥ SYMPTOMS Similar to anaemia from other causes, but there are some additional features:
JAUNDICE occurs because haemoglobin released from the red blood cells is changed into bilirubin, a pigment.
The child's body has to manufacture extra red blood cells to compensate for those broken down. If the bone marrow cannot cope, the liver and spleen will help, but they become enlarged as a result. This may cause a chronic, dull ABDOMINAL PAIN.

▥ ACTION Some of the causes of haemolytic anaemia are inherited disorders. If there is a family history, tell your doctor.
Folic acid is lost when red blood cells are broken down, and this needs to be replaced. Your child may have to take a vitamin syrup or tablets containing folic acid.
For details of treatment and outlook, see THALASSAEMIA, SICKLE-CELL ANAEMIA and GLUCOSE 6-PHOSPHATE DEHYDROGENASE DEFICIENCY.

HAEMOPHILIA

An INHERITED DISORDER causing lack of Factor VIII in the blood. Factor VIII is needed for normal clotting; deficiency results in a tendency to uncontrolled bleeding.

▥ SYMPTOMS may be mild or severe. In the mild form, bleeding only occurs after a definite injury. In the severe form, symptoms begin in early infancy and bleeding can occur for no apparent reason.
In milder cases, the first sign may be bruises when the child is starting to crawl or walk. Bleeding into the joints and muscles starts as an ache and then develops into severe pain in the affected areas. The joint or muscle is swollen and movements are limited. NOSEBLEEDS are common. ABDOMINAL PAIN can be caused by bleeding within the abdomen. Bleeding from the kidneys and bladder results in urine which is very dark.

▥ ACTION If you have a family history of haemophilia, consider GENETIC COUNSELLING before having children. It is possible to detect whether a woman is a carrier of the abnormal gene that causes the condition, and ANTENATAL DIAGNOSIS can confirm whether the foetus has haemophilia.
If your child starts to bruise easily, get medical advice.

A bracelet stating that the child is haemophiliac can be life-saving in an emergency.

Pain associated with bleeding can be treated with paracetamol. Aspirin should not be used – it can aggravate the bleeding.

Activities may need to be limited, depending on the severity of the disease. Some sports can be played by children with mild haemophilia, but in severe cases all possible causes of injury must be avoided.

Care of the teeth is important: having a tooth out can lead to prolonged bleeding. A child with haemophilia should never have an injection into a muscle.

▓ TREATMENT Factor VIII can be given as a small transfusion into a vein at the first sign of bleeding. Prompt treatment is essential as it prevents further bleeding and pain, and minimizes permanent damage to joints. A BLOOD TRANSFUSION may be needed if blood loss has been excessive.

Sometimes home treatment with Factor VIII is practical, so that treatment is started early and fewer trips to the hospital are needed.

When there is bleeding into a joint, it needs to be rested until the bleeding has stopped. After this, physiotherapy is essential to ensure that the joint does not stiffen up.

Severe nosebleeds are treated by packing gauze into the nose to put pressure on the bleeding area. Factor VIII, derived from human blood, may also be necessary.

Cuts should not be stitched until Factor VIII has been given. Excessive pressure on areas of bleeding can also cause further injury. Factor VIII must be used before and during any surgical procedure to prevent excessive bleeding.

Factor VIII derived from human blood has, in the past, contained the AIDS VIRUS. In Western countries, all blood is now tested for this: haemophiliac children should ideally avoid travel in countries where there is any question of blood stocks being contaminated.

▓ COMPLICATIONS Bleeding into joints can cause severe damage, resulting in deformity of joints and chronic ARTHRITIS, but this can often be prevented by prompt treatment with Factor VIII. Bleeding into the brain is a rare complication.

▓ OUTLOOK depends on severity. Recent advances in treatment have resulted in a much better quality and duration of life.

HALITOSIS
This is not a medical term, but it is nonetheless commonly used by doctors to describe bad breath.

▓ CAUSES 1 INFECTIONS of the mouth or throat, such as TONSILLITIS. Even a severe COMMON COLD can cause halitosis for a short time. 2 'Gum disease' (GINGIVITIS), and tooth decay (dental caries) and chronic SINUSITIS can cause a more persistent unpleasant smell.

▓ ACTION For a short-term infection a mouthwash and thorough tooth brushing will help. However, if the problem persists and your child appears to be brushing his teeth properly, consult your doctor or dental hygienist.

HALLUCINATIONS
May be defined as seeing, hearing or smelling things which do not exist in reality, but which the individual perceives to be real. In young children, it

may be hard to distinguish hallucinations from figments of a vivid imagination. Children are prone to hallucinations when they have a high temperature; when the temperature drops, the hallucinations cease. In older children, hallucinations in the absence of fever, particularly if they occur in the daytime, may be symptomatic of a serious underlying disorder; if in doubt discuss the matter with your doctor. See also *NIGHT TERRORS, EPILEPSY, SCHIZOPHRENIA,* and *SOLVENT ABUSE.*

HARELIP
See *CLEFT PALATE.*

HAY FEVER
A group of symptoms in susceptible individuals due to ALLERGY to various pollens, especially from grass and trees, occurring through the summer months. It is perhaps the commonest form of allergic rhinitis and CONJUNCTIVITIS (irritation, congestion and secretion from the linings of the nose and surface of the eyeballs).

▓ SYMPTOMS Sneezing, blocked running nose, itchy or streaming eyes. This may be accompanied by wheezing – ASTHMA.

▓ CAUSE Many airborne pollens, because of their very small size, are capable of being inhaled and react with the lining of the nose and eyes in an allergic way. The tendency to this type of allergy runs in families.

▓ TESTS Skin and BLOOD TESTS can identify particular pollens or allergies. However, this is hardly ever necessary, since the connection between the symptoms and exposure to grass pollen is usually obvious.

▓ ACTION **1** Take common-sense precautions: beware of the particular pollen and take note of the day-to-day pollen count; when possible, avoid exposure to freshly mown grass or hay (if they aggravate your child's symptoms). As far as possible and when appropriate, keep your child out of the 'fresh pollenated' air. Places where pollen is likely to be minimal include air-conditioned rooms, boats at sea and swimming pools. Dark glasses don't help the conjunctivitis: they don't keep pollen out of the eyes. **2** Antihistamine syrup or tablets may be of some help: although they are available over the counter, you may initially wish to discuss their use for your child with your own doctor. **3** Get medical advice if symptoms are sufficiently troublesome to disrupt the child's life.

▓ TREATMENT Antihistamines are usually of some (limited) help in relieving both rhinitis and conjunctivitis. Astemizole and terfenadine are relatively new antihistamine drugs that do not cause drowsiness. Chlorpheniramine is cheaper to buy over the counter, but does cause drowsiness. Antihistamines are usually recommended for use over a few days. They may be used for longer periods of time if medically advised.

Both rhinitis and conjunctivitis can be treated with preventive drugs, given by spray or drops. Such an approach requires the medication to be given daily throughout the pollen season.

▓ SELF-HELP Anticipating, if possible, the hay harvest and starting preventive treatment before the pollen count rises. Desensitizing injections are now rarely recommended: they carry a risk of grave adverse reaction in children, and they are not particularly effective.

■ ALTERNATIVE TREATMENTS
Homoeopathic doctors prescribe agents such as teucrium, sabadilla and mixed pollens for hay fever.

■ LONG-TERM MANAGEMENT
There is no effective way of 'curing' hay fever, but regular use of preventive treatment can keep the misery of summer at bay.

■ OUTLOOK Better and safer treatments are being developed each year. Many children grow out of hay fever.

HEAD BANGING

Repetitive banging of the head against walls, furniture, and so on. This is a COMFORT HABIT which some toddlers display while settling to sleep. It may also occur during temper TANTRUMS, or as a result of frustration or boredom. It may constitute an effective means of attracting parents' attention. Although it is disturbing to witness, it is physically harmless; your best strategy is to ignore it. However, it is prudent to cover sharp corners or objects adjacent to the bed or cot. During the daytime, attempt to distract the child's attention if you can anticipate when head banging might start. If you consider that this habit indicates that your child has worries or anxieties which may be addressed, discuss with your doctor.

HEAD INJURY

May be caused by a direct blow, a missile, by shaking, acceleration and deceleration; among the commonest causes of severe head injury in childhood are road traffic accidents. See CAR SEAT BELTS. All children bump their heads at times with no serious consequences. Moderate head injury may result in CONCUSSION.

■ SYMPTOMS of head injury will depend on the severity and location of the brain injury and may include UNCONSCIOUSNESS, PARALYSIS, loss of speech, abnormality of eye movements, incoordination and CONVULSIONS. There may be loss of memory for events immediately preceding, as well as following, the incident in proportion to the severity of the injury, with a tendency for improvement with time.

■ ACTION See ACCIDENTS IN THE HOME, ACCIDENTS OUTSIDE THE HOME. If a child is unconscious from a head injury for more than a few seconds, take him to hospital for assessment and observation. Bleeding inside the head may occur following the injury and cause a deterioration in the child's condition over a matter of hours. If the doctors judge it safe to allow a child home after a head injury, instructions on observing the child over the next few days will be given.

■ TREATMENT A blood clot causing raised pressure inside the skull may require surgical removal. The child's overall neurological state is the most useful guide as to the nature and severity of the intracranial injury. The presence of a fracture does not affect management unless it is depressed, or causing leakage of cerebro-spinal fluid.

■ OUTLOOK BRAIN DAMAGE may occur at the site of injury, or on the opposite side if the brain was compressed against the skull bones ('contrecoup' injury), or as the result of bleeding. The long-term effect depends on the severity of the injury and part of the brain affected. Personality change, including impulsiveness, irritability and loss of inhibition are common, but may be temporary. Recovery is usually progressive over many weeks or months, and rehabilitation involves many disciplines. HEADACHES are a common sequel for months after serious head injury.

HEADACHE

Pain in the head which may be sharp, tight or thumping is common in children. One child in 20 has one headache per month. One in 100 has one a week.

■ CAUSES Commonly these are the result of worries, tiredness, FEVER, the COMMON COLD, hunger, rushing around, bright sunshine or oversleeping. Most children who have regular headaches have a family history of the problem. Periodic headaches can occur for weeks or months after a mild or moderate HEAD INJURY. See also *MIGRAINE IN CHILDHOOD*.

Diet and eye problems are often blamed for headaches, and although they may be true for individuals, such factors are uncommon. SINUSITIS can cause acute headaches, but is not a common cause of chronic or recurrent headache in children, whose sinuses are relatively undeveloped compared with those of adults.

Headaches are rarely an indication of grave disease. (The rare, serious type of headache is completely different from a run-of-the-mill headache, much more severe and disabling. Typically, raised pressure in the head causes sudden onset of brief, bursting pain associated with vomiting first thing in the morning. See also *MENINGITIS*, in which severe vomiting, fever and headache may occur.)

The longer a child has been experiencing headaches and the longer they last, the less likely it is that there is a serious underlying cause. They are more likely to reflect tension or fatigue in scalp muscles.

■ SELF-HELP Occasional headaches respond to a drink and a biscuit and sitting or lying down quietly. Paracetamol syrup or tablets will probably help the headache which fails to settle. Aspirin is not suitable for children under 12 – see *REYE'S SYNDROME*. If your child has frequent headaches, try to identify and resolve underlying causes of ANXIETY. Encourage regular eating and sleeping habits and methods of relaxation, especially at bedtime. Distract him: heads hurt less when preoccupied with pleasant thoughts.

■ OUTLOOK Headache is a very common symptom, tending to come and go: headaches are more frequent in term-time than holidays, on weekdays than weekends, especially for conscientious children. Some children's headaches have a reverse timing, and these are known as relaxation headaches.

HEART-DISEASE

One child in every hundred has some form of heart-disease. The range of conditions involved are described in detail under CONGENITAL HEART-DISEASE, HEART FAILURE, ARRHYTHMIA, MYOCARDITIS or CARDIOMYOPATHY. It is essential to read this entry in conjunction with the entries listed above. RHEUMATIC FEVER, once a leading cause of heart-disease in children, is now rare in much of the Western world, although still rampant in many developing countries.

■ SYMPTOMS See the separate entries listed above. The most general symptoms of heart-disease in childhood are breathlessness and blueness, the latter especially in the lips.

■ ACTION If your child is breathless or blue, or has any of the symptoms given under the entries listed above, get medical advice. You will probably be referred to a paediatrician or cardiologist.

■ TESTS include ECG, X-ray of the chest and an ULTRASOUND SCAN of the heart (echocardiogram). Admission to hospital may be necessary for other tests such as cardiac catheterization.

■ TREATMENT See the entries listed above. Recent advances in heart surgery have led to a much lower risk for all types of operation, particularly in very young children. Operations are now being performed for heart problems which were previously considered inoperable. In some cases, more than one operation will be necessary.

Make sure you thoroughly understand your child's treatment by discussing all aspects of it with the family doctor. You should understand the risks of any operation, and what is likely to be achieved.

■ LONG-TERM MANAGEMENT The severity of heart-disease is very variable. Some abnormalities are so mild that they only require a check-up every few years. Sometimes medical treatment is needed and continued for many years. Heart surgery may be indicated but not performed until your child is older.

Make sure that any specialists who see your child write to your family doctor and keep him or her fully informed. Your doctor is likely to be the person you will turn to if you need to discuss difficult decisions. He or she can only advise with all the facts at hand.

If your child has a severe heart problem, he may gain weight more slowly than normal. He may also be slow to sit and walk. Such great restriction and developmental delay may not improve until after successful surgery. However, even in extreme cases, the child usually makes normal intellectual progress, although his range of experience may be constrained by physical limitations. A child with heart-disease will instinctively rest when he is tired, so activities need not be limited (with the exception, for some children, of most competitive sports, which demand great physical exertion or stamina). His greater need for rest should be made clear to teachers. (The degree of disability will, of course, vary enormously depending on the heart problem in the individual child.)

Your child should be IMMUNIZED at the normal times unless he is ill, in which case it should be done as soon as he improves.

Children with many types of heart-disease should have an ANTI-BIOTIC when they have dental treatment, and also for some other operations, to prevent INFECTION.

■ OUTLOOK Heart-disease in childhood sounds grave, but in most cases the outlook is surprisingly good; depending as ever on the nature of a particular child's problem, the odds are your child will lead a more or less normal life.

HEART FAILURE

The heart is unable to pump the blood around the body to meet its needs effectively.

■ CAUSES HEART-DISEASE of any

kind, if severe, can result in heart failure.

■ SYMPTOMS include BREATHLESS-NESS, caused by blood pooling in the lungs: this makes the lungs stiff and breathing becomes more difficult and more rapid than usual. In a baby, this is most noticeable during feeding. He may not be able to finish his feeds (and may be noted to sweat with the effort) and fail to gain weight at the normal rate (see *FAILURE TO THRIVE*). An older child may become more breathless than expected during exercise; and may spontaneously limit his activities. If heart failure is severe, he may be breathless while resting. OEDEMA is also a feature. Sluggish circulation leads to fluid leaving the capillaries and collecting in the soft tissues of the body. This results in swelling, most noted in children as a puffiness around the eyes. In a baby, heart failure can result in a sudden increase in body weight due to fluid retention. Enlargement of the liver may also occur as a result of back pressure of blood from the heart. This can cause abdominal swelling.

■ TREATMENT Digoxin and some other drugs will help the heart muscle to beat more strongly.

Diuretics such as frusemide will help the kidneys remove the excess water from the circulation.

■ LONG-TERM MANAGEMENT will depend on the cause of heart failure. If it is due to CONGENITAL HEART-DISEASE, surgery may be necessary. If the cause is an ARRHYTHMIA, this must be treated with drugs. If there is muscle damage as in MYOCARDITIS or CARDIOMYOPATHY, drug treatment is usual. If medication is not effective, and an operation will not help, a heart transplant may be considered.

■ OUTLOOK has improved over the last few decades because of advances in both drug and surgical treatment.

HEART MURMURS
Noises made by the heart in addition to the normal heart beats. Murmurs are usually caused by defects in the structure of the heart. However, 'innocent murmurs' can be caused simply by the turbulence of blood passing through the heart. This type of murmur can be heard in about half of all children at some time, especially during FEVER.

■ SYMPTOMS See *HEART-DISEASE*. If your child has an innocent murmur, he will have no symptoms related to his heart. The murmur is only detected when he has a routine check-up, or is examined for another illness.

Innocent murmurs usually have characteristics that make them easy to distinguish from heart-disease. Occasionally this is not the case, and your doctor will refer your child to a paediatrician or cardiologist.

■ TESTS include an X-ray of the chest, an ECG (ELECTROCARDIOGRAM) and occasionally an ULTRASOUND SCAN of the heart (echocardiogram).

■ TREATMENT An innocent murmur requires no treatment. It usually becomes softer with time and may eventually disappear. If it is due to heart-disease, the exact abnormality will be determined and appropriate treatment given.

HEAT RASH
Transient redness of the skin attri-

buted to overheating. This is not a disease, rather the natural effect of sweat and heat on the skin.

■ SYMPTOMS The redness is especially evident in skin folds, such as those on a baby's neck and groin.

■ ACTION Careful washing and use of talc may help. It is easy to dismiss a RASH as a heat or sweat rash. If in doubt, especially if your baby is in any way unwell, get medical advice.

■ TREATMENT None is necessary.

HEAT STROKE

A rare condition most likely to occur in the very young; very old or those debilitated by disease or by a febrile illness. The body's heat-regulating mechanism fails. Rush the child to the nearest hospital. Cool him as best you can during transport.

HENOCH-SCHÖNLEIN PURPURA

Inflammation of the tiny blood vessels (capillaries) of the skin and other organs of the body, particularly the bowel or kidneys. Cause unknown.

■ SYMPTOMS A RASH, beginning as URTICARIA, with raised weals, mainly on the buttocks and limbs. This is followed by tiny, pin-point haemorrhages into the skin. These too are found mainly on the arms and legs, but they can occur on the trunk and face. There may be joint pains and swelling.

ABDOMINAL PAIN can be caused by tiny haemorrhages into the bowel wall. This is usually an intermittent pain similar to that of COLIC, and it may be associated with vomiting.

The kidneys are occasionally affected. Tests will reveal blood in the urine; occasionally the child's urine looks dark because of the excess blood. NEPHRITIS may develop as a complication.

■ ACTION Any rash associated with bleeding should be checked by a doctor.

Pain in the joints or abdomen can be treated with paracetamol. Aspirin should not be used without a doctor's prescription in any child under 12 years of age because of the risk of REYE'S SYNDROME.

While the rash is severe, the child should probably be in bed: activity seems to make the rash worse.

The child may suffer from DEPRESSION for a few months after the illness. There is no specific treatment, except loving support and understanding.

■ TREATMENT is confined to alleviating the symptoms, but if inflammation of the kidneys is severe, it will be the same as for NEPHRITIS.

■ OUTLOOK is generally good, except in a few cases where the kidneys are affected.

HEPATITIS

Inflammation of the liver caused by a number of different VIRUSES. See also *CHRONIC HEPATITIS.*

It is particularly common in developing countries and occurs at any age in childhood.

The viruses (known as hepatitis A, hepatitis B and non-A non-B hepatitis) spread in different ways, including contaminated water and food.

■ SYMPTOMS initially ANOREXIA, ITCHING, NAUSEA and VOMITING, and possibly DIARRHOEA and FEVER. Several days later JAUNDICE develops, together with the passage of DARK URINE and pale BOWEL

MOTIONS. There may also be a RASH and painful joints. There is often ABDOMINAL PAIN below the right lower ribs. There may be BRUISING due to damage to the liver and low production of clotting factors.

There may be a history of contact with a person who had jaundice; or the illness may follow a BLOOD TRANSFUSION.

Some illnesses mimick hepatitis and several infections and toxic effects on the liver can give similar symptoms; a doctor must consider them all when trying to make the diagnosis.

■ PREVENTION Control of hepatitis A requires high standards of personal hygiene and proper sewage disposal.

Injection of human immunoglobulin (specific protein ANTIBODY) can be given to people in high risk situations, for example, travel in countries where the condition is common, or early after exposure to the infection. This should prevent hepatitis A.

Prevention of hepatitis B infection requires vaccination, (three doses at least one month apart) and blood screening. This is not usually necessary for children.

■ INVESTIGATIONS Physical examination for jaundice, an enlarged, tender liver and sometimes an enlarged spleen. BLOOD TESTS; tests for the virus involved.

■ TREATMENT The child with major symptoms such as persistent vomiting, general tiredness, bruising and ascites (fluid in the abdomen) will need to go into hospital; also if the diagnosis is in doubt. Hepatitis B is more severe than hepatitis A, and the child will need to be nursed by staff immune to this

infection. A patient with hepatitis A is infectious for up to ten days after the appearance of jaundice. The virus is passed in bowel motions.

Improvement is usual by the end of the second week, but full recovery may take months.

■ OUTLOOK Most children with hepatitis A and hepatitis B, and a large proportion of those with non-A non-B hepatitis, recover completely. Complications include further similar episodes, but this is rare. Severe hepatitis with liver failure is rare but dangerous, and needs full support in a special hospital unit (see *CIRRHOSIS*).

HERNIAS

Protrusions of organs through openings occurring at points of muscular weakness, either internally between the chest and abdomen, or externally through the abdominal wall. There are several different types:

– **Inguinal hernia** arises from a channel in the muscles of the groin through which the testes or female ligaments migrate during foetal development. It should normally close off, but premature babies are prone to this type of hernia. There will be an intermittent swelling in the groin, which can become firm and tender. The bowel and its lining will have protruded through the muscular gap and become trapped, in some cases limiting the blood supply to the bowel. An infant with an obstructed inguinal hernia may be irritable, with ABDOMINAL PAIN and VOMITING.

– **Umbilical hernia** occurs in infancy. It is characterized by an especially prominent, swollen umbilicus or navel, which may contain a portion of bowel. This can become trapped in a similar way to an inguinal hernia, but this is rare. Only if the hernia is large, or the bowel becomes irreducible (cannot be pushed back easily), will surgery be necessary. Small umbilical hernias will not need an operation and will usually heal without treatment before the age of two years.

Supra-umbilical hernia (hernia above the umbilicus) and epigastric hernia, (higher still, in the upper part of the abdomen) may become painful, and often need surgery.

– **Diaphragmatic hernia** is a protrusion of the intestinal contents through the diaphragm (the muscular partition between the chest and abdomen). It occurs mostly on the left side of the chest and can have grave consequences, but is, fortunately, rare.

A new-born baby with this type of hernia will have difficulty with breathing, which will not respond easily to oxygen.

The baby's abdomen may be flat and the chest may emit bowel sounds (heard through a stethoscope), indicating that the bowel is in the chest. The heart may be pushed to the right (dextrocardia).

Artificial ventilation may be necessary, and also measures to keep the bowel empty of gas. Emergency surgery will probably be essential to repair the diaphragmatic hernia and to replace the bowel in the abdomen. The outcome depends on how well the lungs work. A lung may be hypoplastic (poorly developed) on the side of the hernia.

This can be a fatal condition, either at birth, or after operation; but babies whose lung hypoplasia is not too serious can do well. See also *HIATUS HERNIA*.

▓ ACTION Any suspicious swelling in the groin, scrotum (the sac containing the testes) or labia (the female genital area) should be reported to a doctor.

▓ TREATMENT Any inguinal hernia will be operated on in infancy, especially if symptoms such as vomiting and pain suggest an obstruction. The operation is simple with no major risk unless there has been a delay in reporting an obstructed hernia, and the bowel is seriously damaged. Treatments of other types of hernia are described above.

HERPES INFECTIONS
See *COLD SORES*, *CHICKENPOX*.

HIATUS HERNIA
An uncommon hernia of the stomach through the diaphragm (the muscular partition between chest and abdomen), at the point through which the oesophagus (food pipe) passes.

The stomach can slide up slightly into the chest, or may roll up next to the lower end of the oesophagus.

When the stomach empties, gastric juice passes upwards and leads to superficial ulceration and swelling of the oesophageal lining (oesophagitis).

▓ SYMPTOMS Persistent VOMITING in infancy starting often in the first week of life and usually related to feeding. The vomiting may occur mostly at night in an older child. There may be mucus (a slimy substance) mixed with the milk.

Brown staining of the vomit due to blood (haematemesis) and blood in the stools which are black (melaena) can occur after bleeding of the ulcerated areas. The baby or child may be pale due to ANAEMIA from acute or chronic BLEEDING. CONSTIPATION is common. There may be CHEST PAIN from the acid reflux. There is often FAILURE TO THRIVE and occasionally the child may become DEHYDRATED.

An infant may have a choking episode from the reflux, or he may wheeze and suffer repeated CHEST INFECTIONS from inhalation of milk; but these are rare.

■ ACTION Discuss your child's vomiting with the family doctor.

■ INVESTIGATIONS Barium meal with X-ray follow-up; in some hospitals, special acid- (pH)- measuring tubes passed into the oesophagus may help quantify the degree of acid regurgitation.

■ MANAGEMENT Small frequent feeds; antacid medication; feeding and nursing in an upright position for several months may be needed.

Thickening the feed with special preparations may be recommended. The vomiting should improve when solids are well established.

Surgery will be necessary in those children with major problems. These include continuing failure to thrive, persistent bleeding, or repeated chest infections. The surgery is not as extensive as that required for a diaphragmatic HERNIA.

■ OUTLOOK Most improve with time.

HICCUPS (HICCOUGHS)
Sudden, involuntary, jerky contractions of the diaphragm muscle, occurring in bouts, often after food. Usually trivial, but often a nuisance, hiccups are of course common in children of all ages. They are usually caused by stretching or irritation of the stomach, either by too much food eaten too quickly, or by a specific food or drink.

They may be a symptom of serious disease, when they tend to be persistent, but this is a very rare occurrence.

■ ACTION Hiccups usually stop of their own accord, but simple measures such as breath holding, blowing the nose, or tickling the back of the throat with a soft rubber tube may help.

HIP, DISLOCATION
See CONGENITAL DISLOCATION OF THE HIP.

HIRSCHPRUNG'S DISEASE
Narrowing of the large bowel due to lack of ganglion (nerve) cells in the wall (aganglionosis). It may involve a short section of the rectum (large bowel), or it may extend throughout the large bowel into the small, but this is rare.

■ SYMPTOMS Delayed passage of MECONIUM in infancy. CONSTIPATION in infancy which may be associated with ABDOMINAL SWELLING and VOMITING. DIARRHOEA and enterocolitis (severe diarrhoea mixed with blood) may occur and is an emergency.

■ INVESTIGATIONS Abdominal X-ray may show an obstructed bowel. A barium ENEMA reveals dilated bowel above a narrowed section. Balloon pressure studies (manometry) may detect a characteristic pattern. Rectal biopsy shows an absence of ganglion cells.

■ TREATMENT Surgical removal of the affected area of bowel with rejoining of normal bowel ends.

■ OUTLOOK Good if there is a short segment only. Poor if there is extended aganglionosis into the small bowel. Hirschprung's disease carries a small chance of occurring in relatives, principally siblings or children of the sufferer.

HIVES
See *URTICARIA.*

HOARSENESS
See *LARYNGITIS.*

HODGKIN'S DISEASE
See *LYMPHOMA.*

HOLE IN THE HEART
See *CONGENITAL HEART-DISEASE.*

HOSPITAL, CHILD IN
Going into hospital is a worrying proposition for most adults. For children, to whom the presence of family and familiar things is essential, and who have less understanding of illness and pain than adults, it can be very frightening indeed. A child may show his fears through difficult behaviour either in hospital or on return home. It is quite common for children between 18 months and five years to show the effects of separation even after they go home if a parent has been unable to stay with them in hospital. These usually take the form of increased clinging, needing extra attention and perhaps reverting to bedwetting. Unpredictable resentment may surface.

▨ HOSPITAL – THE PROBLEMS
– Separation from parents: Studies in the 1950s confirmed that short parental visits simply could not compensate for being alone in hospital. Nowadays, children's hospital wards are organized so that parents can stay.
– New and frightening procedures: Children over seven years are likely to have greater worries about medical procedures than the younger child. In fact, children can have strange ideas about how their bodies work until well into their teens, indeed they may suffer from primitive terrors about investigations and operations. Out-patient investigations are no exception.
– Children are very sensitive to their parents' anxieties: anything parents express can worsen their fears.

▨ ACTION Since many hospital admissions are planned, take advantage of the waiting time by preparing your child for the experience.
Tell him a couple of days before admission that he is going into hospital. This is a sensible time lapse – not too long, not too short; you will have several opportunities to go over it together. You might play some hospital games to explain routines and introduce the idea of doctors and nurses; or you might show him a hospital book designed for children. Some hospitals have public visiting days on paediatric wards.
Give the child familiar objects to take into hospital, so that he is reminded of home. If you are unable to stay with the child, tell the nurses about any routines he is used to, and any special words used, for instance about going to the lavatory.
It is generally best to warn, without giving it undue emphasis, that a painful procedure will hurt for a little while.
See also *SEPARATION ANXIETY, BLOOD TESTS, X-RAYS.*

HYDROCEPHALUS
A condition in which intermittent or persistent raised pressure of fluid within the head causes stretching of the brain.

▨ SYMPTOMS In older children, hydrocephalus causes HEADACHES or

HYDROCEPHALUS

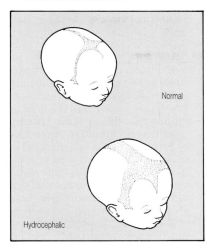

Normal

Hydrocephalic

loss of vision. In babyhood, when hydrocephalus is most common, the softness of the skull allows expansion, and leads to an abnormal rate of growth of the head, before causing signs of raised pressure.

■ CAUSES Excessive fluid production in the ventricles (fluid chambers in the brain); obstruction to the flow of fluid within or outside the ventricles; failure of reabsorption of fluid. But the commonest cause is obstruction to the escape of fluid.

Narrowing of the canal between the third and fourth ventricles (aqueduct stenosis) is found, especially in boys.

Many children with SPINA BIFIDA have some degree of hydrocephalus. Other causes include the consequences of MENINGITIS, brain haemorrhage and HEAD INJURY. There is an inherited sex-linked form affecting half the sons of women who are carriers.

■ TREATMENT Some cases resolve of their own accord. If pressure is raised persistently, fluid can be drained through a valved tube (a shunt) into the abdomen, or into a large blood vessel. This prevents undue head enlargement or death from excessive pressure and, indeed, blindness from stretching of the visual pathways in the brain.

■ OUTLOOK depends on the degree of hydrocephalus and the associated disabilities, for example spina bifida and visual impairment. Most children with hydrocephalus go to mainstream schools and are chatty, sociable children. They tend to be clumsy, to have limited understanding of language and to suffer from poor visual-spatial ability. Their intelligence ranges from high to low – see *MENTAL HANDICAP* and *LEARNING DISORDERS*. As adults they are mostly able to live independently, but spina bifida or mental handicap are the main obstacles to this.

HYDROCOELE
A soft, non-tender swelling in the scrotum caused by fluid from the abdominal cavity entering via a channel in the scrotal neck.

A hydrocele does not damage the testicle, and causes no long-term problems. The channel that connects the abdominal cavity and scrotum normally closes during the first year of life; if it remains open, a small operation may be needed to close up the channel.

HYPERACTIVE CHILD
An abnormally and excessively active child with poor concentration, restlessness and impulsiveness, often accompanied by a minimal requirement for sleep. He is easily distracted and often disruptive. The more severe

degrees of this state are sometimes called hyperkinetic syndrome or attention deficit disorder.

■ INCIDENCE Ten per cent of boys show some degree of hyperactivity; hence, to some extent, it is a variant of normal behaviour, influenced by the family environment, the tolerance of the parents, and inherited temperamental factors. Less than 1 per cent of children have something approaching hyperkinesis. It is very rare in girls.

■ CAUSES In otherwise normal children, no cause is usually identified. Serious degrees of hyperactivity may be seen in children with established BRAIN DAMAGE, EPILEPSY, and severe MENTAL HANDICAP. Most research on FOOD ALLERGY, preservatives and ADDITIVES shows *no* link with hyperactivity.

■ SYMPTOMS Many young children are extremely active and may be difficult to control, but the behaviour of the truly hyperactive child will be noticed by all his different carers at all times, in all settings, and will distinguish him from his peers. He may have difficulty relating to other children, a difficult temperament generally and learning problems. AGGRESSION and other BEHAVIOURAL DISORDERS often accompany hyperactivity.

■ ACTION Give a pre-school child clear instructions, and only when you are sure you have his attention. Praise him when he has concentrated well. Active play out of doors whenever possible will help to use up some of the excess energy. If the problem interferes with the child's learning, friendships and family relationships, ask professionals at nursery school or health clinic for help.

Get medical advice: help from a psychologist, social worker or child psychiatrist may be needed in such cases.

■ TREATMENT For most hyperactive children, BEHAVIOURAL TREATMENT will be suggested. If the child is on medication for a condition such as epilepsy, changes in the dose or the drug may be suggested. For very severe cases, stimulant drugs may be prescribed, of which methylphenidate is currently the most commonly used. This drug may speed up the heart rate but quietens down the behaviour to some degree. Loss of appetite, depression and slowing of growth are possible side-effects which cease when the drug is stopped, but require careful monitoring. Most drugs, such as tranquillizers, make the symptoms worse and hinder learning.

■ OUTLOOK Many hyperactive children improve when they start school, although for the severely affected, school poses new difficulties. Fortunately, almost all degrees of hyperactivity diminish considerably in adolescence.

HYPERGLYCAEMIA
See *DIABETES MELLITUS*.

HYPERLIPIDAEMIA
A high level of fat (lipid) in the blood. This can result from a diet high in animal fat, or from the body's inherited inability to remove fats efficiently from the blood. Cholesterol is one of these fats: persistent lifelong high blood cholesterol levels are associated with an increased risk of CORONARY ARTERY DISEASE in later life. If an individual child is shown to have a particular type of hyperlipidaemia, then

an adjustment to daily diet may be of benefit. Animal fats (found in red meat, eggs, butter and cream) should be kept to a minimum. This is especially important if there is a history of coronary artery disease among young to middle-aged members of the family. Blood fats can be measured by a series of complex BLOOD TESTS. This is not usually necessary during childhood, unless there is a history of young members of the family developing coronary artery disease.

HYPERTENSION

BLOOD PRESSURE above the normal for a particular age. This is relatively uncommon during childhood, but can be due to kidney disease or COARCTATION OF THE AORTA.

HYPERTHYROIDISM

Over-production of the hormone thyroxine, the function of which is explained under HYPOTHYROIDISM. Rare in children.

■ CAUSES The body's immune system may produce ANTIBODIES that stimulate the thyroid. The reason for this is not clear. It may occur at any age during childhood and is more common in girls. A mother who has hyperthyroidism may pass antibodies to her foetus during pregnancy. The new-born baby may then have hyperthyroidism which will be transient, lasting up to three months.

■ SYMPTOMS include restlessness, weight loss, palpitations and poor concentration. The child may have grown rapidly and be tall for his age. Some children have a tremor and some a GOITRE.

■ TREATMENT A BLOOD TEST will

confirm a high thyroxine level, and the child will usually be given anti-thyroid drugs initially. If drugs fail to control the condition, or the goitre itself is troublesome, surgical removal of part of the thyroid gland may be recommended. If complete removal of the thyroid is performed, the child will need thyroid replacement therapy (thyroxine tablets) lifelong.

HYPERVENTILATION

See OVERBREATHING, STRESS SYMPTOMS.

HYPOGLYCAEMIA

A low level of glucose in the blood.

■ CAUSES Hypoglycaemia may occur when a baby is born to a DIABETIC MOTHER, is PREMATURE or SMALL-FOR-DATES. In older children hypoglycaemia may be a symptom of underlying hypopituitarism, certain ADRENAL DISORDERS, or serious failure of liver function. More commonly it occurs in children with DIABETES when their dose of insulin is too high relative to their intake of food and exercise.

■ SYMPTOMS A new-born baby becomes 'jittery', feeds poorly and, if the blood sugar level is very low, may develop FITS. An older child may behave abnormally or aggressively, and appear pale and sweaty. Very low levels of blood glucose lead to loss of consciousness or coma.

■ TREATMENT The aim is to raise the blood glucose level. This must be done without delay – as soon as symptoms are recognized – to prevent unconsciousness. A high-sugar food or drink is given to the child, or, if that is not appropriate, glucose is given by an intravenous injection or drip.

HYPOIMMUNOGLOBULINAEMIA

The term covers a range of diseases, usually congenital in origin, caused by a complete or partial lack of immunoglobulins. These are proteins (also called ANTIBODIES) which play a vital role in the body's defences against INFECTION.

▧ SYMPTOMS some patients with congenital deficiency remain surprisingly free from symptoms until later in life. Others may suffer repeated infections such as CONJUNCTIVITIS, SINUSITIS and chest infections. Skin disorders are very common in this condition, typically ECZEMA, skin abscesses and coarse skin. DIARRHOEA may occur as a result of either *giardia* infection, SUGAR INTOLERANCE or MALABSORPTION. There is also a slightly increased frequency of cancer in this group of children.

Auto-immune illnesses (conditions where the body's defences attack their own cells, for example, RHEUMATOID ARTHRITIS) are strongly associated with complete deficiency, and also partial deficiency, of one particular immunoglobulin called IgA.

▧ TESTS are easily performed by measuring the level of immunoglobulins in the blood. Results must be interpreted with caution in the baby's first year of life because of the high levels of certain types of antibodies passed to the baby from the mother, and of barely detectable levels of other types of antibody. The baby with this problem also tends to suffer an unusually large number of infections in the first year of his life.

▧ TREATMENT None may be needed if symptoms are mild. Intravenous injections of immunoglobulin given roughly once a month will usually provide adequate protection against infections. Monitoring of blood levels will show the best interval between injections.

Children with this problem should have their lung function monitored annually because of the risk of lung disease. In some cases, continuous ANTIBIOTIC therapy may be necessary to give the necessary protection against infection.

HYPOSPADIAS

A condition in which the opening of the urethra is on the under-surface of the penis, instead of at its tip. Sometimes there is also a downward curvature of the penis. A mild degree of hypospadias is common, and may run in families. It requires no treatment. An operation to correct the abnormality is necessary when the opening of the urethra is far from the tip of the penis. This may be done in two stages, usually after the child is out of nappies, but before he starts school.

HYPOTHERMIA

Low body temperature – 95°F or 35°C. This is a particular risk for all newborn babies, especially those of LOW BIRTH WEIGHT. The condition has been described as neonatal cold syndrome. Hypothermia immediately after birth increases the chances of a baby developing RESPIRATORY DISTRESS SYNDROME. Cold stress may also cause the baby to use up calorie reserves to produce heat, with the risk of developing HYPOGLYCAEMIA. Since heat is lost rapidly from the skin if the baby is wet, naked and in a cold, draughty environment, the labour ward needs to be kept as warm as possible. Immediately after birth the baby should be dried with a warm towel, and kept wrapped up. A small baby may need nursing under a heater or in an INCUBATOR (see *INTENSIVE CARE*).

HYPOTHYROIDISM

Low production of the hormone thyroxine, which is produced by the thyroid gland in the neck. Thyroxine controls the rate of energy production by the body's tissues. It is also involved with growth and mental development. Iodine is needed for its synthesis by the body. Hypothyroidism in babies may be called cretinism, and in children, juvenile myxoedema.

■ CAUSES The condition may be congenital – a baby may be born without a thyroid gland or with one that is unable to produce enough thyroxine. This sometimes causes a GOITRE. Deficiency of iodine may also cause a goitre.

Some children manufacture ANTI-BODIES that act against the thyroid, causing it to function poorly (auto-immune thyroiditis). A much rarer cause is hypopituitarism: under-function of the pituitary gland in the brain, which has control over the thyroid.

■ SYMPTOMS Cretinism can be recognized in the first few weeks of life. The baby may have a dry skin and hair, hoarse cry, CONSTIPATION, JAUNDICE and abnormal lethargy. He may be slow to feed. If the problem is not diagnosed, he is likely to suffer retarded development.

Symptoms of hypothyroidism developing later in childhood are poor growth (the child becomes short for his age), dry skin and hair, a general slowness, and a tendency to feel cold. A goitre may or may not be present.

HYPOTHYROIDISM

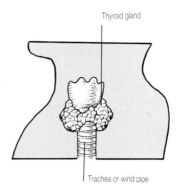

Thyroid gland

Trachea or wind pipe

■ TESTS A BLOOD TEST will be taken to measure the level of thyroxine in the blood. Also to test whether there is a high level of the pituitary hormone, Thyroid Stimulating Hormone (TSH), produced by the body in an attempt to induce the thyroid gland to make an adequate quantity of thyroxine. Occasionally, a scan of the thyroid is useful.

■ TREATMENT Thyroxine is given as tablets.

■ OUTLOOK Provided treatment is started in the first weeks of life, there is a reasonable chance that growth and mental development will be normal.

The biggest advance in the treatment of congenital hypothyroidism has been the introduction of routine blood testing (as part of the GUTHRIE TEST performed on all babies in the first week after birth) for thyroid function. (TSH is measured from the blood spot on the filter paper sample.) This has allowed early diagnosis and treatment and, with very rare exceptions, should make undiagnosed cretinism a condition of the past.

I

IDIOPATHIC THROMBOCYTOPENIC PURPURA

A blood disease of unknown (idiopathic) cause – although it often follows a VIRAL INFECTION. It is most common in children between two and eight years of age, and involves a decrease in the number of platelets in the blood (thrombocytopenia). Platelets are important for normal blood clotting, so the condition makes the child prone to uncontrolled bleeding.

▨ SYMPTOMS A RASH, consisting of tiny haemorrhages into the skin, mainly of the trunk.

There is also bleeding from the nose, gums, in the bowel and bladder and, in rare instances, into the brain. In most children the illness is mild, with no severe bleeding.

▨ ACTION Any rash with bleeding should be seen by a doctor.

Try to prevent any injury likely to cause bleeding. It may be necessary to keep your child off school if minor injuries are causing bleeding.

If the symptoms are severe, your doctor may recommend that the child is admitted into hospital for a short stay.

▨ TESTS include a BLOOD TEST and possibly a bone marrow examination.

▨ TREATMENT In mild cases, no treatment is necessary. If the number of platelets in the blood is low, or if the bleeding is severe, a steroid can give marked improvement, although symptoms may return when the course is finished.

Sometimes the spleen is removed surgically to decrease the platelet count. Severe bleeding may require a BLOOD TRANSFUSION.

▨ OUTLOOK is usually good. Recovery takes three to six months. Attacks occasionally recur, but with decreasing frequency. The only real hazard is haemorrhage into the brain in the early stages.

IMMUNITY

A defence mechanism of the body which combats the effects of invasion by foreign substances. When an infecting organism enters the body, large molecules on the wall of the organism (called ANTIGENS) stimulate the body to produce ANTIBODIES. The antibodies react with the antigens, thereby potentially neutralizing their effect or assisting other cells in destroying the invading organism, thus fighting the INFECTION. This response is usually of benefit, but occasionally the reaction leads to undesirable side-effects. ALLERGY is one such instance when the antigen (such as pollen) stimulates the production of antibodies, interaction with which leads to a chemical sequence with discomforting clinical effects. Another harmful result of this reaction is the rejection of a TRANSPLANTED organ.

Immunity is specific. An antibody will only react with one particular type of antigen. These antibodies remain in the body, or can be produced very rapidly again, so subsequent infection by the same organism will induce a rapid defensive response. Unfortunately the COMMON COLD and INFLUENZA are caused by a number of different VIRUSES and although the body develops an immunity to one, other organisms may still lead to similar patterns of illness.

Babies acquire a degree of immunity passively from antibodies transferred from the mother across the placenta before birth, and via breast milk after birth. This passive immunity decreases over the first six months after birth; as this wanes, the child actively has to build up his own immunity. This happens as a result of natural exposure to antigens and infections, and by IMMUNIZATION.

IMMUNIZATION

Protection against INFECTIOUS disease, achieved by giving the child a weakened strain of a VIRUS or BACTERIUM. This stimulates the body to produce ANTIBODIES so that the child develops immunity without becoming seriously ill. It is sometimes necessary to have more than one dose of a vaccine to gain full immunity, especially if the vaccine is not a 'live' strain.

All children should be immunized against POLIOMYELITIS (POLIO), TETANUS and DIPHTHERIA. With a few exceptions, the risk of ENCEPHALITIS from WHOOPING COUGH immunization is far less than the risk to a child from the illness.

▨ TRIPLE VACCINE of diphtheria, tetanus and whooping cough is a combination given by injection in three doses during the child's first year. The first injection is usually given at three months. If a baby is PREMATURE, immunization starts later. Following immunization, the child may be FEVERISH. The injection site may be red, and a small lump may remain for several weeks.

▨ BOOSTER INJECTIONS of diphtheria and tetanus are necessary. From five years of age, a tetanus booster is advisable every ten years after that.

▨ POLIOMYELITIS (POLIO) immunization is given by mouth at the same time as the triple vaccine. There is a theoretical chance that breast milk may inactivate the vaccine, but this has not been found in practice. Side-effects include fever

or diarrhoea. Live virus is excreted in the stools, so adults caring for the child should be immunized. A booster is given at five years, and again on leaving school.

▨ MEASLES remains a serious illness and can cause death from PNEUMONIA and ENCEPHALITIS. Immunization is advisable, nowadays in combination with MUMPS and *RUBELLA* vaccine (see below). Side-effects – fever and a rash – may occur about a week after the injection.

▨ *RUBELLA* vaccine should be given to girls at about 11 years of age to prevent the disease occurring during pregnancy, as this could result in congenital *Rubella* syndrome – see *RUBELLA*.

Side-effects, including fever, rash and swollen glands, can occur about two weeks after the injection.

▨ COMBINED MEASLES, MUMPS and RUBELLA immunization is now available and is intended to replace the measles-only vaccination in the U.K. It is recommended to be given during the second year of life. A further immunization against *Rubella* is nonetheless currently recommended for girls during adolescence since it is not known whether *Rubella* vaccine given in early childhood will protect against infection right through the child-bearing years.

Side-effects of the combined immunization are the same as for simple measles and *Rubella* immunization.

▨ TUBERCULOSIS (BCG) vaccine is recommended to be given at about 11 years. A skin test is done first to establish whether the child is already immune. See TUBERCULOSIS. If there is no immunity, BCG is given. In areas where tuberculosis is a significant risk, BCG can be given soon after birth. (BCG stands for Bacille Calmette Guerin, the French scientist who was responsible for developing the vaccine.)

■ SMALLPOX vaccine is no longer necessary since the disease has been eradicated.

■ WHERE TO GET YOUR CHILD IMMUNIZED Health authority clinics, G.P.s and school medical services can all provide immunization, and will give you up-to-date information.

■ WHICH CHILDREN SHOULD NOT BE IMMUNIZED? Contra-indications to immunization are few and many children remain unnecessarily vulnerable to preventable disease.

If your child has a fever or diarrhoea, wait until he is better. A cold, or snuffly nose, is no problem.

If he has a chronic medical condition, discuss immunization with your doctor. Most of these children need all the protection they can get.

Whooping cough vaccine is usually avoided if a child had severe CONVULSIONS during the neonatal period. A history of EPILEPSY in close relatives should be mentioned to your doctor.

A previous FEBRILE CONVULSION is sometimes a contra-indication to whooping cough and measles immunization.

ALLERGY to eggs or egg products is no longer considered a contra-indication unless the child has had a very severe allergic reaction.

Rubella and polio vaccines should not be given to pregnant women; definite precautions should be taken to avoid pregnancy for a few months after *Rubella* immunization.

Children who are HIV (AIDS) positive should be immunized as usual because of their increased vulnerability to infection. However, they will not be given immunization against tuberculosis, and those with lowered immunity may be given an inactivated form of polio virus.

IMPERFORATE ANUS
See *ANUS, IMPERFORATE*.

IMPETIGO
A common, highly contagious skin infection, characterized by golden-yellow crusts over a spreading red rash.

■ SYMPTOMS The first sign is usually a small itchy spot, often on the face, (but it can occur anywhere), which quickly enlarges and becomes weepy, sometimes with blisters. If the rash is in contact with another part of the body (for example the face and neck) a second rash appears at the point of contact. Children are more commonly affected than adults.

■ CAUSES *Staphyllococcus aureus* is the BACTERIUM chiefly responsible for impetigo, while another, *Streptococcus*, is often also present. The rashes of HERPES (cold sores), CHICKENPOX, SCABIES, and ECZEMA can also become infected with this bacterium ('secondary impetigo'). The infection is easily carried by the fingers to other parts of the body, and to other people.

It is also spread by bacteria carried on cups, towels, or other objects. The germs enter the skin through tiny cracks, or scratches.

■ ACTION At the first sign of any redness of the skin, a simple antiseptic cream can be applied, and in mild cases may prevent any further spread of infection. If this fails see a doctor for ANTIBIOTIC treatment. You will be advised to carefully wash the skin with soap and water to remove all crusts.

To prevent impetigo spreading, it is important to isolate cups, towels, and other personal items used by a child with the infection.

■ TREATMENT Milder cases respond to antibiotic creams; an antibiotic by mouth will clear up more extensive impetigo.

■ OUTLOOK There should be no permanent marks on the skin.

INCUBATION PERIOD

The time between contact with an INFECTIOUS disease and the onset of the illness. After an infecting organism (such as a VIRUS) has entered the body, it multiplies. During this process, the child remains well. But during the few days before the symptoms develop, the child can pass the infection on to other people.

The incubation period varies for different infections; details are given under individual entries.

INCUBATOR

If you have a PREMATURE baby, the chances are that he will spend time in an incubator in the hospital's special care unit. Someone else will do the caring; you have to sit and watch. This is not an easy situation for the new parent; a few, irrationally but understandably, take it as a judgement on some inadequacy. Try and accept that this is simply a period of limbo, nothing more sinister; and that all uneasy feelings will vanish as soon as you have the baby at home.

INFECTION

Illness associated with an invasion of the body by micro-organisms such as VIRUSES, BACTERIA, PARASITES or FUNGI.

■ SPREAD OF INFECTION How this happens depends on the type of infection. It can be by direct contact, droplets, spread of infected saliva or contact with infected blood, urine or stools. Infection can also occur when organisms are swallowed.

After infection there is a period when the organism multiplies in the body: the INCUBATION PERIOD. The child appears well, but may in his turn be spreading the infection. Hence it is often impossible to prevent the common childhood infections from spreading within the family. There are theoretical advantages to your child contracting certain infections such as RUBELLA and CHICKENPOX, as symptoms are more severe if they are contracted during adult life. (However, the elimination of such infections by wholesale immunization of the childhood population, as may happen with MEASLES, MUMPS and Rubella, is a preferred option.)

Occasionally, a child may be carrying an organism, but not be ill. This child is a carrier who can pass on the infection to others.

■ SIGNS OF INFECTION vary according to the type of disease, but many infections have similar symptoms. These may include FEVER, skin RASH, DIARRHOEA and general malaise. Swollen glands indicate reaction to an infection.

■ RESISTANCE TO INFECTION is achieved by the body in various ways. The skin, nose and tonsils are natural barriers to infection; and intestinal barriers including stomach acid help to exclude swallowed organisms. The body also develops IMMUNITY to infection. ANTIBODIES and white blood cells help to destroy the organisms. The lymph nodes and spleen play a part in this process. Immunity can also be stimulated by immunization. BREAST FEEDING enhances a baby's resistance, as antibodies are passively passed in the breast milk (also ingestion of micro-organisms from bottles and formula milk is avoided).

Resistance to infection can be diminished by diseases which affect the body's ability to develop immunity such as MALNUTRITION, MEASLES and AIDS (AQUIRED IMMUNE DEFICIENCY SYNDROME).

INFECTIOUS MONONUCLEOSIS
See *GLANDULAR FEVER.*

INFECTIOUS POLYNEURITIS
See *GUILLAIN-BARRE SYNDROME.*

INFLUENZA
The acute, highly INFECTIOUS illness caused by the influenza VIRUS. There are many different strains of the virus, and infection by one does not give IMMUNITY to the others. The virus is spread by droplets in the breath, and 'flu' tends to occur in epidemics because infectious carriers are generally out and about, feeling well, in the days immediately before developing symptoms.

■ SYMPTOMS include FEVER, HEADACHE, VOMITING, shivering and muscle pain. Loss of APPETITE, COUGH and listlessness can occur. They usually last between two and seven days.

Complications include PNEUMO-NIA, EAR INFECTIONS and SINUSITIS, which result from secondary BACTERIAL infection. Rare complications in children include MYOCARDITIS and ENCEPHALITIS.

■ ACTION The fever, headache and muscle pain can be treated with a simple analgesic such as paracetamol. Aspirin should not be used in children under 12 years of age because of the risk of REYE'S SYNDROME. A cool bath is the most effective way of bringing down the temperature – see FEVER.

Vomiting is not usually severe, but encouraging your child to take plenty of clear fluids will help to prevent DEHYDRATION, which could be aggravated by the fever.

The child may feel more comfortable in bed while the fever and muscle pain persist.

Get medical advice if the fever does not respond to treatment or if there are any symptoms that particularly worry you.

Your child may start to feel better after three or four days, but you may find that he tires easily. Strenuous activity should be avoided because this can delay recovery.

Older children and adolescents may be tired and moody for a few months after the illness.

■ TREATMENT ANTIBIOTICS will only be necessary if pneumonia or any other secondary bacterial infection occurs.

Management of the other complications are discussed under individual entries.

■ IMMUNIZATION against influenza is recommended for children over four years suffering from a chronic disease, and in whom the complications are likely to be serious. The injection is given during autumn and contains strains of influenza virus most likely to cause epidemics at that particular time. It protects against about 70 per cent of infections, and is effective for about 12 months. Side-effects include redness at the injection site, fever, malaise and muscle pain beginning six to 12 hours later, lasting for one to two days.

■ OUTLOOK after influenza is generally good, apart from the few serious complications.

INHALERS

Devices used in the treatment of ASTHMA, which deliver small doses of various drugs directly to the small air passages in the lungs.

■ HOW THEY WORK All forms of inhaler create a fine spray of tiny particles, either as powder or as liquid droplets, which is carried by the air flow into the lungs. (Some of the spray is deposited in the throat, where steroid inhalers occasionally cause unwanted soreness due to

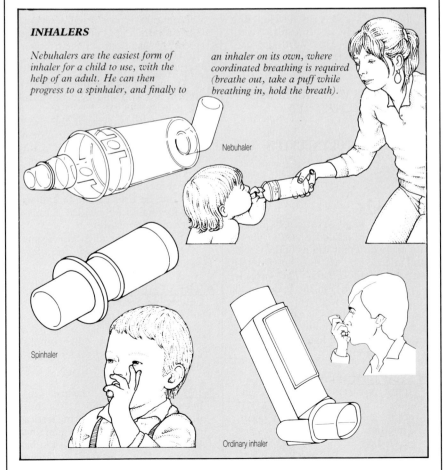

INHALERS

Nebuhalers are the easiest form of inhaler for a child to use, with the help of an adult. He can then progress to a spinhaler, and finally to

an inhaler on its own, where coordinated breathing is required (breathe out, take a puff while breathing in, hold the breath).

Nebuhaler

Spinhaler

Ordinary inhaler

THRUSH.) There are three types of drug commonly used in inhalers: bronchodilators, which open up narrowed air passages; steroids, which help to prevent attacks of asthma; cromoglycate, which also helps to prevent ALLERGIC asthma.

■ HOW TO USE THEM It is essential that children who have been prescribed inhalers know how to use them effectively. A health professional should ensure that the child is taught, but you should always check that the child is still using his inhaler properly. There are several varieties of inhaler, some designed specifically for younger children, so if your child cannot manage one, it is well worth trying a different type.

INHERITED DISORDERS

These are caused by abnormal GENES or CHROMOSOMES, which are passed on from parents. They can also develop for the first time when a gene or chromosome is altered as it is passed to the child. This is called mutation. The abnormality may then be passed on to future generations.

Genetic disorders may be inherited from the genes of one or both parents. Single gene disorders are due to one abnormal gene. This may result in a dominantly or recessively inherited genetic disorder. If an abnormal gene is dominant, there will normally be a 50 per cent chance of the child displaying signs of that disorder, as in ACHONDROPLASIA. Only one of the pair of genes is abnormal; hence there is a one in two chance of an affected parent passing the condition to the child. If an abnormal gene is recessive, the child will have to inherit two abnormal genes, one from each parent (both of whom are carriers of the abnormal gene), in order to develop the disorder. Such diseases include CYSTIC FIBROSIS

and THALASSAEMIA. If a child inherits only one abnormal recessive gene, he will usually have no signs of the disease, but will be a carrier. If both parents have a recessive disease, each child has: a one in four chance of inheriting both abnormal genes, and showing signs of the disease; a one in four chance of receiving no abnormal genes; a two in four chance of receiving one abnormal gene, and becoming a carrier.

It is usually not possible to test whether a person is a carrier. If parents are related, there is a greater chance of inheriting abnormal recessive genes from a common ancestor.

Abnormal genes can be carried on the sex chromosomes (usually the X or female chromosome). These sex-linked inherited disorders are usually recessive, so, if the child is a girl (XX), there will be no signs of the disease. This is because the normal gene on the other X chromosome overrides the effect or the deficiency arising from the abnormal gene. The chromosome make-up of the male is XY. Thus boys have only one X chromosome; if the abnormal gene is on this chromosome, the smaller Y chromosome does not carry a paired normal gene and hence does counter the effect of the abnormal gene. Common examples of such conditions are HAEMOPHILIA and Duchenne MUSCULAR DYSTROPHY. A woman who is a carrier for such a gene will pass it on to half of her sons, who will show signs of the disease. The other half of her sons will be clinically and genetically normal. She will also pass on the abnormal gene to half of her daughters, who will then become carriers.

Chromosomal abnormalities present in the ovum or sperm may be incorporated at the time of conception. Such abnormalities may cause spontaneous abortion early in pregnancy or result in a CONGENITAL ABNORMALITY, such as DOWN'S SYNDROME. Study of the chromosomes of the affected foetus or child may, depending on the particular abnormality, help in predicting the risk of a similar problem in a future pregnancy.

There are many diseases which have no clear pattern of inheritance, but are nonetheless more common in some families than others. These include DIABETES, CONGENITAL HEART-DISEASE and CONGENITAL DISLOCATION OF THE HIP. Environmental factors are presumed to play a major part in the causation of these disorders.

Parents who have a family history of a particular illness, and who plan to have further children, should consider seeking advice or GENETIC COUNSELLING. This also applies to parents who are related, since there is a greater chance of them both carrying similar abnormal recessive genes. Tests can often be carried out to determine the risk of an inherited disorder (see *ANTENATAL DIAGNOSIS*). Treatment of children with inherited disorders has improved greatly in recent years, but the aim is still to prevent them from occurring.

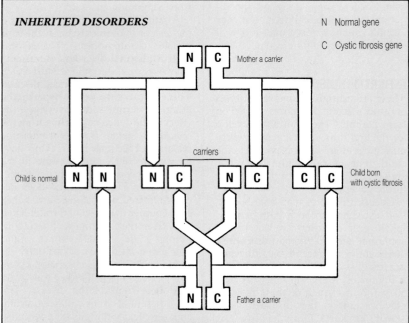

INHERITED DISORDERS

N Normal gene

C Cystic fibrosis gene

Mother a carrier

carriers

Child is normal

Child born with cystic fibrosis

Father a carrier

Inheriting a disorder: CYSTIC FIBROSIS

At the root of most grave inherited disorders is a single defective gene, which is usually recessive. This means that only if both parents contribute the gene at conception is the child born with the disorder. If a child inherits one C gene and one N gene, he will not suffer from cystic fibrosis; but he can be a carrier, and if he has offspring with another carrier, there is the chance but not the certainty that they will have a child with cystic fibrosis. About one in 20 people are carriers of this defective gene without knowing it.

INSOMNIA

Spending much of the night awake, unable to fall asleep. Young children are rarely troubled by insomnia (although their pattern of waking and sleeping at night may not meet with their parents' expectations, and thus be a concern for the parents). Older children may suffer from insomnia when worried or upset. See *SLEEP PROBLEMS*.

INTELLIGENCE

Of course, there are many definitions of intelligence, just as there are many forms of it. Here, we use the conventional one for the context of child development: the ability to absorb and remember information and then to use it to solve problems.

Intelligence is partly inherited, but also influenced by the environment in which a child grows and learns. The most important environmental factors are good antenatal conditions, loving care, suitable stimulation of language, encouragement with play and later, support at school. Children from very deprived backgrounds suffer intellectually as well as emotionally and socially.

Long-term exposure to high atmospheric levels of LEAD seems to cause children to achieve less well. There is some controversial evidence that extra vitamins can improve intelligence slightly in children; however this is not a serious consideration for children on a balanced diet.

Children pass through a number of stages on the way to developing the adult form of intelligence in mid-adolescence.

Up to about two years, a baby understands the world in terms of the here-and-now – what he can do with objects, how they feel, sound, look and taste. Objects are forgotten as soon as they disappear.

Towards the end of this stage, with the acquisition of language, the toddler has some idea of objects when they are not present, and begins to understand how objects can be mentally sorted into groups with similar characteristics. Primitive reasoning now begins and the child develops pretend play and enjoys surprisingly complicated games.

During the infant school years, the mental capabilities increase, so that, for instance, the child begins to manipulate numbers without relying on physical counting. He begins to understand that liquid in different vessels, or indeed modelling clay, may change its shape but remains the same in quantity. However, he still sees the world strongly from his point of view.

In early adolescence, children start to manipulate ideas as well as events and objects. They can imagine things that they have not experienced, organize things systematically, think deductively and see both sides of an argument. From now on they are developing the adult's ability to solve complex problems: a process that must continue with experience.

See also *I.Q., LANGUAGE DEVELOPMENT, LEARNING DISORDERS, DEVELOPMENTAL DELAY*.

INTENSIVE CARE

Continuous detailed observation and care of an ill baby or child, by specialist staff. Intensive care of new-born babies (see *PREMATURITY* and *LOW BIRTH WEIGHT*) takes place in a neonatal or special care baby unit. In such units or nurseries, babies are often nursed in INCUBATORS or under heaters, to keep them warm while allowing close observation. Older children who need intensive care (for example after a serious accident or major operation), will be admitted to a paediatric intensive care unit (I.C.U.) or an adult I.C.U. In addition to close observation, specialized equipment may be used to assist breathing and feeding, and to monitor the child's condition.

The child may be supported by a ventilator until he can breathe for himself. A tube is passed through his mouth or nose into the trachea (the upper air passage), and is connected to the ventilator, which expands his lungs in a regulated fashion with air enriched with oxygen to meet his exact needs. The child may receive physiotherapy, and the tube will be cleared by suction to remove lung secretions. A child who is ventilated may need sedation.

Most children in an I.C.U. need an intravenous drip or infusion, because they are unable to drink or eat normally. Fluids that may be enriched with nutrients such as fat or amino-acids are given into a vein through a plastic tube known as a cannula. Other equipment, used in an I.C.U. includes monitors for heart rate, respiration rate, blood pressure and temperature. Many children, but more particularly premature babies, will also have their blood oxygen monitored, either by a skin electrode or by regular BLOOD TESTS.

Parents are encouraged to be with their children and to help look after them in intensive care. Stay with your child and talk to him as much as possible. It is helpful to understand about your child's condition and the equipment that is being used. Ask the staff anything you want to know. You may feel guilty about your child's illness or anxious that he will be left damaged or weak. Try to share your fears and worries with your partner and the staff. It is helpful if you both take part in any discussions. Your other children may also be worried and upset, so try to involve them in the care of their brother or sister.

INTENSIVE CARE

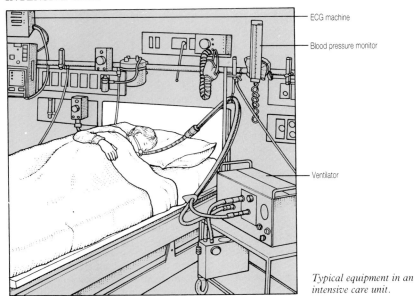

Typical equipment in an intensive care unit.

INTESTINAL OBSTRUCTION

The gut, or intestine, consists of a long continuous tube running from stomach (or, strictly, from mouth) to anus. Obstruction at any point will sooner or later block the passage of food down the intestine. This occurs in childhood most commonly in INTUS-SUSCEPTION and VOLVULUS.

INTESTINAL OBSTRUCTION

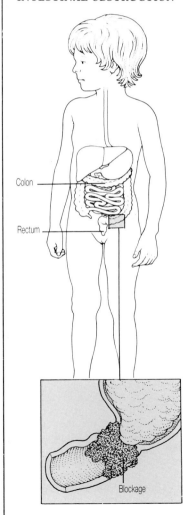

Colon

Rectum

Blockage

■ SYMPTOMS will vary with the nature of the blockage. If this is sudden in onset, as in a volvulus, the presentation may be pain or even shock rather than the signs of obstruction. If it is more gradual in onset, as with PYLORIC STENOSIS, then the signs of upper intestinal obstruction will predominate – VOMITING. Unrelieved complete obstruction of the intestine will lead to ABDOMINAL SWELLING, CONSTIPATION, vomiting, proceeding to perforation and PERITONITIS.

■ TREATMENT depends on the cause, but the usual procedure, once in hospital, is to give fluids by intravenous drip, and to drain the stomach by a tube to reduce vomiting. Then the blockage itself is treated, often by surgery.

INTOEING
See PIGEON TOES.

INTUSSUSCEPTION

A result of inflammation of the lining of the small bowel. The bowel inverts into itself (like the finger of a glove). This may lead to INTESTINAL OBSTRUCTION. The problem is uncommon and occurs mainly before the second birthday, often in the last half of the baby's first year.

■ SYMPTOMS ABDOMINAL PAIN, COLIC, VOMITING, rectal BLEEDING.

■ ACTION If these symptoms occur, get medical advice. Your doctor will have the child admitted to hospital.

■ INVESTIGATIONS/MANAGEMENT 1 Examination: the doctor may feel a swelling (the intussusception) in the abdomen. 2 Intravenous fluids (a 'drip') may be required if the child is DEHYDRATED. **3** X-ray of the abdomen may show abnormal intestinal gas patterns. **4** Barium ENEMA: this diagnoses the intussusception, which appears as an obstruction. Gentle pressure with barium usually reduces the swelling, but if this fails, or there is evidence of PERITONITIS, an abdominal operation will be necessary.

▓ OUTLOOK Once an intussusception has been reduced either by barium enema or surgically, there is only a 5 per cent chance of it happening again.

INTUSSUSCEPTION

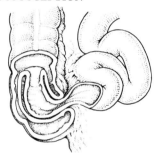

IRON
See *ANAEMIA*.

IRON DEFICIENCY
See *ANAEMIA*.

ITCHING
Not all itching is due to skin disease: normal skin will itch when certain chemicals or materials come into contact with it. Some babies and young children will find wool unpleasantly itchy, and will not wear it. Important medical causes of itching include: ECZEMA, URTICARIA, INSECT BITES, SCABIES, HEPATITIS, JAUNDICE, DIABETES, some forms of LEUKAEMIA, and some types of WORMS.

▓ ACTION If the cause is known, and the itching not severe, as for example with some insect bites – See *BITES AND STINGS* – no action is needed. If necessary, an antihistamine can be given by mouth without consulting a doctor for minor but persistent itching when the cause is known. Promethazine or chlorpheniramine are suitable. Otherwise, get medical advice and your doctor will consider the various possible causes.

▓ TREATMENT This depends on the cause: most of those listed above have specific treatments, in addition to which an oral antihistamine medicine may be prescribed. For long-term management and outlook, see the separate entries.

I.Q. (INTELLIGENCE QUOTIENT)
A number or score obtained from an intelligence test, which compares an individual child's score with the scores from a large number of children of the same age. The I.Q. represents a composite result from tests of a range of skills. The average I.Q. is 100; 68 per cent of people have I.Q.s between 85 and 115. I.Q. scores are limited in their value as predictors of future academic success, because many other factors, such as interest and motivation, are important in learning. They are particularly unreliable for pre-school children, because of the wide variation in rates of development at this age. They can, however, be useful predictors of performance in skills such as reading. Nowadays, educational psychologists tend to concentrate on the overall range of a child's abilities, and aim to diagnose particular strengths and weaknesses, so that teachers and parents can plan for an individual child's education. See *INTELLIGENCE*.

JK

JAUNDICE (IN BABIES)

The yellow discoloration of the skin and eyes, which occurs to some degree in up to 50 per cent of normal newborn babies. It is usually at its most noticeable between the third and sixth days after birth, and may be slightly more common in breast-fed babies.

▓ CAUSES The yellow colour, known as bilirubin, is a pigment produced in the body by the breakdown of red blood cells. It is normally disposed of by the liver as bile, which drains into the bowel, and passed out of the body in the faeces. In the new-born, this process is 'overworked' because of especially rapid breakdown of red cells, and the relative immaturity of the disposal system of the baby's liver. The bilirubin level in the blood rises, and can be seen as a yellowing of the skin. Most jaundice in the new-born is harmless and normal. More severe jaundice may be caused by INFECTION, HYPO-THYROIDISM and the rapid destruction of red blood cells that occurs in RHESUS or ABO BLOOD GROUP INCOMPATIBILITY.

▓ ACTION In most babies, no investigation or treatment is required. Jaundice usually disappears by the tenth day after birth.

Investigation and possible treatment may be required if the jaundice is severe, or the baby is otherwise ill; or if the jaundice appears during the first 24 hours of life, suggesting Rhesus or ABO blood group incompatibility; or if it persists beyond two weeks of age.

▓ TESTS A BLOOD TEST can determine the level of bilirubin in the blood; other tests may be used to determine the underlying cause.

▓ TREATMENT Adequate feeds are necessary, because dehydration may worsen the jaundice. If the bilirubin level is high, PHOTOTHERAPY is required. For dangerously high bilirubin levels and for babies not responding to phototherapy, EXCHANGE TRANSFUSION is required.

▓ OUTLOOK is usually excellent, providing there is no serious underlying cause.

JAUNDICE IN CHILDREN

The symptoms (and underlying process) causing jaundice in children are similar to that of JAUNDICE IN BABIES.

▓ CAUSES of jaundice in childhood range from an inflammatory process in the liver (HEPATITIS), or an abnormality of red blood cells which contain bilirubin (haemolytic ANAEMIA) to an obstruction of bile drainage. Acute jaundice may be due to VIRAL INFECTION inflaming the liver – see *HEPATITIS*.

JEALOUSY

The only antidote to jealousy is learning to share: to share not only possessions, but attention and affection. Sharing is a social skill, learned rather than inborn, though affected to a degree by the individual's personality and temperament. Any new situation (new baby, new school, new parent) will increase a child's need for attention; with parental skill (and some luck), attention and love can be distributed without engendering jealousy in one or other child. See also *SIBLING RIVALRY, DIVORCE, FAMILY PROBLEMS*.

JOINT PAINS

See *ARTHRITIS*.

JUVENILE CHRONIC ARTHRITIS

The term describing a group of ill-nesses responsible for repeated epi-sodes of ARTHRITIS. The problem may also be described as Still's disease. Its causes are unknown.

▓ SYMPTOMS Painful swelling of certain joints, particularly those of the hands, wrists, elbows, ankles and knees. The neck and hip joints may also be involved. You may find that your child has stiff, painful joints in the morning, which im-prove later in the day. He may also have a pale pink RASH, mainly on the trunk, face and limbs.

A slight FEVER is often present and there may be small swellings (nodules) under the skin.

The lymph glands may be en-larged, noticeably so in the neck or under the arms. The child may also be pale and have ANAEMIA.

▓ ACTION The joint swelling is a cue for an early visit to the doctor. Diag-nosis is not always easy, or quick. Tests are necessary (usually BLOOD TESTS and X-rays), and the pattern of the illness needs to be watched for a few weeks before a reliable verdict can be reached.

▓ TREATMENT The aim is to let the child lead as normal a life as pos-sible. To achieve this, the pain must be controlled and damage and defor-mity of joints kept to a minimum. Muscles must be kept active to pre-vent them becoming weak.

During the episodes of severe joint pain, some rest is necessary. Wrist and knee joints can be kept in splints at night to prevent them from becoming fixed in positions which make them difficult to use. The child should also lie on his abdomen with his feet over the edge of the bed for ten to 15 minutes every day to prevent deformity of the hips and knees.

Pain relief is important. Your doctor may prescribe aspirin: one of the few occasions when it is justified in children (see *REYE'S SYN-DROME*). It is highly effective at relieving joint pain and indeed in allowing joints to function normally again. It should always be given with food, and never in more than the prescribed dose.

Alternative anti-inflammatory drugs may sometimes be used and occasionally steroids are necessary when all other treatment fails.

Once the pain and swelling im-proves, a physiotherapist needs to show the child exercises to streng-then muscles that have become stiff. Some of these can be painful, but they are essential to prevent defor-mity. This can develop rapidly if the joiints are not kept moving. Exer-cises in a warm swimming pool are particularly useful and can be fun.

An occupational therapist can help the child with games and activi-ties that keep joints mobile: if an exercise is a game, the child hardly needs motivating.

If deformity has already occurred, the occupational therapist can help with appliances and modification of the home.

Children with this condition may also suffer from anxiety and depres-sion. Do ask for medical help with this: it is part of the illness.

▓ ALTERNATIVE TREATMENTS Acupuncture, homoeopathy, spec-ialized diets and many other reme-dies have all been recommended to relieve the symptoms of juvenile chronic arthritis. None of these have any proven effect, but faith in a spe-cific treatment will often produce some relief of symptoms, and it can-not do harm unless medical recommendations are abandoned and joints are allowed to become stiff and useless.

▨ OUTLOOK is variable, but in most children the symptoms gradually improve during adolescence and the arthritis does not continue into adult life. Thus, if damage to the joints is kept to a minimum, the outlook is usually good. Children with chronic arthritis are rarely known to suffer educationally.

KELOID
See *SCAR*.

KIDNEY FAILURE
See *RENAL FAILURE*.

KIDNEY TRANSPLANT
See *RENAL FAILURE*.

KLINEFELTER'S SYNDROME
A rare chromosomal abnormality where there are three sex CHROMO-SOMES (XXY) instead of the normal two. Babies born with Klinefelter's syndrome have normal male features at birth, but at PUBERTY tend to be tall without the sequence of development of normal male sex characteristics. Instead, affected boys may develop breasts and a feminine body shape. The testicles remain small and do not produce sperm, resulting in infertility. There may be a minor degree of MENTAL HANDICAP.

If you have one child with Klinefelter's syndrome, there is little risk of having another child affected in the same way. You will, however, want to discuss this with your own doctor and it would be helpful to consult a geneticist for further information and counselling.

KNOCK KNEES
The child's knees tilt inwards. When he stands, his knees touch and the ankles remain apart. For the majority of cases there is no cause, apart from the fact that the ligaments which support the knee are more lax than usual. The problem is commonest in OBESE children and those with FLAT FEET, and can occur with RICKETS.

▨ SYMPTOMS, apart from the knock-kneed appearance, don't really exist. But it is possible to measure the severity of the problem. Get the child to stand up straight with his knees together, and measure the distance between the ankles. If it is more than 2 in (5 cm), see your doctor.

▨ ACTION In most cases, particularly in children under six years, no treatment is necessary. However, it is advisable to encourage your child to sit cross-legged on the floor.

If your child is overweight, a return to a normal weight for height will usually cure the problem.

Your doctor may suggest an X-ray to check for RICKETS.

▨ TREATMENT In the most severe cases, it may be necessary to raise the inner border of the heel of the shoe slightly to correct the tilt. In the unusual cases where the problem persists after the tenth birthday, an operation may be recommended.

▨ OUTLOOK Knock knees usually recover without treatment.

KOPLIK SPOTS
The name given to the small white spots which occur inside the cheeks, close to the molar teeth, in the early stages of measles.
See *MEASLES*.

LACTOSE INTOLERANCE

Impaired absorption of the sugar lactose, caused by a deficiency of the enzyme lactase in the bowel lining. There are two types, primary and secondary.

■ SYMPTOMS Watery DIARRHOEA from birth in the primary type or after GASTROENTERITIS in the secondary form, which is much commoner. Primary alactasia is a rare INHERITED DISORDER. Small bowel biopsy (as in COELIAC DISEASE) will reveal low lactase levels. Secondary lactose intolerance occurs in association with many gastro-intestinal disorders, particularly GASTROENTERITIS.

Lactase deficiency may also be associated with protein MALNUTRITION and COW'S MILK ALLERGY, and is commoner in PREMATURE infants, particularly those who have an infection, have been short of oxygen, or who have had abdominal surgery.

■ SYMPTOMS Fluid diarrhoea, starting when normal feeds are reintroduced after therapy for simple gastroenteritis. The BOWEL MOTIONS are passed forcefully, with wind, and there is irritation of the buttocks. There may be fluid loss and DEHYDRATION.

■ INVESTIGATIONS Stool tests; trial with lactose-free milk. The feeds may be changed back to ordinary milk after recovery, as a 'challenge'.

■ OUTLOOK Primary lactose intolerance is lifelong. Secondary intolerance may be brief, or last for some months, but full recovery is the rule.

LANGUAGE DEVELOPMENT

The road to speech starts well before a baby's first words. Babies communicate with familiar adults from birth, responding and being responded to as in conversation. Interacting with their mothers, babies use complex sequences of facial expression and movement. A mother responds by copying the expressions or talking to the baby; in turn, the baby responds. This fine tuning of responses continues naturally through the period of language development. By about four months, most babies make some sounds during these 'conversations' and soon after will start discriminating between familiar voices.

The babbling which develops from six to 12 months involves word-like sounds with varying pitch and is often used as if in conversation. During this period, the baby's understanding of names of people, objects and actions is increasing. Many babies will be saying their first words at around 12 months, although this can vary substantially, even in 'normal' children. The vocabulary of single words increases slowly at first, then rapidly. The toddler than starts to string these together in two-word sentences from about 18 months.

Over the next three or four years, language develops as a social tool and is encouraged and influenced by opportunities to hear and use it. However, the process is essentially innate and follows similar patterns, though at varying rates, in all children except those with severe MENTAL HANDICAP.

Children who are born deaf babble normally until about eight months, then stop. At this stage they can learn some signs for objects, or, if hearing can be restored, continue to develop language normally. Children brought up hearing two languages may take longer to increase their vocabulary for the obvious reason that they have to learn two names for everything.

Delay in language development tends to run in families and is commoner in boys than girls. It is rarely a cause for concern, but your child should have regular development checks, by a doctor or health visitor, or your local WELL-BABY CLINIC, up to school entry. Seek advice as soon as you are worried – there may be a simple remedy.

See also *DEAFNESS, LEARNING DISORDERS, INTELLIGENCE, SPEECH DISORDERS, DEVELOPMENTAL DELAY.*

LARYNGITIS
Inflammation of the larynx, or voice-box.

LARYNGITIS

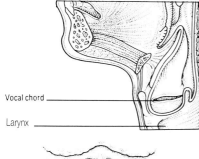

Vocal chord _____

Larynx _____

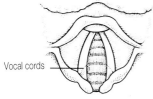

Vocal cords _____

View down throat to vocal cords

■ CAUSES VIRUSES or BACTERIA. The problem may be part of a wide-spread INFECTION, such as LARYNGO-TRACHEO-BRONCHITIS, INFLUENZA, or even a COMMON COLD.

■ SYMPTOMS Hoarseness and a SORE THROAT, often with a raised temperature.

■ ACTION For younger children (under five years), see *CROUP.* Above this age there is much less risk of obstruction to the breathing because the air passage is larger. The sore throat can be relieved by suitable doses of paracetamol, while inhalations of steam (carefully supervised), may be soothing. The hoarseness will be made worse by speaking, so the child should be encouraged to keep quiet.

■ GET MEDICAL ADVICE if the child has any difficulty in breathing or a high temperature.

■ TREATMENT Most laryngitis in children is due to viral infections, which have no specific treatment. Antibiotics are not usually required.

■ OUTLOOK Complete recovery in one to two weeks.

LARYNGO-TRACHEO-BRONCHITIS
The commonest cause of CROUP, affecting babies and young children. The lining of the air passages from the larynx to the lungs may be affected.

■ CAUSES The para-influenza VIRUSES, and some others.

■ SYMPTOMS The cough sounds like the bark of a sea-lion (once heard, never forgotten). The cough is often worse at night. The child may have a running nose, sore throat and hoarse voice or cry; this may be accompanied by noisy breathing or STRIDOR. Some children also run a temperature, and are generally unwell. This may progress to difficulty in breathing, with a heaving chest and indrawing of the space under the ribs.

■ ACTION 1 You may find that your

child gains some relief from sitting in a steamy atmosphere. **2** Get the child to drink plenty of fluids. If he appears unable to swallow, get urgent medical advice. **3** If breathing appears difficult or the child is distressed, get urgent medical advice, even in the night. Be prepared for the doctor to tell you to go to the local hospital casualty department.

▦ TREATMENT Milder cases may be treated at home by your doctor. As the condition is due to a viral INFECTION there is currently no specific ANTIBIOTIC which is effective. Fluids and paracetamol are comforting. Occasionally a drug such as salbutamol may help to relieve wheezing. More severe cases, especially in younger children, are treated in hospital, where an oxygen tent may be used. Occasionally, if there is severe obstruction to breathing, a tube may be inserted into the trachea through his nose or mouth, and artificial ventilation initiated.

▦ INVESTIGATIONS A chest X-ray and BLOOD TESTS will be done in hospital, but are unnecessary for milder cases.

▦ OUTLOOK Complete recovery, with no long-term effects.

LAZY EYE
See *SQUINT*.

LEAD POISONING
Less of a hazard nowadays than it used to be, because many countries now ban lead-containing paint on toys.

▦ SYMPTOMS The most worrying effects are on the nervous and digestive systems: spasmodic abdominal pain, a metallic taste in the mouth, vomiting, diarrhoea and constipation are associated with lead poisoning; as also are headaches, irritability, convulsions and possibly coma. The risk that long-term exposure to lead is a cause of DEVELOPMENTAL DELAY and LEARNING DISORDERS in urban children is worrying. Research still goes on to substantiate a direct link. Lead poisoning can also cause ANAEMIA.

▦ TESTS BLOOD TESTS to measure the amount of lead in the body, and X-rays, may be made to confirm the diagnosis.

▦ TREATMENT in hospital will include ensuring a high fluid intake to protect the kidneys; anticonvulsants if there is a danger of convulsions; and specific treatment with a 'chelating agent' which removes the lead from the bloodstream. Further tests will be necessary to monitor the success of the treatment.

LEARNING DISORDERS
These are suspected when, despite adequate teaching, a child acquires skills or knowledge at a rate that is much slower than expected for his age and INTELLIGENCE. The problem may be general or specific (limited to one area in particular, such as reading, spelling, or arithmetic). Specific disorders are not usually identifiable until the age of seven or eight. This is because of the wide variation in children's learning capacity, particularly for reading, and it is not until this age that slowness becomes a cause for concern. See *LANGUAGE DEVELOPMENT, DEVELOPMENTAL DELAY*.

▦ CAUSES General learning problems may result from a short attention span, easy distractability or emotional disturbance. A child gains encouragement from success or the mastering of a skill; persistent failure discourages and may further impair learning. A sudden slowing of progress is frequently the result of emotional distress, but may be the first sign of a serious physical disorder.

There is no consensus of opinion as to the cause or causes of specific learning disorders. They are more common among boys than girls and often run in families. Such children appear to have a particular inborn difficulty with one or more fundamental processes, for instance that required to deal with symbols in sequences, match sounds to symbols or memorize from sight. The problem may be compounded by experience of failure.

■ ACTION Meet the child's teacher to discuss progress and your concerns. In general, aim to boost your child's confidence and to reward success.

■ INVESTIGATIONS Thorough assessment of the nature of difficulty by an educational psychologist or specialist teacher is a necessary first step. Alternatively, your doctor may suggest referral to a child psychiatrist.

■ TREATMENT depends on the specific nature of the problems identified. Special teaching methods may tackle a particular difficulty and classroom programmes help set the scene for learning (see *BEHAVIOURAL TREATMENTS*). Remedial teaching in small groups is provided in some schools, but withdrawing the child from normal class activities may create other prob-

lems. In a minority of cases, you may be advised that your child's best interests will be served by attending a special school.

■ OUTLOOK Provided the child's self-esteem and behaviour do not suffer, he should respond well to appropriate teaching methods.

LEFTHANDEDNESS
A preference for using the left hand, most evident during specific activities, such as eating, writing or sport. Up to the age of five years, uncertainty about hand preference is common. One in three children will demonstrate cross laterality – the ability to use both hands for many common activities.

■ CAUSES More than 90 per cent of children of two right-handed parents are right-handers. Only half the children of left-handers are left-handed. In Western countries it is typical for 10-12 per cent of children to be left-handed for writing.

■ OUTLOOK There is no essential disadvantage in being left-handed. Left-handed children may have some difficulty with certain manipulative skills since so many tools (for example scissors) are specifically designed for right-handers. When writing, the left hand covers what has been written, unless the child is taught to rotate the page clockwise.

About one in 20 left-handed children are exceptionally poor at right-handed activities. Some reports suggest an excess of left-handers in special classes and remedial services. These children may have suffered a disturbance of the left cerebral hemisphere, having been genetically programmed to be right-handed.

LEUKAEMIA

Cancer of the white blood cells. The child's bone marrow produces large numbers of imperfect, malignant white blood cells which cannot effectively fight INFECTION. The normal production of red blood cells and platelets is also reduced, leading to ANAEMIA and a tendency to bleed.

The cause of leukaemia is unknown, but there is an association with exposure to radiation and certain genetic disorders such as DOWN'S SYNDROME. The disease has a tendency to run in families.

There are different types of leukaemia, depending on which kind of white blood cells are involved. Acute lymphoblastic leukaemia is the commonest type in children, and responds well to modern treatment.

■ SYMPTOMS The child is usually pale, with the other symptoms of anaemia. He may bruise easily and have a RASH consisting of tiny bleeding spots on the skin. He may develop a severe infection. FEVER can occur, not always in association with infection. Occasionally, the child complains of pain in the bones. The doctor may find that the liver and spleen are enlarged, as they try to produce normal blood cells to counter the overgrowth of abnormal cells.

■ ACTION If you suspect anaemia, or find that your child bruises or bleeds too easily, get medical advice. Don't ignore symptoms because you feel that you could not face up to a serious disease. Early diagnosis (see below) gives the best chances of cure: nowadays, the majority of children *are* cured.

■ TESTS are necessary to make the diagnosis. A simple BLOOD TEST usually shows a large number of abnormal white blood cells. The number of red blood cells and platelets is reduced. To confirm the diagnosis, a bone marrow examination is necessary: a needle is inserted into bone under anaesthetic, and a tiny wedge of bone marrow is drawn out. Other tests such as X-rays and ULTRASOUND SCANS may be necessary; and sometimes a LUMBAR PUNCTURE too. The tests are also used to try to determine whether the child is likely to respond quickly and successfully to treatment, or whether the disease may be more difficult to treat. Thus treatment can be tailored to the child.

■ TREATMENT This has been one of the success stories of paediatric medicine in the last few decades. Previously, the disease was incurable.

The aim is to destroy all the cancer cells. Unfortunately, anticancer (cytotoxic) drugs damage normal as well as abnormal cells, and this gives rise to side-effects. For this reason, a number of drugs are used in combination to minimize the side-effects of each drug. Another reason for using different drugs is to insure against the abnormal cells developing 'resistance' to a single drug.

Side-effects include loss of hair, anaemia, a bleeding tendency and decreased resistance to infection. Some drugs cause nausea, vomiting and diarrhoea: these can be treated with further drugs.

Another problem with treatment is the need for repeated tests to assess whether the drugs are working.

Treatment is given in phases: **1** Inducing a remission: this means clearing the body of all detectable cancer cells. Three or four drugs are usually used over a period of weeks, given either as tablets or by injection. If there is a risk of the disease occurring in the brain, radiotherapy to the head, and injection of drugs into the spinal cord are done as a preventive measure. 2 Maintenance therapy is continued once a remission has been achieved. The object is to destroy any undetected leukaemia cells that may start to multiply and cause further disease. This treatment is usually continued for about three years. 3 During maintenance treatment, and for many years later, tests are done to look for signs of relapse. If this occurs, further treatment is given. 4 During the whole period of treatment, the specialist will be on guard against anaemia, infection and NUTRITIONAL problems. 5 If the leukaemia is resistant to treatment, it is sometimes possible to give a bone marrow transplant. If a suitable donor (usually a brother or sister) is found, a large dose of drugs and radiotherapy is given to destroy all the leukaemia cells. It also destroys all the normal bone and marrow cells, which are then replaced by the healthy bone marrow transplant.

▓ SELF-HELP It will be hard for you to be positive, but you must try. If the child feels that you have doubts, he may not trust the treatment. Reassure him that the treatment is necessary to make him well, and that all the family are involved.

Psychological support is available for families going through the ordeal of childhood leukaemia. Don't feel that your problems cannot be shared with staff at the specialist unit treating your child. They are there to help in all ways, not just medically.

Treatment of childhood leukaemia tends to change quite rapidly as new developments occur – and also as a result of the child's response. So don't worry if treatment is different from what you have heard or read about – you will soon become an expert.

Ensure your child's teeth and gums are clean and healthy during treatment to minimize infection.

Alert schoolteachers to the child's condition: he ought to avoid contact with CHICKENPOX or MEASLES, as far as possible. Tell the doctor immediately if he does encounter other children with these infections. Routine immunizations are usually avoided while on treatment.

When the child's blood count is low, keep him away from crowds and other demanding situations. On the other hand, he should carry on with school and other activities whenever possible. Don't over-protect him, despite the potential gravity of the condition – it will make life even more difficult in the long run.

If your child is old enough, encourage him to ask questions too. He may have worries that have not occurred to you.

▓ OUTLOOK At times the discomfort of tests, the side-effects of treatment, and the stress of the illness can seem unbearable. Remember that in most cases, the result of modern treatment is a long-lasting cure.

LICE

Tiny insects that feed on blood. Head lice are common in children, often being recognized by their eggs, properly known as nits. Body lice are rather uncommon; symptoms and treatment are similar to those for head lice.

▓ CAUSE The head louse, *Pediculus capitis*, spreads from person to person as a result of close body contact. The bite itself causes no symptoms initially, but after a few months the child may become ALLERGIC to the insect when an intense itchy reaction may develop. This leads to scratching, and sometimes to secondary INFECTION (IMPETIGO).

▨ SYMPTOMS Itching and scratching of the head are highly suggestive of lice. Inspection of the child's hair will reveal the characteristic oval eggs, firmly fixed to the hairs. Live eggs are brown, and not easily seen; white nits are actually empty egg cases, and signify past infestation. Since the eggs are fixed to the hairs at their roots, the distance of the nits from the skin shows how long the eggs have been there. Hair grows at about ½ in (10 mm) per month. It is sometimes possible, by parting the hair quickly, to see the insects.

▨ ACTION Effective treatment is easily obtained from the chemist. It is not necessary to keep the child away from school. It is usually advisable to treat the hair and scalp of all family members.

▨ GET MEDICAL ADVICE if there are sore patches on the scalp, or painful lumps in the back of the neck – both signs of impetigo.

▨ TREATMENT There are two effective treatments – malathion and carbaryl. Both are applied as a lotion to the scalp, and left on overnight. (Shampoos are available, but are less effective.) In order to prevent the lice from becoming resistant to the drugs, the two are used in rotation in different areas of the country: your local chemist will know which one is in use in your locality at the time.

If impetigo has developed, your doctor will prescribe an ANTIBIOTIC.

▨ OUTLOOK Head lice are common in schoolchildren, and do *not* indicate deprivation nor poor personal hygiene. Treatment is easy and safe, and may be repeated from time to time if necessary.

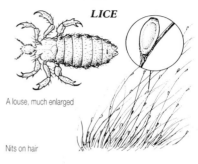

LICE

A louse, much enlarged

Nits on hair

LIES AND FIBS

Until their teens, children do not fully understand, in the adult sense, the meaning of right and wrong. Up to the early school years, a child may tell a story which represents what he would have preferred to have happened without necessarily intending to deceive. At this age, it is quite common for children to indulge in vivid fantasies about their own activities, and is not a cause for concern. As children grow older, they begin to understand the difference between fantasy and reality. All older children, like adults, distort the truth at times, to try to protect themselves or others. Generally they will learn to value truthfulness to the same extent as their parents. Persistent lying is often a sign of problems with relationships and self-esteem. This often goes with other worrying behaviour and parents should seek advice, in the first place, from the family doctor. He or she should have a clear idea of whether the problem needs referral to a child psychiatrist.

LIFE SAVING

See *DROWNING, EMERGENCY RESUSCITATION.*

LIMP

An uneven walk, in which the weight is carried more on one leg than on the other. This is usually caused by pain in one leg, but there is such a thing as a painless limp.

▦ CAUSES A painful limp can be caused by:
 – Injury to the leg (most commonly the foot).
 – A badly fitting shoe.
 – A WART on the sole of the foot.
 – ARTHRITIS of one of the joints of the leg.
 – PERTHE'S DISEASE of the hip.
 – OSGOOD-SCHLATTERS DISEASE of the knee.
 – A BONE TUMOUR.
 A painless limp is usually caused by a problem in the muscle or nerve to the leg, as in
 – POLIOMYELITIS (POLIO);
 – CEREBRAL PALSY; or
 – if one leg is shorter than the other, due to injury or OSTEOMYELITIS.
 – CONGENITAL DISLOCATION OF HIP.

▦ SYMPTOMS The child takes his weight on the 'good' leg for as long as possible while walking. This makes him tilt towards the good leg.
 There is usually pain, which may help to indicate where the problem lies. However, the pain does not always occur exactly in the place which is causing the limp. In addition, muscles can be strained as a result of the limp, causing yet more pain.

▦ ACTION If a limp persists for more than a day, and if you cannot find a simple cause, see your doctor.

▦ TESTS may be necessary.

▦ TREATMENT and OUTLOOK depend on the cause: see separate entries mentioned above.

LOCK-JAW

The common name for tetanus arising from the disease's tendency to severely affect the jaw. See *TETANUS*.

LONGSIGHTEDNESS

The eye sees well in the distance, but has difficulty focusing on near objects. The globe of the eye is healthy, but misshapen – 'shorter' from front to back than it ought to be. It is the commonest eyesight problem in children, and usually becomes apparent at around three years.
 It may be associated with a SQUINT. An EYE TEST will determine which SPECTACLES are needed to correct the child's vision.

LOW BIRTH WEIGHT

This is defined in the Western world as weight at birth of less than 5½ lb (2.5 kg). Low birth weight babies are either premature – see *PREMATURITY* – or born small in relation to the duration of the pregnancy, see *SMALL-FOR-DATES BABY*. Some babies may be both premature and small-for-dates.

LUMBAR PUNCTURE

A medical investigation in which cerebro-spinal fluid is obtained by passing a needle, under aseptic conditions, through anaesthetized skin on the lower back, into the spinal canal.

LYMPHOMA

CANCER of the lymph glands, which may also involve the liver and spleen. It usually starts in one group of glands and spreads to others nearby. The cause is unknown. There are various forms of the disease in adults; one that occasionally occurs in children is known as Hodgkin's disease or Hodgkin's lymphoma. It is very rare under the age of three years.

■ SYMPTOMS Swollen glands, especially those in the neck, are usually noticed first. Some children have weight loss, FEVER and sweating at night. There may be a decreased resistance to INFECTION.

■ ACTION Glands in the neck may be enlarged for many reasons, including scalp or EAR INFECTION, TONSILLITIS and GLANDULAR FEVER. If there is no obvious cause, you should get medical advice and say why you are worried.

■ TESTS If your doctor finds no simple explanation for the enlargement of the glands, he or she may recommend a BLOOD TEST and possibly a biopsy. This involves removing the gland under ANAESTHETIC and examining it for abnormal cells. If the biopsy reveals lymphoma, further tests are necessary to find out the extent of the disease. These include X-rays, ULTRASOUND SCANS and further blood tests.

An exploratory operation on the abdomen may be suggested to determine the exact spread of the disease within the glands of the abdomen, and also the liver. Special scans may eventually replace the operation. During surgery, the spleen is removed to prevent the cancer spreading to it.

These measures are known as 'staging' the disease; accurate staging can improve effectiveness of treatment in up to one third of affected children.

■ TREATMENT Largely due to careful staging, results of treatment have recently improved significantly. If it is known exactly which lymph glands and organs are involved, the correct treatment can be directed at all affected areas at once.

Anticancer (cytotoxic) drugs are used in combination to destroy the cancer cells. See *LEUKAEMIA* for an explanation of the technique, and for side-effects.

Radiotherapy is also used, depending on the findings of the staging tests. The side-effects are similar to those of the drugs; growth, fertility and the thyroid gland may be affected.

If the spleen is removed, there is an increased risk of BACTERIAL infection. ANTIBIOTICS are used to prevent this and a vaccine against pneumonia may be given.

Occasionally, a bone marrow transplant can help in treatment. See *LEUKAEMIA*.

The cancer is most likely to return in the first two years after treatment has been started, so blood tests, X-rays and ultrasound scans are all carried out on a regular basis. If necessary, further treatment is also given.

■ SELF-HELP Unpleasant tests and treatment put a great strain not just on the child, but on the whole family. Staff in specialist centres that treat conditions such as lymphoma are well aware of this and have considerable experience of helping. Take advantage of the support they offer. Discuss any worries that you have and encourage your child to do the same. See also *LEUKAEMIA*.

■ OUTLOOK varies a great deal, depending on how far the cancer has spread at the time of diagnosis. But the cure rate has improved greatly in recent years, as has life expectancy in those whose disease cannot be eradicated.

M

MALABSORPTION

The child has large, pale frequent BOWEL MOTIONS, ABDOMINAL SWELLING and poor growth (FAILURE TO THRIVE). Adequate digestion of food requires sufficient length of bowel, correct bowel movement (peristalsis), the right enzyme-containing digestive secretions from the pancreas and bile duct system, normal bowel BACTERIA, normal bowel lining (villi), and the transportation of digested food products into the bloodstream and lymph vessels.

Disturbances of any of these essential mechanisms may result in an abnormal bowel pattern, usually indicated by DIARRHOEA and malabsorption, which is either generalized or limited to certain substances.

▨ CAUSES There may be an abnormality in the lining (mucosa) of the bowel. This can be associated with MALNUTRITION, or occur after prolonged GASTROENTERITIS. There may be infestation with *GIARDIA* or associated COELIAC DISEASE (permanent or temporary); COW'S MILK ALLERGY; or previous drug or X-ray therapy.

There may be a rare abnormality of lymph drainage or inadequate enzyme production, (see *SUGAR INTOLERANCE*); or the cause may be one of a number of unusual biochemical deficiencies.

BILIARY ATRESIA, HEPATITIS, CIRRHOSIS and bacterial overgrowth may also affect absorption. Previous bowel operations are another possible cause.

Toddler diarrhoea or 'irritable colon syndrome' may be due to rapid transit in the intestine leading to incomplete digestion; undigested food is found in the bowel motions, but this is not true malabsorption.

Inflammatory bowel disease, including ULCERATIVE COLITIS or CROHN'S DISEASE, may have malabsorption as an early symptom.

▨ INVESTIGATIONS A clear history is essential. Plotting the child's GROWTH PATTERN; physical examination to detect poor growth or abdominal swelling; observation and investigation of the bowel motions for infection; BLOOD TEST to determine ANAEMIA and VITAMIN DEFICIENCY; sweat test (see *CYSTIC FIBROSIS*) or jejunal biopsy (see *COELIAC DISEASE*) may help. A barium meal X-ray may be needed to exclude an abnormality of the bowel following surgery, or due to a CONGENITAL ABNORMALITY.

▨ TREATMENT depends on cause. It may include improving the diet (as in malnutrition) or exclusion of food that cannot be tolerated, as in coeliac disease, cow's milk allergy, or food intolerance. ANTIBIOTICS may be required to fight *Giardia* or bacterial overgrowth. Replacement of vitamins, pancreatic enzymes, or drug treatments, may be necessary.

▨ OUTLOOK depends on the underlying condition, but children usually grow out of toddler diarrhoea and cow's milk allergy in the first few years of life.

MALARIA

A common tropical INFECTION caused by a PARASITE transmitted via mosquito bites. The parasites multiply in the liver and red blood cells.

▨ PREVENTION Any child going to a part of the world where the disease occurs must be protected by taking anti-malaria tablets beforehand and during his stay. The type of tablet will depend on the area, and may change from time to time because

MALARIA

Contracting malaria

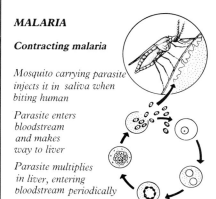

Mosquito carrying parasite injects it in saliva when biting human

Parasite enters bloodstream and makes way to liver

Parasite multiplies in liver, entering bloodstream periodically

When parasite matures, red blood cells rupture, causing fever and malaria symptoms

the parasite tends to develop resistance to anti-malarial agents. The treatment should continue for at least six weeks after leaving the area. Some anti-malarial drugs may be unsuitable for children, but finding a safe one is usually no problem. Breast-fed babies must also be treated because although drugs taken by mouth pass through into breast milk, the amount is too variable to be relied upon to protect the baby.

Mosquito nets, and protective clothing, especially around dusk, are also essential preventive measures. Don't put too much faith in 'insect-repellent' sprays – they are no guarantee against bites and may give a false sense of security.

The INCUBATION PERIOD is nine to 30 days and the first symptom is usually FEVER. The vomiting and diarrhoea that follow can cause DEHYDRATION and the child is usually drowsy and listless. He may become pale as ANAEMIA develops. Treatment usually results in rapid improvement if the diagnosis is made early enough, so get medical advice quickly if you suspect that there is infection.

MALNUTRITION

Generally taken to mean undernourishment – see also FAILURE TO THRIVE. Undernourishment is associated with poverty, insufficient food supplies and ignorance, psychological disturbance or profound low intelligence of the parents. It may also result from insufficient food intake due to loss of APPETITE or *ANOREXIA NERVOSA*, recurrent VOMITING and CHRONIC ILLNESS (this may reduce appetite and/or cause a 'wasting' process). Overeating and diets consisting largely of low-fibre 'junk food' with a high energy density (as sucrose and fat) lead to *over* nutrition, the leading *mal*nutrition in the industrialized Western world.

■ SIGNS of undernutrition: **1** Weight loss, or failure to gain weight, resulting in a tall, skinny body shape (in infancy, undernutrition in the chronic and extreme form is known as *Marasmus*). This chronic process needs to be distinguished from sunken eyes and weight loss associated with acute DEHYDRATION. **2** Apathy, listlessness and irritability. **3** Poor hair growth, dry skin. **4** Changes in distribution of fluid in the body: chronic undernutrition from protein-deficient diets results in puffiness (OEDEMA) of feet, hands and face (*very* rare in the U.K., but known as kwashiorkor in Africa, where the condition was first identified). **5** See *VITAMIN DEFICIENCIES*.

■ ACTION Malnourished children and their families may need intensive care and rehabilitation from a team of different professionals, including dieticians and doctors. If the origins of the condition are social rather than medical, then the professional skills and leadership of social workers will be of paramount importance.

■ OUTLOOK, with treatment, is good.

MARFAN'S SYNDROME

A rare INHERITED DISORDER which tends to run in families. Bones, ligaments, eyes and heart are affected.

■ SYMPTOMS The child has unusually long legs, arms, fingers and toes. He may develop a SCOLIOSIS and an abnormality of the breast bone. Joints have a greater range of movement than normal. FLAT FEET are common.

Abnormalities of the eye can occur. Most children with Marfan's syndrome are SHORT-SIGHTED, and there may be other eye problems such as CATARACTS.

There may also be weakening of the walls of arteries, and possibly HEART FAILURE may result.

It sounds like a grim catalogue, but these features may be mild rather than severe, and not all of them occur in every case. In addition, early detection and treatment can substantially lessen their effect.

■ PREVENTION If there is a history of the condition in the family, consider GENETIC COUNSELLING before getting pregnant. If either parent carries the gene, there is a 50 per cent chance of each child being affected.

■ ACTION If your child has Marfan's syndrome, he will require regular examination to look for the abnormalities mentioned.

■ TREATMENT Scoliosis, flat feet and shortsightedness are treated in the normal ways.

Activities with a risk of blows to the head should be avoided because of the risk of retinal detachment.

If there is evidence of a leaky heart valve, the child may need an antibiotic before dental treatment and certain other operations.

Contact sports and lifting heavy objects should be avoided because of the weakness of the large arteries.

If one of the heart valves leaks severely, it may need to be replaced with an artificial valve.

■ OUTLOOK is improving. Most symptoms can be treated, and the recent advances in heart surgery have greatly improved the prospects for those with significant heart-disease.

MASTOIDITIS

A serious infection of the mastoid bone (the boney prominence behind the ear). It is a rare complication of MIDDLE EAR INFECTION.

■ SYMPTOMS The child becomes very ill, feverish and irritable. The mastoid bone is tender and red.

■ TREATMENT ANTIBIOTICS; uncommonly an operation is required, a mastoidectomy, to clear out the infected bone.

MASTURBATION

Handling genitalia to gain pleasurable sensation. Children become aware of their genitals from about two, and discover in time that fondling them leads to a pleasurable feeling. Children use masturbation, as adults do, to soothe and relieve tension. Though most do not experience sexual excitement, children are capable of achieving orgasm, and those who discover this may well repeat the experiment. A child who is found flushed and panting in bed may well have been doing this.

Most children masturbate at some

time or other; they may do so regularly, or they may do so for short periods and then forget about it. In neither case is it harmful. Boys in particular are aware of their penises, obviously so since they stick out, and it is quite normal to handle them. Only if a child masturbates compulsively and furtively should you be concerned: there may be an underlying emotional cause for which you should seek help; otherwise you should not worry about it and not draw your child's attention to it. It is all part of his SEX EDUCATION which should be kept as natural as possible.

MEASLES

A VIRAL INFECTION spread by exhaled droplets. It is highly infectious from just before the beginning of the illness to about four days after the rash appears. The INCUBATION PERIOD is eight to 14 days.

■ PREVENTION Measles should be prevented by IMMUNIZATION, because the complications can be grave, and occasionally fatal. Immunization is usually given at about 12-15 months, nowadays in combination with MUMPS and *RUBELLA* vaccine, but measles can occur in the first year of life. If a baby is at high risk of catching measles, a 'starter' immunization can be given at six months with a BOOSTER at 18 months. Measles can occur in a mild form even after immunization, but in such cases there are no serious complications.

Keeping suspects in quarantine is not particularly effective because the carrier is highly infectious before symptoms occur, and the disease spreads rapidly.

■ SYMPTOMS First, a very runny nose, red eyes (CONJUNCTIVITIS) and

a dry COUGH. FEVER is mild before the rash develops, but then the child's temperature can rise dramatically.

The rash appears about four days after the onset of symptoms, starting behind the ears and rapidly spreading over the face and body. As the red areas of the rash merge, the skin has a blotchy appearance. The rash fades to a brownish colour over a few days, and the skin becomes dry and scaly.

Koplik spots occur in the mouth in the early stages. Typical of measles, these are small and white, and develop inside the cheeks, close to the molar teeth; they stand out against the red, inflamed membranes of the mouth.

■ ACTION If you suspect measles, get urgent medical advice. It is important to confirm the diagnosis. Measles can be diagnosed accurately at the start, but this is more difficult later.

The fever should be treated immediately with paracetamol and a cool bath. See also *FEBRILE CONVULSIONS.*

CROUP, conjunctivitis and DIARRHOEA often go with measles: see the separate entries.

The child may feel ill enough to want to stay in bed, but this is not essential.

Bright light may hurt his eyes, so a shaded room can help; however, the room does not need to be in total darkness. Music or tape-recorded stories can help to relieve the boredom if the eyes are very painful.

■ COMPLICATIONS, ranging from mild to severe, are common. They include PNEUMONIA, EAR INFECTIONS and ENCEPHALITIS. Occasionally, the croup may be life-threatening. All complications tend to be more severe in undernourished and chronically ill children, so it is particularly important that such children are immunized against measles. Children at risk include those with CYSTIC FIBROSIS, CONGENITAL HEART-DISEASE, KIDNEY DISEASE, DOWN'S SYNDROME and FAILURE TO THRIVE.

■ TREATMENT ANTIBIOTICS are not routinely used, but secondary BACTERIAL infection is common, and they may well be necessary at this later stage.

Children with depressed immunity should be given an immunoglobulin injection if they come into contact with measles. This helps to boost immunity.

■ OUTLOOK Most children recover completely, but prevention is better than cure.

MECONIUM

The sticky green-brown substance produced in the baby's bowel when in the womb. It is usually passed by the baby in his first stool after birth. If the unborn baby is distressed or asphyxiated, he may pass meconium which stains the amniotic fluid.

MENARCHE

See *PUBERTY*.

MENINGITIS

Infection of the membranes lining the brain and spinal cord by BACTERIA or VIRUSES.

■ SYMPTOMS The infection can be preceded by a SORE THROAT. FEVER, HEADACHE and VOMITING usually evolve within hours. Neck stiffness, CONVULSIONS, PARALYSIS, SQUINT and COMA may follow.

■ ACTION Get medical advice if you are worried about meningitis; it is a medical emergency and will require prompt treatment. The signs of meningitis are not always obvious at first, so if a sick child is not improving with treatment for any of the symptoms above, meningitis should be considered. If in doubt, take the child to hospital.

■ CAUSES Infection usually reaches the meninges through the blood, but bacteria can spread from the sinuses or the ears. Bacterial meningitis may also arise as a complication of skull FRACTURE or of SPINA BIFIDA.

■ INVESTIGATIONS   LUMBAR PUNCTURE; sometimes swabs or BLOOD TESTS can help.

■ TREATMENT Bacterial meningitis is treated with ANTIBIOTICS, mostly given by injection. Some children may need INTENSIVE CARE support if the illness is severe. Fluids may be given by intravenous drip and it may be necessary to monitor pulse rate, blood pressure and temperature frequently. There is no specific treatment for viral meningitis, which is usually a milder illness than the bacterial type. IMMUNIZATION is available against some strains of bacteria involved.

■ OUTLOOK Nearly all children suffering viral meningitis make a complete recovery, but some with bacterial meningitis die or survive with disabilities such as hearing impairment, EPILEPSY, HYDROCEPHALUS or CEREBRAL PALSY. Before antibiotics were available, bacterial meningitis was generally fatal.

MENTAL HANDICAP

The social consequence of mental retardation. Children whose general intelligence lies within the lowest 3 per cent in the population are considered to have some degree of mental retardation. The definitions used to classify 'moderate' and 'severe' retardation are to some degree arbitrary and reflect no more than society's ability to cope with the problem.

▨ CAUSES A substantial proportion of 'moderately retarded' children are simply the least able of the normal range in the population. There may be no identifiable cause of their problem. However, more than two-thirds of the severely retarded children have identifiable disorders such as CHROMOSOMAL abnormalities (for example, DOWN'S SYNDROME). Other causes include malformation syndromes, INHERITED DISORDERS, INFECTION or damage by RUBELLA, ALCOHOL or other agents in the womb, very severe BIRTH ASPHYXIA or serious illness or injury in childhood.

▨ SYMPTOMS Mental handicap may be suspected from birth if a specific condition such as Down's syndrome or MICROCEPHALY is present. Usually, delayed MOTOR DEVELOPMENT and, especially, LANGUAGE delay raise suspicions. Severe EPILEPSY in early childhood is likely to be associated with mental handicap, and a third of children with CEREBRAL PALSY turn out to be mentally retarded. Conversely, one in three severely mentally retarded children has epilepsy, and one in five has cerebral palsy. Psychiatric disorders such as ANXIETY, DEPRESSION and AUTISM are relatively common in retarded children, but may be difficult to manage because of the disordered or very limited communication abilities of these children, and because of the lack of appropriate facilities for assessment. Two-thirds of severely retarded children have a degree of visual impairment and one in six has appreciable hearing loss.

▨ ACTION If mental retardation is suspected, the child should be referred to a specialist team which may include a paediatrician, paediatric neurologist or paediatric geneticist.

▨ INVESTIGATIONS include chromosome tests; amino-acid chromatography; BLOOD and URINE TESTS for intra-uterine infection or biochemical problems, and EEG RECORDING. A CAT SCAN does not usually give a specific diagnosis, except when detailed physical examination suggests a particular disorder.

▨ TREATMENT
The question of residential care: In the latter part of the 19th century, and indeed in the early 20th century, it was common to offer long-stay institutional asylum not only for a proportion of severely mentally retarded children with multiple disabilities, but also for young people of low normal or borderline ability who were rejected by their families. This led to overcrowding of underfunded, understaffed, impersonal institutions, some of which scandalized public opinion – though good institutions did exist. From the 1950s to the 1970s the number of residents in, for example, the U.K., had fallen by half, and in the U.K. it is planned to close all large institutions in due course in favour of care in the community. However, there are some severely and multiply disabled retarded children, and some children with serious psychiatric disorders as well as severe retardation, who are likely to profit from specialist hospital care from time to time, especially if their families can-

not cope with full-time care. Indeed, those with intractable seizures or who need tube feeding require frequent nursing attention.

Schooling for the mentally handicapped child: There have been considerable improvements in the schooling offered to mentally retarded children, some of whom were considered uneducable until the early 1970s. Recently, there have been moves towards integration of retarded and disabled children into mainstream schools. Many pupils in special schools would benefit from the wider curriculum and range of social behaviour in mainstream schools, provided special teachers are available.

GENETIC COUNSELLING is important for families. The recurrence risk of mental retardation is 10 per cent unless a specific cause is found.

Treatment of visual or hearing problems, or epilepsy may lead to improvement. Physiotherapy can help motor development; speech therapy is useful for communication problems, and clinical psychologists and child psychiatrists may be able to help in the management of BEHAVIOURAL or psychiatric disorders and, indeed, for distress suffered by their families.

In the U.K., financial help for parents or carers of mentally retarded children has made home care possible where it had not been before. Local health authorities have professional multi-disciplinary teams available to help support mentally retarded people. However, because educational and health services for children are much better developed than those for adults, mental handicap teams have tended to begin their involvement with adolescents or school-leavers.

■ OUTLOOK Most mentally retarded children improve with time and teaching at their own rate, but often reach a plateau at puberty. Autistic children with mental retardation show particularly slow progress, whereas some children with language problems continue to improve into adult life. A few with severe seizure disorders (for example, Lennox-Gastaut syndrome) deteriorate in adolescence despite all treatment.

MENTAL RETARDATION
See *MENTAL HANDICAP* and *LEARNING DISORDERS.*

MESENTERIC ADENITIS
Swelling of the lymph glands in the abdomen, in response to INFECTION. Mesenteric (abdominal) adenitis may result from a local abdominal infection, or from a general VIRAL infection. It is thought to be a cause of tummy-ache in childhood. However, this is rarely certain as there is no visible, external sign of the internal inflamed glands.

■ SYMPTOMS The features of this condition are vague. The tummy-ache is mild or moderate, and there may be a slight FEVER. The child can move around without much discomfort, and does not look unduly ill. There are no specific tests, but if a blood count is done, it will show a raised white cell count as in any infection.

■ ACTION The child may gain some comfort from fluids and paracetamol, bed rest and the judicious use of a warm (not hot) water-bottle to hold to his tummy. But if the pain persists, or the child cannot move easily, or he is sick, you should contact your doctor, in case he has APPENDICITIS.

■ OUTLOOK Mesenteric adenitis is a vague condition. It may recur. It may represent part of the range of conditions which are best grouped together under the term RECURRENT ABDOMINAL PAIN. Always get medical advice, however, if you suspect appendicitis.

MICROCEPHALY
A child with an abnormally small head (and brain). This may be a GENETIC disorder, with a one in four recurrence risk; a non-genetically determined CONGENITAL ABNORMALITY (caused, for example, by infection of the foetus with RUBELLA) or acquired after birth as, for instance, following profound BRAIN DAMAGE from trauma or cardiac arrest. Most microcephalic children are MENTALLY HANDICAPPED.

MIDDLE EAR INFECTION (*OTITIS MEDIA*)
An INFECTION by BACTERIA or VIRUSES often representing an extension from the nose and throat up the Eustachian tube to the middle ear. Commonest in younger children, particularly those under five years. Some children are especially vulnerable, including those prone to HAY FEVER, and those with overlarge adenoids or CLEFT PALATE.

■ SYMPTOMS EARACHE, DEAFNESS; also more general symptoms (especially in infants) including FEVER, VOMITING, ABDOMINAL PAIN and HEADACHE. If the eardrum perforates, a discharge of green or yellow mucus may be seen coming from the ear. The perforation usually heals, and long-term hearing is undamaged. (However, if your child's ear does discharge, he should be seen and followed up by a doctor because of a slight risk of lasting deafness.)

■ ACTION Always get medical advice if you suspect your child has an ear infection. See also *EARACHE.*

■ TREATMENT Mild forms of middle ear infection, when accompanied by a cold, are caused by VIRUSES; your doctor will probably give no specific treatment. If the appearance of the eardrum or the severity of the symptoms suggest that there is a BACTERIAL infection, then he or she will prescribe an ANTIBIOTIC. A relatively short course (say, three days) may be effective, but the doctor should check your child's ears at the end of the course to ensure that they have recovered. If your child also has nasal obstruction, your doctor may also suggest a decongestant, in the hope of decongesting and therefore helping drainage down the Eustachian tube.

■ OUTLOOK For infants and younger children, there is a slight risk of hearing impairment for a while after an ear infection; if in any doubt, ensure that his hearing is checked one or two months after.

MIGRAINE IN CHILDHOOD
Migraine is severe, recurring headache, usually affecting only one side of the head at a time, often preceded by visual disturbances (typically flashing lights), and accompanied by nausea and vomiting. The child may look pale and complain of a nausea and stomachache. Migraine often runs in families, and is commoner in older children.

■ CAUSES Unknown. Individuals

may identify specific triggers, including stress and some foods (such as chocolate and cheese).

■ INVESTIGATIONS There is no specific test for migraine, and all children complaining of headache do *not* have migraine. Severe, recurrent or persistent headache in a child requires medical assessment and advice. It is important not to overlook migraine (some episodes may prove a nuisance for the child at school). Conversely it is important not to call every headache migraine, which may in fact be an appeal for attention or the sign of brain disease.

■ TREATMENT Give paracetamol as soon as possible. Taking an analgesic (painkiller) early may prevent a full-blown attack in some children. During an attack the stomach may empty more slowly than usual: for this reason some doctors recommend metoclopramide, which speeds stomach emptying, to enhance painkiller effectiveness.

There are powerful anti-migraine drugs, but they tend to be used as a last resort in children because of side-effects.

■ SELF-HELP Encourage the child to lie down in a darkened room.

■ OUTLOOK Many children grow out of migraine.

MILK SPOTS
New-born babies frequently have crops of tiny red spots on the face and neck. These come and go rapidly, often appearing and disappearing the same day. They are presumably caused by a skin reaction to warmth, moisture and/or milk (breast or bottle), but are not painful or sore, and do not require treatment.

MINIMAL BRAIN DAMAGE
It is common for some developmental or behavioural difficulties in children to be ascribed to 'MBD' without evidence of actual damage. However, children who have suffered perinatal ASPHYXIA and subsequently display neurological abnormalities, are more likely to have impaired language, co-ordination and attention in later years. Similarly, children who have suffered major HEAD INJURIES are likely to show memory difficulties, irritability and impulsiveness. It cannot be inferred, conversely, that children who sleep badly, make a slow start at school or have tantrums, have suffered brain damage.

Children with relative language delay or disorder are better described as having a specific developmental language problem than MBD. Children who are verbally fluent but immature, or incompetent at motor or perceptual-motor activities, are best described as having a specific MOTOR DEVELOPMENT problem – see *CLUMSINESS*. See also *ASPERGER'S SYNDROME*.

Indeed, it is arguable whether the term 'minimal brain damage' has any meaning scientifically, or any value clinically to the doctor or the child and his family.

MOLES
All pigmented spots and patches are called moles, and most are harmless, but can be unsightly.

■ INCIDENCE 95 per cent of people have some sort of pigmented mole.

■ TYPES OF MOLE Apart from the normal, small, flat, brown moles, there are larger moles, which may be covered with hair ('giant hairy naevi'). These are usually found on the trunk. Also abnormal are the widespread 'café-au-lait' spots, pale brown patches, which may be an otherwise harmless feature of a rare condition called neurofibromatosis. Malignant melanoma, a form of skin cancer, is very rare in children, but can develop in any large pigmented mole.

■ ACTION Nearly all moles are harmless, but if you are worried about a mole, get medical advice. If any mole is seen to be enlarging, bleeding, itching, or changing its appearance in any other way, then don't hesitate to seek immediate medical advice.

■ TREATMENT Large moles can be removed surgically: your doctor will advise about this. Occasionally a mole becomes infected, usually through being scratched. Simple ANTIBIOTIC treatment is the remedy. Itchy moles are often not true moles, but so-called histiocytomas, benign dark spots which may be the result of injury or insect bites. No treatment is needed, but occasionally they are removed surgically if there is suspicion about their nature.

MONILIA
See THRUSH.

MORO REFLEX
An automatic response by a new-born baby to a sudden noise or movement. The baby throws out his arms and legs, and then brings them back together with slight shaking movements. The reflex usually disappears by the age of three months. The Moro reflex is interesting to observe. However, it frequently appears to distress the baby, causing him to cry out and be unsettled. For this reason, the reflex should not be elicited without good reason.

MOTION SICKNESS
Much worse in some families than in others, and some cars provoke it more than others. Children often start to suffer from travel sickness around five or six years of age, and stop in their teens. Prevention is effective, using specially formulated antihistamines (sold over the counter: note dosage instructions for children carefully). Most antihistamines cause drowsiness, but children vary in their susceptibility.

■ SELF-HELP Avoid reading or close work while travelling. In public vehicles, sit near the front preferably with some fresh air and free from cigarette smoke. Don't give a child heavy or fatty meals before or during a journey. Make sure the child faces forwards, and looks out of the window if in a car or train. On boats, try to get the child to lie flat or, failing that, to keep his eyes on the horizon. Small, frequent meals can help reduce nausea.

MOTOR DEVELOPMENT
Most children follow a sequence of sitting (five to 12 months), crawling (six to 14 months) and walking (nine to 19 months). This is generally regarded as normal motor development.

About one child in 20 does not crawl, but instead creeps on his tummy, rolls over and over or shuffles on his bottom. Such children may sit and walk a little later than average, but eventually have no motor or performance deficit. Some children stand and walk as their first means of mobility.

Many specific patterns of motor development tend to run in families. Boys tend to be a little slower in their motor development than girls.

MOUTH ULCERS
Common at any age, painful small

white oval ulcers may occur on tongue, gums or anywhere in the mouth, and can cause fretfulness and real difficulty in eating. They are probably caused by a VIRUS, and may be associated with illnesses, or simply be associated with fatigue or psychological stress.

■ ACTION Lozenges or gels used for teething in babies can be helpful, because of their local anaesthetic content; there are also prescribable medicines containing mild steroids, which can help the healing process. Get medical advice if they last longer than a week or two, or recur frequently.

MULTIPLE PREGNANCY

A pregnancy with more than one baby. It is suspected if the womb seems large, or if more than one heartbeat is heard. It can be confirmed by ULTRASOUND SCAN.

Twins occur in about one in every 100 births. They may be produced from either one fertilized egg constituting monozygotic or identical twins; or from two separate fertilized eggs, forming dizygotic or non-identical

twins. The latter is more likely when there is a family history of twins, or if the mother has taken a fertility drug.

Triplets occur naturally in about one in 6,000 pregnancies. However, they are becoming more common as a result of the use of fertility drugs and test-tube (*in vitro*) fertilization.

■ ANTENATAL CARE of women with twins or triplets needs especially careful management, because complications such as ANAEMIA and high BLOOD PRESSURE occur more frequently than in single pregnancies. In general, the mother will gain more weight and need more rest. Additionally, the individual babies may have problems of their own. For example, one baby may not receive as good a blood supply from the placenta as the other, and may grow more slowly than his twin. The premature onset of labour is more common in multiple pregnancies: the average length of pregnancy for twins is 35 weeks.

■ LABOUR AND DELIVERY In 70 per cent of twin pregnancies, the first twin lies head down and is born

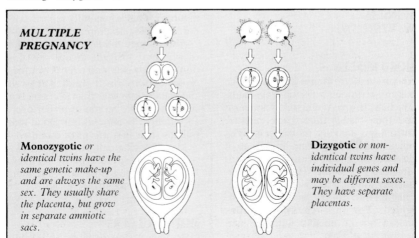

MULTIPLE PREGNANCY

Monozygotic *or identical twins have the same genetic make-up and are always the same sex. They usually share the placenta, but grow in separate amniotic sacs.*

Dizygotic *or non-identical twins have individual genes and may be different sexes. They have separate placentas.*

normally. The midwife or doctor may then need to rupture the sac around the second twin to facilitate his delivery. The birth of the second twin usually follows ten to 15 minutes after the first birth. If the first twin lies head up in the womb, or there are other complications, delivery is likely to be by CAESARIAN SECTION. Triplets are more frequently delivered by Caesarian section.

▓ BREAST FEEDING more than one baby is difficult but can be successful. The mother must consume sufficient calories and fluids daily: this cannot be prescribed precisely other than to encourage the mother to eat and drink to her fill. It may be possible to breast feed the babies together or separately, or to use a bottle alternating with breast feeds. The various options are best discussed with the midwife.

▓ TWIN CLUBS have sprung up in many places, offering a valuable self-support group (equipment, know-how, friendship and gossip) for parents with multiple births.

MUMPS

A VIRAL INFECTION, spread by exhaled droplets. Close contact is necessary to spread the infection, but even so not all contacts will result in mumps. Mumps is most common between five and 15 years of age and tends to be more severe in adults than in children. The sufferer is infectious during the week before he develops symptoms; and he remains infectious for about a week after onset. The INCUBATION PERIOD is 14-21 days.

▓ SYMPTOMS The illness begins with FEVER, feeling generally unwell, HEADACHE and loss of APPE-

MUMPS

The main symptom: swollen glands in the neck and behind and in front of the ears.

TITE. Swelling of the salivary glands below and in front of the ear (the parotid glands) and under the chin begins a day or two later and lasts for about a week. Eating is painful because it causes movement and stimulation of the inflamed glands. The cardinal sign of mumps is the disappearance of the 'angle of the jaw' because of firm swelling beneath the ear.

VOMITING and ABDOMINAL PAIN sometimes occur.

▓ ACTION The pain and fever can be treated with an analgesic, typically paracetamol.

A fluid diet is often necessary until the pain subsides. Certain foods, particularly those that are sour, stimulate secretion of saliva, and these should be avoided as they can cause intense pain.

The mouth should be kept clean with a regular mouthwash.

Complications are rare, but if there are symptoms of drowsiness, pain in the testes in boys, or any unexpected symptoms, get medical advice.

Keep the child away from school until the swelling has subsided (usually about seven days from the beginning of the illness).

IMMUNIZATION is now available against mumps in combination with MEASLES and RUBELLA, and is given during the second year of life. It is thought that the protection will continue into adolescent and adult life.

▨ OUTLOOK Mumps seldom causes serious complications; MENINGITIS or DEAFNESS are very occasional risks. Inflammation of the testes can sometimes cause sterility, but rarely.

MUSCULAR DYSTROPHY

Progressive weakness due to degeneration of muscles. There are different types, all inherited. Duchenne and Becker's dystrophies are inherited on a recessive GENE at a known site on the X chromosome so only boys are affected, though girls can be carriers.

In limb-girdle dystrophy, a dominant gene is usually involved and one of the parents is affected.

The defect directly causing the condition is thought to be in the voluntary muscle cell membrane where the protein (dystrophin) is either deficient or abnormal.

▨ SYMPTOMS The child may be late in walking and shows progressive weakness over a number of years. Muscles are slowly replaced by fibrous tissue and fat which may make them look bulky. Speech, bowel and bladder control are affected later. A quarter of affected boys do not walk by 18 months, delayed LANGUAGE DEVELOPMENT is common, ability to run, jump, rise from the floor or climb stairs is very limited at any age.

▨ TREATMENT There is no cure, but aids and appliances, suitable seating, physiotherapy, hydrotherapy and suitable education nowadays contribute considerably to making it possible to manage the child at home. GENETIC COUNSELLING is required to make parents aware of the risks to further offspring.

National associations and groups provide literature and support.

▨ OUTLOOK The commonest muscular dystrophy (Duchenne) progressively leads to loss of ability to walk at ten to 12 years, and death from respiratory failure or INFECTION in the late teens.

The milder form tends to give slower deterioration and survival until middle age.

MYALGIC ENCEPHALOMYELITIS

Following an apparently minor viral infection, a few children complain of persistent fatigue, depression, weakness, twitching, lack of co-ordination and other rather vague symptoms, over a period of many months. It is thought that a short-lived illness, at a time of psychological vulnerability, can lead to an extended subjective experience of sickness. Treatment requires a combination of medical and psychological insight, with incentives for recovery. In some countries, societies have been set up specifically to provide advice and support for sufferers.

MYOCARDITIS

A rare but dangerous disease in which there is inflammation of the heart muscles, usually caused by a viral INFECTION. See HEART-DISEASE. The symptoms occur suddenly, presenting with acute breathlessness and general illness: there are signs of HEART FAILURE. Most children recover completely, although treatment is often continued for a number of years. Occasionally the damage to the heart muscle is permanent and specialist long-term care is required.

MYOPIA

See SHORTSIGHTEDNESS.

NAIL BITING

A tension habit common in children (and some adults). The child is often unaware that he is doing it. The habit is generally harmless, but some adults may find it unattractive. Measures aimed at stopping the habit – prompting the child to stop when you see him biting, applying unpleasant-tasting liquids to his nails or giving rewards for unbitten nails – usually fail unless the child himself wishes to stop.

NAPPY RASH

A common and temporary redness with or without raised confluent or discrete spots of the nappy area.

▦ CAUSE Urine turns into ammonia after a short time in the nappy. Ammonia is identifiable by its strong smell. It irritates the baby's skin, making it vulnerable to infection by BACTERIA or THRUSH (*Candida*). Some babies develop nappy rash as an early manifestation of ECZEMA or PSORIASIS.

▦ SYMPTOMS The skin under the nappy becomes red, and later raised areas or raw ulcers may appear. These may be painful, causing the baby to cry. The skin in the folds between the baby's legs and buttocks may be relatively less affected by nappy rash.

▦ ACTION Simple measures often work: **1** Remove the nappy in order to expose the area to open air, for as long as possible. **2** Apply a simple cream such as zinc and castor oil ointment. **3** Avoid close-fitting nappies, and change the nappy as frequently as possible.

▦ GET MEDICAL ADVICE if nappy rash does not clear in a few days following these simple methods.

▦ TREATMENT The doctor will consider the possibility of other skin problems, and may prescribe a cream to clear any thrush infection. This may also contain hydrocortisone to relieve the inflammation.

NAUSEA

The inclination to vomit, often accompanied by churning of the stomach, sweating, pallor, excessive salivation and dizziness. Most commonly associated with GASTROENTERITIS or MOTION SICKNESS; can accompany many illnesses, for example EAR INFECTIONS.

▦ ACTION Nausea as such is difficult to treat. Motion sickness is largely preventable with appropriate medication taken before travelling. Otherwise, keep the child off solid food and give him sips of clear fluids or ice cubes to suck.

NEBULIZER

A device frequently used in the treatment of ASTHMA, which transforms liquid medications into a fine mist, which is then breathed in through a mask. In this way, drugs such as bronchodilators can be directed to their site of action in the airways. Electric and foot-operated types are available.

▦ USES To treat severe attacks of asthma. This may take place in hospital, or in the G.P.'s surgery, or occasionally at home (if the family have had full instructions on the use of the nebulizer). If the treatment fails to settle the asthma within a set period, then a potentially dangerous situation may be developing. Hence parents using nebulizers at home need to be carefully briefed.

Nebulizers are also used to give regular doses at home of drugs that prevent asthma, such as sodium cromoglycate or beclomethasone, if the child is too young to use effectively other sorts of inhaler.

NECROTIZING ENTEROCOLITIS
A serious condition of new-born and especially of premature babies, in which there is a disintegration, or necrosis, of the gut wall. Depending on the severity of the episode, it may carry a variable risk of permanent damage to the bowel, and occasionally have fatal consequences.

▓ CAUSE is not understood. It seems to occur when there has been both BACTERIAL INFECTION and poor blood supply to the baby's gut (as may occur as a complication of ASPHYXIA or RESPIRATORY DISTRESS SYNDROME). The baby becomes unwell, his abdomen swells and feeds are no longer tolerated. He may pass blood in his stools.

▓ TREATMENT consists of ANTIBIOTICS and resting the gut; that is, giving the baby no feeds until the bowel heals. A small number of babies require surgery to remove affected segments of the bowel.

NEONATAL COLD SYNDROME
See HYPOTHERMIA.

NEPHRITIS
A general term referring to inflammation or swelling of the glomeruli in the kidneys. A glomerulus is the loop of capillaries (or fine blood vessels) which function as a cup-like filtration system in the kidney. In these microscopic structures water and waste products pass out of the blood to enter a system of fine tubes, in which some water and filtered chemicals are selectively reab-

sorbed. The term nephritis is often used as shorthand for the more specific disorder of glomerulonephritis. It tends to affect children of school age.

▓ CAUSES Nephritis usually follows two to three weeks after a bacterial throat INFECTION. The ANTIBODIES produced by the body to the BACTERIA cross-react with and attack the glomeruli causing them to swell.

▓ SYMPTOMS The most striking feature in most cases is the passage of bloodstained or 'smokey' urine. This may be accompanied by vague lassitude or headache. Damage to the glomeruli prevents the normal filtering process of the kidney. Salt and water are retained by the body, causing oedema, usually seen as swelling around the eyes and of the feet, and high BLOOD PRESSURE.

▓ ACTION The development of discoloured urine or oedema must be reported to a doctor without delay.

▓ TESTS A URINE TEST will confirm the presence of blood and protein. BLOOD TESTS may detect the antibodies which cause the nephritis. More important, they will show how the kidney is functioning.

▓ TREATMENT Initial assessment usually requires admission to hospital. The severity of nephritis is highly variable – some cases need no treatment, others need medicines to control the raised blood pressure. The amount of fluid your child drinks may need to be carefully balanced against the amount of urine he passes. In the most severe cases, the kidneys may temporarily stop functioning. Some form of dialysis will then be required.

▓ OUTLOOK Normally the kidneys

recover spontaneously and completely. There may be blood in the urine for many weeks; this is not in itself a sign that the nephritis is worsening. Uncommonly the kidneys do not fully recover but progress to chronic RENAL FAILURE over a matter of years. Should this happen the care of the child will be with a paediatric nephrologist, and plans will be made eventually for kidney transplantation.

NEPHROBLASTOMA
See *WILM'S TUMOUR*.

NEPHROTIC SYNDROME
The condition arises when the glomeruli of the kidneys become 'leaky' allowing blood proteins to escape into the urine. (The glomeruli are the microscopic filtering units of the kidney which are largely responsible for excreting waste products from the blood and stabilizing the blood chemistry.) The cause of nephrotic syndrome is unknown.

▓ SYMPTOMS The main symptom is OEDEMA or swelling or puffiness particularly of the face, around the eyes, and the ankles. The child usually does not feel particularly unwell. However, he may be somewhat lethargic.

▓ ACTION If your child develops oedema, you should get medical advice. Your doctor will do a URINE TEST for protein if he or she suspects nephrotic syndrome.

▓ TREATMENT is with steroids. The swelling usually remains unchanged for the first week or two, but usually by six weeks there is a decrease in the protein loss in the urine, an increase in the volume of

urine passed, and a steady dissolution of the swelling.

▓ OUTLOOK Nephrotic syndrome may recur, but most children eventually grow out of it. A small minority of children continue to need long-term care, because of the ultimate risk of kidney failure.

NETTLE-RASH
See *URTICARIA, BITES AND STINGS*.

NICOTINE
See *SMOKING*.

NIGHT TERRORS
The sleeping child suddenly appears to be in a state of intense fear. Unlike NIGHTMARES, he does not wake up, and has no recollection of the event afterwards. Witnessing a child's terror can distress parents, but there is no need to wake him or discuss the event with him. They are not a cause for serious concern, and the child will

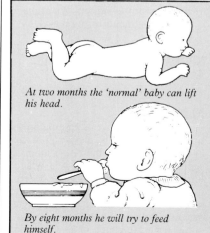

At two months the 'normal' baby can lift his head.

By eight months he will try to feed himself.

have grown out of the problem by the early school years.

NIGHTMARES
Bad dreams that are sufficiently frightening to wake a child: nightmares can be recalled immediately. They are essentially no different from the bad dreams of adulthood. They are sometimes, but not always, related to a recent emotional upset. They are a common reason for night-waking in older children. Many children go through periods of frequent nightmares, which then stop for a time. If your child wakes from a nightmare, calmly reassure him and help him to settle back to sleep, talking about something that will distract him from the fear. There is no need to discuss the content of the nightmare.

NITS
See *LICE, BODY AND HAIR*.

NOISY BREATHING
See *STRIDOR, ASTHMA, CROUP*.

'NORMAL' DEVELOPMENT
The development of 97 per cent of children in growth, co-ordination, language and social behaviour is considered to be 'normal'. The remaining 3 per cent, considered to show FAILURE TO THRIVE or DEVELOPMENTAL DELAY, may require investigation or treatment, typically for motor, language, visual or hearing impairment. In many developed countries, babies and children under five years are checked for correct development as a matter of routine. Health professionals making these checks are trained to take into account family and other special circumstances, and to avoid causing parents unnecessary anxiety when a child falls below 'normal' in some aspect of the testing process.

▨ SIGNS OF ABNORMAL DEVEL-OPMENT Failure to: attend to sounds; to 'fix' with the eyes and follow movements visually in the first year; to walk by 18 months; to use three-word phrases appropriately by the age of three years. All these require expert consideration.

Often enough, though, a child

At ten months he should be able to pull himself up on pieces of furniture.

NORMAL DEVELOPMENT

By twelve months he will be building towers of bricks.

shows delayed development in one of these respects as part of an inherited pattern. For example, the baby who does not crawl, but moves by bottom shuffling, rolling or creeping, may well be late to walk, but usually turns out to be 'normal', especially if his father or mother was the same.

▓ ACTION If your child shows one or more of the signs described above, don't be alarmed, but get medical advice in any case. Ensure that a baby's vision and hearing are checked at eight months, and at 18.

▓ TREATMENT Physiotherapy, speech therapy or precision teaching techniques can help.

▓ SELF-HELP Spend time playing with your child. An excellent book, *Creative Play* by Dorothy Einon (Penguin, 1985), provides endless ideas for constructive activities and games. Variety of experience, sharing your child's interests, ensuring an adequate diet and conversation, within the limit of your child's understanding, all help. Children learn most from adult involvement.

▓ OUTLOOK depends on the cause of the delay, if any. Sight and hearing defects may be remediable. Motor (physical mobility) delay, language delay and SPEECH DISORDERS may well resolve if due to a lag in maturation or a family tendency. But see also *MOTOR DEVELOPMENT, SPEECH DISORDERS, DEVELOPMENTAL DELAY, MENTAL HANDICAP, CEREBRAL PALSY, LEARNING DISORDERS.*

NOSE, FOREIGN BODY IN
Children of two to three years of age

may put a wide variety of objects into their noses, including beads, small toys, paper, wool. These may be less easily noticed than foreign bodies in ears, because the space inside the nose is much larger.

▓ SYMPTOMS The usual sign is a discharge which may become green, brown or foul smelling from the nostril (from that side of the nose containing the object).

▓ ACTION The object needs to be removed by a doctor. This may require the specialist skill of an Ear, Nose and Throat surgeon. An X-ray may help identify and locate the object. He or she will attempt to extract the object with a probe, which may require a general ANAESTHETIC.

NOSEBLEED
A frightening, but seldom serious problem.

▓ CAUSES The bleeding usually comes from a small vein just inside the nostril, on the inner wall of the nose. Such veins can be broken by direct injury, typically falls or playground fights, or indirectly by a COMMON COLD. Generalized VIRAL infections, such as MEASLES, and any high temperature, may also set off a nosebleed. Some children have exceptionally fragile veins in the nose, and bleed without any obvious cause. Very rare causes are those diseases that affect blood clotting, for example HAEMOPHILIA or LEUKAEMIA.

▓ ACTION Almost all nosebleeds can be stopped by simply squeezing the child's nose between the thumb and finger, just below the bony part. Pressure should be just enough to

NOSE BLEED

stop the bleeding and keep the nose completely still, and should be continued for ten minutes, then released, and repeated if necessary. It helps if the child's head is held forward, so that the blood flow can be seen. If tilted back, blood runs down the child's throat, is swallowed, and may later cause vomiting and unnecessary distress. After bleeding has stopped, the child should rest quietly, and avoid blowing his nose or sniffing.

There is no need to apply ice, or put coins on the neck, or to put any sort of plug into the child's nose.

■ GET MEDICAL ADVICE if the bleeding has not stopped after gentle pressure for 20 minutes, or if nosebleeds are recurring frequently.

■ TREATMENT Recurrent nosebleeds can be treated simply by sealing or cauterizing the vein, using either a silver nitrate stick, or some other form of cautery. This is usually done in a hospital clinic, but some G.P.s will do this in the surgery. An antiseptic cream is often prescribed to prevent crusting, and encourage healing of the inside of the nose.

■ TESTS If, besides nosebleeds, there are other signs that the child could have a blood disorder, your doctor will arrange for BLOOD TESTS – but serious disorders accompanying nosebleeds are exceedingly rare.

■ OUTLOOK The amount of blood lost is unimportant, although it may seem to be copious. Children who are prone to nosebleeds can be taught how to manage them by themselves, using the method described above.

NUTRITION
See also *APPETITE, WEANING, VITAMINS.* The ideal diet for a child contains adequate protein for growth and repair of body tissues, plus sufficient energy, mostly from carbohydrates and fats. There should be plenty of unabsorbable vegetable fibre and a liberal intake of fluids. Foods with a high energy density, especially in the form of sugar, should be kept to a minimum. This applies in relation to the developing teeth, the prevention of obesity and the promotion of lifelong, good eating habits and health.

In the first two years of life, much of a child's requirements are met from milk, which is a well-balanced food containing carbohydrate, proteins and fats. In the first six months, this is best provided in the form of the baby's own mother's milk. Thereafter, a transition is made to weaning foods, and latterly to the normal domestic diet with whole (pasteurized) cow's milk as an important component.

Healthy nutrition is easier to define than to implement. The child's diet will reflect the household traditions and habits, later to be influenced by school peer pressures and the media messages.

If you have questions or concerns about your child's diet or state of nutrition, speak to your doctor. He or she may feel that a discussion with your hospital dietician would be helpful.

OBESITY

Deciding when your child is over-weight (obese) is not difficult: if you think he is, you are probably right. (If he thinks he is, he may not be right – see *ANOREXIA NERVOSA*.) He can be defined as obese in terms of his weight in relation to his height.

▨ CAUSES Obesity results from eat-ing more than is necessary for that individual's needs; it is, however, hardly ever due to 'glandular prob-lems' such as CUSHING'S DISEASE – see *ADRENAL DISORDERS*. There may be a long-standing (sometimes family) habit of eating more food than is necessary for nor-mal growth.

▨ OUTCOME Mild obesity may not have serious consequences for future health. However, very fat children may be teased and unpopu-lar at school, less likely to be good at sport and more likely to be fat as adults. It is therefore worthwhile trying to bring the child's weight back towards normal for both pre-sent and future well-being. Obesity carries definite health risks for adults including DIABETES, heart, chest and joint complaints.

▨ AVOIDING OBESITY There is no clear evidence that fat babies invari-ably grow to be fat children. So a healthy, hungry baby who is plump should not go on a diet. However, as the baby becomes a toddler and pre-school child, if the propensity to fat-ness persists, you should try to instil eating habits that avoid sugar-con-taining foods and convenience snacks, of the lemonade, cake, bis-cuit, sweet and crisps variety.

▨ ACTION **1** Mildly overweight, chil-dren often don't need to lose weight; it is enough to hold their weight steady while they grow. Concentrate on small changes in the diet to re-duce calories and fat (perhaps re-placing snacks with fruit, but not cutting them out altogether), rather than trying to make drastic changes which will be hard to maintain. **2** A new pattern of exercise may help the child feel healthy and fit. However, this is only likely to succeed if it is fun, and supported by friends or family. Exercise as a prescription will fail. **3** If your child is definitely obese, get medical advice, and ask to be referred to a dietician. Don't leave this step until too late: once a pattern of fatness is well established, it is very difficult to reverse. And if it is a family feature, then it is a family responsibility to change eating habits.

OBSESSIONS

Many children between the ages of about six and nine years go through a phase of superstitious rituals, such as not stepping on pavement cracks, or dressing in a special way. These seem to help a child feel safe from bad luck in a world which is progressively seen as a dangerous place. These routines can be particularly irritating to parents in a hurry, but are otherwise usually without significance. Some older chil-dren become preoccupied in a similar way when anxious or under stress, for example during examinations. As the stress recedes, normal interests take the place of the obsession.

Usually the parents' best strategy is to ignore the obsession: it will fade as the child grows and becomes more confident. Distracting the child's attention, or offering incentives may sometimes help.

▨ GET MEDICAL ADVICE if an obsession seems to be dominating your child's life, and seriously restricting his activities; or if he seems absolutely compelled to perform the ritual regardless of the situation, and becomes distressed if prevented from doing so; or if family life is being generally affected. Your doctor may refer you to a child psychiatrist. For most children, a few sessions discussing the problem can be helpful. Rarely, more intensive and longer treatment is required. See *AUTISTIC CHILD, FEARS*.

OEDEMA

Excess fluid retained by the body. Normally fluid is removed from the body in a well regulated fashion as urine produced by the kidneys and, to a lesser degree, as sweat and water in the exhaled breath and in the stools. If these regulatory processes fail, the excess fluid passes from the blood into the body tissues. The legs swell and the eyes become puffy. In a baby, oedema may be generalized or show itself as a sudden increase in weight. See also *HEART FAILURE*.

OPERATIONS

See *HOSPITAL, ANAESTHETICS*.

ORTHODONTICS

The branch of dentistry concerned with correcting irregular position of the teeth, and of the way the upper and

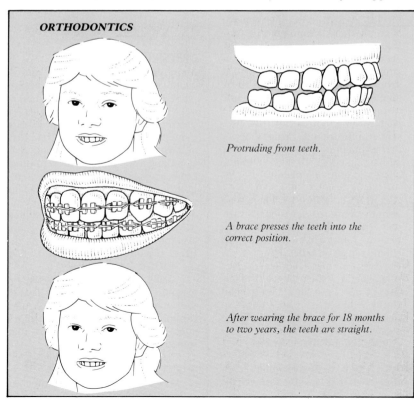

ORTHODONTICS

Protruding front teeth.

A brace presses the teeth into the correct position.

After wearing the brace for 18 months to two years, the teeth are straight.

lower teeth come together when biting. If these are causing problems, treatment usually only begins when most of the milk teeth have been replaced by permanent ones: a successful result is more easily achieved during this period of development than if left until adolescence or later.

■ SYMPTOMS The teeth may seem to crowd the mouth because they are too large in proportion to the jaw. The upper teeth may protrude, or the lower teeth may come together in front of the upper teeth.

■ TREATMENT Crowding of the teeth may simply be treated by removal of some premolar teeth (the teeth immediately behind the pointed canine teeth). The remaining teeth may then move into correct position of their own accord, but usually an orthodontic appliance (a brace) is needed. It works simply by pressing teeth into the correct position and holding them there until they will stay by themselves. Some appliances can improve the bite. The appliance may be fixed or removable, and usually requires adjustment about once a month. It may well have to be worn for between 18 months and two years. Once the child has become used to the presence of the brace in his mouth, it causes no discomfort.

OSGOOD-SCHLATTERS DISEASE

A disease of the bone of the lower leg (the tibia) in the region of the knee. The cause is unknown and the problem resolves by itself after a few months.

Symptoms include pain and swelling around the bone just below the knee. There is usually a LIMP. An X-ray confirms the diagnosis and treatment is rest for six to eight weeks. It is sometimes necessary to put the leg in a plaster cast to enforce adequate rest. There are no long-term complications.

OSTEOGENESIS IMPERFECTA

A rare INHERITED DISORDER. The child's bones are fragile (it is also called fragile bone disease), and fractures are common. The fractures heal normally, but some children suffer many fractures which cause deformity of the bones.

OSTEOMYELITIS

A bone infection occurring most often in the ends of the long bones of the arm or leg. It may occur after a FRACTURE if the bone breaks through the skin.

■ SYMPTOMS The illness usually starts abruptly. The child may complain of severe pain in the bone; he may recently have had a boil or an infected sore on the skin. There is usually redness and swelling of the skin over the infection. He is reluctant to move the painful limb.

Other symptoms include FEVER, HEADACHE, loss of appetite and generally feeling unwell.

■ ACTION Pain or swelling over a bone is always a cue take the child to a doctor without delay, especially if he seems unwell.

■ TESTS include BLOOD TESTS and X-rays of the painful limb. A bone scan may show early signs of the infection. X-rays may not show definite signs of infection in the early stages, but they will indicate the response to treatment.

■ TREATMENT The earlier treatment is started, the better the results. Antibiotics are needed in high doses, usually given into a vein for a few days until the child is better. To ensure all infection has been eradicated, they are usually then continued for about six weeks by mouth.

The pain is treated with analgesics and bed rest.

An operation is often necessary to drain the infected fluid that collects within the bone.

Once the pain has settled, physiotherapy prevents the muscles from becoming weak.

▓ OUTLOOK is usually good if the treatment is started early. Occasionally, the infection causes complications of bone growth, and this must be checked for a number of years after the episode. This problem is commonest in infancy.

OTITIS
See *MIDDLE EAR INFECTION, EXTERNAL EAR INFECTION.*

OTITIS MEDIA
See *MIDDLE EAR INFECTION.*

OVERBREATHING
Breathing more deeply or rapidly than necessary, often through fear or anxiety. Medical term: hyperventilation. This results in excess carbon dioxide being released from the lungs. The body's chemical balance is disturbed, the blood becomes alkaline and nerves and muscles become excitable.

▓ CAUSE Usually the result of anxiety, sometimes reflecting a more serious underlying psychological disturbance.

▓ SYMPTOMS are dizziness, faintness, 'pins and needles', and eventually spasm of various muscles.

▓ ACTION 1 The symptoms are frightening, so reassure the child firmly and calmly. The first time this happens, the child should be seen by a doctor. Only when the diagnosis is sure should parents proceed to try to reverse the disturbance. 2 The imbalance may be reversed if the child breathes in and out of a paper bag, thereby re-breathing his own carbon dioxide.

▓ TREATMENT Try to identify the underlying cause of anxiety and, if possible, relieve it. You may need medical advice for this. Careful assessment of the child's feelings, fears, including enquiry into the family and school backgrounds, may be necessary. Many children experience temporary anxieties during the school years, which pass with no long-term consequences.

OVERDOSE
See *POISONING.*

OVERDUE BABY
Born later than the expected date of DELIVERY (gestation to maturity normally lasts 40 weeks). Also called 'postmature'. The overdue baby often has wrinkled, flaky skin and long nails. He may pass MECONIUM while still in the womb. Postmaturity carries little risk for the baby until the pregnancy reaches 42 weeks. After that, the placenta may begin to fail, and the volume of water surrounding the baby (the liquor) decreases. There is then also a risk of sudden unexplained death of the foetus in the womb, resulting in STILL BIRTH. Almost all obstetricians recommend induction of labour after 42 weeks.

OVERWEIGHT
See *OBESITY.*

PQ

PAIN

The experience of unpleasant, potentially harmful stimuli. Specific nerve endings in the skin and other body surfaces respond to extreme and painful stimuli; and they are distinct from those which transmit 'run-of-the-mill' sensations such as touch, temperature and stretching.

▨ SYMPTOMS Perhaps the most intense, gnawing pain is caused by increased pressure within an enclosed space, for example a bone, ear or dental root. A whole range of lesser pains may be perceived as sharp, throbbing, colicky, burning or tight.

Pain has a protective function: if we didn't feel it, we would not naturally withdraw from danger. Pain also indicates disease. But pain of psychological origin can of course be just as unpleasant as physical pain and may equally deserve sympathetic treatment.

Pain can be acutely and obviously localized in sensitive areas such as the mouth or the hands, but may be more difficult to pinpoint elsewhere. Localizing pain is a particular problem in the very young. Parents can do no more than respond to signs of severe trouble, such as irritability, pallor, vomiting or immobility.

▨ ACTION The first, common-sense step for mild pain is to give the child paracetamol in the pain-killing dose recommended by the manufacturer. People tend to under-use painkillers, unaware of their application in an extraordinarily wide range of conditions from HEADACHES to CUTS AND GRAZES.

Clearly, intense, highly distressing pain requires medical advice.

▨ TREATMENT A bewildering range of painkilling drugs is available today, but most pain in childhood is best treated by a simple analgesic such as paracetamol or codeine. It is generally best to use a single-ingredient remedy because this means you are in control of the dosage. Aspirin should not be used in children under 12 years – see *REYE'S SYNDROME*.

More powerful analgesics are given to children for specific conditions such as post-operative pain, malignant disease or juvenile ARTHRITIS, but under specialist supervision. Some of the powerful analgesics are addictive and are only used for short periods. Opiates tend to cause respiratory depression in babies.

▨ OUTLOOK Children are relatively tolerant of pain. A child will often be active soon after surgery or a fracture. This may be because pain causes less fear in some children, rather than because children are less sensitive to pain.

PAIN IN THE EYE

There are several causes. If it is mild and the eye is red and itchy, it may be due to CONJUNCTIVITIS.

Inflammation of the inside of the eye (as in uveitis) may produce a more severe pain, made worse by looking at light. Your child may also complain of blurred vision. There are a number of conditions associated with uveitis, such as RHEUMATOID ARTHRITIS.

If the pain is severe or prolonged, you should get medical advice without delay. Infections of the eyelids or globe of the eye itself (see *ORBITAL CELLULITIS*) can be dangerous and progress rapidly. Likewise if there is any chance of injury or foreign body in the eye, urgent medical attention is required – if necessary at the casualty department of your local hospital.

PALPITATIONS
See *ARRHYTHMIAS*.

PARACETAMOL
See *PAIN, POISONING*.

PARAFFIN
See *POISONING*.

PARALYSIS
Causes in childhood include diseases of muscle, peripheral nerve, neuromuscular junction, nerve roots, the spinal cord (as, for example, in POLIOMYELITIS) or the brain; biochemical disorders (for example abnormal potassium levels); hormone disorders (see *ADRENAL DISORDERS*) and poisons (see *POISONING*). See also *BRAIN TUMOURS, TETANUS*.

▓ ACTION Paralysis is always a cue to get urgent medical advice.

▓ INVESTIGATIONS depend on the cause and site, and include: muscle biopsy; nerve conduction studies; tests of the neuromuscular junction; myelogram; brain scan (see *CAT SCAN*) and BLOOD TESTS.

▓ TREATMENT depends on the cause, severity, site and duration. It may mean INTENSIVE CARE with respiratory support if breathing is affected; or it may mean rest, drug treatment, surgery, physiotherapy or hydrotherapy.

▓ OUTLOOK Some muscle diseases, such as MUSCULAR DYSTROPHY, lead to deterioration and death in adolescence. Neuromuscular disease may respond to long-term drug treatment or surgery on the thymus gland. Spinal paralysis may respond to spinal surgery, but often does not.

Brain surgery may help acute paralysis (for example after trauma or brain tumour), but not chronic paralysis (say with CEREBRAL PALSY).

PARASITES
Organisms that live off others (the term parasites is often used in contexts outside of medicine and biology). Parasitic organisms may be microscopic, as in the case of MALARIA, or much larger, such as WORMS, which may infest the bowel. Parasites may enter the body in many ways: the child's hands, food or drink may be contaminated; in other cases, the parasite may pass through the skin, as happens with mosquito-born malaria.

PARONYCHIA
An INFECTION of a finger-nail (also called a whitlow). It is usually caused by BACTERIA, but occasionally a FUNGAL infection can occur. The organisms enter the fold of skin around the nail through a break in the cuticle.

▓ SYMPTOMS A painful, red swelling begins suddenly; pus is discharged. Occasionally, a more long-term infection is caused by habitual chewing or picking at the nail folds.

▓ ACTION If the infection is superficial, cleaning and soaking in an antiseptic solution can cure it. If there is swelling, and the finger is throbbing, an ANTIBIOTIC is usually necessary. Early treatment can prevent the nail from falling off.

A fungal infection will require an antifungal cream or tablets.

A chronic infection results in continuing redness and swelling of the skin, with occasional discharge of pus. This also requires antibiotic treatment and continuing damage to the nail fold should be avoided.

■ OUTLOOK is good if the infection is treated early, and breaks in the nail fold are allowed to heal.

PATENT DUCTUS ARTERIOSUS
See *CONGENITAL HEART-DISEASE*.

PEAK FLOW METER
An instrument to measure airflow out of the lungs, chiefly used in the management of ASTHMA, both in the diagnosis and the monitoring of progress during, or between, attacks.

PEAK FLOW METER

Children with severe asthma may be given a peak flow meter to use at home. This is a useful method of following the progress of the condition between consultations with your doctor.

PECTUS EXCAVATUM (FUNNEL CHEST)
A relatively rare deformity in which there is a deep hollow in the centre of the chest.

■ CAUSE Unknown. It sometimes runs in families.

■ SYMPTOMS The deformity does not impair physical health: the problem (if there is one) is parental concern and, occasionally, a psychological one for the child. He may suffer from poor self-image, embarrassment and refusal to take part in sports, especially swimming.

■ TREATMENT A specialist's opinion will always be available, but it is exceptional for an operation to be recommended. The operation is major, and the risks greatly outweigh the benefits.

PEPTIC ULCER
An ulcer caused by inflammation of the lining of the upper intestine (the mucosa), in turn caused by excess acid production. It is uncommon in childhood. The ulcer usually develops in the stomach or duodenum. Such ulcers can arise acutely, or over time. BACTERIAL INFECTION may be a cause. There may be a family history of ulceration, and ulcers are more common in children of certain blood groups.

■ SYMPTOMS Acute: VOMITING blood (haematemesis) after severe infection or trauma, or when using high doses of aspirin (not recommended in children under 12 years – see *REYE'S SYNDROME*). Chronic: vomiting (vomit may contain blood) and recurrent ABDOMINAL PAIN in the upper half of the abdomen. Black stools containing blood may sometimes be produced. Secondary PYLORIC STENOSIS associated with vomiting may develop.
Severe, acute abdominal pain caused by a perforation of the bowel and PERITONITIS is rare.

■ INVESTIGATIONS BLOOD TEST to identify ANAEMIA. Gastroscopy – examination of the stomach with a tube under ANAESTHETIC. Barium meal and follow-through X-ray.

■ MANAGEMENT BLOOD TRANSFUSION may be required; antacids and ulcer drugs, some of which have side-effects, will be necessary for several weeks. Small, frequent meals may help and aggravating foods should be avoided. Surgery may be required for perforation with peritonitis, pyloric stenosis or severe, persistent symptoms.

▓ OUTLOOK Drugs will help to heal the inflamed mucosa. Surgery is not often required, but may be necessary for children with chronic, upsetting symptoms, or major complications.

PERIOD PROBLEMS

A girl starts to menstruate usually about two years after the growth spurt that marks the onset of PUBERTY. But this is variable.

It is important that girls (and boys) understand about menstruation. Girls should not be worried or embarrassed when they begin to have periods, or feel inadequate that their friends have started when they have not.

▓ PROBLEMS If periods begin before the age of ten, or have not started by 16, your daughter should see the family doctor (see also PUBERTY – precocious and delayed). There may well be no abnormality, but it may need investigating.

The first few periods are often

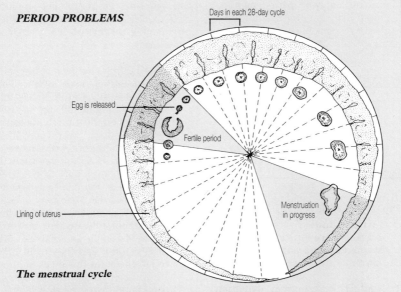

PERIOD PROBLEMS

Days in each 28-day cycle

Egg is released

Fertile period

Lining of uterus

Menstruation in progress

The menstrual cycle

At the beginning of the cycle, follicle-stimulating hormone (FSH) is released by the pituitary gland and stimulates the ovarian follicles, which in turn release oestrogen to enrich the womb lining. FSH drops off and luteinizing hormone (LH) is released in a surge which sparks

ovulation. Another hormone, progesterone, is produced by the follicles to continue the preparation of the womb lining for the fertilized egg. If conception does not occur, the hormone levels drop and the lining is shed at menstruation.

irregular both in timing and flow. This is normal and happens because these first cycles are not 'ovulatory': although menstruating, the girl may not yet be fertile.

Many girls suffer some pain with their periods. The first few cycles may not be painful, but the problem can develop later and is difficult to pinpoint because the pain is often spasmodic. It may be associated with nausea.

It is thought that period pains may be due to hormonal imbalance, leading to high levels of a group of chemicals synthesized by the developing uterine lining. These chemicals, known as prostaglandins, are responsible for uterine contractions during labour. This may explain why period pains are cramp-like; and prostaglandins may also be responsible for contraction of the gut muscle, with attendant feelings of nausea.

▓ SIMPLE REMEDIES Heat (say from a hot water-bottle), massage and simple painkillers (particularly aspirin and ibuprofen, which both inhibit prostaglandins) are often helpful.

▓ MEDICAL TREATMENT If the pain persists despite simple remedies, your daughter should get medical advice. Your doctor may prescribe further painkillers, or, occasionally, a low-dose contraceptive pill or progesterone-only pill.

Pre-menstrual tension is uncommon in adolescent girls. If your daughter suffers from irritability, DEPRESSION, HEADACHES, CONSTIPATION and a bloated feeling due to water retention, two to 12 days before each period begins, discuss it with the family doctor. There are many remedies, but their worth is debatable.

▓ ALTERNATIVE TREATMENTS Rest, reducing salt intake, and taking vitamin B6 are said to work for some women.

PERIODIC SYNDROME
See *RECURRENT ABDOMINAL PAIN*.

PERIODONTAL DISEASE
See *GINGIVITIS*.

PERITONITIS
This occurs when the membrane around the intestine becomes inflamed, as in APPENDICITIS or following a leak or perforation of some part of the intestine. Peritonitis may rapidly spread, leading to SHOCK and life-threatening INFECTION. It is a medical emergency.

▓ SYMPTOMS The signs of impending peritonitis are usually clear. The child is pale, hot and definitely unwell, unwilling to sit up or eat. Depending on the underlying cause there may have been preceding VOMITING, DIARRHOEA or CONSTIPATION. There is severe ABDOMINAL PAIN, which may start in one area and spread as the pain gets worse. The wall of the abdomen is held tense and is tender to touch; the child cannot tolerate any pressure over the abdomen. Internal pressure is also painful, and the doctor may need to check for this by examining with a finger inside the rectum. If unchecked, the pulse rate will go up and the child become distressed or, worse, listless and shocked.

▓ ACTION This is an emergency, and help should be summoned at once.

▓ TREATMENT See *SHOCK*.

PERTHES' DISEASE OF THE HIP

Disease of the upper end of the thigh bone (the femur) where it forms the hip joint with the bone of the pelvis. The cause is unknown, but it is commonest in boys.

■ SYMPTOMS A LIMP is usually the first symptom. The child will complain of pain in the groin or thigh – it may be mild or severe. Sometimes the pain spreads down the thigh, or seems to be coming from the knee. The symptoms can start abruptly, or appear gradually over days, even months.

Occasionally, both hip joints are involved. There is no disturbance of general health.

■ ACTION A limp or joint pain should never be ignored. See the doctor without delay.

■ TESTS An X-ray is needed for the diagnosis, and this will be repeated to measure progress. A scan of the bone can reveal early signs of the disease.

■ TREATMENT The disease gradually gets better by itself. In the past, treatment has included traction and calipers, but neither have been shown to improve the outcome significantly.

In the early stages, bed rest is necessary to allow the pain to settle. In mild cases, no further treatment is necessary, but X-rays are repeated to monitor progress.

Surgery may be necessary if the joint becomes at all deformed.

Sports involving strain on the hip joint are best avoided in severe cases.

■ OUTLOOK About 30 per cent of children continue to have pain or stiffness of the joint once the disease has run its course. A small number will require a hip replacement in later life.

PERTUSSIS

See *WHOOPING COUGH*.

PETIT MAL SEIZURE

A form of EPILEPTIC fit in which the child briefly displays a distant or glazed look, with minor movements of the eyelids and mouth. There is no jerking or loss of posture as in GRAND MAL SEIZURE. Many such episodes may occur daily.

■ CAUSE Abnormal electrical discharge in the brain.

■ SYMPTOMS Eyes glaze or roll up; some facial movements; pallor, episodes last a few seconds only. Occasionally, this type of fit is continuous (petit mal status) giving rise to a false impression of mental deterioration/retardation. Most sufferers respond well to anti-epileptic drugs.

■ TESTS The clinical diagnosis can be confirmed by an EEG, which characteristically shows a three-per-second spike and a slow wave pattern.

■ OUTLOOK If the condition is not diagnosed and treated, learning problems may result. Most inattentiveness in school is due to simple lack of concentration (or day dreaming). Most children grow out of petit mal by middle teenage. In the majority of cases, the condition is innocuous. Occasionally, it is followed by other forms of fits in later childhood and young adulthood.

PHARYNGITIS

See *SORE THROAT*.

PHENYLKETONURIA (PKU)

An inherited disease of metabolism. The child is unable to process a substance – phenylalanine – digested from protein in the diet. Approximately one in 15,000 babies are affected.

▓ SYMPTOMS An untreated child will become MENTALLY HANDI-CAPPED, with signs of DEVELOPMENTAL DELAY by four months. Such children often have blond hair, blue eyes, a funny smell, ECZEMA and poor head growth (MICROCEPHALY). One third will have seizures and many will become HYPERACTIVE and socially difficult.

▓ TESTS All children are screened at seven days of age by the GUTHRIE TEST for phenylalanine levels. If this test is positive, further BLOOD TESTS are needed to confirm the diagnosis.

▓ TREATMENT The aim is to prevent BRAIN DAMAGE in susceptible children. Dietary treatment should begin as soon as the diagnosis has been made. Milk substitutes from which phenylalanine has been largely removed are used in the early months, and parents must follow a special diet once the child is weaned. Natural foods in which the phenylalanine content is known are gradually added. Blood levels of phenylalanine must be monitored.

Dietary control may be relaxed in adolescence, and many adults with the condition will manage a normal diet. Don't, however, underestimate the nuisance which the essential, highly controlled diet can cause to both child and family.

Mothers who suffer from phenylketonuria must return to a strict diet before conception and throughout pregnancy, otherwise the baby may be at risk from microcephaly and CONGENITAL HEART-DISEASE.

PHIMOSIS

A tightening of the foreskin around the tip of the penis. Passing urine will cause 'ballooning' of the foreskin, and the urine stream will be poor, possibly reduced to a dribble. A tight phimosis is an indication for CIRCUMCISION.

Phimosis may be present from birth, but is more commonly caused by recurrent BALANITIS. Pulling back the foreskin with too much force may also cause a phimosis. The foreskin should not be normally retracted before the age of two years.

PHOBIAS

A phobia might be described as a fear that has grown out of all proportion. The child is frightened not only of some object, but also pictures of the object, stories about the object or a place where the object might have been, or anything to do with it. The peak age for children to develop phobias is around three years, when the imagination is extraordinarily vivid.

Developing fear is an essential part of growing up safely. Sometimes a real and reasonable fear (say of dogs once the child has been chased by a snapping dog) develops into a phobia. Some phobias are easier to understand than others, for example fear of the dark. Some, on the other hand, are totally imaginary and may never be explicitly defined by the child. Most fade away as the child's confidence and knowledge of the world increase.

▓ ACTION Don't ridicule your child's fear (and don't let other children tease him). Hold his hand firmly whilst walking calmly past the house with the dog, and talk about looking brave. If he is terrified, calm him down while trying not to rush away. Next time, approach more cautiously; try to deal with the feared situation or object, rather than avoiding it; but don't inadvertently cause your child great or repeated distress in your wish for him to be brave.

Get medical advice if the child's panic is worsening, if the number of phobias increases, or if they don't diminish after a few months.

Phobias in older children are rarer and less easily resolved without help. Isolated phobias of spiders are common and normally not much of a problem; but if the phobia interferes with your child's enjoyment of life and social activities, get medical advice. A consultation with a clinical psychologist or child psychiatrist will probably be suggested.

PHOTOTHERAPY

Treatment by ultraviolet light of a new-born baby with JAUNDICE.

The principle of the therapy is the bleaching effect that light has on bilirubin, the yellow waste product of haemoglobin breakdown. The bilirubin in the tissues below the skin is physico-chemically transformed into colourless and harmless derivatives.

Blue or white light is shone at the baby through the transparent cover of his incubator or cot. The baby is left naked in order to expose the maximum area of skin to the light. His eyes will be covered for protection.

The baby may need extra feeds because phototherapy causes water to be lost from the skin. For healthy term babies, phototherapy will only be needed for two to three days. For the premature baby and the baby with BLOOD GROUP INCOMPATIBILITY, longer periods of phototherapy may be necessary. Side-effects are usually trivial – the baby may have a slight skin rash and loose stools.

PICA

Means eating dirt. There have been cases of children eating paint that contains lead. This can cause ANAEMIA.

PIGEON TOES (INTOEING)

The child's toes are turned inwards. Sometimes one of the bones of the lower leg (the tibia) is involved.

Intoeing actually helps to prevent a small child from falling backwards, so it is normal in children up to three years of age. It can also occur as part of a CLUB FOOT or with some abnormalities of the nerves and muscles of the foot, as in CEREBRAL PALSY.

▓ SYMPTOMS Pigeon toes may make a child trip over his feet, so that he appears clumsy or accident-prone. It is most noticeable when he starts to walk, or wears no shoes.

▓ ACTION In most cases the problem is mild: strong, well-fitting shoes are the simple remedy. In troublesome cases, stretching exercises for the hip and foot can help to reverse the condition.

▓ TREATMENT Occasionally, corrective plaster splints may be necessary. Surgery is rarely needed.

▓ OUTLOOK Intoeing almost always improves without treatment.

PINK EYE

See *CONJUNCTIVITIS*.

PITYRIASIS ROSEA

A skin rash of unknown cause, consisting of oval patches on the trunk, which persists for about six weeks, then disappears.

▓ SYMPTOMS A 'herald patch' is the first sign: a small red patch of skin about one in (2 cm) in diameter, somewhere on the child's chest or tummy. A few days later, numerous oval patches, smaller than the herald patch, cover the trunk. They are red, with a faintly scaly surface. They do not usually itch, but cause great anxiety to parents. The child is not ill, but may have had a mild sore throat during the weeks before the appearance of the rash.

▧ ACTION As this is not an infectious disease, there is no need to isolate the child, or take precautions against infection. It is wise, however, to get medical advice in order to be sure of the diagnosis.

▧ TREATMENT No specific treatment is needed, unless the rash irritates, when a mild hydrocortisone cream may be prescribed.

▧ OUTLOOK *Pityriasis rosea* is not a serious condition, and will completely disappear in two or three months. There are no long-term effects, nor is there a connection with other skin problems. (It is *not* related to PSORIASIS or ECZEMA.)

PLAY THERAPY

At one level, this consists of psychological treatment using play to help a young child express and resolve emotional problems. This would normally require regular individual sessions, with a specially trained therapist.

At another level, play therapy may be utilized in hospital to distract and occupy the small child. This is now recognized as an important and constructive part of the hospital's work with sick children. See *CHILD PSYCHOTHERAPY*.

PLEURISY

An inflammation of the outer lining of the lungs, or the inner lining of the chest wall. Although fairly common in adults, it is rare in children.

▧ CAUSES Any INFECTION of the lungs such as PNEUMONIA or TUBERCULOSIS, can result in pleurisy.

▧ SYMPTOMS In addition to the symptoms of the underlying infection or disease, pleurisy causes pain, which may be felt in the chest, the abdomen or the shoulder. The pain is sharp and severe; it prevents the child from breathing deeply.

▧ ACTION Pleurisy is unlikely to be the first sign of illness in a child: if a child has these symptoms, he should be seen by a doctor for physical examination and tests such as chest X-ray.

▧ TREATMENT and OUTLOOK See the various underlying diseases – *PNEUMONIA, TUBERCULOSIS, LEUKAEMIA.*

PNEUMONIA

An INFECTION of part or all of the lungs.

▧ CAUSES A wide range of BACTERIA or VIRUSES.

▧ SYMPTOMS The child will usually have a COUGH and a FEVER. Very young babies may only display rapid breathing, and appear generally ill. Older children may have no chest signs, but have high fever and delirium; other children (and in other types of pneumonia) may experience pain, or may cough up phlegm, often coloured green or yellow. The child may be BREATHLESS.

▧ ACTION Children with pneumonia

are often seriously ill, and need hospital treatment. In milder forms, pneumonia may be treated at home. However, the term pneumonia always requires medical advice and care: don't hesitate to get medical advice if your child has symptoms of pneumonia.

■ INVESTIGATIONS X-rays of the chest may be performed to confirm the diagnosis, and reveal the extent and type of pneumonia. BLOOD TESTS and tests of the sputum (phlegm) may help to determine the type of infection causing pneumonia.

■ TREATMENT ANTIBIOTICS are often prescribed as many types of pneumonia are due to BACTERIA. They are usually given by mouth. If the child is too ill, they may be given by injection or intravenous drip. Mucolytic drugs may be given to loosen very sticky mucus; their efficacy is questionable, however.

■ PHYSIOTHERAPY 'Tipping' and 'tapping' may help to encourage coughing, shifting mucus or plegm, and improve breathing. The physiotherapist may teach parents how to perform the treatment.

If the pneumonia is severe, the child may be given oxygen through a mask, or in a tent; in extreme cases the child may need life support on a ventilator.

■ OUTLOOK following pneumonia is good for almost all children. Unless there is an underlying cause (such as CYSTIC FIBROSIS), continuing problems are rare. Occasionally, damage to the lung leads to BRONCHIECTASIS, and recurrent infections.

POISONING

Pills and medicines are the most common poisons taken by children, followed by household chemicals, seeds and berries. Eighty per cent of serious accidental poisoning occurs in children under five years, and the accidents often happen when the family is under stress.

■ IMMEDIATE ACTION If unconscious, see EMERGENCY RESUSCITATION.

Pills and medicines: Look for the empty container, and take it with the child to hospital.

Household and garden chemicals: Take the child to hospital, with the container from which the substance came. If there is likely to be a substantial delay, give milk and water. Don't make the child vomit – it can cause further corrosive damage to the gullet.

What to expect at hospital: The toxicity of the poison will be assessed. In some cases, vomiting will be induced to expel any unabsorbed poison from the stomach. This may be brought about by a special syrup; or a tube may be passed into the stomach through which the stomach contents will be washed out. For certain poisons, antidotes are given to neutralize their effect. Many children will be detained overnight in hospital for observation.

POLIOMYELITIS (POLIO)

An INFECTION caused by the polio VIRUS, of which there are three types. The disease is spread by droplet exhalation, or by infected stools. The INCUBATION PERIOD is from three to 21 days, and children are most infectious from a week before to a week after the symptoms appear.

■ PREVENTION IMMUNIZATION is essential, and ought to be routine.

■ SYMPTOMS HEADACHE, FEVER, DIARRHOEA and loss of APPETITE occur first.

These symptoms may be mild and no serious illness may result. However, in some cases, symptoms may become more severe and be associated with muscle pains and stiffness.

In some children, PARALYSIS follows. This can involve the muscles of the arms and legs, or the muscles involved in breathing and swallowing. Paralysis is more common in older children and adolescents; in children who have had an operation or any injection during the incubation period; and in children who have been involved in strenuous physical activity just before the onset of symptoms.

ENCEPHALITIS is a rare but grave complication.

■ TESTS The virus can be found in throat swabs and stool specimens. BLOOD TESTS can also confirm the diagnosis.

■ ACTION Because the symptoms are similar to those of COMMON COLD or INFLUENZA, the diagnosis may not be obvious early in the illness. If your child has any suspicious symptoms and for some reason has not been immunized, always mention this to your doctor.

■ TREATMENT depends on the symptoms. Even if there is no paralysis, rest is helpful to prevent and limit paralysis if it develops. If paralysis occurs, admission to hospital is essential. Splints and physiotherapy will prevent stiffening of joints.

If the muscles of breathing or swallowing are paralysed, the child could well be put on a ventilator to help with breathing.

A child with polio continues to be infectious for a week or more after the illness has started. Everyone looking after the child should be immunized and careful hand washing is essential.

■ OUTLOOK depends on the severity of the infection, but paralysis continues to improve for about a year after the illness. However, permanent paralysis is a possibility.

PORPHYRIA

The porphyrias are a group of diseases caused by inherited deficiencies of enzymes necessary for the production of haem, an essential component of haemoglobin, the oxygen carrier in red blood cells.

■ SYMPTOMS There are many types of inherited porphyria, each with their own set of symptoms. In the types where there is over-production of porphyrins in the blood stream (for example, congenital erythropoeitic porphyria), the child develops striking photosensitivity of the skin. Exposure to sunlight may result in blistering, scarring and in severe cases damage to fingers and toes. Excess facial and body hair and skin pigmentation may also be problematic.

In acute intermittent porphyria, skin sensitivity is rarely a symptom, but patients may suffer sudden ABDOMINAL PAIN and neurological or psychiatric disturbance. Fortunately this condition and the acquired, non-inherited, form of the disease rarely occur in childhood. POISONING with lead and hexachlorobenzene can also produce the condition.

■ ACTION Avoiding sunlight is essential for the photo-sensitive child. In severe cases, the child may need to wear protective clothing and a specially constructed glass helmet which absorbs ultraviolet rays. The home may need special glazing with ultraviolet-absorbent glass, and the child's movements may need to be restricted. Children with a family history of the acute form should avoid certain drugs.

■ TREATMENT Oral beta-carotene may be helpful in reducing photosensitivity. In acute intermittent porphyria, the abdominal pain attacks may respond to a diet high in carbohydrate or glucose solution given intravenously.

■ OUTLOOK With sound preventive measures and prompt treatment, most forms of porphyria can be controlled sufficiently well for the child to grow up to live a useful and happy life.

POSSETING
Babies often bring up a little milk at the end of a feed, accompanied by wind. The milk will appear partially digested. Posseting, as opposed to VOMITING, is, by definition, more of a nuisance than a threat to a baby's health and well-being.

■ ACTION It may help to wind the baby additionally in the middle of each feed.

POST-NASAL DRIP
The flow of mucus from the nose down the back of the throat. This is the usual cause of COUGH when a child has a COMMON COLD, HAY FEVER, or ALLERGIC RHINITIS. The cough is usually described as 'tickly'. It should not be suppressed, as it keeps the mucus out of the child's lungs. If possible, the cause should be treated.

PREMATURITY
Born before 37 weeks of pregnancy. The full term of pregnancy is 40 weeks.

■ CAUSES In the majority of cases, labour begins prematurely for no apparent cause. A baby may, however, have to be delivered prematurely because of maternal or foetal problems. Hypertension developing during pregnancy is the most common reason.

■ PROBLEMS The more premature the baby, that is, the shorter the duration of the pregnancy, the more immature the baby's normal physiology. Thus premature babies have poorly developed sucking and swallowing mechanisms. They tend to regurgitate feeds more easily, and are therefore at risk of inhaling milk into the lungs.

Most premature babies become JAUNDICED, and are susceptible to HYPOTHERMIA, INFECTION and RESPIRATORY DISTRESS SYNDROME. They often develop ANAEMIA when they are two to three months old.

■ TREATMENT Some premature babies (those born around 36 weeks of gestation; not those born after very short pregnancies) can be nursed with their mothers on the postnatal ward. However, feeds may need to be given via a small-bore tube passed down one nostril into the stomach. (If tube feeds are needed then special nursing help will be required, which may be available only in the special care baby unit.) The feeds may be either breast milk which has been expressed (by the mother or a donor if the hospital runs a human milk bank) or formula milk. Because such babies have small stomachs, they need tube feeds of low volume at frequent intervals. Babies born after shorter gestation with very low birth weight will need INTENSIVE CARE.

Premature babies of less than 35 weeks' gestation, together with most babies of less than 70 oz or 4½ lb (2,000 gm), require at least close observation with special attention to temperature control and feeding.

However, sick babies and those below 30 weeks' gestation and less than 18 oz or 1 lb (500 gm), will often need additional or intensive care. This may require one nurse to be assigned at each work shift to observe and care for an individual baby. Additionally, fluids and nutrients may need to be given intravenously, ANTIBIOTICS may be required for infections, other drugs may be indicated to stimulate breathing or support heart function, and frequently a period of artificial ventilation will be called for. The care of such babies is a highly complex form of medicine; it is very technical. But you should ensure that, as parents, your central role in being with your baby is not overlooked.

▓ OUTLOOK For other than the smallest and very sick premature infants, the outlook is generally good. That is, the majority of such babies live and grow up to be normal children. But each baby's problems are highly individual, and you should ask the doctors to discuss with you what they believe the outlook to be.

PROLAPSE, RECTAL
See *RECTAL PROLAPSE*.

PROTRUDING EARS ('BAT' EARS)
Children's ears sometimes stick out to a degree that leads to embarrassment and ridicule. A simple cosmetic operation can be performed, usually in the early school years, to correct the anomaly. A narrow strip of cartilage is removed from the ear to allow the ear to flatten.

However, many parents (and children) choose to live with the problem, perhaps encouraging the child to wear his hair long.

PSORIASIS
A relatively common skin condition of unknown cause, characterized by raised red patches, which tend to come and go. There are several different types: the commonest type in children consists of many small round patches (about the size of a finger-nail or less); less common scalp psoriasis, in which thick scales form on the scalp beneath the hair; and generalized psoriasis, very rare, affecting the whole skin.

Overall, about 1 per cent of the population have psoriasis at some time in their lives. It may run in families, and is less common in children than in adults.

▓ SYMPTOMS The red patches of psoriasis are due to areas of skin with a rich blood supply growing faster than normal skin. The main symptoms are the reddened appearance of the skin, and its scaliness. Occasionally there may be itching and, if cracks occur, pain.

▓ ACTION Children who develop any new rash should be seen by the family doctor. The diagnosis of psoriasis depends on the appearance

professional help. In this case, the casualty should be lying flat on his or her back and the airway should be maintained in this position.

RECOVERY POSITION

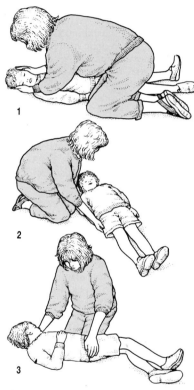

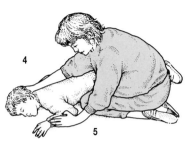

4 *Adjust head once more as shown, jaw forward, to ensure airway is still open. Still support the body against your knees.*
5 *Bend arm as shown.*

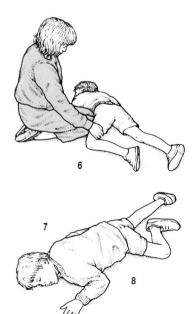

1 *Open airway: see EMERGENCY RESUSCITATION.*
2 *Place the child's arm by his side, then lift his near buttock and place the hand underneath, fingers straight. Grasp the far leg behind the knee and cross it over the near leg; move the far arm across the chest as shown in* **3**.
3 *Support the child's head as shown, and with the other hand get a grip on his clothing in the vicinity of the far hip. Pull the child's whole body towards you, supporting him while temporarily on his side against your chest.*

6 *Bend knee.*
7 *Pull other arm from under the child. Leave it as shown.*
8 *No more than half the chest should be left in contact with the ground. Finally check that the casualty's resting position is stable – one purpose of the recovery position is to prevent him from rolling.*

RECTAL PROLAPSE

A rare condition in many countries. It may occur in states of malnutrition and occasionally in CYSTIC FIBROSIS, and in association with bowel PARASITES. Pressure in the rectum causes a protrusion of bowel from the anus.

■ SYMPTOMS The protruding bowel looks red and moist. Parents are likely to be alerted to the problem in a small child if it causes discomfort when defecating.

■ IMMEDIATE ACTION An ice-pack made from crushed ice in a small plastic bag will reduce soreness, while getting medical advice; your doctor may ask for a stool specimen to check for parasites. Infestations can be eliminated by appropriate medication.

RECURRENT ABDOMINAL PAIN

Some children have bouts of abdominal pain that seem to recur again and again. Sometimes there is a pattern – perhaps at the beginning of term, or just before exams. Usually, however, there is no obvious pattern. Parents sometimes worry that each episode is APPENDICITIS. There may be associated NAUSEA and pallor, but the abdomen is not particularly tender and there are no signs of PERITONITIS.

■ CAUSE There seems to be a link with STRESS, but this is certainly not always obvious; the child may not show any obvious signs of ANXIETY. Discussing the pattern of episodes may help the family come to terms with the idea that the pain functions as a signal of some sort, but is not a sign of appendicitis. Muscles in the bowel may well be contracting in response to tension.

■ ACTION If the family can recog-

nize the pattern, there will be less anxiety and more hope for coping with any underlying problems. The individual bout of pain may be helped by paracetamol, and rest and reassurance, and invariably blows over within a couple of days. Observation at home by a doctor who knows the child well is helpful in establishing the diagnosis. Unfortunately, when the pattern is not recognized, a child may be admitted to hospital and operated on for suspected appendicitis. He then undergoes convalescence from an unnecessary operation, which does nothing to reduce the pain of his anxiety and his next episode.

See also *PUBERTY* for recurrent lower abdominal pain before and during periods; also pain at ovulation time.

RENAL FAILURE

The point at which health deteriorates as a result of chemical inbalance in the body produced by poor kidney function. It may occur rapidly, or gradually over a number of years. Rare in children. See *NEPHRITIS*.

■ SYMPTOMS The child feels unwell, has a poor appetite and passes less urine than normal. He may also become ANAEMIC, develop RICKETS and have high BLOOD PRESSURE. Growth is affected if kidney failure progresses slowly over many months or years.

■ MANAGEMENT A child with kidney failure will be given a special diet low in protein (but high in other energy sources) and low in salt and phosphorus. His fluid intake will be regulated as excess fluid cannot be filtered out by the kidneys. Drugs may be necessary to treat the high blood pressure. He may require blood transfusions for anaemia.

Eventually kidney failure will require dialysis to keep the chemistry of the body in equilibrium. Most children would then be placed on a waiting list for a suitable donor for kidney transplantation.

■ DIALYSIS A means of carrying out the filtering work of the kidneys. There are two methods – haemodialysis and peritoneal dialysis. In haemodialysis, blood is led from an artery in the arm via a piece of fine tubing to the kidney machine where the waste products are removed; the filtered blood is then directed back through another tube to a vein in the arm. This treatment is usually needed for a period of several hours two to three times a week. In peritoneal dialysis, a tube is inserted into the abdomen and a special fluid allowed to run in. The fluid flows over the peritoneum, the lining that covers the bowels and major abdominal organs. The waste products in the blood cross the peritoneal membrane into the fluid, which is then allowed slowly to run out of the abdomen. This cycling of the fluid is repeated until the chemical balance of the body is improved. It can be performed overnight or during the day when the dialysis system is arranged so as to allow the child to be up and moving about.

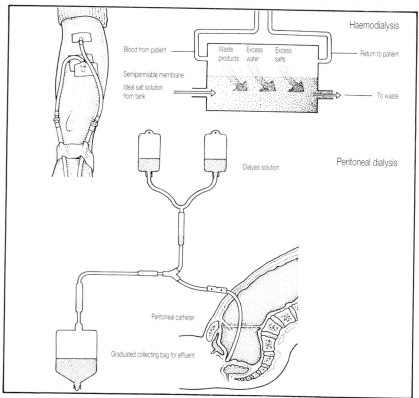

Haemodialysis

Blood from patient — Waste products Excess water Excess salts — Return to patient

Semipermiable membrane
Ideal salt solution from tank — To waste

Dialysis solution

Peritoneal dialysis

Peritoneal catheter

Graduated collecting bag for effluent

▓ KIDNEY TRANSPLANT Replacement of a non- or very poorly functioning kidney by a healthy one. The healthy kidney may be donated by a living person (usually related to the child) or may come from someone who has recently died. The kidneys are carefully matched for tissue type to minimize the risk of rejection. Steroids and drugs that suppress the immune system are also given to help prevent rejection.

In recent years the success of renal transplantation has been dramatic. About three-quarters of transplants are completely successful, and are being undertaken at progressively younger ages (vital for those babies born with untreatable damaged or malformed kidneys).

RESPIRATORY DISTRESS SYNDROME (RDS)

A breathing difficulty of PREMATURE babies caused by lack of surfactant, a chemical that coats the lung surface, preventing both collapse of the small airways and stiffening of the lungs. Surfactant does not appear in the foetal lungs until around 28 weeks of pregnancy, and RDS affects 70 to 80 per cent of babies born at, or before, this time. (See also *PREMATURITY*.) The incidence and severity of RDS decreases with maturity at birth, so that only 10 per cent of babies born around 34 weeks of pregnancy will develop RDS. It is very rare in full-term babies.

▓ CAUSES Prematurity is the major cause. Put another way, immaturity of the lungs is a component of the general immaturity that characterizes the premature baby. However, RDS may occur in full-term babies who suffer BIRTH ASPHYXIA or HYPOTHERMIA, although in many such cases the picture does not simply result from surfactant deficiency.

▓ SIGNS Within the first hours following birth, the baby will have breathing difficulties: he will breathe rapidly, his chest will be drawn in and he will make grunting noises. However, these signs can occur in conditions other than surfactant deficiency such as MECONIUM aspiration, PNEUMONIA or CONGENITAL HEART-DISEASE. A chest X-ray helps clarify why a particular baby is suffering distress with his breathing.

▓ TREATMENT is aimed at keeping the premature baby alive and well until he starts to make his own surfactant. This often begins 48 to 72 hours after birth. Current research aims to find ways to replace the missing surfactant.

Babies with RDS receive INTENSIVE CARE. The oxygen level in their blood is measured at regular intervals by BLOOD TESTS or by the continuous use of a skin monitor, or of an umbilical catheter (a small tube inserted in the artery of the UMBILICUS). If the level drops, oxygen is given either by enriching the air of the INCUBATOR or by ventilation. The latter involves a tube placed through the baby's nose or mouth into the trachea (the upper air passage). The tube is then connected to a ventilator (breathing machine), which takes over the work of breathing. Over the following days, most babies recover sufficiently to breathe without the ventilator. The smallest and sickest babies may, however, require weeks of assisted ventilation. During the course of intensive care, all body systems receive support: thermoregulation; PHOTOTHERAPY for jaundice; fluid regulation; feeding by tube into the stomach; and many other details of care including stimulation and maximal contact of the baby with his parents.

■ COMPLICATIONS may arise with ventilation. These include lung collapse, pneumothorax, PNEUMONIA and chronic oxygen dependency. Very high concentrations of oxygen can damage the retina of the eye, but this can usually be prevented by monitoring the blood's oxygen level. Some babies with severe RDS need long-term ventilation.

■ OUTLOOK Babies whose lungs are not damaged will grow to be healthy, and even those with the most severe lung damage usually recover from breathing difficulties by the time they are 12 to 18 months old.

REYE'S SYNDROME
Severe VOMITING, FEVER, confusion and CONVULSIONS following an upper respiratory tract INFECTION. This is a rare condition, but it is controversial because in some cases it appears to be related to a child taking aspirin. For this reason, never give aspirin or aspirin-containing medication to a child under 12. Use paracetamol instead for pain and fever in children. Reye's syndrome may also be related to CHICKEN-POX or other VIRAL infections.

■ ACTION If Reye's syndrome is suspected, the child will be urgently admitted to hospital for treatment.

■ INVESTIGATIONS Blood glucose is usually low. Other BLOOD TESTS will also be needed.

■ TREATMENT Correction of fluid imbalance. Treatment of convulsions and raised pressure in the brain. Artificial ventilation, management of liver failure and correction of clotting problems will be the priorities.

■ OUTLOOK May be fatal, but full recovery is possible.

RHESUS INCOMPATIBILITY
Destruction of a new-born baby's red blood cells which occurs when the baby is Rhesus positive and the mother Rhesus negative.

Most people have the D-Rhesus ANTIGEN on the surface of their red blood cells: they are Rhesus positive. Those who don't have this antigen are Rhesus negative. During pregnancy some foetal red blood cells cross the placenta. If the mother is Rhesus negative, exposure to the antigen results in sensitization and the production of anti-Rhesus ANTIBODIES. If it is a first pregnancy, the effects may be insignificant. However, in subsequent pregnancies, if the foetus is Rhesus positive, the mother's immune response is more vigorous. Her antibodies cross the placenta, and destroy the foetal red blood cells. If severe, this will result in foetal anaemia and OEDEMA; and after the baby is born, severe jaundice (jaundice does not occur in the uterus because the placenta filters the bilirubin from the foetal blood).

■ PREVENTION AND TREATMENT If the mother has not developed any Rhesus antibodies, then the destruction of the baby's red blood cells can be prevented. The mother is given a substance called anti-D immediately after birth, which destroys Rhesus positive cells (the foetal cells which would otherwise sensitize the mother's immune system, and which cross into the mother's circulation in largest numbers at the time of delivery), and hence prevents the development of antibodies which would cause problems in the next pregnancy. All mothers who are Rhesus negative should be given anti-D after delivery. If the mother has already developed antibodies, then the baby may be deliberately delivered early to avoid excessive destruction of red blood cells.

RHEUMATIC FEVER

A rare disease in developed countries (but common in some undeveloped ones) caused by the same *Streptococcus* BACTERIUM that causes SCARLET FEVER. It occurs mainly in schoolchildren and results in joint pains, FEVER and inflammation of the heart. It can have the unwelcome long-term effect of HEART-DISEASE, and in some cases damage to the heart valves.

If a child has had an episode of rheumatic fever, he should be given the ANTIBIOTIC, penicillin, regularly for several years in order to prevent a recurrence, which can further damage the heart. If he has heart problems as a result of the illness, he will always need the protection of antibiotics when having a tooth out, and indeed if undergoing any other operation, to prevent further heart complications.

RHEUMATOID ARTHRITIS in children is properly described as *JUVENILE CHRONIC ARTHRITIS*.

RICKETS

A curable disease of bone, due to a disturbance in the way calcium is incorporated. This is a process requiring vitamin D, which is formed in the skin when exposed to sunlight. A combination of inadequate diet, cloudy weather and poor housing conditions explains the occurrence of this problem in some urban areas in the U.K., but it is not common now.

■ SYMPTOMS Bone pain, BOW LEGS, weakness and possibly other signs of VITAMIN DEFICIENCIES.

■ TREATMENT Vitamin D is taken for several months.

RINGWORM

A contagious skin infection.

■ SYMPTOMS A circle of itchy, red, scaly skin with a bumpy edge. On the scalp an unsightly bald patch will occur.

■ CAUSE A FUNGAL INFECTION which can be transmitted from either humans or animals.

■ TREATMENT Your doctor will prescribe an antifungal cream. If the infection fails to respond, an oral drug, griseofulvin, may be prescribed. Throw away your child's brushes and combs etc. Keep him off school, try to prevent him from scratching and see that he washes after touching infected areas. If pets are infected, get them treated as well.

ROSEOLA INFANTUM

A relatively common INFECTION affecting children between six months and two years. The INCUBATION PERIOD is about ten days.

■ SYMPTOMS There is a sudden onset of high FEVER; FEBRILE CONVULSIONS can occur. This lasts for a few days and the temperature then returns to normal, whereupon a fine, pink rash spreads rapidly over the body within a few hours.

ACTION The fever is the only real problem, and this should be treated with a cool bath and paracetamol. Some parents mistake the infection for measles. In the case of *Roseola*, the temperature returns to normal when the rash appears and the child looks and feels much better.

OUTLOOK The child always recovers fully.

ROUNDWORM
See *WORMS*.

RUBELLA
A VIRAL INFECTION, also known as German measles, which most commonly occurs between four and 12 years of age.

The INCUBATION PERIOD is 14-21 days. A child can pass on the infection during the week before he becomes ill, and remains infectious for up to five days after the rash has appeared.

SYMPTOMS The illness starts with a rash of fine pink spots over the face and trunk which gradually merge and last three to five days. The lymph glands at the nape of the neck and behind the ears usually enlarge. They are seldom painful, but are easily felt. There may be slight FEVER, a runny nose, CONJUNCTIVITIS and sometimes a general feeling of being unwell.

In young children, the symptoms are often so mild that the diagnosis is never made. Other viral infections can give a similar picture, so the diagnosis is often difficult to make with certainty.

In adolescents and adults, the symptoms tend to be severe and can be followed by pain and swelling of the joints, which usually last for a week or two.

ACTION There is no specific treatment, but the fever should be treated with an analgesic such as paracetamol and a cool bath if necessary.

If the joint pains are severe, aspirin will help but it should not be used in children under the age of 12 years because of the risk of REYE'S SYNDROME.

The child with German measles should avoid contact with pregnant women who have not had *Rubella*, since infection of the foetus in early pregnancy can cause CONGENITAL *RUBELLA* SYNDROME. Children who have been recently IMMUNIZED cannot transmit *Rubella*.

PREVENTION Immunization is now offered as part of MEASLES, MUMPS and *Rubella* immunization, given between one and two years of age. It will in due course reduce the number of infections in the given community. It is not clear whether this early immunization protects throughout the child-bearing years, so reimmunization is recommended to all girls at PUBERTY.

Prior to getting pregnant, all women should be immunized against *Rubella*, or have a BLOOD TEST to determine whether they are immune.

OUTLOOK The joint symptoms don't cause permanent disability. Long-term complications are rare, although ENCEPHALITIS has been recorded in association with *Rubella*.

RUPTURE
See *HERNIAS*.

S

SALT IN THE DIET

Salt intake is a health issue for adults, largely because of its apparent association with high BLOOD PRESSURE. However, for healthy children, salt is more properly considered a normal and essential dietary ingredient. Thus salt loss and dehydration may occur in hot weather, or otherwise through excessive sweating, vomiting or diarrhoea leading to weakness and lethargy.

However, in the light of current views on the long-term relationship between excessive salt intake and adult health, it seems prudent to discourage children from habitually adding salt.

SCABIES

An itchy skin eruption due to infestation with the mite *Sarcoptes scabei*.

■ CAUSE The tiny mite, hardly visible to the naked eye, is 'caught' by close contact with an infected person. It then burrows into the new host's skin. Once installed, the female lays eggs, leaving a track, or burrow, in the skin, which may be visible. The invasion causes an allergic reaction, resulting in a red raised itchy swelling, some millimetres in length.

■ SYMPTOMS Itching, worse at night, and thickening of the skin as a result of constant scratching. Common sites for the lesions are between the fingers, the inside of wrists, the elbows, the genital area and the arms and feet generally. Close contacts (typically of mothers and babies) need to be examined and treated. Secondary INFECTION of the infected site may cause IMPETIGO.

■ ACTION Get medical advice. Your doctor will prescribe a lotion.

■ TREATMENT Benzyl benzoate, or gamma benzene hexachloride are the standard treatments for scabies. It is important to use them correctly: each member of the household, parents and children, should be treated at the same time. The cream or lotion is applied to the whole body from the neck down, ideally after a hot bath. The treatment is repeated after 24 hours. Persistent itching may be treated by the addition of hydrocortisone cream. Wash all clothing worn by the child (or other affected family members); similarly, change and wash bedding and towels.

■ OUTLOOK Correct treatment as described should eliminate the scabies infection; however, itching can persist for up to a week. Scabies can return of course, even after treatment if contact with an infected person recurs.

SCALDS

See *BURNS*.

SCAR

A mark on any part of the body, internal or external, where a natural repair has occurred.

■ CAUSE Scar tissue is the growth of firm, fibrous material which joins together separated tissue, typically after a cut. The scientific term for the fibrous material is collagen, and it is also found in ligaments and tendons. Any injury or cut can lead to scar formation, but the more ragged the cut, the more extensive the scar. An infected or dirty cut will produce more scar tissue than a clean cut, while a widely gaping wound on the skin will produce a bigger scar than a tightly closed wound. Cuts in the skin are thus stitched to give as slender a scar as possible.

Burns to the skin also cause scarring over wide areas where scar tissue entirely replaces the lost skin. For this reason, skin grafts are applied to areas of full thickness burn, and special dressings used to reduce scar formation.

A keloid is a scar on the skin which has become very prominent, and may need special treatment by a plastic surgeon. It is commoner in dark-skinned people than whites.

▓ ACTION To minimize scarring, cuts should be cleaned to remove all dirt and grit (see CUTS AND GRAZES). If the skin edges are separated, they should be brought together either by special skin plasters, or by sutures (stitches) – usually this is performed in a G.P.'s surgery or in the casualty department of a hospital.

▓ TREATMENT If a scar is unsightly, it may be possible to improve it by plastic surgery: your family doctor can advise.

▓ OUTLOOK Scars tend to fade with time, and to become smaller. They are usually red at first, but gradually turn white, over about a year. Permanent scars on the face can be well hidden by special masking creams, available through plastic surgery clinics and skin specialists.

SCARLET FEVER

An INFECTION caused by Streptococcus BACTERIA. It is spread by droplets exhaled or coughed out. The INCUBATION PERIOD is two to seven days.

▓ SYMPTOMS For reasons not fully understood, this has nowadays become a mild disease. It usually consists of a SORE THROAT, FEVER and RASH. The rash appears a few days after onset of fever, and consists of tiny red spots covering the body. The area around the lips is often white and the tongue becomes bright red (strawberry tongue). There may be ABDOMINAL PAIN, loss of APPETITE and VOMITING.

Complications are rare and the infection responds fast to penicillin.

SCHIZOPHRENIA

A rare illness of adolescents (and adults), almost unknown in younger age groups.

▓ SYMPTOMS Onset is often gradual and intermittent. The adolescent loses interest in school work and withdraws from friends, seems to lose touch with reality, and may become preoccupied with unusual ideas. You may notice mood swings which exceed what you would expect for his age. Sometimes the illness appears suddenly (typically at an obviously stressful time) with HALLUCINATIONS and inexplicable behaviour.
See PSYCHOSIS.

▓ ACTION The family doctor will recognize the possibility of schizophrenia, and refer your child to a child or adolescent psychiatrist.

▓ TREATMENT Hospital admission may be recommended and treatment with major tranquillizer drugs (of which chlorpromazine is the commonest, but there are many). The family should also be offered advice to cope with what is often a relapsing illness. Most adolescents recover sufficiently to return to a normal school and friendships after treatment. However, the long-term outlook for some is variable and, in some cases, gloomy.

SCHOOL ATTENDANCE PROBLEMS

Attending school for the first time, or changing school is an ordeal for some children. For the nervous child, it may require special preparation: stress the enjoyable parts of school life; emphasize that you will be looking forward to his return each day.

Reluctance to go to school may be expressed directly or take the form of 'symptoms' such as headaches, feeling sick or tummy-ache just before it is time to leave for school; symptoms which the child is no doubt experiencing, but which disappear once it is clear that he can stay off school. Sometimes what starts as a genuine physical illness may seem to linger on – see *ANXIETY, STRESS SYMPTOMS*. This may reflect something worrying your child at school; it can also be due to changes or worries at home: Is someone ill? See FAMILY PROBLEMS.

It is better for your child to tackle problems rather than hide from them.

▨ ACTION Talk to your child and his teacher; deal with anything in the school routine that your child identifies as worrying.

If the worry is about you or something at home, try to ease his anxieties; but remain consistent and firm (but not unkind) in presenting school attendance as the norm.

Problems may re-surface after a holiday break or an illness; the routine of going to school needs to be re-established quickly.

If reluctance to attend school is accompanied by major distress or continues for more than a week or two, investigate, with his teacher, whether there are LEARNING DISORDERS.

If the problem continues, talk to your doctor, who may suggest seeing a clinical psychologist or child psychiatrist.

SCHOOL MEDICALS

A child entering school for the first time is usually examined by a professional from the local health authority to detect defects of growth, vision, hearing, health or development. This provides an opportunity for a further health check on the whole population of children: it also specifically serves to identify problems which require specific educational provisions. In Britain, a statement of special education needs under the 1981 Education Act requires a medical report. Additional medical examinations may also be called for if teachers are worried that a medical problem is interfering with learning.

Some authorities recommend health checks by school nurses (for example at eight, 11 and 14 years) to detect problems which may require medical investigation or treatment, and (perhaps of greater importance) to contribute to health education, dealing with such matters as cigarette smoking, drug abuse, contraception, AIDS avoidance, preparation for parenthood, and so on.

SCOLIOSIS

Abnormal curvature of any part of the spine. It can be caused by any problem with the bones of the spine (the vertebrae), or the muscles designed to support the spine equally on either side. But sometimes no cause is found.

Scoliosis is most common in childhood. Doctors usually follow the child up for several years as the curve may or may not worsen with time. It may become more severe during periods of rapid growth, and stops progressing when growth ceases.

▨ SYMPTOMS Deformity is usually the only symptom in childhood. The condition can however cause pain at a later stage because of long-standing structural strain. Scoliosis can occur in young children, but it may well appear for the first time at ten to 12 years. Sometimes it is discovered by the school doctor, who routinely looks for the condition during examination.

■ ACTION If you think that your child may have scoliosis, get medical advice. Your doctor may suggest that the child see an orthopaedic surgeon. This does not necessarily mean that the child will need an operation.

Scoliosis in the lower part of the spine is usually not particularly severe, but may be more problematic if it affects the spine in the region of the chest.

■ TESTS X-rays will reveal the degree of scoliosis, and may help to detect the cause. They are also essential, at regular intervals, to monitor progress.

■ TREATMENT depends on many factors:

If the scoliosis is mild, no active treatment may be necessary. Examinations and X-rays done every six to 12 months indicate whether there is any change which requires treatment.

A brace may be fitted to keep the spine as straight as possible.

Sometimes an operation is suggested. Various types are available, but the common aim is to stabilize the spine in the best possible position and prevent further curvature of the spine.

■ OUTLOOK depends on the cause and on the treatment.

SCURVY

Caused by a deficiency of vitamin C in the diet. This could, theoretically, occur in bottle-fed babies, but is very rare in developed countries. Vitamin C is present in most fruit and vegetables, including potatoes, but is partly destroyed by cooking. Symptoms include bleeding gums and slow healing of skin after cuts and bruises. See *VITAMINS*.

SEAT BELTS

For babies, birth to nine months The traditional method is carry-cot restraints: two parallel straps anchored to the chassis of the car, and passing over the carry-cot to hold it in position. The disadvantage of this system is that the straps can tear through the sides of flimsy carry-cots, allowing the baby to be thrown out on impact. If this system is used, the carry-cot must be secured in the *back* seat of the car. The recently introduced rear-facing baby restraint is much safer: a toughly constructed, padded, semi-reclining seat, held in place by an adult seat belt. Legally approved in many countries, it can be used as a reclining seat outside the car. Other variants of the car seat for babies are currently being evaluated and introduced on to the market. Ensure that you select a model from a reputable manufacturer, preferably carrying a British Standards approval tag.

For young children, six months to four years As soon as a child can sit up he can, in principle, use a child's safety seat. These usually have two shoulder and two hip straps and also a strap between the legs, giving a comprehensive support. Always choose a safety seat with four attachment points to the car. Follow fitting instructions carefully: this is usually easy in a saloon, but not always so in a hatchback. Again, look for manufacturer's name and the tag indicating British Standards or other national body's approval.

Older children, four years onwards can use adult seat belts in the back seat, with booster cushions until the seat belts fit correctly. A correctly fitting belt puts pressure on one shoulder and over both hips; the belt should not ride up on to the abdomen. If children use an adult seat belt without a booster cushion, the belt could compress the abdomen on impact, and damage the liver and spleen.

SEPARATION ANXIETY
The normal reaction of babies and young children when separated from parents or familiar carers. Before about seven months, babies allow themselves readily to be held and cuddled by strangers. They then become gradually unsure of anyone new or unfamiliar, and will cry and protest if picked up by them.

As mobility increases, the toddler shows separation anxiety by playing close to carers if in a strange place, or protesting vigorously if left at nursery or crche. He has not yet understood that you are going to return. It is natural for him to be angry with you if he has to be left unexpectedly with strangers for a few hours; but short periods of separation will not damage

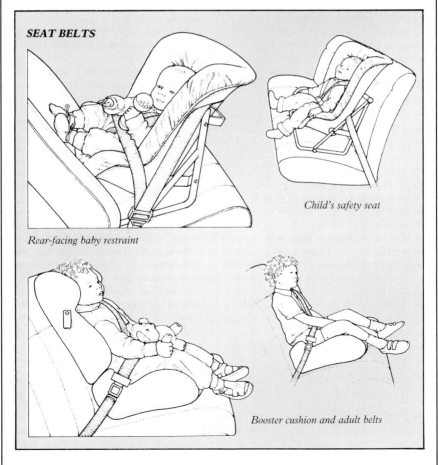

SEAT BELTS

Rear-facing baby restraint

Child's safety seat

Booster cushion and adult belts

him. Well-judged, regular opportunities in his first few years to spend short periods away from his parents are helpful to most children. But some pre-school children are ready to separate earlier than others: it is a matter of temperament, development, parental skill and luck.

By about three years, many children cope with strange places and strange people for short periods, given some encouragement. Some children are naturally more clinging and nervous than others, showing more separation anxiety and for a longer time.

All children regress in their behaviour – go back to behaving younger than their age – if upset by an upheaval such as the arrival of a new baby, or going into hospital. So don't be surprised if such a child becomes unhappy about you leaving him. It should resolve in a few weeks.

SEX EDUCATION

A subject which worries most parents. But in order to grow up safely, your child will need to know facts about his body, the names used for sexual parts of it and how these work; also about sexual feelings and sexual relationships.

He needs this knowledge in the same way as he needs to know about roads and traffic for his own safety. In both cases, what he needs to know changes as he grows. There will be many opportunities to explain the facts in increasing detail as he grows up.

■ A PARENT'S ROLE Facts which *you* give your child have the advantage of being communicated in words which you choose, and of being accompanied by your beliefs and attitudes. This will not be true of playground conversations. It may also be best to have talked as fully as you can with your child before any sex education classes or indeed any other lessons in school which cover related topics. Then he can come back to you afterwards if he is confused, knowing it is something you can discuss together.

There is no evidence that if parents have explained sexual reproduction and feelings to their child, he or she is more likely to experiment than others who know nothing. If anything, a child who has accurate information will be *less* at risk of pregnancy, disease or even SEXUAL ABUSE. He or she will certainly be less fearful about these subjects, which worry many young people, sometimes unnecessarily.

Of course, you will tailor what you say to your child's level of development; he will not understand or remember what is beyond him. There are books (for example, *The Body Book* by Claire Rayner) which help to explain all aspects of the body's working. These can also give the parent a useful idea of the language and ideas a child can understand at different ages. When (or before) your child enters puberty, he may also appreciate an up-to-date book to read for himself, for example *The Teenage Health Freak's Handbook* by Aidan MacFarlane and others. The books are no substitute for explaining your own views, but can make it easier. See *SEXUALITY, PUBERTY, MASTURBATION, PERIODS*.

SEXUAL ABUSE

In the U.K., this term includes the legal offences of incest, unlawful sexual intercourse, and indecent assault, together with other forms of inappropriate sexual experience between adults and children, including fondling, flashing and pornography.

■ INCIDENCE Surveys of adults have shown that between 10 and 25% were sexually abused to some degree during their childhoods. Sexual abuse is actually diagnosed in less than one child per 1,000 each year. Abusers are far more likely to be family members or close family contacts than strangers.

■ SYMPTOMS and signs which might suggest the possibility of sexual abuse include: inappropriate flirtatious behaviour (for the age of the child); infection of the sexual organs with organisms normally transmitted venereally, such as gonorrhoea and syphilis; unexplained abdominal pain; sudden unexplained changes in behaviour; unexplained problems at school and truancy; depression or withdrawal; 'clingy' behaviour in young children; low self-esteem and feelings of worthlessness in older children; bedwetting or soiling if accompanied by other symptoms; attempted suicide or self-injury.

■ OTHER SIGNS Any evidence of injury in a child, which cannot be explained, should lead to questioning about physical or sexual abuse.

■ ACTION If any adult suspects that sexual abuse may be happening, he or she should seek help from a responsible professional person such as a family doctor, health visitor, paediatrician or social worker. *Above all, tell someone.* Sexual abuse that is kept secret goes on harming the child.

■ INVESTIGATION Once an allegation is made, local health professionals will interview the child and others involved, and will decide what is best for the child's safety. This might involve admitting the child to hospital for a while. However, if the person alleged to be responsible for the abuse is not in the family home, investigations will be carried out without removing the child from home. The police will be involved if there are grounds for suspecting that an offence has been committed. Medical examination of a sexually abused child should take place in a pleasant room (usually not available in a police station) by doctors specially trained in child care, and in legal (forensic) medicine.

■ OUTLOOK The sad truth, borne out by long-term studies, is that sexual abuse in childhood causes long-term emotional problems. It is possible that more active counselling at the time of the abuse may help to lessen this. As the taboo on speaking about sexual abuse is lifted, more adults may be able to seek professional help: help with psychological problems arising from childhood sexual abuse; and help with the psychological problems that result in the propensity to abuse children.

■ PREVENTION Increasing emphasis is put on educating children to say 'No' to behaviour that feels uncomfortable, or wrong.

■ FURTHER READING *No More Secrets for Me* by Oralee Wachter (published by Penguin) is a sensitive study.

SEXUALITY
See *PUBERTY, MASTURBATION.*

SHINGLES
See *CHICKENPOX.*

SHOCK

As a medical term this denotes the effects of the circulation failing to reach and deliver oxygen around the body effectively. It occurs after: severe blood loss; excessive fluid loss, as in prolonged VOMITING or severe BURNS; 'poison' in the bloodstream, for example a severe INFECTION, some insect stings; and with HEART-DISEASE.

▓ SYMPTOMS A child with shock is pale, cold, sweaty and anxious, with a fast pulse and possibly rapid breathing. He may also complain of thirst, feel sick, or lapse into unconsciousness.

▓ IMMEDIATE ACTION Call an ambulance, or ask someone else to do so; lie the child flat on his back; stop any bleeding with firm pressure; see EMERGENCY RESUSCITATION and, if necessary, start this without delay. If it seems likely that the child will need an ANAESTHETIC in hospital, withhold drinks and food.

▓ TREATMENT in hospital: Oxygen, intravenous fluid (a drip) and/or blood will be given, along with appropriate drugs. The cause of shock will be treated.

SHORT STATURE

There are many causes of a child being significantly short in height, and these include:
– Deficiency of various hormones, but typically those produced by the thyroid, adrenal and pituitary glands.
– Chromosomal abnormalities such as TURNER'S SYNDROME.
– Chronic illness such as severe HEART, kidney (see *RENAL FAILURE*) or liver disease.
– Disorders of bone development such as ACHONDROPLASIA.
– Steroid treatment for diseases such as JUVENILE CHRONIC ARTHRITIS.

There are many other rare causes; and of course, some 'normal' children are short.

▓ SYMPTOMS will depend on the cause of the problem. See the separate entries mentioned above. The problem, if it is one, may well be recognized at a routine medical examination.

▓ ACTION If you think that your child is significantly shorter than all the other children you know of a similar age, get medical advice. Your doctor will examine your child and accurately measure his height. This is then entered on a percentile chart, which gives the average height and weight for every age and for both sexes.

He will want to know the exact height of both parents, and to get some idea of whether there are many short people in the family.

If there is no obvious medical condition, and if the members of the family are short (in particular the parents) the doctor may decide simply to watch your child's growth to see if it is increasing at the normal rate. Charts are available (based on the parents' height and the child's current height), which will predict the height that the child is likely to reach as an adult.

If there is any possibility of a medical problem, tests may be necessary, performed either by the doctor or by a specialist.

▓ TESTS include X-rays of the bones to discover the child's 'bone age'. This shows how the bones are maturing and can help with diagnosis; BLOOD TESTS to measure hormone levels and to detect CHROMOSOMAL abnormalities; investigations for kidney or liver problems, and also for MALABSORPTION.

■ TREATMENT depends on the cause – see the separate entries mentioned above.

If your child has a hormonal problem, treatment is usually available to replace hormones that are lacking.

Until recently, there has been no effective treatment for children who are 'normal' but short, and for those with chromosomal or genetic abnormalities such as Turner's syndrome or achondroplasia. There is experimental evidence that daily injections with growth hormone can increase the height to the normal range, but there are also convincing arguments against increasing a child's height for cosmetic and psychological reasons. The treatment is not routinely available.

■ OUTLOOK Many short children will eventually reach an adult height within the normal range. For those who do not, developing a positive self-image is essential. However, there is the prospect of new and improved treatments in this field.

SHORTSIGHTEDNESS

When the eye sees distant objects as blurred and near objects clearly. The globe of the eye itself is healthy, but it is misshapen – 'longer' from front to back than it ought to be.

You may suspect your child is short sighted if he sits close to the T.V., holds books close to his eyes, or complains of not being able to see the blackboard at school. The problem can be corrected by SPECTACLES, which are fitted after an EYE TEST.

Because vision changes with age, regular eye tests are important.

SHYNESS

This can be worrying or infuriating, and it rarely responds to reprimand or coaxing. Often best ignored unless it interferes with new activities, or making friends; or suddenly worsens and becomes incapacitating. In these cases, talk to your child's teacher or the family doctor. See also *FEARS, PHOBIAS, ANXIETY*.

SIBLING RIVALRY

It is a rare child who would not like to be the permanent centre of parental attention; learning to share anything, from affection to toys, takes time. Sharing is hardest when one child is ill or upset or feels at a disadvantage. The very existence of a brother or sister can constitute a direct threat and a very apparent need to compete for attention. Often enough, children squabble most and press their demands hardest when parents are busiest. So runs the vicious circle of sibling rivalry.

There is little you can do, apart from being scrupulously even-handed; if you have a favourite, let it be your affair and no one else's.

When a new baby is due, prepare your child or children by talking about it well beforehand. Explain the changes in routine that will be necessary. Make sure you or your partner always has some time exclusively for the first child, ideally when the other parent is busy with the new baby. Don't use special names for the baby which you used to give the older child, and don't always put the baby first. And don't belittle the child whose behaviour regresses when the newcomer arrives. Being jealous of a new baby may make a child aggressive or unkind (sometimes interspersed with being very loving). Remember that a child cannot properly understand that a baby is unable to look after himself. It often takes many months for the bad feelings to settle down.

The relationships between siblings over time show a wide range of patterns: don't expect your own children to relate in the same way as you did with your brothers and sisters. Sometimes bitter fighting early on may be replaced with closeness, but the reverse is also true.

When the going gets rough, remind yourself, and the jealous child, that jealousy, like any other emotion, is something he must learn to handle.

Make sure that visitors don't forget the elder child when coming to see a new baby: if there is a gift for the baby, there should be one for him too – and he should be greeted first.

SICKLE-CELL ANAEMIA

An INHERITED DISORDER, mainly in people of African or Afro-Caribbean origin, caused by abnormal haemoglobin – the blood's oxygen carrier. In this form of ANAEMIA, the red blood cells become fragile and break down, blocking the tiny blood vessels.

■ SYMPTOMS are uncommon under six months. After that, the problem occurs in 'crises': large numbers of red blood cells are broken down, resulting in painful swollen joints, which can involve the hands and feet; backache; intermittent, possibly severe ABDOMINAL PAIN, typically due to damage to the blood vessels in the spleen; and JAUNDICE.

Between crisis periods, the child is usually pale, but may have no other symptoms. Growth and normal development may be delayed.

Children with the mild form of the disease may have no symptoms, the problem only being discovered by a routine BLOOD TEST.

■ ACTION If there is a family history of sickle-cell anaemia, consider GENETIC COUNSELLING before you have children.

Bed rest and analgesics help the pain. DEHYDRATION can make the effects of the disease worse, so encourage your child to take plenty of fluids. Folic acid needs to be replaced.

■ TREATMENT INFECTIONS (and high altitude) can precipitate a crisis so these must be treated early (or avoided).

BLOOD TRANSFUSION may be necessary if the anaemia becomes severe. Damage to the spleen can result in an increased risk of infection. Penicillin is often used on a long-term basis to prevent this. IMMUNIZATION against the pneumococcal bacteria is given at two years of age.

■ OUTLOOK has improved with better treatment in recent years.

SICKNESS
See *VOMITING*.

SINUSITIS
INFECTION in the sinuses; rare in children.

■ SYMPTOMS Pain and swelling over one of the sinuses, usually following a cold. Children with sinusitis may become feverish and quite ill. Pain, redness and swelling around the eye may be due to infection in the maxillary or ethmoid sinuses (and of the eyelids and globe of the eye itself – known as periorbital cellulitis).

■ ACTION Mild symptoms can be treated with decongestant nose drops (for example, ephedrine 0.5%), and paracetamol.

■ GET MEDICAL ADVICE if the pain is severe, there is local tenderness, or FEVER. If the eyelid becomes red and swollen, you should get urgent medical advice.

■ TESTS An X-ray of the sinuses may be performed in order to confirm the diagnosis.

■ TREATMENT An ANTIBIOTIC will be prescribed, together with decongestant nose drops. If this does not effect a cure, your child will be referred to an ear, nose and throat (ENT) specialist. A needle may be inserted into the sinus to remove the infected fluid, and antibiotics given by injection.

■ LONG-TERM MANAGEMENT Sinusitis is not usually a persistent problem of childhood, but milder symptoms caused by ALLERGIC RHINITIS may recur.

SINUSITIS

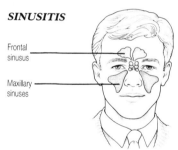

Frontal
sinuses

Maxillary
sinuses

Main symptoms: pain, redness and swelling.

SIX-WEEK CHECK
See *NORMAL DEVELOPMENT.*

SLEEP PROBLEMS
The amount of sleep needed varies enormously from child to child, and from age to age. In the pre-school years, many children have difficulty in settling to sleep, and may wake habitually during the night. In older children, problems may include SLEEP-WALKING, NIGHTMARES, NIGHT TER-

RORS or talking in their sleep. See those entries for further details.

■ CAUSES Difficulties in settling and night-waking may arise in a child accustomed to contact with you at the point of going to sleep. Disruption in routine or illness may start sleep problems in a young child who has previously been sleeping through the night.

However, there is, of course, a range of normal night-time behaviour. Many normal children and parents value the bedtime routines or rituals. And in most instances the 'problem' is the inconvenience caused to parents.

■ ACTION Try to establish a bedtime routine. Be consistent about the pattern and duration of the routine, the story, drink, and so on. It will normally follow as a matter of course over the years that the duration and degree of contact will progressively decline. If your child cries on waking and does not fall asleep again, try to settle him with a minimum of contact, and avoid a complete repetition of the bedtime rituals. If you cannot resolve the problem, ask your health visitor or doctor for advice. A range of sedatives is available, but these are rarely effective for more than a few nights.

Adults should perhaps recall or recognize that for some children (and adults), particularly those with a nervous disposition or colourful imagination, night-time and falling asleep can be worrisome. Such children need consistent sympathetic support and not 'treatment'.

■ OUTLOOK Difficulties in settling and night-waking rarely persist into the school years; but the cumulative effect of broken sleep can take its toll on the parents' capability.

SLEEP-WALKING

Some children are prone to sleep-walking: it may happen particularly at times of stress. There is no need to wake them, just gently return them to bed. Sleep-walking children almost always avoid potential hazards in the house, but with younger children it may be a wise precaution and give you peace of mind to ensure you are woken: attach something to the child's bedroom door that will make a noise if he opens it to leave the room.

SMALL-FOR-DATES BABY

Babies of a LOWER BIRTH WEIGHT than would normally be expected for the length of pregnancy. The size of a baby depends on many factors. There is the size, health and age of the mother – mothers in their teens or over 35 tend to have smaller babies. If the mother smokes, drinks, takes drugs or is severely undernourished during pregnancy, the baby is likely to be small (cigarette smoking is the most serious and avoidable factor in causing poor growth of the foetus). Babies of a MULTIPLE PREGNANCY tend to be small. CONGENITAL ABNORMALITIES and CONGENITAL INFECTION also affect the growth of the foetus, and hence the baby's birth weight.

Most small-for-dates babies have no major problems after birth and will usually 'catch up' in weight and height by the end of their first year. If a foetus has had a prolonged period of poor growth in pregnancy, then he is likely to remain relatively small in later life.

New-born small-for-dates babies are more likely to suffer from HYPOGLY-CAEMIA and HYPOTHERMIA. The smaller the baby, the more serious the risks of other complications. Thus even a full-term baby who weighs under 70 oz or 4½ lb (2,000 gm) at birth will need close observation, if not admission to a special care baby unit.

SMALLPOX

A disease of the past: mass vaccination during childhood appears to have eradicated it; indeed immunization is no longer necessary.

SMOKING

Out of every 100 men in most developed countries, 25 will die prematurely of tobacco-related diseases, mainly cancer and heart-disease. Nicotine, the active drug in tobacco, is extremely addictive, causing intense craving in regular users if stopped. It is also a powerful tranquillizer. The act of sucking on a cigarette, with its echoes of early comfort from breast feeding, is in itself extremely soothing. And the self-conscious adolescent, who does not yet know what to do with his hands in company, can find cigarettes the ideal displacement activity.

These powerful inducements to smoke don't even include the obvious pleasure of doing something of which adults disapprove, and of being part of a group which demonstrates its independence by smoking in secret.

Studies have shown that in some countries about one third of 14-year-olds smoke every day. Many of these will continue to smoke in adult life, when they will greatly increase their risk of cancer, heart attacks, artery disease, strokes, and, for women, the risk of a premature baby.

▩ ACTION Children attach more importance to the immediate effects of smoking – cost, smell on breath, staining of fingers, damage to fitness for sports – than to threat of future disease. So it seems that parents explaining the dangers should emphasize these immediate draw-backs – although of course the long-term health hazards must be stated.

Above all, remember that your child is probably smoking as a result of copying another child. Tackling the problem from this angle is easier said than done, but removing or diverting (even temporarily) the peer group pressure to smoke can be the most effective manoeuvre of any.

SMOKING DURING PREGNANCY

This affects the growth of the foetus causing LOW BIRTH WEIGHT, short length and, to a lesser degree, small head size. As it is not known how many cigarettes a day affect an individual baby, smoking in pregnancy should be avoided altogether.

SOILING (ENCOPRESIS)

An uncommon problem ranging from soiling pants to frank defecation, day or night, in places and at times that are socially inappropriate. See also *CONSTIPATION, DIARRHOEA, TOILET TRAINING.*

Some children just don't learn bowel control by the time they go to school. Children who are exceptionally constipated have difficulty in learning bowel control – the child may 'hang on' and avoid passing a stool if this has been painful in the past; some children resist attempts to regulate bowel action, to use the potty or toilet, particularly if their parents place a high premium on success – they may 'hang on' deliberately, and may soil their pants or pass stools at another time and elsewhere as a result.

Soiling often indicates an emotional problem, particularly in a child who has previously adjusted to the use of the toilet. A minority of children who soil themselves may smear their faeces on the floor or walls, indicating by such antisocial acts that there is a more serious underlying emotional disturbance.

Soiling is embarrassing and upsetting for children, even if they don't

show it. Parents naturally become distressed. However, this in itself can make it harder to resolve the issue. Treat any episodes of soiling in as calm a manner as possible. Punishing the child will not help him to learn bowel control.

Get medical advice if your child is over three years old and soils persistently, soils and seems constipated or appears to be in pain on passing stools, starts soiling regularly after being toilet trained, or soils and smears his faeces. Your doctor may treat any medical problem, or refer him to a paediatrician. If, after medical investigation and the treatment of any associated constipation, the problem persists, help from a clinical psychologist or child psychiatrist may be suggested. Treatment will usually involve a programme of toilet training, which may include rewarding your child for passing stools on the toilet, while paying as little attention as possible to any episodes of soiling. The problem may take a few months and, exceptionally, years to resolve completely. Meanwhile, your child may be upset by teasing or comments at school or nursery. To ameliorate this aspect of the problem, discuss with your child's teachers how you are handling the situation, and the best way of dealing with incidents at school.

SOLVENT ABUSE

Vapours are given off by a range of products used in the home, including adhesives, dry cleaning fluid, aerosol sprays and typing correction fluid. If actively inhaled, these vapours lead to intoxication. In recent years, many adolescents have experimented with these substances, mostly on an occasional or sporadic basis.

Damage as a result of solvent abuse is rare but can be serious or lifethreatening. The major risk is from accidents while intoxicated – inhaling vomit, falling under cars or from high buildings. However, sudden intoxication can alter the rhythm of the heart, and result in sudden death.

If you recognize that your child is abusing solvents, you should address the problem directly. Discuss the changes with him: if in doubt about how to proceed, ask your doctor for help.

SORE THROAT
In children, typically a symptom of COMMON COLD, INFLUENZA or TONSIL-LITIS, also OTITIS MEDIA, LARYNGI-TIS, GLANDULAR FEVER, THRUSH, HAY FEVER and CROUP. May also occur during infections such as CHICKENPOX, MEASLES and RUBELLA. Pharyngitis is the technical term for an inflamed throat; if a common cold mainly takes the form of a sore throat, a doctor may describe it as pharyngitis.

SPECTACLES
Commonly prescribed for children with a variety of eyesight problems including LONG- or SHORTSIGHTEDNESS, LAZY EYE, ASTIGMATISM and SQUINT.

Spectacles are prescribed after an EYE TEST, which needs to be repeated regularly as eyesight changes with age. Spectacles will not only improve the accuracy of vision but may also relieve a headache from 'eye strain'.

Children sometimes don't like wearing their spectacles, but they should be encouraged to do so. In toddlers and young children, it makes sense to buy inexpensive frames and to have a spare pair as accidents are almost inevitable. To help persuade a reluctant toddler to wear spectacles, try showing him how much clearer the television screen is while wearing his glasses. Point out the number of heroes who wear spectacles – from Clark Kent to Postman Pat. Re-

wards and constant encouragement for regular wearing are important.

In older children, the option of fashionable frames or contact lenses may be a helpful inducement to keep wearing spectacles.

SPEECH DISORDERS
By two years, all but one in 15-20 children will have started to talk. Age of uttering first words is not related to social class, but later LANGUAGE DE-VELOPMENT favours children of professional families. By the age of three years, all but three or four in 100 children will be able to utter three-word phrases spontaneously and with meaning (not echoing).

The commonest speech disorder is STAMMERING, common under the age of five when language is being acquired most rapidly. It usually resolves by seven years.

Physiological, psychological and environmental factors are all causes. It is twice as common in boys as in girls; and more than twice as common in children from large families and in children of unskilled parents than in only children or children of professional parents. Identical twins tend to echo each other's speech problems.

Speech disorders can also result from structural abnormalities of the lips, teeth, palate, tongue, throat or larynx; or they can simply be due to difficulty in forming speech sounds or sequences of speech sounds. One in seven children entering school is described as partially unintelligible.

■ SYMPTOMS Poor understanding of speech, HYPERACTIVITY, frustration, delayed or unclear speech.

■ INVESTIGATIONS Assessment by a speech therapist or speech pathologist and a clinical psychologist. Medical examination may show a local cause for articulation difficulties such as a disorder of the larynx or palate. Children with more severe language disorders may require a CHROMOSOME test, an EEG or a psychiatric assessment for, typically, elective mutism (deliberately staying silent for psychological reasons) or AUTISM. Hearing tests are essential, although only two children per 1,000 have a sufficiently severe hearing loss to cause major delay in acquiring language.

■ TREATMENT   Children with speech or language disorders will benefit from speech therapy and a language-based teaching programme with plenty of adult contact. Children with language problems do not benefit particularly from playing with other children.

■ SELF-MANAGEMENT   When you talk to the child, make sure you have his attention. Talk clearly and simply about the child's interests.

■ OUTLOOK   Most children are intelligible by seven years and only one in 40 will remain difficult to understand. But while it is usual for speech difficulties to resolve, the child may well have spelling difficulties later. Severely restricted language development at five years carries a poor prospect for educational success, and many such children are classed as MENTALLY HANDICAPPED, AUTISTIC or both.

SPINA BIFIDA

The commonest major CONGENITAL ABNORMALITY of the nervous system, affecting typically one per 1,000 births. The baby is born with a plaque or cystic swelling over part of the spine (neck or back). This contains fluid and usually some neural tissue – derived from malformed spinal cord and nerve roots.

■ CAUSE   The neural tube, which forms the baby's spinal cord, closes between three and four weeks after conception. If this fails to occur, spina bifida results. Ninety per cent of affected foetuses abort spontaneously. A slight degree of failure of closure of the spinal bony arch is quite commonly found on X-rays of children who have normal skin over the spine. This is spina bifida occulta, which is usually of no significance to the child in later life.

■ COMPLICATIONS   Spina bifida is often associated with HYDROCEPHALUS. In severe cases, there may also be abnormal angulation (kyphosis) or curvature (scoliosis) of the spine and abnormalities of bowel and bladder function. Disability depends on the site and degree to which the spinal cord has been damaged.

■ TREATMENT   Immediately after birth, care is required to prevent INFECTION of the spinal wound and to treat infection if it occurs. Head size needs to be monitored to treat hydrocephalus (by surgical shunt) if it occurs. Thereafter the individual problems need a team approach as a long-term management plan. Mildly affected children will walk independently. Moderately affected children walk with aids and appliances, but severely affected children are chair bound. Bowel and bladder disorder require careful long-term medical and surgical care. Loss of sensation in the feet requires well-fitting footwear and chiropody advice. Loss of sensation higher in the legs carries additional risks such as painless fractures.

Care of the child extends to all

aspects of his physiology and psychology, schooling and employment skills, together with attention to the needs of the whole family.

■ PREVENTION Screening tests are available in early pregnancy for parents who would prefer to abort an affected foetus. A BLOOD TEST, a test of the fluid round the baby (amniocentesis – see *ANTENATAL DIAGNOSIS*) and *ULTRASOUND* can all contribute to antenatal identification of the malformation. GENETIC COUNSELLING is available for further pregnancies.

SPLINTERS
Common-sense treatment – removing the foreign body with tweezers as gently as possible – is the answer unless it is embedded deeply, in which case get medical advice. Don't probe the area. Clean the affected area with soap and water first. Sterilize the tweezers first by passing the tips through a flame. Squeezing the flesh around the splinter can make the outer end rise clear enough of the skin surface to give purchase for the tweezers. See also *BLEEDING*.

SQUINT
When one eyeball looks in a different direction to the other: the child may appear cross-eyed. Normally both eyes move together from time of birth. In about 3 per cent of babies this does not happen, and a squint develops. There is a family history of this problem in about half of all children with squints.

■ CAUSES The commonest is an error of sight in one or both of the eyes. This is most often LONGSIGHTEDNESS, but SHORTSIGHTEDNESS may also cause the problem.

An imbalance of the eye muscles, which move the eyeball up and down and from side to side may also be a cause. One group of muscles pulls more strongly than another.

Occasionally, a squint may be caused by an obstacle to the image transmitted to the brain. This could be because of a CATARACT, or a disease of the retina at the back of the eye.

■ A LAZY EYE is the common complication of a squint. Normally the brain can sort into one coherent picture the separate information brought to it by each eye. If a child is squinting for any of the reasons above, his brain will receive a complicated picture of what he sees, similar to double vision. In an attempt to sort this out, the brain quickly learns to suppress the vision of the squinting eye. If this suppression is maintained for several years, the eye is in danger of functioning poorly – of being 'lazy' – permanently.

■ ACTION In order to prevent this, squints should be treated early. Get medical advice if you suspect a squint. Your doctor will arrange an appointment with an eye specialist. Squints are sometimes more obvious when your child is tired or unwell, but tiredness or ANXIETY can never cause the squint.

■ TREATMENT depends to some extent on the cause. The eye specialist will make a careful examination for underlying eye problems such as a cataract. An EYE TEST will determine if SPECTACLES are needed to correct any visual error. If a lazy eye has developed, this is treated by covering the better eye with a patch to force the child to use the lazy one. If a squint is caused by an imbalance of the eye muscles, or if it persists, in spite of correct glasses and a patch, then an operation is usually needed. This can correct the appearance of the squint, and involves lengthening or shortening the eye muscles.

■ OUTLOOK Most squints can be corrected with spectacles and/or covering the lazy eye.

STAMMERING
Most children will stammer or stutter occasionally (as indeed do adults) under stressful circumstances. If stammering is persistent, get medical advice. Your doctor may suggest seeking the help of a speech therapist. See *SPEECH DISORDERS*.

STEALING
A child's sense of right and wrong develops over a period of years, not only through intellectual development, but through following example. The toddler or pre-school child who takes something often has no idea of what ownership means and indeed makes no distinction between taking and borrowing.

While this is clearly not true of older children, parents do need to think carefully about the context of theft. If faced with the knowledge that a child has, say, been shoplifting, ask yourself whether other children have been influential. A child will steal in order to imitate; to rise to a 'dare'; or because he is forced. He may also steal because he wants an object as compensation for something missing in his life. If the child is stealing from home, family relationships may well be implicated. Jealousy of a brother or sister may be the cause; as can the simple need to attract attention. Children need attention in order to thrive; sometimes the need can be desperate.

■ ACTION Ponder these factors and, if you can, get disinterested advice from a friend before deciding to punish the theft. Base any sanctions on these clear principles:

First, the child should not benefit from the theft: don't let it become an attention-getting device.

Second, the reasons why he stole should be openly discussed and taken to heart.

Third, try to explain *why* he should not steal – you may need to cover this again and again.

If a child steals persistently, discuss the problem with the family doctor, who may suggest further help from a child psychiatrist or psychologist. He or she will help you explore the reasons behind the child's behaviour, which may be difficult for the family to tackle alone, especially if the problem is longstanding.

See also *LIES AND FIBS*.

STICKY EYE
See *CONJUNCTIVITIS*.

STILL BIRTH
The delivery of a dead baby after 28 weeks of pregnancy.

■ CAUSES are mostly unclear; contributory factors include maternal DIABETES and high BLOOD PRESSURE, and CONGENITAL ABNORMALITIES of the foetus.

If your baby is still born you may be asked to give permission for a post-mortem examination in order to try to identify the cause of the death.

■ MOURNING The parental distress following a still birth may be as great as that following the death of an adult: feelings of shock and disbelief may follow, accompanied by intensive bouts of tearfulness; feelings of guilt, despair and anger are common. It may take a year for emotions to settle back to normal, but distress may resurface from time to time, especially around the anniversary.

Psychological studies have suggested, and many parents have found, that seeing and holding their dead baby helps, even though this may seem very painful at the time. Taking photographs and being involved with the funeral arrangements are also important. The doctors and nurses caring for parents normally provide opportunities for discussion about the baby's death, the results of the post-mortem and also, if necessary, GENETIC COUNSELLING. A follow-up visit to the hospital is usually suggested.

■ REGISTRATION AND FUNERAL ARRANGEMENTS All still births have to be registered. Registration of a baby's first name is now also possible. Parents must take the medical certificate of cause of death to the appropriate registration centre where the certificate for burial or cremation required by the undertaker is issued to them.

■ NEXT PREGNANCY It is wise to allow time to mourn the death of your baby before conceiving again; you need sufficient rehabilitation to be able to cope with the anxieties of the next pregnancy and delivery. This may take over a year.

STILL'S DISEASE
See *RHEUMATOID ARTHRITIS*.

STINGS
See *BITES AND STINGS*.

STOMACH-ACHE
See *ABDOMINAL PAIN*.

STRAINS AND SPRAINS
Apply the RICE principle: R is for rest – it helps to stop bleeding, internal and external. I is for ice – apply ice cubes (or frozen peas) in a polythene bag; but take care that excessive cold does not burn the skin. C is for compression – firm bandaging will prevent further bleeding into the tissues. E is for elevation – raising the affected part lets fluid drain away and reduces swelling. See also *FOOT INJURIES, BRUISING, PAIN*.

STRAINS AND SPRAINS

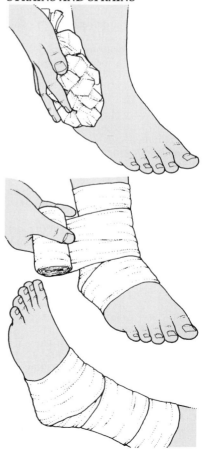

STRAWBERRY NAEVUS
See *BIRTHMARKS*.

STRESS SYMPTOMS
Although children do not usually complain about stress in the same way as adults, they may well experience it in a variety of situations: when struggling at school, when experiencing failure in friendship, when frightened, if there are FAMILY PROBLEMS, illness or a threatened loss or BEREAVEMENT. Often the child cannot express his feelings; instead the stress is felt as a physical symptom: see *RECURRENT ABDOMINAL PAIN, HEADACHE, OVERBREATHING, NIGHTMARES, ANXIETY, BEDWETTING, VOMITING,* having a PAIN anywhere. All are common ways of experiencing stress, and should not be ignored if they persist or keep returning.

▓ ACTION Check with your doctor that there is nothing physically wrong. Think about what could be distressing your child. He may or may not be able to tell you himself, but others (his teacher?) may have ideas. You may know yourself that there are family or other worries but may not have realized that your child has picked up the tension. Reassure the child, but remember the best remedy is to sort out the problem – whether the child's or your own. The family doctor should be able to help, if only by listening.

STRIDOR
The name given to the noisy indrawing of breath.

▓ CAUSES The commonest form in the new-born period is congenital laryngeal stridor. This is thought to result from a relative softness of the cartilage of the larynx. In older infants and children, stridor is often synonymous with CROUP or viral LARYNGITIS. Other rare causes include the inhalation of a solid object sticking at the level of the vocal cords.

▓ SYMPTOMS There may be none other than noise on breathing in (inspiratory stridor). Additional features will depend on the cause of the stridor.

▓ ACTION Stridor present from birth is not dangerous, but medical attention may be needed if the child contracts a respiratory infection. Stridor occurring for the first time should be taken seriously. This could be common viral laryngitis; or life threatening EPIGLOTTITIS; or the child could have inhaled something, in which case turn the child upside down or slap his back and *summon urgent medical help*.

▓ TREATMENT depends on the cause: *very* occasionally surgery may be necessary to relieve obstruction due to malformation of the larynx.

▓ OUTLOOK Congenital laryngeal stridor improves as the child grows, and has usually disappeared by the age of one year, nearly always by two.

STYE
An infection in the base of the eyelash which causes a small, painful boil on the eyelid.

Most styes need no treatment. Bathing the eye with cotton wool moistened with warm water may speed healing.

If your child repeatedly has styes, it is worth discussing the problem with your doctor, who may prescribe an ANTIBIOTIC ointment to prevent reinfection.

SUDDEN INFANT DEATH SYNDROME (SIDS)
See *COT DEATH*.

SUFFOCATION
An external obstruction such as a soft pillow, a plastic bag over a baby's or a child's head, preventing air reaching the lungs.

■ IMMEDIATE ACTION Remove the cause of suffocation. If the child is not breathing, see EMERGENCY RESUSCITATION.

■ PREVENTION Keep plastic bags out of reach; don't give a baby a pillow, and provide a mattress to approved standards. Don't leave animals alone in the room with sleeping babies or toddlers.

SUGAR INTOLERANCE
Impaired absorption of sugar leading to watery DIARRHOEA, flatulence (wind), COLICKY ABDOMINAL PAIN and sore skin around the anus and buttocks. The child may suffer from FAILURE TO THRIVE due to MALABSORPTION. An uncommon condition. See also *LACTOSE INTOLERANCE* and *GALACTOSAEMIA*.

■ ACTION If your child has profuse watery DIARRHOEA either after the introduction of sugar to the diet usually in the first few days of life, or after GASTROENTERITIS, report it to the family doctor. A visit to hospital may be needed for investigations.

■ MANAGEMENT depends on the type of sugar involved and whether the condition is primary (from birth) or secondary (acquired later in infancy or in childhood). Specific sugar(s), usually lactose, are excluded and introduced some weeks later as a challenge (see *LACTOSE INTOLERANCE*). Children with primary deficiency will require long-term special milks to exclude the appropriate sugars. The primary forms are inherited and further siblings have a one in four chance of developing the problem. There is no inherited pattern in the secondary form of sugar intolerance.

■ OUTLOOK Primary types will persist through life and require continued dietary adjustment. The secondary form lasts for a period of months.

SUNBURN
Sunburn is essentially no different to any other sort of burn to the skin surface; it can cause problems varying from slight redness to serious burns.

■ SYMPTOMS The first sign is redness, and in mild cases this may be the only sign. Soreness develops after a few hours, and may be followed by BLISTERING. If the blisters break, fluid weeps from the raw surface of the skin. As the burn heals, ITCHING can be severe, and skin peels away in flakes.

■ CAUSE Ultraviolet rays of medium wavelength (UVB) are the 'burning' element of sunlight. These are not visible as light, and can pass through thin summer clothing, or through hazy cloud cover. The burning efect is greatest between 11 am and 3 pm, when the sun is at its highest, and worst on beaches or in snow, because rays are reflected off the earth's surface.

■ ACTION Prevention is the best approach: whenever sunburn is likely, keep your child covered up with a dark coloured shirt or dress,

SUNBURN

The sunburn process

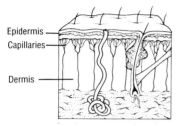

Epidermis
Capillaries

Dermis

The top layer of the skin, the epidermis, is semi-transparent and ultra-violet rays from the sun can penetrate it to reach the dermis, which lies beneath.

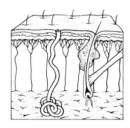

In response to ultra-violet penetration, the capillaries (fine blood vessels) swell, allowing more blood than usual to flow close to the skin's surface. The skin takes on the characteristic redness of sunburn. This eventually subsides.

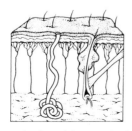

In due course the ultra-violet rays stimulate certain cells in the skin to produce melanin, a skin pigment that colours underlying tissues. Melanin in the epidermis makes the skin look brown or tanned.

and a sun-hat. Sun-screen creams are helpful; choose one with a high sun protection factor (SPF), say 10 or 15, especially if your child has fair skin and/or red hair.

■ TREATMENT If a child does get sunburnt, soothe the pain, and limit the damage by cooling him off in a tepid bath or shower. The pain may be relieved by paracetamol, and the inflammation can be damped down by a 1 per cent hydrocortisone cream, available over the counter.

An antihistamine (or the old-fashioned remedy, calamine lotion) may help the itching. Try to keep blisters intact, but if they burst, pro-tect the skin with a clean dressing and an antiseptic cream.

■ OUTLOOK Even severe sunburn leaves no permanent scars, but over-heating is potentially risky for a baby – see *FEVER.*

SWALLOWED OBJECT

Unless the object is sharp or poiso-nous, it will pass through the body harmlessly and out with the bowel movement within 24 hours.

■ ACTION If the object fails to pass with a bowel movement, see a doctor without further delay. If the object is stuck in the child's throat, see *CHOKING.*

■ RUSH THE CHILD TO HOSPI-TAL if the object is sharp or poiso-nous. An X-ray will determine where the object is and the doctor will decide whether it is safe to allow it to pass through the body or whether an operation is necessary to remove it before it damages the stomach lining or the intestines. See *POISONING.*

TANTRUMS

Most children have outbursts of kicking, yelling and foot stamping from as early as one year; they may continue up to three or four years. View them as angry responses to frustration -- resulting from the child's own limitations, or because desires or a growing wish for autonomy are thwarted. Tantrums diminish as the child's skills, tolerance of frustration and ability to express himself in words increase.

Watch out for common situations when tantrums occur. Some are unavoidable, but some may be deflected by distracting the child's attention. Giving in to the demands of the child can be tempting, particularly in public; but this encourages the behaviour in the long term and should be avoided. Since the child is fired by the anger of the moment, losing your temper or punishing him will not stop the tantrum, or reduce the likelihood of future outbursts. The best response is to ignore the tantrum as far as possible, calmly prevent the child from hurting himself or others, or breaking things, and reassure him when the episode is over. Praise your child in situations where he shows evidence of controlling a possible tantrum. See also *AGGRESSION, BREATH-HOLDING ATTACKS, HEAD BANGING*.

TAPEWORM

An exotic PARASITE of the bowel, much less common than other intestinal infestations. The adult worm is made up of a 'head' portion which adheres to the bowel, and a tape-like 'body' consisting of flattish segments which contain eggs. Individual segments break off and are passed in bowel motions. Each segment can be up to ½ in (0.5 cm) square.

■ TREATMENT Medication such as mebendazole, which loosens the head portion and allows the whole worm to be expelled.

TEAR DUCT, BLOCKED

The tear duct is the tube that drains tears away from the eye; tears are necessary to keep the eye clean and moist. About 2 per cent of babies are born with some degree of obstruction.

■ SYMPTOMS The eye will be watery. If the tear sac becomes INFECTED, the eye may be sticky (especially after sleeping), or the eyelids appear stuck together with yellow pus.

■ TREATMENT Keep the eyes clean. If they are sticky, bathe with warm water using sterile cotton wool. If there is infection, your doctor may prescribe ANTIBIOTIC drops or ointment. If the baby still has problems after six months, a simple operation will relieve the blockage.

TEETH, DEVELOPMENT OF

See *TEETHING*.

TEETHING

A baby's first set of milk teeth starts to erupt, or break through the gums, at about five months. The two lower front teeth are first to appear, and are followed shortly afterwards by the two upper front teeth. The milk teeth are usually all present by the time a baby is three years old. The permanent teeth start to erupt at around five to six years, and this continues until the wisdom teeth come through in late teens or early twenties.

■ SYMPTOMS Your baby will appear irritable, will cry and will probably refuse feeds because of the soreness of his gums.

TEETHING

Milk (baby) teeth: order of appearance.

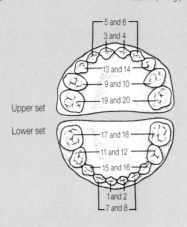

Upper set

Lower set

Permanent adult teeth: order of appearance.

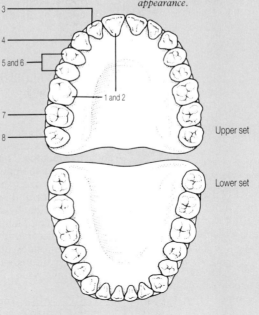

Upper set

Lower set

■ TREATMENT Chewing appears to give some relief, hence the use of the traditional teething ring. Application of a teething gel containing a local anaesthetic may also give some relief. Consult your dentist or local chemist about suitable preparations.

■ ACTION Clean the new teeth with a cotton wool bud at first, later with a soft baby-size brush using a fluoride toothpaste. Babies can try cleaning their own teeth when able to hold a spoon, but tooth brushing should be supervised until he is at least six years old. Find out from your dentist whether the water in your area contains enough fluoride to protect your child's teeth. If it does not, ask your dentist about a fluoride supplement. Regular dental check-ups from the age of two or three years are recommended.

TEMPERATURE
See *FEVER*.

TETANUS
A rare disease caused by tetanus BACTERIA, which lie dormant in soil and can INFECT cuts and abrasions. Tetanus is also found in many animals, whose bites can transmit the disease. It is, however, rare in most developed countries because of IMMUNIZATION and lower risks of infection. The INCUBATION PERIOD is between four and 21 days.

■ PREVENTION Immunization prevents this lethal disease: its importance cannot be overemphasized.

■ SYMPTOMS Muscle pain and stiffness, caused by the tetanus toxin affecting nerves and causing muscle spasm.
   The spasms grow in frequency and cause severe pain; the jaw tends to be particularly affected, hence 'lock-jaw', the common name for the disease.

■ ACTION If you suspect tetanus, rush the child to hospital.

■ TREATMENT Tetanus antiserum and ANTIBIOTICS can lessen the severity. Hospital treatment, including sedation, will help the spasms, but these may be so severe as to also affect breathing.

■ OUTLOOK Poor, despite modern improvements in treatment.

THALASSAEMIA
A form of ANAEMIA caused by abnormal haemoglobin formed in the body in place of the normal one. Haemoglobin (see *ANAEMIA*) is the blood's oxygen carrier. In thalassaemia the red blood cells become fragile and tend to break down. It is an INHERITED DISORDER. If both parents carry the GENE for the disease, they themselves are mildly affected, but there is a one in four chance of it occurring in a severe form in their children.

■ SYMPTOMS appear between six months and one year of age. There is pallor, listlessness and poor feeding. The spleen is always enlarged, as it tries to produce extra red blood cells. In older children, growth is retarded. Children and adults with the milder form of the disease usually have no symptoms, except perhaps slight anaemia.

■ TESTS BLOOD TESTS confirm the diagnosis.

■ ACTION INFECTIONS should be treated rapidly. Extra folic acid is usually needed to replace what is lost as red blood cells break down. If there is a family history of thalassaemia, GENETIC COUNSELLING should be considered. Contact sports should be avoided: the enlarged spleen may rupture, causing severe bleeding.

▨ TREATMENT of the severe form relies on BLOOD TRANSFUSIONS to counteract the acute anaemia. The problem with transfusions is accumulation of large amounts of iron in the body; drugs may have to be used to get rid of this.

Recently, bone marrow transplants have been used to re-establish manufacture of haemoglobin.

Sometimes the spleen needs to be removed: it can grow so large that it causes problems.

▨ OUTCOME The severest form of the disease is fatal, but the recent development of bone marrow transplant gives hope. Milder thalassaemia may be unproblematic.

THREADWORM

Threadworms are the most common bowel PARASITES in children in the U.K. They are not likely to cause symptoms other than an itchy bottom at night, when the adult worms emerge to lay eggs at the anal margin. The worms may be visible as white threads.

▨ TREATMENT consists of medication such as piperazine or mebendazole to paralyse the worms, which are then expelled in bowel motions. It is usually advisable to treat the whole family. Recurrences are frequent – keep finger-nails short to reduce the chance of reinfection through the mouth.

THROAT, INHALED OBJECT IN
See *STRIDOR, CHOKING.*

THRUSH

An INFECTION caused by the *Candida* species of FUNGUS, also known as candidiasis or moniliasis. It thrives throughout the environment, and in the mouth, gastro-intestinal tract and vagina of a healthy person. A baby is often infected by his mother's vagina at birth, but infection can be present in teats of bottles, dummies and anything else that is sucked. In older children, the infection is usually associated with ANTIBIOTIC treatment, which kills normal BACTERIA present in the bowel and allows the *Candida* to flourish. Children with depressed IMMUNITY are also at risk, and certain diseases such as DIABETES, LEUKAEMIA and HODGKIN'S DISEASE can predispose to thrush.

▨ SYMPTOMS White patches or plaques are seen inside the mouth, on the sides of the cheeks and on the tongue. If scraped, the surface may bleed. The areas around the patches may be inflamed and occasionally can hinder feeding.

In the nappy area, thrush is revealed as reddened skin, extending right into the skin creases, unlike the usual NAPPY RASH. There are also small red spots which extend out from the main rash. The rash can occasionally occur in other skin-fold areas such as around the neck and under the arms.

Thrush can occur in a girl's vagina. This usually causes redness, white plaques and an intense itch.

▨ ACTION Thrush is common in babies. Check his mouth from time to time before feeds, particularly if he is reluctant to feed. Because *Candida* are excreted in stools, nappy rash may go together with oral thrush. If you suspect thrush, get medical advice.

If your child has had thrush, mention this to a doctor intending to prescribe an antibiotic. Most antibiotics have a tendency to cause thrush.

If you suspect, during pregnancy, that you have vaginal thrush, make sure that it is properly treated before the baby is born.

■ TREATMENT is simple and effective but it must be continued for long enough to clear the infection completely. Although response to treatment is usually rapid, the infection tends to recur if not fully eliminated.

Oral thrush is treated with nystatin drops in the mouth with each feed (typically four-hourly). Treatment should be continued for seven to ten days. Bottle teats can cause re-infection, so these should be boiled after every feed: ordinary chemical sterilizing agents do not kill *Candida*. If you are breast feeding, the infection can get into your nipples and so pass back to your baby. Nystatin cream will prevent this.

Thrush nappy rash is treated with antifungal cream. As the infection comes from the bowel, it is usual to give nystatin drops by mouth as well. Washable nappies can harbour *Candida* if they are not boiled after use, so it makes sense to change to disposable nappies for a few weeks and boil all towelling nappies before they are used again. These simple measures can prevent nappy rash from returning.

Vaginal thrush can be treated with a special vaginal nystatin cream. Treatment should be continued until one week after the symptoms have disappeared.

If thrush occurs whenever your child is given an antibiotic, treat for thrush at the same time.

■ OUTLOOK Resistance to infection increases with age, so this is a diminishing problem through childhood.

THUMB SUCKING

Many children find thumb or finger sucking comforting, usually when they are tired, bored or tense. A few continue to comfort themselves in this way into their early teens. It is not harmful and is best ignored: children stop themselves when they are ready. See also *COMFORT HABITS*.

TICS

Jerky, repetitive, habitual movements or sequences of movements. Very common in middle childhood; tics of the eyes, face or head are commonest of all.

■ CAUSES Poorly understood, but usually reflect underlying psychological stresses, the origins and nature of which will mostly be unknown to the child and family alike.

■ ACTION Most tics are best ignored, though this is, of course, difficult when they are annoying or worrying for the parent, and embarrassing for the child. Reassure him that tics nearly always disappear on their own in the fullness of time. Ensure that the child's school-teachers avoid unnecessary public comment about the movements.

■ TREATMENT Get medical advice if the number or form of tics is increasing, if your child is being teased about them at school, or if he seems to be developing elaborate rituals and routines around them. The doctor may suggest seeing a psychologist, neurologist or child psychiatrist. BEHAVIOURAL TREATMENT can be effective, working with the child and family to reduce stress.

Very rarely, it can be difficult to differentiate tics from the early symptoms of serious neurological disease.

See also *GILLES DE LA TOURETTE SYNDROME.*

TOILET TRAINING

A child can only become toilet trained when he has reached a particular stage of development. (It remains uncertain, however, what the exact components of development consist of.) This stage is not usually reached until 18 months of age (at the earliest). Most children learn bowel control first, followed by bladder control by day, then by night. There is great variation between children in how and when they gain such control; girls usually learn earlier than boys. Parents often feel strongly about toilet training but if started too early it is likely to fail, and indeed make for conflict and worry over toilet training in the future. Avoid making toilet training a big issue. When the child begins to show he is aware that he is about to pass urine or move his bowels, sit him on the potty, without tension or fuss. Choose times when there is a reasonable chance of success, such as after meals. Praise success, stay relaxed and don't get upset about accidents. When he makes progress, reduce the use of nappies. Take advantage of sunny summer days to allow your child to be without a nappy in the garden, park or on the beach. See also *BEDWETTING (ENURESIS), SOILING, WETTING.*

TONGUE, APPEARANCE OF

Nowadays doctors take the appearance of the tongue much less seriously than they used to – perhaps because they now have access to a wider range of tests of the internal functioning of the body than ever before. Children may have a 'coated' tongue at any time, but it is more common when the child has a FEVER, is DEHYDRATED, or CONSTIPATED. All these conditions, and the appearance of the tongue, will be improved by getting the child to drink clear fluids, as well as dealing with the underlying cause of the problem.

Apart from the 'coated' tongue, another cause of worry may be the 'geographical' tongue which looks like a pink-and-white map. This is not due to disease, and may be a CONGENITAL variant. It causes no problems and is not a sign of illness. White plaques on the tongue and inside of the mouth, which are sore, are usually a sign of THRUSH, and can be treated with antifungal drops. MOUTH ULCERS can also occur on the tongue, and in children with SCARLET FEVER the tongue is often bright red.

TONGUE-TIE

A small skin fold on the under-side of the tongue occasionally preventing full movement of the tip.

▓ SYMPTOMS Usually none; rarely affects speech.

▓ TREATMENT Surgery to release the fold only if there is a marked SPEECH DISORDER.

TONSILLITIS

INFECTION of the tonsils, usually by BACTERIA (such as *Streptococcus*); but may be part of a VIRAL infection of the respiratory tract, as in GLANDULAR FEVER. The condition varies widely in its severity.

▓ SYMPTOMS A very sore throat, FEVER, general malaise, sore neck (from the swollen glands which accompany the tonsillitis); in younger children there may be accompanying VOMITING, STOMACH-ACHE, general irritability or lassitude. On rare occasions, the fever causes a FEBRILE CONVULSION.

■ ACTION 1 Give paracetamol to lower the temperature and relieve the pain. 2 Encourage the child to drink plenty. 3 It is often difficult (for the parents and the doctor) to decide whether a child has a bacterial tonsillitis, or a more mild viral throat infection, or pharyngitis (as in the earliest phase of many COMMON COLDS).

■ GET MEDICAL ADVICE if you think your child has a bacterial tonsillitis. You may look inside the mouth and see bright red tonsils with whitish patches on them: this is typical of tonsillitis. (Do not try to press the tongue down with a spatula or spoon: you may hurt your child or make him sick.)

Note: the size of the tonsils is not a guide to whether they are infected or not – many children have large tonsils as part of their normal make-up.

■ TESTS The doctor will sometimes take a swab from the tonsils in order to test which type of infection is present. This test is not essential but may occasionally be used as a guid as to which ANTIBIOTIC to prescribe.

■ TREATMENT Penicillin is almost always effective against *Streptococcus*, and is the usual first line of treatment. Erythromycin can be given if a child is known to be allergic to penicillin (a rare problem).

Tonsillectomy, the removal of the tonsils, is an operation performed infrequently today compared with a generation ago. It will be advised only if a child is losing considerable time from school, due to repeated attacks of tonsillitis, which are not controlled by antibiotic treatment; or if there are signs of chronic (persistent) infection of the tonsils. The last is rare.

A severe complication of tonsillitis,

quinsy, involves an abscess forming behind the tonsils. This requires hospital treatment without delay.

■ OUTLOOK Tonsillitis normally clears up without trouble, but may recur several times a year. As children grow older, their tonsils become smaller; tonsillitis may, however, still be troublesome in teenagers and adults.

TOOTHACHE

Often extremely distressing pain from the teeth or jaws, which, when it occurs in children, is often associated with eating, but which may in some cases be more persistent.

■ CAUSES In children toothache is commonly caused by tooth decay (*caries*). Poor tooth brushing results in the accumulation of a bacteria-containing film called plaque. The bacteria acts on food debris and produces acids which attack the tooth surface. This eventually results in penetration of the tooth enamel, so that in due course the inner part of the tooth (the dentine), becomes affected and this will almost certainly result in pain. If untreated, the pulp, which is the living part of the tooth, may die and lead to infection of the tissues which support the tooth in the jaw. This is usually the cause of more continuous toothache.

■ TREATMENT Where pain is experienced on eating or drinking, the cause is usually linked with dental decay, and will require early diagnosis and treatment by your dentist. If it persists after eating, the pain may be relieved by using a simple painkiller such as paracetamol. More advanced decay, resulting in full-

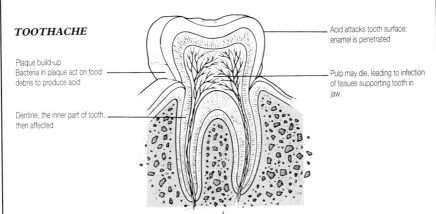

TOOTHACHE

Acid attacks tooth surface; enamel is penetrated

Plaque build-up
Bacteria in plaque act on food debris to produce acid

Pulp may die, leading to infection of tissues supporting tooth in jaw.

Dentine, the inner part of tooth, then affected

blown toothache, will almost certainly require an urgent visit to the dentist. The only way to stop the pain will probably be removal of the tooth.

■ ACTION See *TEETHING*, and talk to your dentist about preventive measures. Regular and thorough toothbrushing with a fluoride toothpaste, and the use of fluoride supplements, where the local water supply does not contain sufficient fluoride, will help.

TORSION OF THE TESTICLE

Twisting of the testicle out of its normal position. This can occur at any age. *Immediate action* is necessary: torsion cuts off the blood supply to the testicle, and treatment must be carried out within hours if the testicle is to be saved.

■ SYMPTOMS are severe pain in the testicle, groin and/or lower abdomen. The testicle will be swollen or tender. If torsion is suspected, get medical advice at once.

■ TREATMENT is by operation to reverse the twist and secure the testicle in a straightened position. If the testicle is irretrievably damaged, it

may be removed. The testicle on the other side may be stitched into position, to prevent the risk of bilateral torsion.

TOXOCARIASIS

Caused by ingestion of the eggs of the dog or cat roundworm, found in dirt contaminated by the animals' faeces. If eggs get into a child's stomach, the parasites settle in different tissues of the body causing inflammation.

■ SYMPTOMS FEVER, ANAEMIA, FAILURE TO THRIVE associated with COUGH and wheeze. CONVULSIONS and generalized weakness may develop. An enlarged liver and spleen or inflammation of the back of the eye (retina) may be detected. The child may have failing vision.

■ PREVENTION Hygiene; regular worming of cats and dogs.

■ TREATMENT Appropriate medication; attempting to eliminate the parasites; treating symptoms.

■ OUTLOOK Blindness may result if the effects on the eyes are allowed to advance. The condition can be lethal, but will respond gradually (over one to two years) to treatment if detected early enough.

TOXOPLASMOSIS

Toxoplasma is a microscopic organism which thrives within body cells. IN-FECTION can occur if, for example, it is breathed in with dust, or swallowed in food. Cats are a common source. It cannot be transmitted from person to person, except during pregnancy, from mother to foetus (congenital toxoplasmosis). This gives different symptoms from ordinary toxoplasmosis.

▓ SYMPTOMS OF CONGENITAL TOXOPLASMOSIS A severe infection early in pregnancy can result in abortion or still birth. Infections later in pregnancy may, rarely, lead to the baby being born with signs of the disease. These may be mild or severe, and may in turn cause:
– Inflammation of the eyes, which can lead to BLINDNESS.
– Brain damage with MENINGITIS, ENCEPHALITIS or HYDROCEPHALUS. This may be obvious at birth, or give rise to CONVULSIONS or MENTAL HANDICAP which are only detected later.
– Inflammation of the liver, spleen and lymph glands can result in enlargement of these organs. JAUNDICE, ANAEMIA and a bleeding tendency can occur.
– A red, blotchy rash.

▓ SYMPTOMS OF INFECTION ACQUIRED AFTER BIRTH This usually occurs after three years. The symptoms may be so mild as to pass unnoticed, or there may be signs of a severe infection. Enlargement of the lymph glands is common, particularly those in the neck. There may be muscle pain.

▓ TESTS BLOOD TESTS can confirm the diagnosis.

▓ TREATMENT In severe cases, a combination of ANTIBIOTICS. Treatment of convulsions and hydrocephalus is described under those entries.

TRACHEO-OESOPHAGEAL FISTULA

A CONGENITAL ABNORMALITY where the trachea and oesophagus fail to separate completely during development. The oesophagus is usually incomplete (oesophageal atresia).

▓ INCIDENCE Very rare: three babies in every 10,000.

▓ SYMPTOMS From birth the baby is unable to swallow his saliva, and drools frothy mucus. Any attempt at feeding results in choking and distress.
    A very few children have a minor form of this abnormality, in which there is a small connection between the oesophagus and the trachea, allowing food to spill over into the lungs. This causes recurrent attacks of PNEUMONIA.

▓ ACTION *Immediate* specialist care is required. Midwives are trained to test for, and to recognize, this condition at birth.

▓ TREATMENT After specialist resuscitation, diagnostic evaluation and stabilization, surgery is required to separate the trachea and oesophagus.

▓ OUTLOOK Babies born at full term, and without other abnormalities or complications, have a better than 90 per cent chance of survival, with an expectation of a healthy, normal life thereafter. If a baby is premature or has a very extensive abnormality, then his chance of survival is smaller.

TRANQUILLIZERS
See *POISONING*.

TRAVEL SICKNESS
See *MOTION SICKNESS*.

TRIPLETS
See *MULTIPLE PREGNANCY*.

TUBERCULOSIS (TB)
An INFECTIOUS disease, common world-wide, but now relatively rare in developed countries. A tubercle, a microscopic mass of tissue, was one of the characteristic findings of the disease noted by early pathologists when examining victims' lungs.

■ CAUSE The BACTERIUM known as *Mycobacterium tuberculosis*, which is transmitted from person to person, but can also be spread through infected cow's milk. The latter source of disease remains a problem even in Western countries where herds of cattle are not tuberculosis free, and milk is sold unpasteurized.

■ PREVENTION In most developed countries, children are tested for naturally acquired IMMUNITY to tuberculosis at some time before or during their school years. If they have not developed immunity, they are vaccinated against the disease. (If a child has a positive test result, it means that he has been in contact with tuberculosis and may have contracted the disease: he will therefore have a medical examination and, if necessary, undergo treatment.) Babies exposed to the infection in the new-born period pose a particularly difficult problem in weighing up the advantages of vaccination versus reserving the test as the earliest index of acquired disease.

■ ACQUIRING IMMUNITY The child, unknown to anyone, catches the infection and develops a 'primary complex' in the lungs. There are no symptoms, although its occurrence may later show on a chest X-ray, or when the child is shown on routine testing to be skin test positive. This first stage of the disease, in itself essentially harmless, gives immunity. However, the infection can spread through the body, causing such infections as tuberculous PNEUMONIA or MENINGITIS, which while uncommon in industrialized countries, can be serious and even life-threatening.

■ SYMPTOMS of active tuberculosis include (early) loss of energy and appetite; (later) cough, sputum, weight loss and nocturnal sweating. Infection from milk (bovine tuberculosis) causes swollen glands which are hard and may produce problems from local pressure or breakdown of the tissues. This affects the glands of the gastro-intestinal tract, most notably those of the neck.

■ TREATMENT is by ANTIBIOTICS specific to tuberculosis. The patient usually has to take the drug for several months.

■ OUTLOOK depends on the type of infection: for tuberculosis of the lungs, and glands, treatment should be completely effective; tuberculous MENINGITIS is a grave disease, carrying a risk of permanent disabilities.

TUMMY-ACHE
See *ABDOMINAL PAIN, RECURRENT ABDOMINAL PAIN, MESENTERIC ADENITIS, APPENDICITIS*.

TUMOUR OF THE EYE
An abnormal mass of tissue in the eye.

The only significant tumour or cancer of the eye in childhood is retinoblastoma. It is very rare, can affect one or both eyes, and usually develops before the age of three years. The predisposition to this cancer may run in families.

■ SYMPTOMS The child may develop a SQUINT; or when light is shone into the pupil, the reflection may appear white rather than red (as is usual). Untreated, sight will deteriorate and the eye become inflamed.

An eye doctor will examine the back of both eyes, usually under general anaesthetic, to investigate the tumour's size and position.

■ TREATMENT Small tumours may be burnt out by laser or treated with radiotherapy. Sometimes, in order to save the child's life, it may be necessary to remove the affected eye.

■ OUTLOOK About 90 per cent of children with retinoblastoma are cured. The radiotherapy may cause CATARACTS, which can be removed at a later date. If the child's eye needs removal, an artificial one can be fitted. Providing the vision is good in the other eye, he will be able to lead a normal life.

TURNER'S SYNDROME

A rare abnormality in girls where there is one sex CHROMOSOME (an X) per body cell, instead of the normal two. Affected girls are of short stature and stocky, and may be of slightly lower intelligence than might be expected from the family background. Sometimes the diagnosis is not suspected until PUBERTY, when the girl's breasts fail to develop and her pubic hair growth is only slight. Periods do not start and she will be infertile. She can otherwise lead a normal life. If you have one child with Turner's syndrome there is no added risk of further children suffering the same abnormality.

TWINS
See *MULTIPLE PREGNANCY.*

TYPHOID FEVER
A grave, INFECTIOUS illness now limited to undeveloped countries, caused by the BACTERIUM *Salmonella typhi.*

■ CAUSE The infection spreads through poor hygiene, particularly by contaminated food or water. Uncooked food such as ice-cream, fruit, or milk products can carry the infection.

■ ACTION Prevention is essential: avoid likely sources of infection, and have your child IMMUNIZED if visiting a danger area. In high risk areas, water should be boiled or treated, and uncooked foods avoided. Small children should be given only boiled or well-cooked food and drink, or bottled or canned drinks.

Immunization against typhoid is safe, and recommended for all children over one year. Babies under a year should be protected by strict application of the precautions listed above.

Consult your travel agent or your doctor, or contact a tropical diseases hospital for advice about whether you need immunization for a particular destination.

■ GET MEDICAL ADVICE if your child becomes ill in any way during or after a visit to a tropical or undeveloped country. Typhoid fever is diagnosed by BLOOD TESTS, and treatment is effective.

UV

ULCERATIVE COLITIS

An uncommon inflammation and ulceration of the large bowel (colon and rectum) and sometimes the small bowel lining (mucosa). The cause is unknown. It occurs mainly in school-age children, but sometimes also during infancy.

▓ SYMPTOMS DIARRHOEA, mucus and blood in the stools, loss of APPE-TITE and of weight, ANAEMIA, generally feeling unwell and FEVER. VOMITING (occasionally), MOUTH ULCERS, joint pains, anal irritation, poor growth, eye inflammation, skin RASHES (particularly red swellings over the shins).

Rarely, acute ABDOMINAL SWELL-ING and distension of the bowel (toxic megacolon) may lead to perforation of the bowel and PERITONITIS.

▓ INVESTIGATIONS Abdominal X-ray to assess gas shadows. BLOOD TEST for anaemia and evidence of inflammation. A barium ENEMA to show extent of abnormal bowel inflammation.

The specialist will need to examine the bowel and back passage, and possibly to take specimens of the lining of the bowel.

▓ TREATMENT Rest and anti-inflammatory drugs. Corticosteroid therapy as enemas, or by mouth. BLOOD TRANSFUSION is occasionally necessary. Dietary changes to exclude any foods that worsen the condition. Intravenous fluids may be necessary at times. Surgical colectomy (large bowel removal) and permanent ileostomy (bowel opening on to skin of abdomen) may be necessary if the colitis does not respond to medical treatment.

▓ OUTLOOK Medical treatment only may be required. Surgical treatment will be necessary for perforation or for severe or chronic symptoms with evidence of complications. Most children accept, and are very much better with, an ileostomy if it is necessary. CANCER in very long-standing colitis is a risk in adulthood, so regular check-ups will be advised.

ULTRASOUND SCAN

A diagnostic technique employing high-frequency sound waves, which are transmitted into the body. On reaching organs, they bounce back and are picked up on a receiver, which converts them into pictures on a screen. Each organ, or part of an organ, has a characteristic appearance, so abnormalities in size or structure can be detected. The scan cannot reveal anything about the function of the organs, however, nor can all organs be clearly seen. The organs most readily examined include the heart, liver, kidneys, bladder and brain. During pregnancy, the foetus can also be examined – see *ANTENATAL DIAGNOSIS*.

To take a scan, the child is asked to lie on a bed and an instrument is placed lightly on the skin. A jelly is used to make contact with the skin. The procedure is painless.

Ulstrasound waves do not cause damage to the body. If necessary, scans can be repeated without worry.

UMBILICUS

The place where the umbilical cord was attached to the baby while in the womb; also called the navel or belly button. The umbilical cord is clamped at birth, and the remaining stump kept clean and dry to prevent INFECTION. If the skin around the ubilicus becomes red or the cord becomes moist, this indicates an infection. If neglected, this can become dangerous: if in doubt get medical help. The stump drops off within ten to 14 days. The technique used to cut and clamp the cord does not affect the final size and shape of the child's navel.

UNCONSCIOUS CHILD

An unconscious child is unresponsive, and the level of unconsciousness can be graded according to how well the child responds to different stimuli, such as talking or touching. A deeply unconscious child will not respond to any stimulus; a less unconscious child may withdraw his arm or speak in response to, say, an injection or a painful procedure.

▓ ACTION 1 Call for immediate help and summon an ambulance. 2 Assess the situation, remembering the possibility of neck injury (see *EMERGENCY RESUSCITA-TION*). If breathing and pulse are absent, follow steps A, B and C in EMERGENCY RESUSCITATION. If breathing and pulse are present, put the child in the RECOVERY POSITION. 3 Keep the child warm and continue to check his pulse and breathing while waiting for the ambulance.

▓ ACTION AT HOSPITAL If necessary, the child will be resuscitated. The reasons for the unconsciousness will then be investigated and treated. Possible causes will include:

– POISONING;
– INFECTION of the nervous system (for example, MENINGITIS);
– HEAD INJURY;
– severe trauma leading to blood loss (see *SHOCK*);
– anaphylaxis (see under the SYMP-TOMS heading in *ALLERGY*);
– EPILEPSY;
– DIABETIC crisis.

UNDESCENDED TESTICLE

A testicle which does not lie in the scrotum. Normally the testicle forms in the abdominal cavity of the foetus, and migrates down into the scrotum by the time the baby is born. However, in 2 per cent of new-born boys, this migration is only completed over the first year of life. In a smaller number, the descent remains incomplete.

▓ TREATMENT The baby's scrotum is examined shortly after birth. If a testicle is undescended, regular checks are made. If it has not descended by the time the boy is one year old, then surgery is advisable and will usually be performed between the ages of one and three years. The operation involves bringing the testicle into the scrotum, and securing it there. The operation is advisable for various reasons: appearance – this is especially important as the boy grows older; fertility, which will decrease if the testicle remains undescended; and there is an increased risk of TORSION OF THE TESTICLE or accidental trauma if the testicle is left undescended.

▓ OUTLOOK There are usually no problems following the operation, and fertility is normally unaffected.

URINARY TRACT INFECTION (UTI)

INFECTION of the urinary tract, caused by BACTERIA commonly originating from the bowel. It is commoner in girls than in boys.

▓ SYMPTOMS Older children will have pain on passing urine, and a feeling of urgently needing to pass urine. They may also have ABDOMINAL PAIN, FEVER and blood in the urine. Babies' symptoms may be more non-specific: CRYING, feeding poorly, VOMITING, DIARRHOEA and fever.

■ ACTION If you suspect your child has a UTI, take him to the doctor, who will request a urine specimen to test for infection.

■ TREATMENT is with a course of ANTIBIOTICS, usually by mouth.

■ FURTHER TESTS Special X-rays, ultrasounds and other newer forms of imaging may be indicated to investigate whether there is an underlying abnormality of the kidneys or the urinary tract. A common problem associated with recurrent or chronic urinary infection in children is ureteric reflux – urine runs up the ureters towards the kidneys when the bladder contracts. This in turn results in urine stagnating in the bladder and ureters where it becomes infected. Furthermore, if the urine is infected this can cause scarring of the kidneys. Fortunately this usually ceases as the child gets older and, providing the urine is kept clear with antibiotics, no further treatment is usually needed.

URINE TESTS

A urine test is required to make or confirm a URINARY TRACT INFECTION. The urine sample must be free from contamination and sent fresh to a laboratory. Easier to obtain from boys than girls – a small plastic bag taped around the penis is usually successful in boys who are still in nappies. Potty specimens from girls must be collected in a sterile (boiled) container. Alternatively, a clean specimen may be 'caught' from the free stream of urine as the child passes water. Rarely, in babies, it may be necessary to puncture the bladder with a needle to collect an uncontaminated sample.

Other urine tests, for protein and for glucose (sugar), can be carried out on ordinary potty specimens. 'Dipsticks' can provide an instant result. Protein is present in the urine if the child has NEPHRITIS; also in NEPHROTIC SYNDROME. Glucose in the urine indicates DIABETES.

URTICARIA

Commonly known as nettle-rash or hives, this is an intermittent, very itchy rash, usually on the trunk, consisting of either small raised lumps or large patches (giant urticaria).

■ CAUSES Broadly speaking, urticaria represents an ALLERGIC reaction of the skin. Children can become allergic to foods, dyes, drugs (such as penicillin), or plants. Other drugs, including ASPIRIN, and food colourings (for example tartrazine), can cause urticaria by directly stimulating the release of histamine in the skin.

■ SYMPTOMS The intensely itchy lumps come and go over a few hours, and clear to leave normal skin. In severe cases, swelling may occur inside the mouth or in the airways, leading to wheezing and difficulty in breathing (angio-oedema).

■ ACTION Most episodes of urticaria will subside without any treatment. It is useful to identify the cause by considering what food, drink or medicines have been taken in the previous 24 hours. In this way recurrence may be avoided.

■ GET MEDICAL ADVICE if the more severe symptoms of wheezing or swelling of the mouth develop, or the child becomes distressed.

■ TESTS Some dermatologists

recommend skin or BLOOD TESTS to try to identify the irritating agent.

■ TREATMENT Avoiding known cause(s) is the first line of treatment. Antihistamine drugs, such as chlorpheniramine or terfenadine, will relieve the symptoms, and may be given until the rash has cleared. Angio-oedema is treated by the injection of adrenalin (which should always be available when skin testing is carried out).

■ OUTLOOK Urticaria is seldom a major problem in childhood.

VAGINAL DISCHARGE

Many girls have an inoffensive white discharge from the vagina from time to time during childhood. It may cause itching and is sometimes bloodstained.

There are many possible causes; the following is typical, not an exhaustive list:
– Infections due to THRUSH (sometimes following a course of ANTIBIOTICS) or THREADWORM.

– If the vulval skin is also red and itchy, the discharge may be part of a DERMATITIS caused by scented soaps, bath oils or nylon pants.

– In a new-born baby girl, a clear discharge is normal, and results from the action of the mother's hormones on the baby's vagina.

– In adolescence it may, as in adults, be a sign of sexually transmitted disease.

– A bloodstained discharge is much less common and may be the result of the child pushing an object, such as a bead, into her vagina.

■ ACTION If your child has a vaginal discharge that is smelly, profuse, itchy or bloodstained, take her to the doctor for investigation. He or she may take a swab of the discharge, and test for threadworms.

■ TREATMENT usually involves an externally applied cream or a drug taken by mouth. If the discharge is bloodstained, the child may have to be given an anaesthetic in order to make it possible to look for, and remove, the foreign object.

VALVE DISEASE OF THE HEART
See *CONGENITAL HEART-DISEASE.*

VARICELLA
See *CHICKENPOX.*

VENTRICULAR SEPTAL DEFECT
See *CONGENITAL HEART-DISEASE.*

VERRUCA
See *WARTS.*

VIRUSES

Viruses are smaller than BACTERIA, and can only survive within living cells. The body produces ANTIBODIES when exposed to a virus, resulting in IMMUNITY to that virus. This usually occurs within a few days, and most viral INFECTIONS are mild and self-limiting. Immunity can also be induced by IMMUNIZATION.

Treatment of viral infections is usually symptomatic: rest, sleep, paracetamol, and drinks and food as the child wishes. ANTIBIOTICS have no effect against viruses. Some antiviral drugs are now becoming available, but as yet are used only for certain specific and serious infections. There is no specific treatment as yet for the commonest of the viral infections, the COMMON COLD.

VITAMIN DEFICIENCY

See *VITAMINS*. Vitamin deficiency is highly unusual in Europe and North America, occurring mainly in certain high-risk groups, such as children with MALNUTRITION, unusual or inadequate diets, disorders such as liver or renal disease or, rarely, in PREMATURE babies.

Disorders may occur singly or together in relation to malnutrition.

■ VITAMIN A DEFICIENCY affects the cornea of the eye and the conjunctiva, the outer lining of the eye, causing dryness and thickening. Night vision may also be affected. In severe cases, daytime sight may eventually be damaged.

The skin tends to be dry and scaly and there may be poor growth and intellectual impairment.

Treatment is by simple replacement of the deficient vitamin. Prevention is by adequate intake of dairy products and vegetables.

■ VITAMIN B DEFICIENCY There are several types associated with various clinical disorders.

Thiamine deficiency causes beriberi, mostly in Asian babies. Unless treated with thiamine injections, this is a serious, indeed rapidly fatal condition.

Riboflavine deficiency is characterized by severe cracking at the corners of the mouth, a sore red tongue and lips, and excess blood vessel formation in the cornea. These clear quickly with daily doses of riboflavine.

Niacin deficiency (pellagra) occurs particularly in maize-eating communities. There is redness, swelling and dryness of skin exposed to sunlight. Thickening and infection also occur. The symptoms may arise in association with other vitamin B deficiencies, and will probably be associated with malnutrition including protein deficiency (kwashiorkor).

Treatment involves doses of all the B group of vitamins and an adequate protein intake.

Deficiency of vitamin B6 (pyridoxine) may lead to ANAEMIA and CONVULSIONS; and a new-born baby who has had prolonged convulsions with no obvious cause might just be pyridoxine-dependent.

Treatment is pyridoxine by injection. The vitamin is present in milk but is inactivated if heated.

Cyanocobalamin (vitamin B12) deficiency is also rare. The substance is necessary for red blood cell production by the bone marrow, and is also concerned with the biochemical processes of the nervous system. The child becomes tired, has a poor appetite and develops anaemia. The tongue may be sore, and neurological complications include ataxia (unsteadiness), paraesthesia (numbness), and poor tendon reflexes.

Treatment is injections of vitamin B12 several times a week.

Folic acid deficiency: some small PREMATURE infants with low folate levels develop anaemia at about eight weeks. Children with MALABSORPTION such as COELIAC DISEASE can also develop mild folate deficiency and anaemia, and when certain anti-convulsant drugs are used. Folate deficiency may also arise as part of a general vitamin deficiency state in malnutrition.

Symptoms include ANOREXIA (loss of appetite), FAILURE TO THRIVE, and liability to infections and gastro-intestinal disturbances.

Treatment is folic acid daily, plus correction of other deficiencies.

▓ VITAMIN C (*ascorbic acid*) DEFICIENCY SCURVY is the main consequence, but this is rare in developed countries except in children on unusual diets. If fruit and vegetables are entirely lacking, there is a risk.

The main symptoms are bleeding gums, pain in the bones and BRUISING in the skin.

Treatment is vitamin C pills daily.

▓ VITAMIN D DEFICIENCY Most infants in developed countries are fed on commercially prepared cow's milk fortified with sufficient vitamin D. Those lacking the vitamin may get RICKETS.

▓ VITAMIN E DEFICIENCY may occur in malabsorption. Premature infants will become anaemic.

Treatment is vitamin E pills daily.

▓ VITAMIN K DEFICIENCY leads to BLEEDING disorders. Bleeding in the first week of life at the umbilical cord site, or into the gut involving VOMITING of blood, or into the intestine may produce SHOCK. Vitamin K deficiency may also occur in older children who have malabsorption.

Treatment by injection of vitamin K may be necessary for a baby. Oral vitamin K for the mother a few days before delivery, or to the baby soon after birth, makes the deficiency unlikely to occur.

Vitamin K needs to be given regularly to children with malabsorption.

VITAMINS

Organic substances occurring in minute quantities in plant and animal tissues. Vitamins are essential for specific functions of the tissues to proceed normally, and must be supplied in the diet or made in the body from dietary products. Deficiency of vitamins leads to particular disorders and disease including RICKETS, SCURVY and BLINDNESS – see *VITAMIN DEFICIENCY*.

The important vitamins are vitamins A, B, C, D, E and K.

▓ VITAMIN A occurs naturally in dairy products, and can be made in the body from pigments occurring in vegetables. Impairment of this process may arise in liver disease or HYPOTHYROIDISM. The vitamin is necessary for the health of the epithelium (skin or tissue lining cavities), particularly that of the eye.

▓ VITAMIN B is concerned with the body's use and production (metabolism) of carbohydrate, lipids (fat) and amino-acids (protein products). In fact it occurs as several different, interrelated chemical compounds including thiamine (vitamin B1), riboflavine and niacin (B2); pyridoxine (B6); cyanocobalamin (B12) and folic acid.

Thiamine, present in liver, kidney and eggs, is important in carbohydrate (sugar) metabolism. Riboflavine and niacin are necessary parts of enzymes involved in the metabolism of carbohydrates, proteins and fats. They occur in dairy products, meat, eggs and vegetables. Pyridoxine is present in milk. Cyanocobalamin needs to be bound to a protein produced by the stomach lining in order to be absorbed properly.

Folic acid, necessary for growth and normal red blood cell production, is present in most milks but is low in goat's milk.

▓ VITAMIN C (*ascorbic acid*) is essential for the formation of the protein

VITAMINS

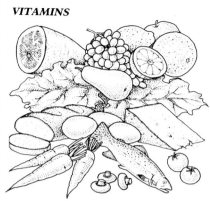

Food products containing vitamins.

structure of body tissues. It is present in human milk, fruit and vegetables, and commercially prepared food.

■ VITAMIN D is present in milk, fish oils, animal fat and in some commercially prepared foods such as margarine. Sunlight acting on the skin can also provide vitamin D naturally. The vitamin increases the absorption of calcium and phosphate from the gut, which in turn are important for bone calcification and growth.

■ VITAMIN E occurs in milk, vegetables and many foods. It is necessary for body processes involving fat, and also for the normal health of muscle tissue.

■ VITAMIN K occurs in milk and green plants, and is necessary for the production of certain clotting factors in the blood.

VOLVULUS

An acute obstruction of the bowel, usually the large bowel (sigmoid colon), caused by a twist in a bowel loop.

■ SYMPTOMS VOMITING, acute ABDOMINAL PAIN, and sometimes passage of blood through the anus. The child may be very ill and develop PERITONITIS.

■ INVESTIGATION An abdominal X-ray shows a large distended loop of bowel and evidence of INTESTINAL OBSTRUCTION.

■ TREATMENT Reduction with a barium ENEMA, or in severe cases surgery, usually leads to cure. There is a risk of death if the diagnosis is delayed.

VOMITING

More common, and fortunately less distressing, in children than in adults – see also *POSSETING*. Vomiting in babies, which is severe, very forceful and 'projectile' may be a sign of PYLORIC STENOSIS. Less specifically, vomiting occurs in infants and young children in association with a variety of INFECTIONS, from COMMON COLDS, COUGHS, ear infections to URINARY TRACT INFECTIONS. When associated with a sudden onset of DIARRHOEA, it usually indicates GASTROENTERITIS and occasionally FOOD ALLERGY. MOTION SICKNESS is another common cause of vomiting. Occasionally vomiting is indicative of more serious disease, as in MENINGITIS or APPENDICITIS.

■ ACTION Observe the child, noting whether the vomiting is followed by other symptoms. Let the child have sips of water, but don't force him to eat. If there is a FEVER, try paracetamol. Get medical advice if there is no improvement, or if the child becomes generally unwell, DEHYDRATED, develops a bad HEADACHE or is unduly drowsy.

W
X

WARTS

Common warts are small, brownish, round lesions several millimetres in diameter, which usually occur on the hands; plantar warts, or verrucas, are flattened warts on the soles of the feet; genital warts are not essentially different from common warts, but occur around the genital area.

▧ CAUSE All warts are caused by VIRUSES known as human papilloma viruses. They are caught from other people with warts, and can be spread by touching.

▧ SYMPTOMS Pain occurs if the warts are in a sensitive place, such as under a finger-nail, or on the sole of the foot. Genital warts can become sore because of their position. Many children, naturally enough, find warts embarrassing.

▧ ACTION Common warts and verrucas can be treated at home with a simple wart paint (see under treatment) from the chemist – but if this fails, and they are troublesome, it is worth getting advice from your health visitor, doctor or chiropodist.

▧ TREATMENT 1 Wart paint usually contains salicylic acid, which works by softening the hard skin of the wart, allowing gentle rubbing with an emery board or pumice-stone to gradually remove the wart. 2 Formalin (5 per cent formalin in water) can be used as a soak for plantar warts, which are then rubbed away as described. 3 Freezing with liquid nitrogen or carbon dioxide snow; the latter tends to be less effective. The wart and the skin around it are frozen solid and then allowed to thaw. This kills the wart virus; the wart then separates from the surrounding skin and drops out, or off. Some children find the process painful; it is certainly uncomfortable. 4 Podophyllin paint is used for genital warts. It is applied by a nurse or doctor at a specialist clinic. It should not be used by patients themselves. Podophyllin is also found in a proprietary verruca ointment that is effective, but can burn the skin.

▧ LONG-TERM MANAGEMENT Since warts are so common, and relatively harmless, parents can usually deal with them themselves. Paints and ointments are easily obtainable from chemists. If the treatment causes pain, it should be stopped for a few days, then resumed. Covering the wart with waterproof plaster helps to soften the skin, and also prevents spread. Some schools require children to cover the feet with plastic socks for swimming if they have verrucas. Children with verrucas need not be banned from swimming.

▧ OUTLOOK Warts eventually go away. The body develops resistance to the virus, and kills it. But, of course, a different virus can still cause new warts.

WATER IN EARS

There is no danger to a child's ears from water, unless the child has a perforated eardrum – see MIDDLE EAR INFECTION. EXTERNAL EAR INFECTION can result from too frequent swimming, or excessive hair washing. If avoiding the problem becomes difficult, you could try giving the child disposable ear-plugs.

WAX IN EARS

It is usual for ears to produce wax, which serves to protect the delicate skin inside the ears from water and dirt. Excess wax normally just drops out. It is not necessary to remove wax from a child's ears, and it can be harmful to do so. Ears only become blocked with wax after it has been pushed into the ears by well-meaning parents wielding cotton-wool buds.

▦ ACTION If this happens and the child becomes deaf, get medical advice. Your doctor may remove the wax by syringeing, or probing, or by advising drops.

WEANING
The transition from the initial milk diet of a baby to the mixed diet of the older child.

'Solids' are usually introduced to a baby between three and six months in response to a baby who is no longer drowsy and satisfied after milk feeds.

A spoonful of rice-based cereal is a useful starter. Since breast and formula milks are sweet, sugary foods are often the most acceptable. But they are not good for the developing gums and teeth, and should be avoided for as long as possible.

The baby will soon, if hungry, take an interest in other tastes: fruits, vegetables and cereals can be puréed and added in slowly increasing amounts to give variety, over the next few months.

At eight or nine months, hard foods such as rusks or crusts are welcomed as teething progresses. As the child learns to chew, chunks of food can be managed and the toddler can be fed some of the normal family diet, chopped up or puréed.

The toddler may wish to continue to drink large amounts of fluid from bottle or cup, but the amount slowly reduces during the second year.

The health risks of this dietary transition are mainly to do with INFECTION and are thus related to hygiene and environment. As with BOTTLE FEEDING, carers must be aware of risks of in-

fection and multiplication of BACTERIA when food is handled, or left out in a warm place.

Weaning is a tricky stage for parent-child interactions, and outside advice may appear to aggravate matters instead of helping. Parents may feel under pressure if their child is not proceeding easily through the stages outlined above. It may help to remember that feeding-time battles are very common – see FEEDING PROBLEMS.

WEIGHT LOSS
See FAILURE TO THRIVE, ANOREXIA NERVOSA, ULCERATIVE COLITIS.

WELL-BABY CLINICS
Usually run by health visitors and community paediatricians. They are available to all parents and children aged nought to five years. As the name implies, they are not intended as a service for sick children, but to provide preventive medicine: IMMUNIZATIONS, development check-ups (see GROWTH PATTERNS and DEVELOPMENTAL DELAY), and advice about NUTRITION, FEEDING PROBLEMS, SLEEP PROBLEMS and any other matters of concern to parents. Many clinics offer a 'drop-in' system. Your doctor or local health authority should be able to provide a list of such clinics in your area.

WETTING
It is common for children, in the early school years, to have occasional 'accidents' during the day, often because they cannot find a lavatory in time. However, wetting can also be a sign of stress in a normally dry child. URINARY TRACT INFECTIONS and other medical complaints can also cause wetting. See also BEDWETTING, TOILET TRAINING.

▦ ACTION Do not over-react to the

incident: all children are embarrassed by wetting accidents, and an angry response may only make the situation worse. Check whether there are any particular difficulties for your child, for example in using the school lavatories, or whether your child is under any obvious stress. If the problem persists or occurs frequently, get medical advice. Your doctor may check for a URINARY TRACT INFECTION; or may suggest seeking the advice of a psychologist or child psychiatrist.

WHITLOW
See *PARONYCHIA*.

WHITLOW
See *PARONYCHIA*.

WHOOPING COUGH (*PERTUSSIS*)
A highly INFECTIOUS disease, caused by BACTERIA and spread through exhaled droplets. It is commonest in pre-school children and most serious in babies under six months. The INCUBATION PERIOD is seven to 14 days. A child is infectious from a week before the onset of symptoms to three weeks after the start of the spasmodic cough: sometimes a total of about six weeks.

■ SYMPTOMS are in three phases, each lasting about two weeks.
First phase: sneezing, a runny nose and slight FEVER. The cough develops gradually, mainly at night to begin with, then becoming worse during the day. During this time the child is at his most infectious, but because the symptoms are so like those of a COMMON COLD, the diagnosis is unlikely to be made unless the child is known to have been in contact with the disease.
Second phase: the cough grows even worse, and comes in spasms lasting half a minute or more. The child's face turns red, and he may

even go blue. Intake of breath after the cough produces the characteristic whoop. The cough may be set off by the slightest movement, crying or even eating. VOMITING often occurs after coughing and the child may have NOSEBLEEDS and small haemorrhages in his eyes. His APPETITE may be very poor and together with the vomiting, this can lead to DEHYDRATION and WEIGHT LOSS. CONVULSIONS can occur, particularly in babies who don't have the typical whoop, but who appear to choke and become blue.
In severe cases this second phase may last about four weeks. PNEUMONIA may develop and chronic lung infections occasionally follow the illness. Lack of oxygen to the brain during the coughing spasms can lead to BRAIN DAMAGE.
Third phase: the cough gradually becomes less frequent and prolonged and the appetite improves. However, relapses can occur and the whooping can re-establish itself alarmingly.

■ TESTS A nasal swab can indentify the bacteria early, but this is seldom performed unless the child is known to have been in contact with whooping cough.
A BLOOD TEST will show an increased number of white blood cells and characteristic ANTIBODIES; but usually the diagnosis is made simply on the characteristic cough.

■ ACTION If you suspect whooping cough, get urgent medical advice. Milder cases can be nursed at home: keep the child in a warm room with an even temperature of about 70°F or 21°C. Steam from an electric kettle can be used to increase the humidity.
Feeds should be small and frequent. Easily digestible, nutritious

food helps to prevent weight loss.

Try to keep the child quiet, as exertion and crying can set off a spasm of coughing.

During a coughing spell, sit the child up, leaning him forwards to prevent inhalation of vomit.

The cough can be frightening for the child, who has difficulty catching his breath. Hold him on your lap and soothe him to minimize anxiety, which could aggravate the cough.

Fever which returns during the second phase of the illness often indicates a chest infection. If this occurs, get medical advice. Your doctor may prescribe an ANTIBIOTIC.

■ TREATMENT Admission to hospital may be necessary if the cough is associated with breathing problems. Oxygen can be given, and nursing staff can help by clearing the mucus at the back of the throat.

Antibiotics are not particularly effective once the cough has started, but can be used to treat bacterial pneumonia if this is a complication.

Anticonvulsants may be necessary to treat convulsions.

■ PREVENTION IMMUNIZATION is effective and in many countries is now given with the three DIPHTHERIA and TETANUS immunizations starting at three months of age.

The risks from the disease are greater than the risk of immunization. The only reason not to immunize is if the child has had a convulsion. It used to be thought that EPILEPSY in the family increased the risks of immunization, but this does not now seem to be the case.

Whooping cough can occur before three months and if an older child gets it, an unimmunized baby in the family is at risk. Mass immunization is tending to prevent

this problem arising, but if you find yourself in this situation, get urgent medical advice.

■ OUTLOOK Whooping cough remains potentially fatal, particularly in children under a year. Younger children are at risk of permanent brain damage, or long-term lung damage after the infection.

WILM'S TUMOUR (NEPHROBLASTOMA)

A tumour of the kidney. It is rare and usually develops before five years. It usually affects only one kidney, although it is not unknown for both to be affected.

■ SYMPTOMS There may be no symptoms until a swelling develops in the child's abdomen. Sometimes the child may complain of pain in his abdomen or pass blood in his urine.

■ INVESTIGATIONS A scan will show the size and position of the lump, and a special X-ray of the kidney may be taken.

■ TREATMENT is specialized, and will be at a hospital where there is a children's cancer unit. The affected kidney will be removed as soon as possible. If both kidneys are affected, or if the tumour is large or if it has spread, then chemotherapy will be given. Radiotherapy may also be used to shrink the tumour (see *CANCER*). The treatment may last six months to two years.

■ OUTLOOK Most children with Wilm's tumour are cured. Even when the tumour has spread, treatment with chemotherapy and surgery cures over 50 per cent.

WORMS

Parasites that live in the bowel.

■ <u>SYMPTOMS</u> only develop when there are large numbers present. These include itching around the anus: the worms venture out of the anal passage in the dark, and it may be possible to catch sight of them while the child is asleep. Some resemble tiny threads, and you can remove them by picking them up on adhesive tape.

The stigma attached to having worms in the family is out of proportion to the usually insignificant nature of symptoms. THREADWORMS are the most common in the U.K. Roundworms are rare, except in the tropics. You can see them in a child's faeces – they look like long, white earthworms. TAPEWORMS are extremely rare in the U.K. They appear as flat, white moving segments in the faeces and call for a visit to a doctor.

■ <u>TREATMENT</u> for the common worms is available over the counter and also as prescription-only medication. See *THREADWORMS*. A single dose of medication, taken by all members of the family simultaneously, may be sufficient – ask your doctor.

■ <u>OUTLOOK</u> If the whole family is ready to comply with treatment – despite naturally indignant feelings on the part of parents – worms are almost always eradicated for good. From time to time there is press publicity about worms caught from faeces of pets. In fact, the risk of children catching worms in this way is not great, even though puppies and kittens do frequently have worms. It makes sense, nonetheless, to have your pet(s) de-wormed by the vet, and not to let children play in places contaminated by pets' faeces.

X-RAYS

These have more uses than many people suspect. An X-ray of the chest will show abnormalities within the lungs, the size and shape of the heart, and the bones of the chest and upper back. An X-ray of the bones will detect fractures or other abnormalities. X-rays of the abdomen will indicate obstructions of the bowel, the position of the stomach and liver, and objects that have been swallowed, such as pins or coins.

Specialized X-ray techniques may involve: injection of a dye which shows up on X-ray to detect abnormalities of the kidneys, blood vessels or heart; or swallowing an X-ray opaque solution to highlight abnormalities of the bowel.

X-rays don't always provide a definite answer to a problem, but they help in the overall assessment.

■ <u>PROCEDURE</u> Simple X-rays cause no more discomfort than having a photograph taken; the child needs to remain still momentarily as the X-ray is being taken. The child should wear a protective lead apron over the genitalia when X-rays of the hips or abdomen are being taken. Reassure your child: the machinery is quite daunting. If you remain in the room while the X-ray is being taken, you should also wear a protective lead apron. If there is any chance that you could be pregnant, it is especially important that you are not exposed to X-rays.

■ <u>SIDE-EFFECTS</u> The radiation risk from a single X-ray is very slight, but small amounts add up. These risks are weighed against the benefit of successful diagnosis. X-rays of children are not taken without careful consideration.

Editorial panel
Professor David Baum
Dr Susanna Graham-Jones

The contributors
Denise Kitchener (who also made a major contribution to shaping the content and approach of the book) studied medicine at the University of Witwatersrand, qualifying in 1970. She trained as a paediatrician at the Red Cross Children's Hospital in Cape Town, has worked in general practice, and as a consultant in paediatric cardiology. Since 1986 she has lived in the U.K. She has two children.

Dr Peter Campion, Senior Lecturer in General Practice at the University of Liverpool and a partner in an inner city general practice in Toxteth, Liverpool. Qualified 1970 at the London Hospital, worked in paediatrics at the Queen Elizabeth Hospital for Children, Hackney, M.R.C.P, 1973; family doctor 1974 to 1980; Lecturer in General Practice at Dundee University before moving to Liverpool in 1985.

Chrissie Verduyn, principal clinical psychologist for children's services, Bolton; formerly member of a multi-disciplinary team in child and adolescent psychiatry in Oxford.

Dr Elizabeth Didcock, neonatal registrar in Birmingham.

Dr Mary Eminson, child psychiatrist in Manchester.

Dr Karen Baker, registrar in Child and Family Therapy, Birmingham.

Ian McKinley, Senior Lecturer in Community Child Health at Manchester University; consultant paediatric neurologist to the Manchester Children's Hospitals 1978-86.

Dr Geoffrey Frost, consultant paediatrician, Kidderminster General Hospital.

The editors and publishers also acknowledge, with thanks, contributions from Dr Tony Costello and Brian Tongue.